The Victorian Reinvention of Race

New Racisms and the Problem
of Grouping in the Human Sciences

Edward Beasley

Routledge
Taylor & Francis Group
New York   London

First published 2010
by Routledge
711 Third Avenue, New York, NY 10017

Simultaneously published in the UK
by Routledge
2 Park Square, Milton Park, Abingdon, Oxon OX14 4RN

Routledge is an imprint of the Taylor & Francis Group, an informa business

First published in paperback 2012

Library of Congress Cataloging-in-Publication Data
Beasley, Edward, 1964–
   The Victorian reinvention of race : new racisms and the problem of grouping in the
human sciences / Edward Beasley. — 1st ed.
      p. cm. — (Routledge studies in modern British history ; 4)
   Includes bibliographical references and index.
   1. Racism.   2. Race relations.   I. Title.
   HT1521.B3823 2010
   305.8—dc22
   2010007694

ISBN13: 978-0-415-88125-8 (hbk)
ISBN13: 978-0-203-84498-4 (ebk)
ISBN13: 978-0-415-65278-0 (pbk)

The Victorian Reinvention of Race

Routledge Studies in Modern British History

To Becky, Sarah, Ron, and Dad

Contents

Acknowledgements

My first thanks go to my parents, Virgil Roy Beasley and the late Ima Jean Beasley; and my roommates and family, namely Rebecca Lea Hartmann Frey (my once-in-a-lifetime best and dearest friend, my most wonderful housemate, companion, and counsellor, and the gifted editor of this book), my beautiful, brilliant, and beloved goddaughter Sarah Frey, who likes names and stories, and the ever-patient Ronald Zavala. I must also thank my mentor and once-upon-a-time research sponsor and dissertation advisor, the late John S. Galbraith; and my co-advisor back in graduate school, Judith M. Hughes, for suggesting that I read Tocqueville. Now more than twenty years later I have not stopped doing so.

I am grateful to Peter Catterall for reading distant ancestors of Chapters 7 and 8, and James Ralph Papp for hosting me in New York and thus making possible some of the research for Chapter 9. My former officemates Barry Joyce, Bill Ashbaugh, and Bruce Castleman listened to the early plans for the book, as did Ross Dunn. My other colleagues in the history department at San Diego State University deserve my thanks as well, which go especially to my chair in recent years, Joanne M. Ferraro; my former chair, Harry McDean; the chairs of my hiring committee, Elizabeth Cobbs Hoffman and Lawrence Baron; and the chair of my tenuring committee, David Christian. I am also grateful to the history department's administrative coordinator, Adriana Putko, and her staff, including Bonnie Akashian, Jan LeBlanc, and Robert Wallace. My thanks as well to the College of Arts and Letters and the SDSU Research, Scholarship, and Creative Activity faculty grant program.

At Routledge, I am grateful to Laura Stearns, Stacy Noto, and the anonymous reviewers. My thanks also to Terence James Johnson at IBT Global.

I could not have written this book without the wonderful booksellers and library staffs of San Diego and London—my special thanks to the British Library, San Diego State University's Malcolm E. Love Library, and the Adams Avenue Bookstore in San Diego. I should also like to thank the New York Public Library. And my thanks go to the San Diego Circuit and Link+ systems that send me books.

1   Introduction
Reinventing Racism

To classify the peoples of the world, we sometimes invent races. What I mean is that we cut the human continuum into discrete groups, each with a biological identity that we think of as passed down from one generation to the next. We then assign characteristics to these groups: Whites are good swimmers and blacks have rhythm. One period when racial categories like these were invented to mark the differences between human groups was in the middle of the nineteenth century in England. How the idea of 'race' gained adherents in England at that time is the central focus of this book.

The idea that 'races' exist was indeed invented then, or rather *re*invented. For what the 'races' are and who fits into each one are not things that every culture agrees on. Nor does any one culture at any particular period (such as the mid-nineteenth century in England) have to inherit its ideas of race in a direct line from its ancestors; racial ideas sometimes die out or become dormant, and there is room to reinvent them.

Slavery and xenophobia certainly existed in the English-speaking world on both sides of the Atlantic in the eighteenth century. But despite all of that there was no idea of race as we have come to know it—no widely shared theory of biologically determined, physical, intellectual, and moral differences between different human groups. The most common assumption was that climate made people different and physical inheritance did not—for everyone had to be related to everyone else as fellow descendants of Adam (and although she was less often mentioned in this context, Eve).[1]

Then in the nineteenth century came the creation of ideas about separate, stable, physically distinct, and physically inheritable races, with different mental and moral characters. Race in this sense was *re*invented in England in the 1850s and 1860s, as it had been reinvented twenty years earlier in the United States, and long before in France. In Great Britain in the age of abolitionism, the racist ideas that came out of slaveholding America won few converts. Only at mid-century did the idea that the world is divided into several large, physically inheritable colour-races become widespread in England. The 1850s and 1860s saw a hardening of the rhetoric of race prejudice in some quarters, and a new insistence by such men as Richard

Burton and James Hunt on the significance and heritability of overarch-ing racial essences.[2] Yet even then many other men—and for a time per-haps most English thinkers on the subject—openly rejected the new idea of race.[3] At the same time, as this book will show, racial ideas very similar to those of Arthur de Gobineau in France were introduced into English opin-ion by Walter Bagehot, the editor of the *Economist*, and by none other than Charles Darwin. In using race to classify the peoples of the world, Bagehot and Darwin would influence far more English opinion-makers than Burton and Hunt ever did.[4]

By the 1870s, a belief in race was more widespread. And yet even in twentieth-century England, the racial categories of (more or less) black, white, and yellow were less than universal. In the 1980s I watched a Brit-ish man who seemed to be of Chinese extraction complain of bad service in a London shop. He asked the clerk: 'Is it because I'm black?'[5] Along these lines, the historian Bernard Lewis recalls joining the British Army in 1940 and being required to specify his race. He had never before seen the word in an official document. He wondered whether to put 'Aryan'—but remembering that he was signing up to fight the Nazis and not become one, he decided to ask what his choices were. The British Army, he was told, recognized four races: English, Scottish, Irish, and Welsh. Apparently the Central and Eastern Europeans who were becoming British officers in large numbers just then—but who had no particular tie to Scotland, Ireland, or Wales—could simply choose English.[6]

Certainly the word 'race' was well enough known in England before 1850. It was used as a description for a family- or clan-sized group with common descent. But in early Victorian Britain (Victoria came to the throne in 1837), people did not as yet have the major colour-races in their heads. They applied the word 'races' to whatever groups they wished, with *or without* any idea of common descent. To use 'race' in that way today, one might speak quite literally of the race of London taxi drivers, or the race of Californian professors. In calling groups of such widely different sizes and descriptions 'races', the early Victorians were quite as serious about finding physical differences between people as the late-Victorian colour-racists might be in discussing the characteristics of blacks, whites, and yel-lows. In his carefully researched, multi-volume account of London social groups in the 1850s and 1860s, Henry Mayhew famously discussed the dirtiness and the life conditions of the children of different vocations in London, but also the mental characteristics and indeed the skeletal shapes of the 'race' of chimney sweeps, and the 'race' of trash-gatherers, and so on, all of these groups fitting within his two larger composite 'races' of 'wanderers' and 'settlers'. He looked at how groups of children in some trades showed an earlier attainment of puberty than medical men thought possible in humans. Different vocations seemed to breed heritable physical differences.[7] For other writers in the middle of the nineteenth century, the 'dark races' included the Italian peasantry.[8]

This early Victorian way of trying to divide people into races for analytical purposes, and dividing people into races of wildly varying sizes and kinds, was not entirely perverse. Historians and social thinkers *must* try to divide people into persistent groups. So must anyone who pays attention to the world. Many well-meaning people would agree that certain human cultural groups differ from each other in ways that seem to be inherited—culturally—from one generation to the next. What else does it mean to discuss the way that Europeans are, or Germans, or Bavarians, or people from Munich?

Even if we have purged from our minds any idea of human races as biological categories, we still need to categorize people in order to think about them at all analytically. If our analytical categories are to have any stability, we must assume that their characteristics run from one generation to another because of the consistent effects of environment and culture. What else does it mean to describe the cultures of America or France?

Or must we always keep foremost in our minds the fact that every human being is unique, and never analyze any unit greater in scale than that of the individual? Can't we talk, however carefully and informedly, about what Americans are like, or French people, or people from the north of England?

GROUPS, OR RACES?

Each individual may be unique, but as individual scholars and thinkers we do not live forever, and we cannot stop to give equal weight to all the individuals of America, France, and so on. We must be able to classify and generalize about the groups that people fit into, while we continue to test our generalities against whatever evidence of individuality that may present itself.[9] Jorge Luis Borges made this point in his famous story of a sickly recluse of a young man, Funes the Memorious, who could remember the individual details of every moment, his thoughts at the time, and the precise angle of the sun on each leaf of each tree at each fraction of a second:

> Without effort he had learned English, French, Portuguese, Latin. I suspect, nevertheless that he was not very capable of thought. To think is to forget a difference, to generalize, to abstract. In the overly replete world of Funes there were nothing but details, almost contiguous details.[10]

Racism comes in when we decide that the particular social and psychological characteristics that we have used to divide people up for some analytical purpose or another are, in fact, indelible. That is, we invent races when we decide that the characteristics that we have used to divide people into groups—when we could divide people in other ways, for other purposes—mark *real* groups that are out there in the world, and whose characteristics are passed down from one generation to the next.

One can erect these categories upon the idea of recurrent environmental conditioning or underlying heredity. Either way, one has entered a confused region that the literary critic Vincent Pecora has identified in contemporary thought: In talking about cultures and ethnicities, he points out, we often allow the blood to merge into the culture and the culture into the blood.[11] The English have a stiff upper lip; Italians are hot-blooded.

If one decides that human cultures constitute types that partially or largely outweigh what individuals make of themselves, and that these categories more or less persist down the generations, one has invented a race. If one forgets that the race in question is an invention, and that a different set of analytical categories for dividing people up could be used to group people in another way—perhaps who eats grits (some American Southerners, and a few Americans outside the South), or who likes to watch stock-car racing (some other Americans, many outside the South)—then one has invented a race that can last not just for a day, but over a lifetime of thought. The race of grits-eating, stock-car-watching American Southerners will pop out at you from everywhere. You will forget how clever you were in first recognizing it, and you will forget that you are clever enough to make up all kinds of other racial groups if you want to (all Americans, all Alabamans, all English-speakers from big democratic countries, people who live in London and New York and go to museums, people with Greek ancestry, people who move their home from city to city every decade or two, people whose families have been in the same town for generations, cat-lovers, people of a certain range of skin colours—what have you). You will have become a racist—merely in trying to set up a categorization that would allow for social analysis, and in letting your *ad hoc* analytical groups run away with you.

But is it really that simple? George M. Fredrickson stresses the importance of one 'racial' group having disproportionate power over another if true racism is to exist; but in this matter I agree with the position of Harry Louis Gates, Jr.: I do not think that hostility is key for creating racism as an attitude or a belief system. It is key for what Fredrickson has in mind, which is the erection of a full system of racist social and political structures, as in the history of the United States.[12] But races are easier to create than all that.

Meanwhile, I take Ann Laura Stoler's point that categories and power relations keep changing and destabilizing one another. But in this book I want to explore the process of categorization when it *does* produce racial categories that will remain more or less stable for some considerable period of time. I think that focusing on this special case of stable categorization will be fruitful enough, and I don't want that aspect of things to get lost.[13]

'VICTORIAN ENGLAND' AS AN ANALYTICAL GROUP IN EXAMINING 'RACE'

It is better to question one's categorizations and groupings than to take them as read. So let me question my own categorizations. In looking at the history of race, an idea that has been invented many times and in many places, why should I focus on British people in the middle of the nineteenth century? Why should I focus on that group instead of some other?

Here are two reasons: (1) For the first time in the history of the planet, one area (the Euro-American metropole) was in routine contact with all the other areas of the world and the people in them; the Victorians had more people to categorize. (2) Out of the nineteenth-century attempts to classify the human world came the major forms of modern racist thinking—what the races supposedly are and what their social and psychological character-istics might be.

The Victorian picture is still more interesting because certain thinkers of the time also saw the problem—that the reification of analytical categories into heritable races was invalid.[14] And they saw that this problem might be avoided, if one took categories for postulates and not for discoveries, and if one continually retested and redefined one's categories in dialogue with the evidence. This constant redefinition of the categories into which we divide people would allow for fewer obvious comparisons between one place or people and another, for there would be fewer pieces of directly comparable social data—fewer than if different social researchers all used the same headings. If the categories change for each culture that is studied, it will be harder to make a comparative social science. But what is discovered about the cultures might have the advantage of being true.

To proceed in this fashion, to change and float one's categories on the tide of evidence, might upset certain critics. But as Alexis de Tocqueville recognized—and he has been accused of exactly this sin of unstable defini-tion[15]—redefining one's categories according to the evidence at hand was a way of remaining faithful to the tradition of care in scholarship, of staying true to the evidence. Despite Tocqueville's critics, the more *ad hoc* and self-adjusting version of classification that he practiced would seem to be exactly the kind of thing recommended by modern information theorists.[16]

Tocqueville and his rejection of the concept of race is the subject of Chapter 2 of this book. Looking at Tocqueville will make clear that the idea of careful, *ad hoc* categorization was a real alternative to racism in the nineteenth century, and that important and very well-known thinkers were conscious of this alternative. Our detour to France to examine Tocqueville will help make the English sections of this book clearer.

What 'race' meant in Tocqueville's work depended entirely upon con-text, and so he did not succumb to racial dogmas. He could recognize the special pleading in the more consistent racial views of his secretary, Arthur de Gobineau, whom I will look at in Chapter 3, where our French detour will conclude. Gobineau was the inventor of the full-blown system of physical races and the idea of the superiority of Aryans. How was his way of thinking about social groups different from that of Tocqueville, his mentor? Their methodological differences were so deep that Tocqueville can stand as an example of how to avoid racial thinking—while Gobineau, through the 'Gobineau Societies' of late nineteenth-century Germany, became an inspiration for Nazi racial thought.

Although the fact is seldom noted, racial views very similar to Gobineau's were reinvented in England—largely because of the work of Walter Bagehot (Chapters 4 and 5 in this book). Bagehot wanted to create a comprehensive theory of human grouping, and what he wound up doing was reproducing the worldview of Gobineau. Bagehot was a major author. English acceptance of the major colour-races did not stem entirely from the wilder and more controversial views of Robert Knox and James Hunt. Although they are more often cited by modern historians of race, Bagehot was more often read.

From Bagehot, the trail of modern race invention leads to Charles Darwin in *The Descent of Man*. Darwin's earlier work on human race had been more careful and more evidence-based, as I will show in Chapter 6. Then Darwin adopted racist thinking. In *The Descent of Man*, Darwin credited Bagehot with enlightening him on the real importance of race in the human realm.

It should be said here that there were other contributors to the reinvention of racism in England in the mid-nineteenth century. Carlyle contributed his share to the process, as did Anthony Trollope, who included a large amount of racist material in his *West Indies and the Spanish Main* (1859). Also contributing to the new focus on racial categories among intellectuals were a number of less eminent, more specialized authors, men such as James Cowles Prichard. We will review them later on, as necessary. But the particular set of racial views shared by Gobineau, Bagehot and Darwin was an important part of the picture. More than that, their shared approach to race can show us something larger: How easy it is to reinvent races when one is merely trying to identify categories of people for social analysis.

For in this volume I am also trying to make an argument about methodology. In the first instance this book is meant as a historical contribution, adding a new strand to the story of the growth of racism in England. But in addition to and by no means instead of 'telling the truth about history', *The Victorian Reinvention of Race* also attempts to use the historical picture to suggest how we should and should not put people into groups when we are writing history or doing social science.

That said, we should return to the story that the book means to tell: Tocqueville saw the danger in reifying one's analytical categories into heritable, biological races. He warned Gobineau not to fall into this trap. Gobineau fell in anyway, and so did Bagehot, who pulled Charles Darwin in with him.

But as we will see, certain English thinkers saw the dangers inherent in grouping peoples, just as Tocqueville had seen these dangers in France. The Duke of Argyll—often dismissed these days, unread, as a 'degenerationist'—took Darwin and the Darwinian anthropologist John Lubbock to task for exactly this mistake of racial reification, echoing Tocqueville's objections and adding some of his own.

But again, don't people have to be classified and grouped if they are to be understood (and administered)? As secretary of state for India, Argyll the anthropological thinker needed stable analytical categories for Indian and imperial society. His Indian policies further revealed his thinking. Argyll's criticism of Darwin and Lubbock, and his experiences as a racial sceptic governing India, are the subject of Chapter 7.

Beyond the special case of Argyll, to what degree does the model of racial reinvention explored in the earlier chapters of this book really seem to apply in the world of imperial governance? In Chapter 8, I will look at the career of Frederick Weld, New Zealand prime minister and later governor of what is now Malaya and Singapore. His career spanned the mid-nineteenth century transition when the major colour-races were reinvented. He reflected these intellectual changes in his writings and in his actions. A new age of racism had been born.

Then, in Chapter 9, I will briefly examine how a very atypical colonial governor of Weld's period, Arthur Gordon, looked at the groups of people under him in a way very much his own. Gordon's thinking suggests the continued viability of a different approach to grouping people—the Tocquevillean approach.

Our starting point, in Chapter 2, will be how Alexis de Tocqueville did it. He defined groups of people carefully enough to reveal patterns bigger than the individual. Yet at the same time he refrained from allowing his groupings to become ends in and of themselves. He avoided inventing or reinventing the races. But before we turn to him, it may be helpful to review how recent and how odd it is to think in racial categories in the first place. Once that is done it will be possible to say more about the general background of nineteenth-century racism.

But first I have a final confession, or admission. I am interested in the narrow (but I hope not overly narrow) problem of how races are invented and reinvented. But as a number of scholars have pointed out—more than I can list here, given the voluminous scholarly literature on the subject—'races' can rise above being mere concepts, mere intellectual figments. People act on their racial stereotypes. Then 'races', however fictional, have social and economic consequences. Some of these consequences are easy to see. The visible evidence of socioeconomic inequality feeds back into the idea of racial distinctiveness. In some societies, people who look a certain way often wind up living in a certain way—and in turn people who live in a particular way are more likely to have a particular range of skin tones.[17]

So, yes, races have real effects. But at bottom they are fictional. It is worth looking at what that means.

ON 'RACES'

The main scientific view on 'race' is this: Any idea of what the supposedly separate human races might be is arbitrary, or at least culturally determined.[18] As members of a single human race, we have been alone on earth for 30,000 years. There are no underlying physical races that underpin cultural differences. If you use skin colour to divide the continuum of humanity into black, white, and yellow, what you will have discovered about your groups—besides the differences in skin colour that you started with—will be precisely nil, just as dividing all the books in the library between those that have blue covers and those that have some other colour will tell you nothing about the insides of the books. 'Books that are blue' and 'people who are yellow' are definable sets, but they are not very useful ones. The philosopher Kwame Anthony Appiah explores how racial definitions that have no predictive power—beyond predicting the categories used to sort people into them in the first place—are circular and nugatory, merely empty words.[19]

Naturally, some sets or groupings can be useful; groupings can have predictive power, where one characteristic goes with another. Knowing the breed of a dog tells you something. The shape and size of a terrier go with an interest in digging holes and trying to find animals in them. A dog that looks like a sheepdog will most likely be interested in sheep. But if you sorted people out by skin colour, they would be all mixed up in every other way, with people who are short and people who are tall, people who follow the financial page and those who don't, good cooks and bad, the tone deaf and the musical prodigies, Type O blood and Type A blood, all being mixed together.

So why are we different colours? Away from the equator, the higher frequencies of light are screened out. Sunlight has to penetrate the atmosphere at an angle, so it travels through the atmosphere for a longer distance and hits more molecules, scattering along the way. People who migrated to these northern lattitudes had to absorb more of the remaining light in order to synthesize Vitamin D. So because of the greater health and child-rearing success of those individuals in the north who happened to be born lighter, the northern populations as a whole became lighter—except for people who moved far enough north to put on furs and adopt a diet centring on fish rich in Vitamin D. They stayed darker.

Early peoples who lived near the equator had more than enough light to make all the Vitamin D their bodies needed. And the darker people in the equatorial populations were more successful than the lighter in screening out mutagenic ultraviolet light. The darker individuals remained more successful and more prominent in the population, so that tropical peoples retained humanity's originally dark colour.

As a result of these adaptations, skin colour before the migrations of the last several centuries corresponded well with the areas to which peoples migrated 10,000 to 20,000 years ago. Some groups may have lightened and darkened more than once in their preagricultural wanderings. In the estimation of Luigi Luca Cavalli-Sforza, there are twenty-seven of these underlying biological groups. The groups who were closest together geographically were the more closely related genetically—so that blacks from West Africa are closely related to Europeans, not to blacks from South India or from the wonderfully named area of Melanesia.[20]

The underlying genetic differences between our twenty-seven groups *predate* these colour changes. So our different groupings beneath the skin do not correspond with popular ideas about what the skin-colour races should be. Underneath the skin, the blacks of Melanesia and Africa are not closely related, whereas the more recently established skin-colour gradients of West Africans and Europeans do not belie the close genetic relationships between these peoples.[21] '[B]ecause of its high degree of responsiveness to environmental conditions, skin pigmentaton is of no value in assessing the phylogenetic relationships between human groups.'[22]

If one wants to call the multifarious and subtle genetic groups that do exist 'races', one can. But these 'races' do not correspond to skin colours or any other obvious surface differences. So if there are human races in the biological sense, they are at the molecular level, and they are invisible to us in history and in the street. Even then, these groups are now crossed and recrossed with one another in fantastically complicated ways resulting from travel and migration. Cavalli-Sforza had to use complicated regression analyses to separate them out.

THE EIGHTEENTH-CENTURY BACKGROUND

The idea that there *are* biological human races in the more familiar sense, that blacks, whites, yellow, and perhaps one or two other groups are the major subdivisions of biology *and* culture, belongs to a particular historical period. The 'races' familiar to us in the modern West were invented and elaborated after the decline of faith in biblical monogenesis in the early nineteenth century and before the maturity of modern genetics in the middle of the twentieth. While words for different groupings of people go back to the ancients, usually distinguishing between those who were part of a political or religious community and those who were not,[23] 'races' in the eighteenth century were no more than any group of people (or of animals, or of plants) with a common descent. Often your 'race' was your family tree, going however far back you wished. The farther you went back toward

Adam, the more of his contemporary descendants you would encompass in your race.

Even in colonial situations where black and white populations were sometimes distinguished under those names, the two groups 'black' and 'white' were often called 'nations', 'peoples', even 'complexions', as Carl Nightingale has shown, but never 'races'. In the British Empire, that word began to connote colour groups only in the late eighteenth century.[24] Until at least the middle of the eighteenth century, the same lack of an idea of race marked the French world as well.[25] But even the new focus on 'race', pioneered by natural historians such as Buffon, was inconsistent and unclear. 'Nations', continental groups, 'tribes', and other groups (formed by external conditions and changing moral or legal arrangements) were vying with heritable 'races' as the concept of choice.

Legions of Enlightenment figures were writing on the supposed biblical ancestors of the different peoples across the globe. They wrote about how climate and level of civilization may have changed a people's colour, or they grouped different peoples by the supposed similarity of their earliest religious beliefs to those of the Jews. Except in the works of David Hume and the Jamaican apologist for slavery Edward Long,[26] and debatably in the works of Thomas Jefferson, Lord Kames, and Immanuel Kant,[27] there was no adoption of anything resembling the more recent idea of the race, where clearly demarcated colour groups inherit different intellectual and moral characters.

Not until the early nineteenth century would polygenetic and racialist theories win many adherents. In the mid-seventeenth century, Isaac la Peyrère had proposed other, pre-Adamic creations of humanity; the Jews descended from Adam but no one else did. This view was not thought to be acceptable, and La Peyrère was forced to recant. Paracelsus had suggested polygenesis and so in the eighteenth century would Voltaire, but not with the elaboration of La Peyrère.[28] The dominant view in the eighteenth century was of a human unity-across-colours, with the colour differences coming from degeneration: The various human groups had degenerated from the common stock of Adam, probably because of climate and environment. These differences were by no means set in stone. For Johann Friedrich Blumenbach, who with his collection of skulls was the first systematic physical anthropologist, the five different geographical races that he identified were changeable. They merely represented poles within one human field—that is, one group shaded off into the others with no clear breaks between them. Change was easy and fast. Because everyone had Adam and Eve as their common ancestor little more than 6,000 years before, colour changes had happened very quickly, with each of the five racial types changing in some way.[29]

As Kathleen Brown, Carl Nightingale, and Roxann Wheeler have pointed out, modern historians sometimes take for granted the real biological existence of the colour-races. They assume that premodern discussions of types and colour differences involved the progress of Western science towards the discovery of certain colour-based racial groups that have an objective reality, and that were just waiting to be discovered.[30] This search for evidence about colour in history—because 'we' know that colour is key to the *real* races[31]—involves taking historical evidence out of its context and making more of it than it deserves. Finding evidence of discrete colour-races too far back in the past means imposing later (and completely artificial) categories on earlier ages, obscuring what was really going on.

And what *was* going on, then, with colour and discrimination in the eighteenth century? In a world of many nations and peoples, Europeans tended to judge themselves superior to others on the grounds of religion, technology, or even clothing, but not by colour, even though they noticed colour differences along the way.[32] The result of these distinctions could be discrimination and murder and intergroup hatred. A few scholars have argued that because these status distinctions between Europeans and others had bad consequences, they are the same as later ideas of physical race and so they should be called racism.[33] I cannot agree that status groups equal racial groups. As Ladelle McWhorter has put it: ' . . . the logic of this early concept of race did not entail [an] all-encompassing type of rac*ism*, any more than the existence of twelve different tribes of Israel entails what we might call "trib*ism*" '.[34]

RACIAL REINVENTIONS

Ideas about humanity and its groups began to get more complicated around 1780, especially with the work of Georges Cuvier and others at the turn of the century. Biblical monogenesis was subject to question in this age of revolution and scepticism. Because of the work of Blumenbach and then of Cuvier himself, there was a new focus on collecting skulls and trying to measure and classify the physical differences between peoples. As the biblical consensus fell away and new kinds of evidence accumulated, speculation about human origins and the unity of humanity ran in new and contradictory directions. Maybe blacks and other kinds of people were not descended from Adam and Eve after all.

The rise of science itself meant that there would be new attempts to classify people (as Tzvetan Todorov has pointed out[35]). After Linnaeus propounded his taxonomy, the question of what a 'species' was became a locus of debate. Were the different kinds of animals, plants, and even people really particular and discrete types, or did they shade off into one another?[36] In works dating from 1813 to 1847, the most influential British author on race in the first half of the nineteenth century, James Cowles Prichard, seemed to go back and forth on monogenesis and polygenesis, and on the related question of whether the human 'races' were fixed in character or subject to continuing modification. Over time he moved away from focusing on the skull measurements and skin colours of the Cuvier school to focus on defining races by language groups. This was his mature position, that people should be characterized by language groups, and he maintained it in the last two decades of his life (and fame) in the 1830s and 1840s.[37]

The more stable late nineteenth- and twentieth-century ideas of colour-races did not exist in England in the first half of the nineteenth century.[38] But the idea of colour-races had emerged earlier elsewhere. Anti-black racism had reared up from time to time in the Islamic world, and this form of racism was carried forward into early modern Spain.[39] Medieval Spain also produced a full and clear idea of heritable blood races (Jewish and Christian).[40] David Nirenberg argues that Spanish racism—complete with a belief in the inheritance of different psychological characteristics—was reinvented in Spain out of the desire to categorize the mix of peoples and religions; it was not inherited from some earlier time.[41] Later on, Spanish rule in the New World would yield a rather different system of inherited racial gradations and racial characterizations; in this new system of races, skin colour mattered more than religious heritage, which was the opposite of the situation in peninsular Spain, where religion mattered most. The 'casta' paintings showed the skin colours, the facial features, and the different ways of furnishing a home of people from each of the various degrees of racial crossing. These carefully labelled paintings indicated which third- or fourth-generation crossings produced albinos, and which crossings looped back to produce pure Spaniards. All kinds of human crosses were named, from the major categories of *español/española*, *indio/india*, *negro/negra*, *castizo/castiza*, *mestizo/mestiza*, and *morisco/morisca*, to *coyote*, *lobo/loba* (wolf), and, yes, *albino/albina*. Character was thought to be inherited along with skin colour. Races were not a continuum but a carefully worked-out set of discrete and heritable units predicting behaviour—in theory.[42] In reality, the census categories used in colonial Latin America did not always have the same number of named gradations as the theoretical tables; and comparisons of one census with the next show that many people eventually passed for another 'race', as people will do.[43] The increasing fluidity of the situation only produced greater attempts at specificity on the part of those doing the classifying.

If race had been invented and reinvented in early modern Spain—whose racial policies in the New World were energetically condemned in Protestant England—the idea of biological race was also invented in the French colonies in the early eighteenth century.[44] It was invented again in a sharply different way in metropolitan France beginning in the 1780s. Sue Peabody argues that as the idea of equality spread among the French in the Revolutionary era, a rationale had to be developed about why the slaves of the very profitable Caribbean plantations should *not* share in this equality; Tzvetan Todorov would argue the same. Then, as other scholars have shown, racial categories and a strongly racist ideology were worked out by anthropological thinkers almost without dissent in France in the first half of the nineteenth century, perhaps in some degree as a response to the Haitian Revolution.[45]

So our story is merely *re*invention of racism in nineteenth-century England—as racism can be reinvented again and again as we look about the world.[46] Thus I disagree with Ann Laura Stoler on one key point. In my view the fact that scholars have found ideas of 'race' reinvented or transformed in different places in different centuries says less about the scholarly process of finding origins for things in the period in which the scholar happens to specialize—and it says more about the real existence of what so many scholars have found in their different periods: 'Race' keeps getting reinvented or rediscovered.[47] Taking a different tack, Kathleen Wilson maintains that the multiple origins which have been argued for 'race' show that race itself is more of a positional relationship than a worked-out ideology or identity. There is truth in this. But I think that people very frequently reify their positional relationships into racial ideologies and identities.[48] Sociologists studying contemporary examples of this process have given it the name 'racialization'.[49]

In nineteenth-century Britain, too, race was reinvented. No more than fragments or echoes had been passed down from earlier periods. When the Chartists (active between 1838 and 1848) protested 'aristocracy', 'caste', the exploitation of the 'working classes', and 'the "National" hatreds which had hitherto divided . . . one family, the human race', nowhere in the litany of human divisions was there any mention of race or colour.[50]

It does not seem that the British had inherited any physical ideas of race from the period of colonial slavery in North America, before the independence of the United States. For no worked-out theory of race or races had been present there. In his massive study of the American attitude toward blacks from the earliest colonial period till 1815, Winthrop Jordan thought that the hints of a conscious idea of physical race in eighteenth-century America were rare and 'embryonic'. Until the 1830s at the earliest, even the slave owners in America had said little about blacks as a physical or heritable race. Instead, they believed that environment—nurture, not nature—is what set one group of people apart from another. American Southerners often confessed that slavery existed because of economic needs and unequal levels of power; no one in this fallen world is entirely free, and some are less free than others. Southerners would admit that they kept slaves because they had the power to do so, and because they profited by it, not because it was right. Or they claimed that by enslaving Africans they were bringing fellow human beings to civilization.[51]

In the era of the American Revolution, there is some evidence that a belief in physical races arose among journalists in the South who were seeking to justify slavery against the arguments of abolitionists. They went so far as to insist that black people were not human.[52] But few American Southerners would give up biblical monogenism even when many in the North adopted polygenist theories.[53] This Northern adoption of polygenist racism, an American *re*invention of 'race', dates from the 1840s and 1850s. It was led by the theorists Samuel G. Morton (who had studied at Edinburgh alongside Robert Knox), George Robins Glidden (an Englishman related to Leigh Hunt, he was the son of the American minister to Egypt and was himself an Egyptologist), and Josiah Clark Nott (an Alabama physician).[54] The Northern polygenist school echoed certain—and in their own time much ridiculed—suggestions by the Englishman William Lawrence in 1818.[55]

Turning to the development of less supposedly scientific, more popular racial attitudes and their effect on the reinvention of race in America, James Brewer Stewart argues that in the increasingly industrialized society of the American north after 1830, distinctions of wealth became more keenly felt. Lower-class whites, he shows, wanted to maintain solidarity with the upper class by distinguishing all whites from the richer blacks. Meanwhile, new urban musical and theatrical entertainments in the cities picked up on the desire for the marginalization and caricature of blacks, and continually reinforced it. So much may also have been true of England, too, about two decades later, as we shall see presently. Stewart also argues for another factor that does not seem to have had an English parallel: Abolitionists tried to move *immediately* to a colour-blind society of integrated and respectable blacks and whites. One unfortunate result of this movement was the widespread burning of black-owned houses, businesses, factories, and churches, and the burning of the white-owned properties where blacks and whites came together.[56]

THE GROWTH OF RACISM IN ENGLAND
BY THE END OF THE 1850S

What then of the *English* reinvention of race? In the middle of the nineteenth century in Great Britain, at the centre of the world's first modern communications network, ideas of racial difference began to crystallize dramatically. There appeared the full set of supposedly permanent races covering the globe, the set of races so familiar from the last third of the nineteenth century to the last third of the twentieth. The standard colour-races began to emerge in the thinking of an increasing number of people.

But the rise of racism in the American North after 1830, made 'scientific' by Morton, Nott, and Glidden in the forties and fifties, played little part in this. The self-serving racial theories of provincial thinkers in the slave-holding United States found little purchase in an England proud of its abolition of slavery in the 1830s, and with little recent tradition of skin-colour racism domestically. The American racist thinkers themselves complained of their rejection in Great Britain.[57]

Before the middle of the nineteenth century, as Douglas Lorimer has shown, black people in Britain did not face discrimination because of skin colour. Those with money moved in the highest circles, those with less money moved through the streets unmolested, and those without money were dependent on employers, patrons or—yes, masters. They suffered and died, as did white Britons with a similar lack of money or connections.

Hierarchy and individual status mattered and race did not.[58] Enlightenment ideas of the universality of human nature and the noble savage meant that blackness was not confused with baseness. By the mid-nineteenth century, the idea of individual responsibility reinforced this principle: Discrimination abounded, based upon socioeconomic status and individual fortune but not upon heritable skin-colour groups. Certain racist theorists can be identified in this intellectually rich but confused period, but even in the 1860s the more overtly racist among them could be treated as marginal figures.[59]

The 1850s saw a hardening of the rhetoric of race prejudice in some quarters in England. One element of this was a new way of understanding the word 'civilization'. As Mark Francis has shown in looking at Great Britain and Canada, 'civilization' had referred to a certain level of education and morality attainable by any properly educated person in the world. By the middle of the nineteenth century, 'civilization' was increasingly defined as the collective inheritance of a whole society—middle classes and the aristocracy together. Uncivilized peoples abroad did not share in that inheritance.[60] But the hardening of race rhetoric was most notable in the new insistence by such men as Robert Knox and James Hunt on the significance and heritability of overarching racial essences.

Feeding into colour-based racism were certain changes in society and mass culture. As Christine Bolt points out, some men who looked back on this period from later in the century believed that the widening of popular readership after the 1830s had led to less careful and more sensationalistic portraits of cultures and races.[61]

Indeed, as Patricia Anderson has demonstrated, it was the period from 1830 to 1850 that marked the first mass-produced high-quality illustrations affordable by the common people, who in earlier times would have been able to see (much less purchase) only the crude and often reused woodcuts of the broadsides. By mid-century, steam-driven printing presses and the *Penny Magazine* and its competitors had brought realistic illustrations to the masses—pictures of flamingos, Buddhist stupas, the paintings of Murrillo—and what people looked like on the other side of the world.[62] We can add an element to her argument: Almost all of the illustrations were in black and white. Thus people could be graded along a single continuum of lightness and darkness, despite differing from each other across many only partially overlapping ways.

The new periodicals began creating and in turn pandering to racist stereotypes in the 1840s, popularizing some of the racist visual stereotypes of black people developed by the early nineteenth-century cartoonists who sold comic prints to the elite.[63] Meanwhile, in the 1840s the missionaries and abolitionists stepped up their propaganda that most blacks were down-trodden and dehumanized. Richard Burton blamed the missionaries for portraying Africans in this way—or rather he did so in his earlier writings, at a time when he would briefly mention skin colour but focused his attentions on culturally rather than physically constituted groups.[64] The missionaries and abolitionists may have been well-meaning in producing their myriad texts and images of nonwhites who needed rescuing, freeing, uplifting, and/or converting, but they popularized an image of nonwhites as weak and helpless.[65]

As Lorimer has shown, this message was reinforced by the publication of the fantastically popular *Uncle Tom's Cabin* in 1852, and the increasing frequency and popularity of exhibitions by such men as George Catlin and P.T. Barnum of American Indians, Africans, and others for the fee-paying public. Blackness and powerlessness came to be associated with one another, as it was among the Baptist missionaries in Birmingham studied by Catherine Hall. And from 1848 to 1873, better economic times and an increasingly urban population saw the birth of a new world of mass popular entertainment in music halls and theatres. Many of the venues featured blackface minstrels. Their racist portrayal of American blacks was as often as not taken for truth.[66]

And there were new stereotypes for whites as well as for blacks. As Lorimer and more recently Catherine Hall have argued, very few trades-men and professionals, however much they rose in the world, could hope to join the English aristocracy themselves, even if in the stable and prosperous mid-century world their children might. Yet such people were free to think of themselves as a part of the same superior, Anglo-Saxon, globe-encircling race as the finest families in the land.[67] Here in a process that we have seen recalls that in the American North, there was constructed a *völkisch* belief in the now-racial unity of the different social classes that was not apparent in the sect-ridden England of fifty years before, in the time of Walter Scott.

It has been argued that Walter Scott's romantic focus on race had been more influential on the continent than in the British Isles themselves.[68] But later popular works would indeed advance the cause of racism. Hall maintains that from the end of the 1850s the works of David Livingstone and Anthony Trollope reflected and reinforced the idea that English people as such were morally and intellectually superior to nonwhites, in ways inherent to the bodily constitution of each group; this new racism may have stemmed in part from Thomas Carlyle's *Occasional Discourse on the Negro Question* (1849).[69] This is a bit unfair to David Livingstone, who saw and treated people as individuals, and who sympathetically describes incidents in the daily life of African cities and towns.[70] But Hall is right about the views of Trollope. For Trollope, writing during his tour of Jamaica in 1859, 'God, for his own purposes—purposes which are already becoming more and more intelligible to his creatures—has created men of inferior and superior race'. Part of the explanation was nurture, but part was nature: 'In many ways the negro's phase of humanity differs from that which is common to ours, and which has been produced by an admixture of blood and our present state of civilization', Trollope said, referring to an 'us' and on 'ours' that extended to Englishmen and perhaps to whites in general.[71]

Meanwhile, there were new ideas of race in science. To paraphrase Nancy Stepan's analysis, by the end of the 1850s there was a new idea of race among theorists interested in the subject. It included (1) a graded scale of value (certain races being above others), (2) innate differences between the brains of different races (measurable from the shape of the head), and (3) a strong element of determinism, rejecting of the idea that any of the supposed differences between 'races' were due either to the environment or to the inheritance of acquired characteristics.[72] And moving away from the loftier reaches of science, the shift from a cultural or mutable idea of race to a physical one begins to be apparent in the writings of certain of the more communicative imperial officials and in English literature more generally from the 1850s.[73] As David Arnold has shown, in British India there was a notable change as well. The earlier idea was that dark-skinned Indians were fellow Caucasians, physically different from the British only because they grew up in a different climate, wore lighter clothing, and ate different foods. The new consensus was that there was an inherited Indian racial identity marked by skin colour; the new thinking can be seen as early as 1830 and it had become widespread by mid-century.[74]

In some of the other colonies with a long tradition of European-controlled slavery or European-native conflict, the idea of 'races' became common earlier than it did in England. As Alan Lester argues, the colonial press in Australasia and South Africa felt aggrieved that the British people did not see races as the colonists did.[75] This colonial racism, growing from the contempt that the dispossessors felt toward the dispossessed, does seem to have been on the rise by mid-century.[76] And sometimes adding to this contempt was a religious component. By the 1840s in South Africa, even the British missionaries were becoming racists. Many had grown disillusioned by the slow rate of conversion, and they began to resort to racial categorization to denigrate their flocks. As Hall has shown, some of the Baptist missionaries in Jamaica had reached the same level of frustration by the late 1850s, if not quite the same level of overt racism.[77]

In England, in any case, racism was newly in evidence at mid-century. Even the publication of *The Origin of Species* in 1859 marked no epic in the consolidation of racial thought. It did not need to. Besides, Darwin had carefully avoided the question of whether people evolve through natural selection in the way the plants and animals do. It was a subject to which he would return later, as we will see.

INTO THE 1860S: A MIX OF VIEWS

By the 1860s, then, the idea of separate physical races was already wide-spread among those who studied the question. Missionary propaganda, a new visual culture in popular periodicals, changes in science, and a desire to unite the unenfranchised together with the enfranchised to create single special English nation had all contributed to the creation of new ideas of racial colour difference. Yet fixed races still remained controversial. Bagehot, Darwin, and many of the figures in this book faced a confusing range of views as they tried to work out their own opinions. Language differences seemed to some thinkers to be at least as good a way of dividing people up as differences in skin colour.[78] At the 1863 meeting of the Royal Asiatic Society, the idea that Europeans were better than Asians and that Asians were better than Africans—and that these divisions were very meaningful in the first place—was soundly rejected, even ridiculed. A similar scene was played out at the meeting of the British Association in Newcastle in the same year.[79] Indeed, the idea of dividing the human world into a few skin colours was rejected even at a number of meetings of Hunt's own Anthropological Society of London in the mid-1860s.[80] And the argument that there was a uniform-looking black race of smelly, prognanthous, pointy-toothed people unable to write books provoked widespread laughter at the meeting of the British Association in Birmingham in 1865, where it was presented—in all seriousness—by John Crawfurd, the polygenist president of the mostly monogenist Ethnological Society. Someone pointed out that he had a shelf of 150 books written by black people. Hunt, also a polygenist, himself criticized Crawfurd's formulations that day.[81]

However, the idea of physical (and physically and morally unequal) races is rightly associated with the work of the same, infamous James Hunt, disciple of Robert Knox. Hunt's racism was so extreme as to put people off. His Anthropological Society (founded in 1863) was famous chiefly for its disrespectably explicit discussions and its display of African body parts. Not until Hunt's death in 1869 would the society back away from such effrontery and achieve social acceptance for its activities, and for physical as opposed to cultural anthropology generally.[82]

The scandalous Richard Burton took things further with his crudely racist (and anonymously published) *Wanderings in West Africa* in 1863, the same year in which he associated himself with James Hunt in founding the Anthropological Society. Dane Kennedy argues that Burton's experience in West Africa changed the opinion that he had developed of nonwhites in East Africa only a few years before.[83] Hunt's other close associate in the Anthropological Society (and at times his secret co-author) was Henry Hotze, formerly a resident of Mobile, Alabama, and while in England a paid agent of the Confederate government. Hotze supplied British journalists and leader-writers with proslavery and anti-black, polygenist propaganda. Back in Alabama, he had also been Gobineau's translator.[84] But

Hunt, Burton, and Hotze in the rabid racism went far beyond acceptable English opinion at the time.

While different thinkers debated the question of whether to divide humanity by physical characteristics or by language, and whether to interpret the resulting groups as many species or as one, it was not hard to find legions of others who kept to the discourse of moral universalism and human unity, grounded in the Christian religion. For the president of the Royal Geographical Society in 1860, African-American explorers were doing good work in advancing geographical knowledge in their expeditions into West Africa. These expeditions (he further explained) were facilitated by the local black African Anglican hierarchy in the person of Bishop Samuel Ajayi Crowther. The 'African descent and appearance' of these explorers allowed them to gain trust with the natives, and he looked forward to the further work of African-American explorers.[85]

This innocent acceptance of dark-skinned Americans as equal participants in the creation of the archive of imperial knowledge about West Africa was not to last. Nor by the end of the century was the authority of Bishop Crowther still accepted by local Europeans. The debate between the adherents of the new racism and the older view of basic human uniformity, which held to the equal aptitude of any group to become civilized if properly educated, first became notable during the Governor Eyre crisis from 1865 on. As Bernard Semmel has shown, the British troops in Jamaica regarded the fighting as a race war, killing and torturing thousands and forcing blacks to kneel and curse their race as such. With widespread beatings, house burnings, and executions, all determined by colour and not resistance to the authorities, the soldiers carried out a racial war to suppress the supposed rebellion. Back in England, the controversy over these actions was also framed in explicitly racial terms.[86]

The controversy over the new racism was especially acute because a key part of the old view was still very common in the 1860s: Any group whom one wished to examine was a race. That is, a 'race' was any group with a common identity down through the generations, whether that commonality was due to nature or due to nurture. And for those who wanted to make the intellectual jump, commonalities due to nurture could become commonalities due to inborn nature after as little as one generation. Most people, Darwin among them, believed in the inheritability of acquired characteristics.[87]

Nor did one have to wait for a new generation to see an astonishing plasticity in the human form. Back in the 1830s, Captain Fitzroy of the *Beagle* believed that he had seen the skulls of the three living Fuegians whom he had taken to Europe assume one form in England and another very different and less civilized shape when these individuals had returned to live among their own people in Tierra del Fuego. Charles Darwin's father believed that the intellectual work and adventures of five years on the *Beagle* had quite changed the shape of his son's skull, and Charles Darwin himself accepted his father's observation as valid, also putting the change in the look of his skull down to the thinking that he had been doing (and not at all to his own increasing baldness).[88] The idea of skulls changing shape in the course of a single lifetime, as African tribes became civilized, also appeared in the popular press in the 1840s.[89] One English observer believed that the shape of foreheads, noses, and lips in Jamaica had changed markedly within a few years of emancipation. Foreheads were no longer sloping.[90]

And even some decades later there was no reason to doubt that acquired characteristics like these changes in the shape of the skull or face would become inherited. In the last two pages of *The Origin of Species* (1859) Darwin was quite clear that acquired characteristics are inherited. Robert Chambers's much noted *Vestiges of the Natural History of Creation* (1844) had argued that while the basic culture-and-language groups tend to persist, whole populations large and small have changed their colour and the size of their jaws from one basic racial type to another, and are continuing to do so; change comes from moving to a different climate or, short of that, adopting a higher or lower mode of living.[91] This view survived the publication of *The Origin of Species* in 1859 and persisted long after. As late as 1868 Charles Dilke in his widely selling *Greater Britain* believed that whites could be changed in their height and build by one generation of living in the colonies. He did not go as far as Robert Chambers had done; the whites would still wind up looking quite distinct from the natives, who were of a different basic race (and who were doomed to extinction, which was 'a blessing' in Dilke's view). Dilke could see strong and in his opinion undoubtedly heritable physical changes in the settlers of arid South Australia, where already the men were born thin and fine-featured, the women small and pretty, but 'burnt up'.[92] Other thinkers continued to believe in the inheritance of acquired characteristics up to the end of the nineteenth century.[93]

RACE AFTER 1870

By the 1870s, however, there was an increasingly pan-Western consensus in favour of fixed, heritable, and intellectually unequal skin-colour-based racial groups.[94] For the average Briton (if such a concept is possible) later in the nineteenth century, blackness meant *ipso facto* servitude, and mental and moral weakness—a weakness that earlier generations would have associated with lower-class blacks *and* whites. Now, large, colour-based 'racial' groups were of key significance.[95] These major colour groups could be subdivided into smaller heritable identities—as with the supposedly warlike Gurkhas and Sikhs[96]—but there was an overall pattern of black, yellow, white, and perhaps one or two more.

The racial categories that came to be constructed in this new era of explicit racialism and proud tropical imperialism overrode all else. Every part of the Old World and some parts of the New had their ancient history retold according to the fantasy of race.[97] No darker people could ever borrow or improve upon any cultural or technological development, much less invent such a development for themselves; any sign of cultural advance showed that the people in question had been invaded by lighter and more advanced groups from the north, supposedly the key to the history of every continent and region save Antarctica.[98] Meanwhile, some scholars erected the main colour races into fully Platonic types—races that recurred around the globe even without sharing a particular descent.[99] Blackness, even when it was found in apparently unrelated people on opposite sides of the world, always carried with it a certain set of physical, psychological, and moral consequences. A mixed descent could dilute but not erase a mixed racial heritage. For some thinkers, the essential type would eventually come back as strong as ever, even in the face of continued interbreeding with whites.[100]

There were occasional hints that the 'races' were not obvious facts but rather categories that a person had to be taught.[101] But by and large the consensus was to try to explain away any signs of our biological continuum as merely the evidence of the crossing of the underlying essential races.[102] This turn to essentialism meant that by the late nineteenth century the field of anthropology would occupy itself in trying to define or uncover the original types in this mixed world. But with the greater accuracy of skull and brain measurements came greater frustration with the results—such measurements refused to clump up into races.[103]

That particular age of racism is over. The development of genetics and molecular biology since the 1960s has shown what the devout Christians of the mid-nineteenth century already knew: There is only one human race. The biological differences *between* the so-called races are far smaller than the differences *within* each supposed group. Thus, statistically—whether one is looking at morphology, intelligence, or most recently the genome itself—the racial groups have no real existence. If we count each breeding zone, with its slightly different statistical frequencies in a few genes, all shading and blending into one another, there are on the order of 10,000 to 100,000 groups, none of much more than 500,000 individuals. Research shows that this is the maximum size of the more uniform and stable of the social/geographical breeding groups from which the most homogenous of pairings can occur.[104] We are simply not divided into three or four large colour-races. It may be traditional to sort medical research data by those large 'races'—especially in the United States[105]—but the better practice is to sort the data by the very different and far more numerous genetic groups that do have a biological grounding. When medicines are marketed to only one 'race', it is a matter of marketing, not biology.[106] Some people insist that human genetic difference *must* sort itself out into continental groups, despite the actual findings of the studies they are quoting[107]—but we know that biologically the human races do not exist.

Some people knew this a long time ago. Long before the work of Luigi Luca Cavalli-Sforza and others on human genetic difference, Franz Boas and his followers, among them Ruth Benedict and Ashley Montagu, made the case that there are no biological races. As Boas observed before the First World War, the descendants of immigrants to the United States who landed at Ellis Island in New York Harbor matched other native-born Americans in size and shape much more than they matched the records of their immigrant parents. American nurture proved more significant for how these children looked than their supposedly racial nature as immigrants.[108]

Standing outside anthropology, W.E.B. DuBois had also pointed out the shifting grounds and questionable statistics used to define or characterize races during his education in America and Germany in the late nineteenth century. Nonetheless, there was this consensus, which at the turn of the century he still shared: 'The world was divided into great primary groups of folk who belonged naturally together through heredity of physical traits and cultural affinity'. By 1940, his view was that science had not yet determined whether there was any inner physical difference of character or constitution between blacks and whites.[109] His conclusion was this:

> Human beings are infinite in variety, and when they are agglutinated in groups, great and small, the groups differ as though they, too, had integrating souls. But they have not. The soul is still individual if it is free. Race is a cultural, sometimes an historical fact. . . .
>
> 'But what is this group, and how do you differentiate it; and how can you call it "black" when you admit it is not black?'
>
> I recognize it quite easily and with full legal sanction: the black man is the person who must ride 'Jim Crow' in Georgia.[110]

As late as the 1960s the idea that the major colour-races really existed, and in the physical sense, rather than Dubois's cultural, historical, and legal sense, was hard to escape, despite the best arguments of the Boas school. Books on Victorian England published in that era often assume that the colour-races are natural divisions to discover and elaborate; so that one can take isolated early- to mid-Victorian quotations that seem to refer to these colour divisions, and isolated thinkers who believed in something only arguably like them, and discern a coherent early Victorian idea of race.[111]

Yet once again I am arguing that up until the middle of the nineteenth century there were a variety of ideas regarding monogenesis and polygenesis, the effects of climate in differentiating people, and the possibility of the degeneration of one stock of people into different stocks. Even at mid-century, discordant voices defined the great colour-races in many different ways, or denied that they existed; and popularized versions of these views further confused the general discourse on race.

Much of this is well known. I am less interested in sifting through the mid-nineteenth century for all the incipient specks of the later racist ways of looking at the world. Other scholars have taken on this (yes) vital task. I am more interested in the processes out of which those specks of later racisms were themselves first formed. I am interested in the synthesis of 'races' from the process of trying to find neat categories for dividing up and analyzing the people of a confusingly diverse world. The very confusion of the mid-nineteenth-century picture of humanity is of key importance. There had already been moments elsewhere in history of the clear 'racial' categorization of people into groups thought to be heritable, as in the blood racism of Inquisition-era Spain.[112] But self-consciously Christian and abolitionist Britain of the early to mid-nineteenth century had moved away from those clear racial categories; nor would they import them from the France that they had defeated in 1815 or recall them from the cruel Spain of the Black Legend—the traditional British complaint of Spanish cruelty to the American Indians. Nor indeed would they listen to the self-serving racist doctrines of colonial slaveholders or planters, whether in independent America or in the colonies that remained under the British Crown. So what matters in this book is the re-creation of heritable racism in a period and a place that did not did not initially possess such a belief. Our focus is this synthesis and reinvention of racism more or less from scratch, by people who were trying to make sense of human diversity, or who were trying (to put it another way) to do social science.

Besides the emphasis on the continual problem of reinventing racism— once again, reinventing it in order to classify people into groups that are stable across generations, a reinvention of 'race' that continues to this day—there is also the particular story that this book tells: Alongside a new British tradition of racial thought from Robert Knox and Thomas Carlyle in the very late 1840s, Anthony Trollope in the later 1850s, and Burton and Hunt in the 1860s, there was another tradition, leading from the parallel views of Arthur de Gobineau and Walter Bagehot, and from Bagehot to Darwin himself. Bagehot and Darwin were more influential (and less scandalous) in their racism than Trollope and even Carlyle were; Bagehot, in his widely selling *Physics and Politics*, and certainly Charles Darwin were vastly more influential than Knox, Burton, or Hunt. Having explored all of this, in the later chapters of the book we can examine how the new ways of classifying people by race were relevant to the thinking of certain key imperial officials.

2 Tocqueville and Race

In *Democracy in America*, Alexis de Tocqueville did not see how a multi-racial society could be constructed in the United States. He thought that a race war was inevitable in North America unless the blacks were given a country of their own. And this was not the only time that he indulged in less than egalitarian racial views. In his writings on French Algeria, Tocqueville came out in favour the destruction of the farms and foodstuffs of the Arabs in the name of pacification and colonization. So, was Tocqueville a racist in the modern sense, as a few scholars have indeed argued?[1]

In fact, Tocqueville was for most of his life a model for how to think about human groups *without* turning them into supposedly inheritable 'races'. He had a formal methodology, keeping national and racial aggregates constantly in question and under constant revision. But when he turned to the French empire he sometimes slipped away from this methodology. As the sociologist David Reisman pointed out long ago, there is a danger in reifying one's analytical groups, a danger in no longer questioning them.[2] And even Tocqueville succumbed to this danger in his later writings on Algeria.

If we are to appreciate the possibility of nonracist social science in the nineteenth century, it is all the more important to examine the nonracist way that Tocqueville used categories in his earlier work. Other scholars have looked at parts of the picture.[3] And Harry Liebersohn has analyzed what Tocqueville wrote on the Ojibway before he composed *Democracy in America*; Liebersohn confirms the fluidity of 'race' in Tocqueville's thought.[4] One thing that is new in the present book is a fuller examination of what 'race' really meant for Tocqueville in the bulk of *Democracy in America*, when he had left the Ojibway behind. As a matter of broader intellectual history, as we have seen, 'race' had yet to settle into its current meaning,[5] with some people using it for large colour groupings and some—including Tocqueville himself—using it quite differently.

It is important to note that indeed the case was not, as Curtis Stokes would have it, that Tocqueville was muddled in his thinking about certain obvious racial categories, categories that should have seemed as clear in his mind as they did to a modern American.[6] We cannot judge Tocqueville by looking at what he said about what *we* might call races: American Indians, blacks, whites.[7] We must look throughout *Democracy in America*, at the wide variety of groups to which *he* applied the concept of 'race' even where we would not—and we need to look at his methodology in doing so.

This emphasis on Tocqueville's methodology in constructing races in *Democracy in America* will also help to shed light on why his later writings on Algeria advocated race war. Melvin Richter, in the earliest careful analysis of Tocqueville's imperialism, and Jennifer Pitts in one of the latest, both argue that Tocqueville supported a racist and murderous conquest of Algeria in order to bolster French pride. By giving the French something to be proud of in Algeria, Tocqueville sought to firm up the French popular will to pursue democratic government in France itself. In addition, Pitts argues that Tocqueville came to see the French colonists in Algeria as still more of the overseas Europeans whom he had observed in America.[8] These are valuable perspectives. But our look at race and how he defined it in the *Democracy* will allow us to identify other strands of thought in Tocqueville's Algerian writings.

For Tocqueville, the Algerian colonists did not yet make up a viable community on the model of the North Americans. Rather, it was other aspects of his picture of America that Tocqueville saw replicated in Algeria—namely, the relative social position of the different races of the United States and the presence of an American-style race hatred between the groups.

And then there was the matter of the way he defined races in the first place. When Tocqueville was closest to defining groups according to the careful methodology that he had employed in *Democracy in America*, his Algerian imperialism was less shocking. His imperialism became more ruthless in those writings in which he ignored his own careful methodology. Perhaps by that time he had become famous and did not feel the need to question his own categories too deeply. Yes, Tocqueville's racism in Algeria was inexcusable. But it can be understood better after examining his earlier, very different methodological care when dividing people up into categories for social analysis.

Alexis de Tocqueville provides a model for how to think about human groups, and how not to. In later chapters we will see how that model was replicated or ignored by different thinkers in England.

THE BACKGROUND: RACISM IN FRANCE

As an abolitionist and an anti-racialist, Tocqueville stood out in the France of his time. Feelings about slavery and race were very different than they were across the channel. Abolitionism in England was constant and broad-based, but as Seymour Drescher has shown, in the France of 1789 to 1848 abolitionism was no more than a sporadic urge on the part of the elite. And there was a key difference between racial opinion in abolitionist

England and the normal way of thinking about the subject in France. In Great Britain, most people rejected the belief that blacks and whites were fundamentally different from each another, while the idea of an essential difference won broad acceptance among the French. For the English, the minds and bodies of blacks had been damaged by slavery—an environmental rather than an essential distinction between whites and blacks. In England, indeed, a belief in permanent black inferiority was not something that one professed, but something that one accused others of professing. British abolitionists charged the slaveholders of the West Indies with believing that blacks were separate and inferior. Most of the slave owners bitterly denied that they thought any such thing. They said that they believed in a common humanity. In taking blacks out of Africa, they had removed them from barbarity to a higher level of civilization. The few British authors of the early nineteenth century who maintained that blacks were inferior were careful to add that they did not believe in slavery.[9]

In France, on the other hand, the one writer who denied black inferiority and who catalogued black achievements was the Abbé Gregoire—who was mostly ignored on this subject during his lifetime.[10] Bitterness over the rebellion in Haiti, the relative lack of familiarity with blacks (.02 percent of the population, perhaps as little as one-tenth the British figure), and the influence of the naturalist Georges Cuvier fed widespread racism. Blacks were not the same as whites. They were inferior mentally and emotionally. A substantial literature was produced on this point throughout the first half of the nineteenth century and beyond.[11]

Alexis de Tocqueville never referred to any of this literature. Twenty-six when he toured America, he had been schooled in the rather different literature of national character. For one thing, he knew his Montesquieu, who had stressed in the mid-eighteenth century that different factors, from climate to custom to laws to 'mores', had to be carefully considered to see which explained the most about a people. But not all of Montesquieu's ideas were serious. They had about them the wit of the eighteenth-century salon: It was climate that had shaped the English, giving them their characteristic distemper, Montesquieu noted. That is why they constantly commit suicide even when they are happy. Their unsettling climate is also why the English have developed government by consensus—they are so constantly dissatisfied that they need a government in which no one person is to blame.[12]

Before they went to America, Tocqueville and his travelling companion, Gustave de Beaumont, had considered the more useful of Montesquieu's ideas. They had also looked at the ideas of Montesquieu's predecessor Henri de Boulainvilliers, who believed that a hereditary ethnic character set the Frankish aristocracy of France apart from the rest of the nation.[13] The young Tocqueville also knew the late eighteenth- to early nineteenth-century Romantic tradition of French travel writing in North America—represented by authors such as Hector St. John Crévecoeur, Constantin-François Volney, and chief among them in literary fame, François-René de Chateaubriand, who was part of Tocqueville's extended family and an important figure in the life of Tocqueville's father. Perhaps with the exception of Volney, these men portrayed the persecuted North American Indians as natural aristocrats not unlike themselves, exiled from the Revolution or, after 1815 (as after 1763), defeated by Anglo-Saxon civilization.[14] Even Volney in his most critical passages—on the hardship and shiftlessness of the lives of North American Indians—nonetheless believed that people are shaped by their environment and not by hereditary race.[15]

Tocqueville knew all of this, having read Chateaubriand, Volney, and perhaps others.[16] But his education did not seem to include either the Abbé Gregoire or, on the other side of things, the leading racist writers of Napoleonic and Restoration France, such as the brothers Augustin and Amédée Thierry and the Gallicised Jamaican Englishman William Edwards (all three had their major publications in the late 1820s). Nor, once he had come home from America, would Tocqueville deign to notice the newer racist or proslavery writings of such men as Victor de Courtet de l'Isle, Louis-Jean-Armand de Quatrefages, and the rest of the Société Ethnologique. Nor would he pay any more attention to his own colleagues in the Académie des Sciences Morale et Politiques by 1840, none other than William Edwards and Amédée de Thierry.[17] And yet in this period of his life Tocqueville worked for the abolition of slavery in the French imperial possessions. Since he was fighting against the proslavery faction, he would doubtless have heard of the corpus of racist writing in France.[18] But he neither mentions any such writings, nor any arguments about the essential characters of the different races of Europe or of the world. Tocqueville does not seem to have had any more time for the racist tradition after he came back from America than he did before he left.

For he had a different approach to the subject of race: An open mind.

METHODOLOGICAL CONSIDERATIONS IN *DEMOCRACY IN AMERICA*

Democracy in America was published in two parts, the first in 1835 and the second and more philosophically analytical part in 1840. Early in the second part, Tocqueville makes a statement on the American approach to philosophy:

> To escape from the systematic spirit, the yoke of habit, family maxims, class opinions, and, up to a certain point, national prejudices; to take tradition only as a source of information, and existing facts as something useful to study only in order to make things out differently and better; to seek for oneself and only on one's own part the reasons for things, striving for results without allowing oneself to become

enchained to a method, and aiming at the foundations beneath out-ward forms: these are the principal traits of what I shall characterise as the philosophical method of the Americans.[19]

In these words on America, Tocqueville also identifies important aspects of his own methodology: To use pre-existing analytical categories ('family maxims, class opinions, and . . . national prejudices') as points of origin, a 'source of information' only, so that the thinker quickly moves beyond them, 'to seek for oneself and only on one's own part the reasons for things'. One does not ignore class or national characteristics, but one uses these chestnuts of received opinion about social groups 'only in order' to think about things 'differently and better'.

Whether or not many Americans rose to this philosophical level, Toc-queville himself certainly did. People often get an abstract idea that may or may not represent the evidence fairly, and then they run with it: Ger-mans are like this, Americans are like that, the postmodernist condi-tion is like such-and-such. Tocqueville was more careful. As his papers and letters show, his full method was (1) to take what he could from the received sociological categories that divide the peoples of the earth into different analytical categories; (2) to use these categories only as prompts to give shape to a program of guided observation; (3) to orga-nize his categories into notebooks of alphabetized headings under which he immediately organized his field observations; (4) to attempt, once in the field, to induce new generalizations and categories that might further stimulate his observations; and then (5), back home, to lock himself away with these voluminous notes—both the notebooks of alphabetized head-ings and his other notes and letters home; and (6) to make new analyti-cal indices for them, while (7) stimulating his mind and his recollections with a heavy program of reading in secondary sources and in the clas-sics of politics and philosophy.[20] With his notes spread about him and a writing desk on his lap, as he tells us, he attempted to intuit a general pattern.[21]

When Tocqueville had sorted enough of his carefully gathered evidence to intuit the applicability of such intellectual categories as 'classes' or 'races' in the particular historical context that he had researched, he would use such terminology. But, as he claimed in discussing whether one ought to employ the idea of social 'classes', he would not set up any such abstrac-tions as permanently valuable reifications.[22] One had to demonstrate that the abstraction fit the evidence in a particular case.

It was with this level of careful fact gathering and careful analysis that Tocqueville first approached the question of permanent racial types. In Sag-inaw, Michigan, where he first saw the way differences persisted between the French and the Anglo-American settlers, he played with the idea that certain cultural traits were indeed inheritable. As Seymour Drescher has pointed out, the heritability of cultural traits would mean that social conditions were *not* so important and that Tocqueville's whole method of analyzing social phenomena was misguided. But indeed Tocqueville's habit of voluminous observation-*cum*-induction would not let him conclude the whole question of heritability from a few observations in one part of North America. He went on to find a number of counterexamples, not least among the French of Louisiana, who had inherited none of the cultural or moral traits of the Quebecois. This showed Tocqueville that history and environment counted for most everything.[23]

Tocqueville's methods freed him from the inherent danger of falling into racialist thinking. His categorizations were always tentative, part of a life-long process of learning and guided observation. Racial categories could not long exist in such a mental universe (the universe of continual revision) unless there really were human races determining the contents of our minds and hearts. There are not.[24]

In *Democracy in America*, Tocqueville did put people into groups, as with the concept of 'Americans' itself—but he did so provisionally and with self-awareness and care. Witness his scepticism:

> God does not think about the human race [*genre*] in general. He sees in a single glance, separately, each of the individual beings of which humanity is composed, and he sees each of them with the resemblances that unite them and the differences that set him apart.
>
> God therefore has no need of general ideas; that is to say, he never feels the need to enclose together a very large number of analogous objects under a single category [*forme*] in order to think about them more conveniently.
>
> This is not the case with man. If the human intellect attempted to examine and judge individually all the particular cases that made their impressions on it, it would soon become lost amidst the immensity of details and see nothing more; in this extremity it has recourse to an imperfect but necessary procedure that makes up for its weakness as well as demonstrating it.

And that imperfect but necessary procedure called to mind these considerations:

> General ideas do not attest to the strength of human intelligence but rather more to its insufficiency, for there are no exactly similar beings in nature; no identical facts; no rules applicable without distinction and in the same manner to several objects all at once.
>
> General ideas are admirable in that they permit the human intellect to make rapid judgments about a great many objects at one time; but on the other hand they never furnish the mind with anything but incomplete notions, and what they give us in breadth they lose in exactitude.[25]

So generalization is inherently flawed but it is inevitable if one is to think. Certainly Tocqueville himself did not shy away from generalizing about large groups of people. It is a wonderful Tocquevillean paradox; he was regretful that generalization is necessary, but he wrote hundreds of pages of it, even producing generalizations about which groups of people were guilty of the most generalization: '[T]he English demonstrate much less aptitude and taste for generalization than their American offspring, and much less indeed than their neighbours the French. . . . '[26]

The contradiction between being sceptical about generalization and doing it anyway is not a fatal one; it is merely a reflection of the human condition.

Besides, the flaws that generalization introduces into one's thought can be minimized, and a web of powerful thoughts can be achieved after all:

> It is necessary to distinguish between these sorts of ideas. There are those which are the product of the slow, detailed, and conscientious labour of the intellect, and these enlarge the sphere of human knowledge.
>
> There are others that spring easily from the first rapid effort of the intellect, and lead only to notions that are highly superficial and highly uncertain.'[27]

So what then of the categories into which we divide each other? For Tocqueville, a 'people' is defined at its earliest origins by language, and also by the spirit of governance, democratic or otherwise, that grows up among each new generation as it works its way through life.[28] But the definition is never final. We do not live in a world of final definitions or finished schemes of races, countries, or other such abstractions: 'and as to the forms of things which are called constitutions, laws, dynasties, classes, I can say that for me not only that they have no value but no existence independently of the effect they produce'.[29]

This nominalist scepticism about the real existence of the abstractions that we talk about makes settling out a scheme of particular fixed 'races' both impossible and undesirable. Knowledge is a set of approximations to be continually transcended and refined; knowledge about humanity—which must mean knowledge in the form of a continual process of learning and not a fixed scheme—cannot be tallied up and ossified into predictive 'races'. So, it does not make sense to try to sort the instances of the word 'race' in *Democracy in America* into those involving skin colours and those that point to different kinds of white people. One must not read into *Democracy in America* any such assumption that black, white, and brown races-as-cultural-and-biological-inheritance groups *do* exist as a part of everyday reality, fixed in character. Avoiding the mistake of injecting modern perspectives into what Tocqueville wrote can be difficult. Even James T. Schleifer's *The Making of Tocqueville's Democracy in America*, a magisterial book, imposes the modern idea of 'race' on Tocqueville's work.

Schleifer draws together Tocqueville's apparent references to colour-races and analyzes them accordingly, while in contrast in *Democracy in America* itself these references are intermixed with other uses of 'race' (chiefly for cultural groups) and scattered throughout the book.[30]

RACIAL CONCLUSIONS IN *DEMOCRACY IN AMERICA*

In the first half of *Democracy in America*, the characteristics that make what Tocqueville describes as a 'race'—'[e]ducation, law, origin, and even their exterior form'[31]—do not add up to much that is passed down inside the body. Neither do the characteristics that define national, occupational, and social groups. Instead, the characteristics of the race, class, or nation in question are the result of the continual re-exposure of each new generation to the conditions that had produced the same characteristics in its predecessors. That is why American Indians, whether considered as a whole or as separate tribes, had the group characteristics that they did. These characteristics were changing as European settlers chased away the game and made the Indians' previous way of life impossible. Meanwhile, the American blacks, whose original languages and national identities had been erased by slavery, had so many characteristics in common with one another because all their conditions of life were imposed upon them by their masters.[32] None of these characteristics was physical. The blacks had no special ability to work in a hot climate, for whites were able to work outside in southern Italy. American whites in the south had simply acquired the habit of laziness, especially in the face of field crops that required more constant attention than those in the north.[33]

In using such categories as black and white, Tocqueville is summing up the effects of a people's environment on each new generation.[34] The words 'race' [*race*] and 'stock' ['*souche*'] do appear,[35] and they sometimes refer to heritable skin colour,[36] but most of their salient characteristics are *not* heritable. If a race shares certain characteristics, that is because each new generation has reacquired these characteristics under a similar set of external conditions. Race, then, is merely one of the several identities into which we are socialised.[37] The Tocqueville of *Democracy in America* was by no means the 'racist' or an 'essentialist on racial questions' that he is sometimes made out to be.[38]

Tocqueville's analytical units—the socially conditioned groups that he perceived—ranged in size from very large ones, such as the blacks, the Indians, and the whites or Europeans, down in scale to the Anglo-Americans, then down further still to more specific European groups such as the Spanish, the English, and the Americans, and on a still smaller scale the English of the Northern states and the English in the slave states, various 'Indian races', and smallest of all the poorer English emigrants from the old slave states who had moved on to form the leading element in the town populations of the Mississippi Valley.[39] Nowhere in the book did he set out any picture of the overall racial structure of the world. He did not set out how many other races there might be other than those he had seen in America, or whether the American races of white, black, and Indian were part of some basic threefold or fourfold or *n*-fold distinction of the basic racial categories of the human world, or how many levels of sub-races and sub-sub-races there might be, or of how one could tell.

But he did put forth a theory of the world history of groups, not races.

He went down this path because of his concern over the future of American Indians. Can a racial group of this kind change its characteristics, thereby resocialising itself, or resituating itself within society? If the American Indians could not defeat European society, could they join it? No, for groups like the American Indians had *never* settled. Tocqueville introduced a theory of the stages of civilization reminiscent of Condorcet a generation before and 'social evolutionism' a generation after[40]—his idea was that different cultural groups in the contemporary world were illustrations of the stages of social development through which the more advanced Western societies had already passed. But he made no assumption that the social or psychological characteristics of his groups were biologically inheritable.

Tocqueville began by rejecting the then popular idea that the Germanic peoples of the forest had brought with them, when conquering the Roman provinces, a love of liberty and self-government that was bound up in their race, and that would prove central to the development of Britain and France.[41] No, instead of there being something especially German and racial about this love of liberty, 'the same cause produced, in the two hemispheres, the same effects. . . . In each of what we call the German institutions, I am thus tempted to see nothing but the habits of barbarians, the opinions of savages in what we call feudal ideas'.[42] History shows that dissimilar peoples become similar because of similar environments. As Tocqueville put it on the last page of the 1840 half of the book,

> I am not ignorant that some of my contemporaries have thought that peoples here on earth are never their own masters, and that they necessarily obey I know not what insurmountable and unthinking force born of anterior circumstances, whether of race or soil or climate.
>
> These are false and mean-spirited doctrines, which can only produce feeble men and pusillanimous nations: Providence did not create the human race [*genre*] either entirely independent or entirely enslaved. She traced, it is true, around each man a fatal circle that he cannot go out of; but within these vast limits man is powerful and free; so are peoples.[43]

The only way the American Indians could survive would be to join European-American society, which would mean settling down to cultivate the land. But this they would not do; the change required would be too great, and so the Indians were doomed to disappear.[44] But there is no inborn racial characteristic that might decree that the Indians cannot be civilized; the reason is that they are all freeborn, socially conditioned, freedom-loving barbarians, natural aristocrats—a traditional view of them in French thought.[45] For Tocqueville, the phenomenon was not a racial one but something familiar in the Old World. 'The peoples among whom civilization has the most difficulty establishing its empire are the hunting peoples'.[46] So:

> When the conquered people is enlightened and the conquering people half-savage, as with the invasions of the Roman Empire by the peoples of the North, or of China by the Mongols . . . the barbarians end up by bringing the subject peoples into their palaces, and the subject peoples in their turn open their schools to the barbarians. But when those who possess the material force also enjoy intellectual superiority, it is rare that the vanquished are civilized; they either retire away or are destroyed.[47]

RACIAL CONFLICT

In America, Tocqueville saw the many kinds of destruction that race prejudice caused. In the *Democracy*, he stressed that prejudice was worse in the North because there the black population had something like legal equality; therefore they were repressed socially. Race prejudice was less severe in the South, where the legal restrictions on blacks allowed the whites to be less fearful of informal interracial contact. If the blacks were freed in the South, they would suffer from the more strict, more Northern style of prejudice, and the continuing distinction that skin colour would draw between who was descended from slaves and who was not would prevent the merging of the two peoples.

Without the divide of skin colour, a better outcome might have been conceivable; Tocqueville cited the slow forgetting of who was slave in origin and who was not that followed the collapse of ancient Roman civilization. But in America the memory of who came from slave stock would remain encoded in the skin. Tocqueville was pessimistic about the possibility that the American blacks and the American whites would ever live together in freedom.[48] Prejudice would remain too strong: '[T]his stranger whom servitude has introduced among us—hardly do we recognize within him the common features of humanity. His visage to us seems hideous, his intelligence appears limited, his tastes are low; we come close to taking him for a being intermediate between brute and man'.[49] Here Tocqueville adds a footnote: 'For the whites to give up the opinion that they have conceived of the intellectual and moral inferiority of their former slaves, the negroes must change, and the negroes cannot change while that opinion exists'.

Prejudice therefore has real effects on social opportunity and self-esteem; the races are different, but only because society continues to produce these differences. After the abolition of slavery, the continuing colour difference would still leave the need to 'destroy three prejudices that are harder to take hold of and more tenacious: the prejudice of the master, the prejudice of race, and the prejudice of the white man'.[50] Strictly speaking, then, we can see that in Tocqueville's view the problem is not race, but racial prejudice, starting with the very idea in the minds of Americans that races exist. Americans then act upon this mistaken belief.[51]

The question of colour could not escape Tocqueville in North America, even if he wanted to focus on the nature of democratic equality. Thus, 'While the negro remains in servitude, he can be kept in a state bordering on brutishness; free, he cannot be kept from teaching himself to appreciate the extent of his wounds and to catch a glimpse of the remedy.'[52] Those on the bottom will try to force society on toward equality, whether they are the European masses of Tocqueville's introduction or the emancipated blacks of this passage. That is, everywhere human history has the same motor, which is the impetus on the part of the many to catch up to the privileged few. This is the uniform, underlying human nature that Tocqueville has been striving for through all of his studies; races are not. Races do not exist except insofar as certain groups share a common set of experiences down through the generations.

THE DEVELOPMENT OF TOCQUEVILLE'S VIEWS ON ALGERIA

While he was still finishing *Democracy in America*, Tocqueville turned his attention to the French colony of Algeria. Algiers had been acquired in 1830, and ten years later the rest of the country was taken and large-scale colonization was begun—this included the forcible dispossession of much of the Arab population, starting along the coast.[53] Support for this move ran the political gamut from Frederick Engels and the Saint-Simonians on the left to French generals such as Thomas Robert Bugeaud on the right.[54] Tocqueville and his brother, along with Gustave de Beaumont, each considered becoming colonists themselves. This prospect is what prompted their first visit to Algeria in 1841. Tocqueville would also make another extended journey there in 1846. He made himself into one of the main Algerian experts in the Chamber of Deputies, and he wrote a number of articles in which he analyzed the relationship of the colonizers to the colonized.[55]

It should be stated at the outset that Tocqueville was by no means in favour of political or social equality for the colonized Arabs and Berbers. Other scholars have shown this.[56] One argument from liberal scholars is that Tocqueville was so *strongly* liberal that he wanted equal Frenchness for everyone and so became blind to the human costs of French colonial expansion.[57] George Frederickson also cites this French universalism of 1789, but he adds a Christian missionary element to Tocqueville's supposedly universalist imperialism.[58] Frederickson's interpretation seems unlikely, for Tocqueville's Christianity showed less of a proselytizing zeal than a cool attachment to what he thought was a necessary moral teaching.[59]

Faced with this problem of Tocqueville's Algerian imperialism, another response is that his liberalism simply lapsed somehow,[60] or that his so-called liberalism was always compromised by a lifelong fondness for imperial adventure.[61] Richard Boyd argues that it is fortuitous for Tocqueville's liberal reputation that his conclusions as a social scientist took him in a liberal direction when he studied America and France; for when Tocqueville studied the immoral French presence in Algeria, the essential amorality of his methodology revealed itself in his illiberal conclusions.[62] But for all the complexities of Tocqueville's thought,[63] surely he had deeply liberal convictions, as Boyd indeed details in a later work.[64] For Michael Hereth, the unusually illiberal, Algerian Tocqueville was espousing a blurry passion for right and country. And as Mourad Ali-Khodja has argued,[65] Tocqueville in his Algerian writings was indeed indulging in a blurry orientalist vision of the Islamic world. Hereth argues that Tocqueville was deliberately indulging in all this emotionalism and blurriness as a means to excite the healthy (and very blurry) passions of the French.[66]

Most recently, Cheryl B. Welch has shown that that Tocqueville did indeed see very clearly—and not in some blurry haze—how deeply he was violating his own beliefs. She has catalogued the rhetorical dances that he used to avoid facing up to his own argument for inequality and oppression in Algeria.[67] But we should recall that is some ways his thought had not changed all that much since his American days. Tocqueville did not favour equality for the peoples of Algeria, and he did not believe that Anglo-Americans, blacks, and Indians could live together in equality in the United States. He had predicted race war between black and white if the slaves were ever freed, because they would want more in the way of equality than the colour-prejudiced whites would ever be prepared to give. The most the blacks could hope for would be a country of their own, should the United States fragment; and the Indians would disappear. If they remained hunters they would lose their hunting grounds; if the Indians settled into farming they would be absorbed by the whites.[68]

Tocqueville was not *advocating* either race war or Indian removal as courses of action. Instead he was recognizing that white prejudice was the main problem. Given the recurring and degrading conditions in which the nonwhite races of North America were placed, the whites would keep developing racist prejudices against them. Tocqueville's pessimism regarding the future of race relations in America came from what he saw of the real social effects of racial prejudice in creating 'races' of different characters.

But from that way of understanding the world—what Liebersohn has called Tocqueville's 'socioeconomic interpretation of race',[69] which was still

Tocqueville's position in his first Algerian writings—he would move to a position of apparently racist, even genocidal imperialism in his later writings on Algeria.

Having devoted so much effort to adducing his own categorization of groups and races in America, Tocqueville applied them rather lazily to Algeria. He did not rebuild or re-derive his categories with full intellectual rigor. This methodological lapse is, I think, the key to understanding the nastier parts of his Algerian writings. We need to explore these aspects of his thinking.

*   *   *

In 1837, when Tocqueville was still writing the second volume of the *Democracy*, he published his first two articles on Algeria. He had yet to visit the country, and he does not make clear what the majority of his sources were, beyond continual references to his opponent in debate, the anti-imperialist deputy Amédée Desjobert,[70] whom he addresses directly throughout the essays. Certainly he had heard much from his cousin and frequent correspondent, Louis de Kergolay, who had been a soldier in the conquest of Algiers,[71] but this source is not mentioned in any of Tocqueville's Algerian articles; the impression that one gets from them is that Tocqueville was drawing on the same kinds of government reports, gentlemanly conversation, and metropolitan journalism that informed so many of his observations on America. Here, however, he is drawing upon French rather than American sources, and so he does not feel the need to name them. His only specific citation is to the work of the Institut de France on the origins of the Berber farmers of the Atlas—the Kabyle 'race'. He makes fun of the members of the Institut for their various racial speculations on whether the Kabyles are descended from the Gascons, the Arabs, or the Vandals: 'You may be sure, sir, that no one knows anything at all about their origins. But in truth this hardly matters. It is the Kabyles of our day that we need to know, not their ancestors.'[72]

For him, what matters about this race and the only thing that keeps them distinct from their neighbours is their current mode of life: 'The Kabyles live in the Atlas, the Arabs in the valleys. . . . In this way the two races are always intermingled, but they never become one.'[73]

And race-as-socially-determined type remains, not surprisingly, Tocqueville's preferred working definition. It was the definition that he was using at the same time in the second half of *Democracy in America*, which he was still engaged in writing. Defining races by their socioeconomic positions means that one can ignore tribal or other smaller divisions between similarly situated peoples. Indeed, Tocqueville did just that—he employed socioeconomic categories and explicitly rejected the importance of the hereditary Arab tribal structure. One can also see another procedural advantage to remaining with the idea of race-as-socially-determined type:

Such races can be read from social conditions, carefully considered but considered at a distance, while exploring races-as-lineal-descent groups would require detailed and accurate genealogical or biological knowledge. Tocqueville was able to reject the popular ideas of the nature of the Arab race that were common, he said, in the France of his day.[74]

Further, he was able to employ a key concept from his American work, that of 'mores'. Their shared 'mores'—along with their shared origins, memories, and opinions—showed that these 'tribes' were once one 'people', one 'nation'.[75]

And it is mores that as a political thinker and not a biologist he is chiefly interested in. In Algeria one finds the 'general traits of the Arab character'—the sensuality, the shrewdness, and the changeability. The Arabs are 'a mobile and indomitable race that adores physical delights but that places liberty above all the pleasures and would sooner flee into the desert sands than vegetate under a master.'[76] All these characteristics were 'known for many centuries'. So Tocqueville is beginning by reporting the common appreciations—the first step in his methodology, as we have seen. But in thinking about race in Algeria, will he look through these received forms to make headings and observations of his own?

For the moment, it seems so. He still refers to smaller level groupings as 'races'. Tocqueville is even careful enough to note that children can be of different races than their parents. He explains that the Turks did not trust their own children by the local women. 'Preferring their race to their family, they had no desire whatsoever to recruit among their sons. But every year they sent to Turkey for new soldiers.' Their children by the Arab women were called *coulouglis*, and along with the Jews they formed another strand of the town population.[77]

The second of Tocqueville's 1837 letters on Algeria, written a month after the one that we have been following, is concerned with how to rule the Algerians; it is to that end that he has gathered the information that we have been reviewing. And yet if the French authorities in Algeria learn the lessons that he is trying to teach them, then the familiar racial characteristics of the Arabs known for so long would no longer remain apparent. The way he describes them, the racial characteristics that he has been detailing would no longer be reproduced from one generation to another. The Arabs would then be living in permanent settlements, and therefore they would grow up with different racial characteristics. Again, this is the socioeconomic view of race. These culturally transformed Arabs would be more like the people already living in Algeria's towns, the people known as the Moors. The Moors themselves, as Tocqueville says at the end of the first letter, 'belong to various races', but the majority of them were indeed simply that portion of the Arab population which had preferred the settled and prosperous life of the towns. Thus, moving into a town meant changing one's racial category from Arab to Moor, seemingly in the very next generation.

Meanwhile, the civilizational or social-evolutionary chasm between the nomadic but highly cultured Arabs and the French settlers did not seem so great to him as the chasm standing between the North American Indians and the modern Anglo-Americans. The Arabs were nomads, but they also divided up their land into carefully documented, carefully marked-out, individually owned parcels. Some of these they planted individually while most they used for the grazing needs of the whole tribe. If the Arabs living under this system were not quite sedentary, as they were still living out in their tents, nonetheless they were very much more sedentary than the freely roaming 'hunting peoples' of North America.[78]

Nor was there in the gap between the non-Arab, Berber farmers of the mountains (the Kabyles) and the French, however wide that gap might be, the extreme, colour-coded gulf between America's black slaves and its free whites.

While Algeria, like America, had three groups—one nomadic, one non-white but sedentary, and one European—the outcome of the interaction of the three groups of Algeria was still indeterminate. Without the racial pessimism of *Democracy in America*, then, Tocqueville's 1837 Algerian articles were free to reveal more of his own hopes. If the settlers took or bought the land that the Arabs used least, 'without violence', he looked forward to

> a time in the near future when the two races will be intermixed in this way throughout much of the regency . . . finally to form a single people from the two races.
> Everything that I have learned about Algeria leads me to believe that this possibility is not as chimerical as many people suppose.[79]

Tocqueville has imported some of his American categorizations, but so far he is holding to his careful method of re-categorization; race is still a fluid and a situational thing.

TOCQUEVILLE EMBRACES GENOCIDE

The racial optimism and analytical open-mindedness of his earlier writings on Algeria did not survive the experience of actually visiting the country. In an unpublished 1841 essay on Algeria that he wrote after his first visit, an essay that Jennifer Pitts has carefully explored, Tocqueville was already in favour of the violent reduction of the Arabs in order to expand French settlement as soon as possible. If the French did not take Algeria, someone else would—and so France *must* take it, and keep it, or the French must accept that they were a nation in decline and that all the world would know it.[80] Continually defeated at home and abroad, the French tended to grovel before the tyrant who promised material comfort in exchange for curtailing liberty. The settlement of Algeria was a great project that would rebound to the glory and thus the freedom and political maturity of the French people.

What did that mean for the colony? What about the political maturity, the self-esteem, the feelings of the colonized instead of the colonizers? That side of things did not seem to matter.[81] Native resistance must be suppressed. Again, whatever needed to be done to secure and further French settlement *must* be done for the good of the psychology of France.

Tocqueville listed the specific measures that he thought justified. They included seizing unarmed women and children, burning villages, going on *razzias* (French military raids of destruction, which had killed a tenth of the population of the country in a few years), destroying most of the villages, and preparing for years of war not with an identifiable enemy but with the whole colonized population.[82] The savagery was tremendous,[83] and to him it was justified.

Four years before, Tocqueville had denied that the coming together of the races of Algeria was 'chimerical'. Now that was exactly what it was. The Arabs and Muslims were slowly dying off—here Tocqueville does not mention by whose agency—while the Christian population kept growing. 'The fusion of these two populations is a chimera that one only dreams of when he has not been to these places.'[84]

Yet while we may know *why* Tocqueville took up the cause of French expansion in Algeria, namely for the glory of France, what about the *how*? How did he reconcile his situational ideas about race with his new position of embracing racial conflict? Where was his methodology now?

*   *   *

While most of Tocqueville's notes from Algeria record what he was told by different officials and private gentlemen, the notes begin with two strong and vibrantly expressed impressions of his own. His first note concerned the bustle of races—races defined in the old way, by mores and by culture. In Algiers, there was a '[p]rodigious mix of races and costumes, Arab, Kabyle, Moor, Negro, Mahonais, French. Each of these races, tossed together in a space much too tight to contain them, speaks its language, wears its attire, and displays different mores.'[85] The bustle and level of building activity of the place reminded him of Cincinnati.

Tocqueville's second major observation going in was the level of violence. It stood out very starkly as soon as he had left Algiers proper to see one of the neighbouring villages. He travelled on a '[s]uperb road that seems as though it must lead to the provinces of a vast empire, and that one cannot follow more than three leagues without being beheaded.'[86] Algerian settlers faced a far higher level of violence than they did in the New World. The plains Arabs had to be defended against with pillboxes placed a cannonshot apart around every French-controlled town or port. Sometimes the enemy were the Kabyles of the mountains; but most of the time on the flat land where the French wanted to carry out their operations and settle, it was the Arabs themselves.[87]

Unfortunately, that left the French colonists huddled under the shadow of their own military. And the French military officers were forbidden from owning colonial land, so in defending the colony they were not defending their own interests. They despised the colonists, whose lands and goods they arbitrarily seized whenever they wished. The development of civil society in the colony was crippled.

If French civilization were to advance in its overseas form, as English civilization was doing in the United States, Algeria must be reformed. Tocqueville argued that the French government of the colony had to be put on a more democratic footing, so that decisions could be made locally, not in Paris. And the colonial government should not simply seize the property of absent Frenchmen, away in France for several weeks of vacation, whenever it wanted money.

But *must* French civilization advance overseas? A colonist named de Saint-Sauveur advised Tocqueville that the country would be far more productive if French colonization were abandoned and the Arabs were set to work farming the now-underworked Turkish estates. The French should rule but not settle a more prosperous Algeria.[88] Tocqueville noted the man's ideas in detail, but he rejected them. Nonetheless, Tocqueville acknowledged that French colonization would mean a long war with the distrustful Arabs. For Tocqueville, the level of violence was already so high, and Arab distrust of the French so deep (because of blunders on the part of French commanders), that doing what Saint-Sauveur advised and allowing the Arabs to keep their territory, allowing them to prosper, was in fact impractical. The level of mutual distrust would not allow the Arabs to believe that this was what the French were really doing.[89] So, Tocqueville argued, the French might as well confirm the worst fears of the Arabs and take their land.

Indeed, the attempt to cooperate with the Arabs would mean building up a level of trust that was impossible—because the French side could not restrain itself. That is, there would be occasional lapses in the policy of not killing Arabs, dooming any attempt to implement a policy of cooperation.[90] Therefore, there should be no such attempt. In other words, because as in America the whites were so violently racist (literally, for they were carrying out racist violence), they should get what they wanted out of that racism; they *would* get what they wanted, the removal of the previous tenants. And in Algeria the best should be made of this now inevitable situation, to make a better colony and a better France. Conquest should be undertaken hand in hand with as rapid a colonization as possible.

Tocqueville seems to have turned away from his racial scepticism for a time. Or if race was situational, the only situation that mattered was that of the French as a whole *versus* the natives considered *en masse*.

Certainly he was still capable of deeper analysis, at least when a finer-grained disaggregation of the term 'Arab' might serve French interests.[91] Even in this 1841 essay, Tocqueville knew full well that the terms 'Arab' and 'race' were inadequate: Arabs soldiers do not make good infantry because they do not like being in the infantry,[92] not because of some ineffable quality in the Arab racial mind; meanwhile, *French* officers in Algeria who are permanently stationed in the country like being there much more than those posted there for a limited time, and the result is 'that one would think they formed two distinct races'—one set of Frenchmen energetic, and with a passionate desire to conquer the country, and the other weak, demoralized, and ill.[93] Even the Arabs make what seems to be a racial distinction between themselves and those who live in the towns, with whom they deny any common origin or 'generic name' [*nom générique*].[94]

Tocqueville's prejudices loom over his analyses. Algerian colonization was world-historical in its inevitability: 'Africa has henceforward entered into the movement of the civilized world and will never leave it'.[95] As in the *Democracy*, his conclusion was that the racism of the world-dominating, expanding whites was so severe that there was no hope for peaceful cooperation between settlers and original inhabitants. And so the original inhabitants were doomed. What was different about the two situations was that in the French case he advocated the acceleration of that doom. Tocqueville admitted that his idea of subduing the natives, destroying towns, burning crops, killing large numbers of people, and colonizing the country was the path of 'iniquity' and violence, but it was also the necessary path if France were not to be humiliated by having to withdraw from Algeria, and see Algeria fall into the hands of another power.[96]

It has been argued that Tocqueville could afford the luxury of a humanitarian position only in his more abstract works.[97] There is much to be said for this view. Tocqueville did see a distinction between the science and the art of politics; the clarity possible in political philosophy was not something to look for in the artful dodgings of the active politician, captive to public opinion.[98] But ultimately Tocqueville the thinker and Tocqueville the statesman still had much in common. In the 1841 essay on the practical questions facing the French in Algeria, Tocqueville the politician still took America as his point of departure, he still had the same world-historical picture in mind that he had for America, and he employed the same ideas about the civilizational stages of different peoples that he had employed in the *Democracy*. Above all, he had the same idea of the problem to be faced: not that races exist, but that Europeans think they do, and act accordingly. But rather than sticking to this methodological insight into the nonexistence of fixed races, he began lumping people together as either colonizer or colonized. He even used racial categories, and counselled actions based upon looking at the world in a racist way: '[t]he quarrel is not between government and government, but between race and race'.[99]

Tocqueville did not lapse from his philosophical ideas when he was writing about Algeria; he lapsed from applying them—in the end, he lapsed from applying his own methodology of continually reconstructing his ideas and categories, the methodology that had allowed him to see through the idea of race. Perhaps that is why he did not publish the essay.

BEYOND ALGERIA

And Tocqueville did revisit the question of imperial morality. In 1843 he devoted a series of articles to the French sugar islands and advocated the emancipation of slaves in the French Empire. Here his analysis returned to its moral centre. In these articles he let his belief in racial mutability fly free.

As he would do in his later work *The Old Régime and the French Revolution,* in this series of articles Tocqueville focused on his key themes while nonetheless carefully working through primary-source evidence, reshaping his conclusions according to what he found.[100] In this case, Tocqueville took his evidence largely from the voluminous reports issued by the British government regarding the great project of abolition. Great Britain had abolished slavery in its empire over a few years following the Slave Emancipation Act of 1833. He thought that its terms ought to be the model for France.

The French planters predicted anarchy and ruin from abolition under any terms, as the English planters had predicted in their turn.[101] But events in the English colonies had proved the planters wrong, as Tocqueville saw it. Even those British colonies that remained French in language and culture shared the more or less happy fate of the English-speaking colonies. Yes, abolition had brought problems to the British sugar islands. The unplanned move of many former slaves into farming or their own businesses had caused a labour shortage and a rise in wages in the sugar industry, which resulted in an economic depression among the planters. But as the blacks set up their households, they bought a variety of British goods. The overall picture of British emancipation showed the freed people behaving morally and industriously, trying to make comfortable lives for themselves.[102]

Indeed, now that they were no longer slaves, '[t]he Negros seemed . . . perfectly like all other men'. Indeed, '[p]lace English or French workers in the same circumstances, and they will act in precisely the same manner'.[103]

If, as Tocqueville had argued in the *Democracy,* the North American Indians could not adapt quickly enough to modern conditions to survive, the blacks of the Caribbean had made their leap (from slavery rather than hunting, to settled agriculture) much more quickly. The suddenness of the change put paid to racial ideas, and to the inevitability of the conflict caused by European racial prejudices: 'In an instant almost a million men together went from extreme servitude to total freedom, or better put from death to life. Just a few years were required to accomplish something that Christianity could only do over a great number of centuries.'[104]

There was no reason that France should not make the jump and emancipate its slaves, and every reason for doing so: England had usurped the place of France at the vanguard of freedom by freeing the slaves of its empire; the glory of France required that she should retake her rightful position as the exemplar of values that were French in origin.[105] The glory of France here came allied to the cause of humanitarianism, unlike the situation in Algeria.

＊   ＊   ＊

While Tocqueville's Algerian views cannot be disguised, his socioeconomic definition of race as a continually reproduced set of effects on a people growing up under certain circumstances is probably the best way to think about 'racial' groups. In later years he would examine the apparent stability of national character,[106] but he would never embrace the idea of colour-races.

And yet as a young man elected to the French Academy in 1841, and moving into politics, he did not stop to question his categories deeply enough when he turned his attentions to Algeria. It is significant that he made his old categories from North America do double duty, and more significant yet that in the end he fell back to a crude French *versus* native distinction. He did not re-create or re-distil his categories as he ought to have done. As we have seen, he did not forget how to analyze constructed social groups like the 'Arabs'—he simply chose not to make the effort as often or as deeply as he should in a matter regarding France. Perhaps one problem is that it would indeed have taken a special effort to get to know the Arabs very well. When Tocqueville created his categories of the nomads and farmers and Indians and such of North America, he had been able to speak to the people involved in English and French. When he reused his categories in Algeria, he had not been able to speak to the Arabs and the Berbers in their own languages. He had done some research before his voyage, but only in applied colonial and Islamic law, not in the nature of the people—and he could not interview them on the subject.[107] Ultimately in his mind (in the essay in question) the various groups of Arabs and Berbers were simply non-French, lumped together as a foil for French national pride.

One solution in an intellectual situation like this (besides learning Arabic) might be to put a greater stress on methodology when the subject of national or racial categories comes up. For even when one's intellectual categories are long established, they continually need to be properly derived and questioned—even in small works on Algeria, and even when you have already written the great book on America.

3 Gobineau, Bagehot's Precursor

Tocqueville's views on race were utterly rejected by his friend and secretary, Arthur de Gobineau. Gobineau argued that the human races are real, biologically separate, highly unequal, and in permanent conflict, and that the Aryan race is responsible for all civilization. For him, racial conflict and conquest are required to retard cultural decay; race is the key to history. Later, in England, Walter Bagehot would come to all of these conclusions, and in a strikingly similar way.

How did they both come to this new way of looking at race? We will start with Gobineau, and in the next chapter we will turn to Walter Bagehot.

RACE, OR CHAOS?

Arthur de Gobineau would rise to fame by denying the effects of environment upon race and culture. But his own cultural position was strongly affected by the unusual environment of his youth. Born outside Paris in 1816, this French boy received a thorough grounding in the German language and the German *Weltanshauung*. Then, from the ages of fourteen to sixteen, Gobineau attended a German-language school in the bilingual Swiss town of Bienne (or Biel). His love of the Germans would always mark him.

After his schooling there was a short period when he lived with his father. The object was to prepare the young man for a military career, but it was not to be. He spent his time reading. The young Arthur had become too enamoured of literature and languages, not only German but now also Arabic, Persian, and Hindi. He was bookish, a Romantic, a budding Orientalist. And he enthused over the Germanic aspects of his supposed genealogy—*'Je descends d'Odin!'* he exclaimed.[1] In 1855 the pull of Romanticism was so strong that he would award himself the title of count.

In 1835, with no systematic or professional education after the age of seventeen, Gobineau settled with his uncle (the real count) in Paris. This was the year that Tocqueville rose to fame with the first volume of *Democracy in America*. Gobineau did not yet know him. The young Gobineau frequented his share of salons, looking for his opportunities; meanwhile, he worked by day as a clerk in a gas company until he went to work for the post office in 1839.[2]

In 1843 he moved into journalism. In looking at Gobineau's journalistic output, Michael Biddiss has argued that Gobineau always found the modern world to be decadent and in terminal decline. In Biddiss's view, Gobineau constructed his theory of racism so as to justify his own pessimism.[3] However, Biddiss admits that in his early journalism Gobineau was not always so pessimistic, not always so sure of the decadence of his age as he would one day become.[4] Perhaps another reason for Gobineau adopting a theory of racial determinism was that he was trying to find a simple principle to bring order to his studies and his journalism—which were in danger of becoming a jumble of efforts on literary and political themes.

Becoming a journalist was not Gobineau's only career breakthrough in 1843. In the same year none other than Alexis de Tocqueville hired him as a researcher, seeking out his knowledge of German. Tocqueville set him to the task of reading and preparing notes on different organs of law and finance in the German states, on the major German idealistic philosophers, and also on a number of British political economists. By the end of 1843 Gobineau complained that he was confused by all the variety and detail. He thought he was merely labelling things rather than finding any clarity in them.[5] He wanted a pattern, and he wanted it more quickly than Tocqueville's careful research methods would allow.

When Tocqueville became Foreign Minister in 1849, he took Gobineau along as his secretary. The clerk at the gas company had come a long way in ten years. Although Tocqueville lost his own position a few months later, Gobineau stayed on in the Foreign Ministry for what was to become a three-decade career in minor diplomatic appointments. He was posted at Berne until he was sent to Frankfurt in 1854. In the neat, German-speaking environment of Berne in 1851 he seems to have conceived the idea of a huge book that would finally make clear the whole pattern of the world history and culture, and the central role of Germans in all human achievement. Under the title *Essai sur l'inégalité des races humaines*, it was published in five volumes between 1853 and 1855.[6]

Let us turn to what he said in it, for it was meant to be a complete alternative to Tocquevillean thought.

EVIDENCE AND RACE

In the nineteenth century, Gobineau believed, there was almost too much information coming out about the rest of the world and its peoples. Ethnologists could hardly make sense of it all: 'Every year brings [ethnology] even richer contributions.' These contributions poured in from so many different fields of knowledge that 'only with some trouble is it possible to take in and classify discoveries as quickly as they accumulate.'[7] For guidance in this age of upheaval, 'to soundly decide the characteristics of humanity, history has become the only competent tribunal'.[8]

But was there enough evidence to support what Gobineau had in mind? For he was about to set up a system of detailed historical generalizations about the inner character and psychological makeup of all the societies of the world since the origin of civilization. Was there really enough evidence for this? Tocqueville had thought that America was unusual in part because its origins remained clear; one could follow a chain of evidence from the first days of the American colonies all the way to the present. One could not do that with the countries of the Old World, as Tocqueville had pointed out.[9]

But Gobineau maintained that one could do just that. There was so much evidence that one could construct firm, fine-grained generalizations about every society, going all the way back. Research in Assyrian and Vedic archaeology, however fragmentary and however lacking in precise chronologies, had yielded knowledge of a kind far more important than any chronological table: 'the revelation of customs, the manners, of the very portraits and costumes, of vanished nations. We know the condition of their art. We know their whole life, physical and moral, public and private. . . . ' Gobineau believed that he had the evidence to understand even more than that: '[I]t becomes possible to reconstruct, by means of the most authentic materials, that which constitutes the personality of races and the main criterion of their value.'[10]

In place of Tocqueville's idea that racial groups of different sizes are constructed by their varying social experiences, Gobineau argued that each of the major colour-races has a fixed 'personality', constant since the most ancient stages of history. These lineal descent groups are themselves indivisible, but they can come together to form more complicated racial mixtures. Gobineau meant to undertake 'a kind of historical chemistry'.[11] He wanted to 'dissolve' the obscurities and look at the discrete racial substances underneath.

Gobineau tells us early in the book of a time when he came to see race as the most important human characteristic, the key to history. But then he was 'struck with the crushing thought, that in my haste I was advancing a proposition that was entirely without proof. I began to search for it. . . . '[12]

And as often happens in such cases, he found what he was looking for:

> It was thus, by induction after induction, that I allowed myself to become fully convinced by the evidence that the ethnic question overshadows all other problems of history, and holds the key, and that the inequality of the races from whose confluence a nation is formed suffices to explain the whole chain of events of its destiny. Every one must already have been struck by some glimpse of this sparkling truth. . . . [13]

Cultures rise when and only when a more energetic race conquers a settled people:

> Everyone must have seen how certain groups of people have descended upon a country in olden days, and by their sudden action they have transformed its habits and its way of life; and that where torpor had reigned before their arrival, they have shown themselves able to cause an unknown activity to gush forth.[14]

But underneath the mere idea of the admixture of conqueror and conquered there was an even more important fact about just who the energetic conquerors were. Gobineau's discussion of his main chain of reasoning concludes this way:

> Having recognized that there are strong races and weak ones, I preferred to examine the former, to unravel their dispositions, and especially to recover the links of their genealogy. By following this method I satisfied myself in the end that everything great, noble, and fruitful in the works of man, in science, art, and civilization, the observer can trace back to a single starting point, and comes from the same seed [*germe*] and a single thought; it belongs to only one family whose different branches have reigned in all the civilized countries of the universe.[15]

And their name was Aryan. Of the ten great civilization-races of the earth, nine were begun or led by energetic Aryan conquerors. The only one that was not Aryan in origin was the 'Assyrian' race of the Jews and Phoenicians. Their greatness stemmed from their absorption of elements of the Zoroastrianism of the Aryan Iranians. In other words, the Jews only stole what others had; they did not create.

To be clear, Gobineau argued that the Aryans were the conquerors and race founders of all but one of the ten key race-civilizations of the world. The Chinese are descended from the Aryans, the Aztecs are descended from the Aryans, and the Inca are descended from the Aryans. So were the American Indians of the Alleghenies. All of these peoples became what they were through the contribution of the blood of the Aryan conquerors. Gobineau believed that the three American civilizations were descendants of people of Mongol stock, but very mixed and wanting in racial quality (as the Polynesians also were). The more purely Aryan blood of some individuals shone forth in conquest and in the founding of the three Native American civilizations.[16] Four more Aryan-descended race-civilization groups were the people of India, the Egyptians (for Gobineau, Egypt was founded by Aryan colonists from India), the Greeks, and the Italians.

And then there was the tenth race-civilization group on the list, the Germans—but really they are the first on the list, for they *are* the Aryans.

Aryan-ness, then, would seem to transcend time (the Aryans of India, who arrived there in 1500 BCE, would seem to have gone back thousands of years before to have founded Egypt); to transcend space (as in the case of Aryan elements transported through overly mixed, racially decadent, almost entirely non-Aryan Pacific to conquer and shine once more in a few places in the New World); and to transcend skin colour (as in the case of such nonwhite Aryans as the Americans, the Chinese, and a good number of the Indians and Egyptians). But in fact Aryan-ness, while indeed transcendent in many ways, did *not* transcend the most basic divisions of skin colour as Gobineau saw them. Gobineau imposed a basic pattern of three races on the world: white, black, and yellow (the three-way division that Cuvier had chosen). Gobineau stressed that two of these colours were *not* conducive to civilizations. No black people had ever created a civilization, even after Aryan conquest and the admixture of Aryan blood, and no yellow people could sustain a civilization once their Aryan blood had been too far diluted.[17]

Given all of that, and given Gobineau's fondness for waxing on in torpid prose about the Aryans of long ago in their forest glens, it is often said that *The Inequality of Races* reads like an earlier version of *Mein Kampf*. There is much to be said for this view. The key differences between the two books are that Gobineau is less poisonously and repetitiously anti-Semitic, and—above all—that Gobineau sees *all* of contemporary Europe, including Germany, as racially mixed and in terminal decline as a civilization. European civilization as we know it will be replaced someday by a future Aryan-invigorated culture, the eleventh creative civilization in the history of world and probably the last new civilization that would ever arise, as Aryan blood itself was becoming too intermixed to have its old effect.[18]

Gobineau did not go on to conquer Europe, to invade Russia, or to commit genocide; he spent the last decades of his life as a popular romantic novelist. And we must not let the aptness of the comparison with *Mein Kampf* distract us from the essential issue. That issue is that there may be something of permanent interest to learn from the research methods, the habits of mind, and the ways of dividing up and thinking about humanity that sent Gobineau down a different road than Tocqueville. Both men were trying to explain the fall, or possible fall, of the European aristocratic civilization that they knew. How did these two thinkers come to such different conclusions about the immutability and character of races?

GOBINEAU DECLARES HIS INDEPENDENCE

As we have seen, Tocqueville did not consult contemporary French thinking on the physical races of the world. He set out to derive his own ways of categorizing people. He paid no attention to the racism, much less the polygenism of ethnological thinking in France in the first half of the century.

Gobineau does seem to have paid some attention to it. 'Aryans', his favourite group, were frequently referred to by those Frenchmen who followed Sir William Jones in India in dividing the world linguistically. And while Tocqueville and other major thinkers had no time for such theorists of physical race types as Victor Courtet de l'Isle,[19] Gobineau seems to have consulted him, although he refused to admit the fact in his book.[20] But Gobineau wrote nothing on the subject of linguistic classification or race in his years in Paris in the 1840s. For all of his literary and journalistic activity, on the surface the racist writers do not seem to have come into it—they were people whom one could at least pretend to ignore.[21]

The Société Ethnologique (founded in 1841), then, never counted Gobineau a member.[22] But what might he have heard about it, assuming that he had in fact been tracking the work of Courtet de l'Isle? The Société began a famous set of enquiries into the differences between races in 1847; its members believed that there were indeed racial differences. The Société's enquiries were meant to complement the continual debate on slavery in the Chamber of Deputies.

Before the Société, the abolitionist Victor Schoelcher lengthily and bitingly dismissed the racial knowledge under discussion as nothing more than a set of ungrounded assumptions. But most of the speakers stood by their guns. The accomplished blacks whom Schoelcher cited to refute racist thinking were themselves dismissed as irrelevant to the question by Courtet de l'Isle himself. For Courtet de l'Isle, Schoelcher's accomplished blacks must have been of mixed race, or they must have been copying the achievement of their betters—for everyone knew that in identity and in character the pure races were exactly what everyone knew them to be, so there could be no valid evidence to the contrary.[23]

The tenor of ethnological thought in France as Gobineau turned to the subject of race was this: Races were so separate and dissimilar that they usually could not mix with or otherwise change one another. Individuals might mix, but races could not mix to any significant degree. In the many conquests of one 'race' by another in European history, 'race' was too persistent to undergo change. There were never enough people among the conquerors to make much of a difference.[24] Gobineau argued the opposite. He believed very strongly that races were mixed. The fact was central to his theory: Aryans mixed their blood with others to create civilizations. What he may have taken from the tradition of Courtet de l'Isle and others is the assumption that races are naturally antagonistic toward one another, and that the races themselves are unaffected by climate. From certain aspects of Courtet de l'Isle's thought specifically, Gobineau may have taken *something* of his idea of racial mixing, although he is one author whom Gobineau never openly cites.[25]

Gobineau does cite—in order to dismiss—the thinkers of the skull- and face-measuring school, namely such figures as the eighteenth-century Dutchman Petrus Camper, the turn-of-the-century Frenchman Georges

Cuvier, the American Samuel Morton, and Morton's German follower Karl Gustav Carus. These men entered Gobineau's writing chiefly so that he could criticise their statistics and deny polygenism, or so he could cite the random fact.[26] Gobineau also draws from William Edwards and the (more humanistic) brothers Thierry, although he disagrees with the Thierrys over his own insistence that moral character inheres in physical race.[27]

* * *

Gobineau was anxious to distance his work from that of any possible intellectual forbears. Part of doing so meant spending the first part of the book arguing against what he said were the familiar classical and modern explanations for the fall of the civilizations. Three explanations, namely fanaticism, luxury, and moral corruption, fell straightaway. Gobineau pointed out that the Aztecs—who acted with 'a ferocity the modern physiologist recognizes as being a general characteristic of the races of the new world'— were by no means weakened by their fanaticism, and their empire would have continued for some time if not for the Spanish.[28]

A fourth traditional explanation for social decline, political strife, got a chapter of its own—but this new chapter was more theoretical, and only about three pages long. Here Gobineau was not so much using historical examples as trying to define away the need to do any real factual research.

In this short fragment, Gobineau argued that, by definition, politics could never be the cause in the fall of a civilization. Political faults could only lead to the fall of a *state*, and since Gobineau was interested only in the fall of that larger entity, the *society*, he was not interested in political analysis.[29] Thus Gobineau has explained the complete lack of Tocqueville or of Tocquevillean analysis in *The Inequality of Races*—save for a footnote referring to what Tocqueville had said about the Cherokee.[30] Gobineau claimed that he was looking at the life, death, and essential nature of civilizations, a 'more grave' question.[31] And so it was, in dismissing political science, that Gobineau escaped the need for the close analysis of political structures— the many details about inheritance law, administrative centralization, the structure of the press, and the like—that one would have to examine if politics were not subordinate to race, and entirely explained away by it.

But to escape the anxiety of Tocquevillean influence, Gobineau had to escape more than Tocqueville's focus on political specifics. He also had to escape Tocqueville's main idea: that the rise of social equality is the unstoppable central feature of the modern world. At one point Gobineau seemed to agree with Tocqueville that the feudal orders, with their formal inequalities of power, had been replaced by a society characterized by the growth of equality.[32] Some people—and coyly Gobineau does not say who—saw America as heralding the future of democratic progress.[33] In fact, America demonstrated only the growing decadence of the old-world races. All the democratic pretensions of the United States come to naught when compared to how it treats its nonwhites.[34] Besides, it will not be the Anglo-Saxon element that will determine the future of America. The real story of America is one of racial heterogeneity: 'The intermixture of all these degenerate types will inevitably give birth to new ethnic disorder. . . . [F]rom this no result can be imagined short of that horrible confusion which can be the only consequence of the incoherent juxtaposition of such degraded people.'[35]

Tocqueville was wrong not only about America being worthy of study, but also about the importance of social equality itself. Central to the Tocquevillean view is that equality shapes many of the characteristics of the societies in which it is expressed. Gobineau spent a whole chapter refuting these ideas.[36] He began with what he took for a piece of popular wisdom, namely that everybody knows that racial inequalities exist. And all groups are racially prejudiced against all the others. The idea that one group might be equal to another grew only in highly urbanized, highly sophisticated societies. So the idea of social equality was not a world-historical phenomenon characteristic of the modern era, but a mere epiphenomenon that had popped up here and there in the history of civilizations entering their cosmopolitan, mixed-blood, and thus decadent phase:

> To the degree that the groups begin to meld and fuse, they grow great and civilized, and begin to consider each other more benignly, because they find each other useful; then do we see among them that the absolute principle of the inequality and mutual hostility of the races is vehemently attacked and debated. Then, when the majority of citizens have mixed blood flowing through their veins, that majority transforms into a universal and absolute truth that which is only true for themselves, and feel called to affirm that all men are equal.[37]

Moved as well 'by a laudable dislike of oppression', the thinkers of this stage of civilization would proclaim grand principles of equality—an equality that does not describe even their own superior selves, much less the different races that they are speaking of.[38]

But if all men are equal in mind and heart, Gobineau marvels, then:

> the cerebellum of a Huron Indian contains quite the same germ of intellect as that of an Englishman or a Frenchman! Why then, in the course of ages, has he not invented either printing or steam power! I should be justified in asking him, this Huron, if he is equal to our compatriots, where out of the warriors of his tribe there has never come a Caesar or a Charlemagne, and by what inexplicable negligence his singers and sorcerers have never become Homers and Hippocrates's?[39]

Here Gobineau fails to acknowledges several points: First, that until very recently the Europeans had no more steam power than the Hurons did; second, that he had no idea what sort of society the Hurons *had* made; third, that settlement patterns, the density of population, and the availability of domesticable plants and animals might have some effect on the speed of social advance in any one direction.

Gobineau does go on to acknowledge the last of these points—that the settlement patterns and natural resources of the Hurons might be different from those of Europe. But he rejects not only the idea of social equality but now also an even larger idea, the idea that social conditions can influence the characteristics of a people. This idea, that social conditions influence the assumptions, the behaviours, and the identities of the people growing up under them, was fundamental to Tocqueville's thinking as a whole, and it was also fundamental to Tocqueville's views on race formation in particular. But Gobineau—having assaulted his Huron over the lack of Huronic steam power—will have none of this, none of the criticism that peoples are influenced by their surroundings. So much for the ridiculous view that

> an island will not see the same social marvels as a continent; the north will not be what the south is; forests will not allow the developments favoured by open country. What else? The humidity of a marsh will push forward a civilization which the dryness of the Sahara would infallibly suffocate![40]

We have seen that Gobineau rejected Tocqueville's analysis of political details; that he rejected the key Tocquevillean idea of equality as a world-historical force; and now that he rejected Tocqueville's idea that races are produced only by the social conditioning of each new generation. Gobineau believed, instead, that influences flowed from race to society, and never from the society to the race or the individual. Gobineau also rejected Tocqueville's method of looking past received principles to frame his field research so as to refute or refine what people thought they already knew. For Gobineau, all that matters is race. Everyone talks about the national characteristics of their own group, or of the Greeks, or whatever group they might like. And what 'everyone says' is Gobineau's sole evidence so far. Everyone knows that the Hurons don't have steam power, and everyone knows that races hate each other, and so on. So, says Gobineau, everyone acknowledges that pre-existing racial groups are key, and that the environment plays no factor at all in forming the groups about whose characteristics we speak.[41] Gobineau will not bother checking what everyone knows.

He does not need to. For him, a people is not a group of individuals re-creating a civilization in itself as it grows up; instead, a people is born once in history, with its characteristics already formed for all generations until its blood is diluted away. The basic human groups are static, and their characteristics are clear.

Gobineau concludes his chapter on the noninfluence of the environment with two extended examples of peoples who had ill-fitting, racially inappropriate institutions: the Hawaiians and the Haitians. These were nonwhites who had European-style governments, but their governments had not changed the underlying non-European character of the people. The Haitians and the Hawaiians did not run their countries well. The Hawaiians were, in truth, dominated by the missionaries who gave them the political and material benefits of white civilization.[42] For their part, the Haitians mouthed European ideals, but underneath they were murderous buffoons in bright red rags with gold trim. They spent most of their time sleeping, and they would not even farm.[43] The European-style institutions had not changed and would not change the clear race character of the people.

And the character of Gobineau's own unchanging assumptions on race is clear as well.

DEGENERATION

It remained for Gobineau to detail the *right* way of looking at the decline of civilizations. He mentioned that there was a new explanation for social decay floating about. As all good explanations should, it rejected environmentalism in favour of examining the inborn character of a people. This new explanation was called degeneration. But the biologists who had written about degeneration had not gone far enough with the concept. They had described social decay but they had not explained it.[44]

Gobineau's great achievement, then—in his own mind—was to discover the explanation for the degeneration of a whole people. And that explanation is simply this: The blood of the people's glorious ancestors had become more and more diluted. Not much was left of the founders' particular talent in meeting and beating their inevitable epiphenomenal social problems. The society was no longer made up of the sons of the great; it was composed of the nephews, and then cousins, and then the more distant cousins, as the original strengths of the society thinned along with its original blood down through the centuries.[45]

Gobineau argues that the earlier Aryan leavening was superior and less racially diluted than the Aryan blood of today. Thus, the modern control over energy and science cannot mask a brutality and artlessness that makes the current civilization of Europe sink in comparison to the other great periods and places of history. Besides, modern scientific knowledge is mere classification, not discovery. By contrast, the arts and poetry of most historic civilizations, including the nonwhite ones, are far superior to those of the modern Europeans. (But nonwhites in general, those who are not artists, are like dull, miserable animals making their way across the landscape.) As for liberty being a modern achievement, it has existed in ancient Mexico and most everywhere else; it is neither a modern nor a Western discovery.[46]

The Aryans have made a great civilization in the modern era; and so they have conquered and absorbed too many other peoples, and they have lost their character in the very act of fulfilling their largest imperial destiny. Only when the common people come to accept the values of their rulers is a civilization truly civilized. Gobineau's example is China, where books are much cheaper than in Europe and the humblest peasant understands and accepts the foundational principles of the state. Europe is too mongrel for this, with too many undigested common peoples. No institutions can be crafted that will satisfy so diverse a population. In Europe, the peasants do not care to learn to read and to share in their own so-called culture. Nor do the peasants share even the same basic values from one outlying province of France to another. Modern Europeans are like the Romans of the Empire, presiding over a majority population of barbarians. Only now there was no further population of unmixed Aryans to come and save the day, and extend history.[47] History is near its end. Degeneration is nearly complete.

Clearly, Gobineau was not above setting down a very specious chain of reasoning, one supported by bluster rather than evidence. Let us follow him down another such chain: '[T]he historian has clearly established the irreconcilable antagonism between the races and their modes of life.' He says in the same extended sentence, with its many 'ifs', that if 'the European cannot hope to civilize the negro, and succeeds in transmitting to the mulatto only a very few of his own capacities'; and if mulattos intermarry with white women, and their children are still incapable of anything but 'a mestizo culture slightly advanced toward the ideas of the white race'; then

> in that case, I am right in saying that the different races are unequal in intelligence.
>
> I repeat again here one should not disturb things at all by sinking to the unhappy and ridiculous method so dear to the ethnologists. I will not discuss, as they do, the moral and intellectual value of individuals taken separately.[48]

He adds: 'So let us leave these puerilities, and compare not men but groups'.[49] He is proud of his chain of ifs, and refuses to test it against the puerility of individual cases. Here is the *coup de grace* for the nominalism of Tocqueville. For Tocqueville, individuals are tangible and the groups are imaginary, the shortcuts of our sublunary minds. For Gobineau, one's long chains of assumptions about groups are the highest wisdom, and they cannot be refuted by mere evidence.

GOBINEAU'S RACES

He has stated his method—to erect generalizations without facts. It remains to examine the picture of races that his method produced.

He began this way: First, Europeans are more attractive than anyone else. By contrast, the negroes of the different parts of the world are, all of them, monkey-like. There is an overall, eminent category that unites all blacks, so they should be treated together—even though they must then be distinguished by who has inherited what kind of blackness where. Thus

> We come next to the tribes whose aspect is still less flattering to the self-love of humanity than that of the Congo negro. Oceana has the peculiar merit of furnishing pretty nearly the most degraded, the most hideous, and the most repulsive of these miserable beings, formed it would seem to serve as the transition between man and the brute pure and simple. Set against many of the Australian tribes, the African negro himself rises to a value that seems to reveal a better ancestry. In many of the unfortunate inhabitants of this lately discovered world, the bulk of the head, the excessive thinness of the limbs, the famished shape of the body, present a hideous aspect.[50]

This material sets the tone, but it does not answer all the questions. The key dispute in the established literature, Gobineau reports, is between monogenesis and polygenesis. Are the races originally one species or more than one? Gobineau moves into a careful discussion of contemporary opinions about the alleged differences in the anatomy or character of human races, and he looks at the famous table of racial skull measurements produced by Samuel Morton.

Gobineau rejects Morton's separation of the 'yellow' category into 'Malay' and 'Mongolian', and he rejects Morton's erection of a separate category of 'Redskins' for Amerindians.[51] For Gobineau, the three races have been constant from Genesis on, because no one can prove that they haven't been. And no one could ever prove that they haven't been, if all contrary evidence is explained away by throwing in the concept of racial crossing, as Gobineau does.[52]

Gobineau's argumentation through all of this has an odd ring. He looks carefully at Morton's data and finds several flaws. And he winds up admitting that two key arguments for monogenesis—the fertility of interracial crosses, and the somewhat ambiguous testimony of Genesis—are ultimately unanswerable.[53] Thus, at the level of logic and dry argumentation, Gobineau cannot dismiss monogenesis, and he comes down on that side. But he calls those who argue on his own side 'unitarians', and he makes no secret of his disdain for them.[54] Technically he may agree with them, but he prefers to stress the *biological* distinction between the three main races of black, white, and yellow still exists, albeit within an originally single species.

Despite his insistence that there is a huge gulf between the lowest person—all people have souls—and the highest animal, nonetheless his belittling of 'unitarianism' sets the tone. For every assertion on his part that we are all of essentially *human* intelligence comes an ungrounded and crude insult against the intelligence or character of one or another brutish, hideous, or monkey-like group.

Meanwhile, the three overall groups that inform Gobineau's vocabulary—the black, the yellow, and the white—themselves float through, unscathed, unaffected by all the different arguments about how to classify skulls and other body parts. Gobineau never critically examines his own subdivisional categories, beyond the one moment when he substitutes his three-way split for Morton's five-way split because it seems to fit the evidence in Morton's table somewhat better.

GENERATIONS OF RACES

Gobineau does write two other scattered chapters on *how* the different races came about despite our single origin. In these chapters, Gobineau accepts environmental conditions as having produced the permanent distinctions between peoples. And yet earlier he had made his lengthy refutation of the effects of the environment. He attempts to resolve the contradiction by positing catastrophism: While today's environment has no effect on the long-unchanging races, there was once an age of environmental catastrophe that made all the difference. Long ago the earth was unstable geologically, and conditions were much more extreme. Thus the *higher* and *denser* populations of the prehistoric age—for our world is degenerate and much less populous than it was in the remote past—were forced into the three main racial groups:

> The contest of earth, water, and fire led to rapid and decisive reversals in humidity, drought, cold, and heat. The gases expelled from the still trembling earth worked irresistible changes on living beings. All the causes that enveloped the globe with the air of battle, of suffering, of sorrow, naturally redoubled the pressure that nature exerted on man—and so the influences of environment and climate possessed an entirely different power to produce effects upon on our earliest kindred than today.[55]

The earth's axis was displaced; mountains rose and fell with great speed.[56] Gobineau claimed that the period of mutability had lasted for about the first half of the six to eight thousand years of human existence—in a world immeasurably older than humanity, as he had learned from contemporary geology.[57] Up until three or four thousand years ago, a volcanic earth led to a level of human mutability quite different from that of the modern world. This was the origin of the three main categories of black, white, and yellow.[58] The groups could continue to interbreed and produce fertile offspring, but otherwise they were entirely different. Their character was fixed forever at the end of the catastrophic period.

Individuals do not transmit their characteristics; the races do, and they will always return to type.[59]

The original blacks, yellows, and whites were the secondary races, then, as distinct from the unified and unknowable primary form of mankind. Ever since the origin of these secondary races, many blacks have remained more or less unchanged, but whites and yellows have become too interbred for even a sense of the original secondary types to be known. Today's whites and yellows, and probably most of the blacks, are the further interbred races of the 'tertiary' stage. But even these tertiary races have not remained constant in character. Advanced cultures always conquer and interbreed to make new apparent or local types—although these types, the racial and national groups with which we are familiar, are still within the tertiary stage:

> We have a very weak historical understanding of these [original] tertiary races. Only in the misty beginnings of the chronicles of humanity can we catch a glimpse, in certain places, of the white species at this stage, which seems nowhere to have lasted very long. The essential inclination to civilize of this elite race continually pushed them to mix their blood with other people's. As for the black and yellow types, those found in the tertiary stage, they had no history then, for they were merely savages.[60]

There are also certain more fully interbred 'quaternary' races, such as the Polynesians (said by others to be the cross of the Caucasian and the Asian; Gobineau believes this to be a misprint for Caucasian and Negro.[61]). But it is hard for such fourth-stage groups themselves to meld into new races with new characteristics, and the resulting fifth-stage races can never settle down into unity and productivity.[62]

And, after all of this, the reason humanity should be divided into black, white, and yellow is never openly considered or defended. For Gobineau, these categories are basic and their validity is unexamined.

But otherwise the picture, with all of its interbreeding and all of its hard-to-distinguish stages, is fiendishly complicated, and it will allow Gobineau in subsequent volumes to cite almost anything in favour of one or another aspect of his thought. Even Gobineau refers to this complexity: The original characteristics of the races, he says, 'tend to disappear in the confusion.'[63] The more interbreeding, the more confusion, so that one person will have light skin and curly hair, another straight hair and dark skin, and so on. Yet a physical uniformity can be produced in an overall population given sufficient time. And the pure essence of the races is unquestionable if irrecoverable and unobservable.

What we have here, in sum, is an encyclopaedic (and thus in every sense selective) model of scholarship, skipping about the world. It stands apart from the monographic or primary-source-based approach that Tocqueville had used in *Democracy in America* and *The Old Régime and the French Revolution*. One advantage of Gobineau's method is that his conclusions can take flight of any real evidence.[64]

RACIAL HISTORY AND GENDER

Gobineau was unafraid of adding even more complexity. Along the way he revealed just how arbitrary his method of categorization was.

Gobineau defined three levels of human groups: Tribe, nation, and civilization. Most groups are mere tribes. Most tribes would never go on to conquer others. A tribe that does embark upon conquest will create a new mixed-blood community with the new characteristics that could define a nation or ultimately a civilization.[65] The highest level of social organization, the civilization, arises when a full nation resists being conquered by other full nations in the only possible way—by making wide conquests of its own, and mixing its blood even further afield.

Civilization reaches its highest level when a race is so powerful that it can and will absorb all in its wake. Thus, some civilizations are by their nature empires.[66] But not all civilizations are like this. At each level, the tribe, the nation, and the civilization, there are different kinds of peoples, above and beyond the differences in colour-race. Some peoples are more practical and others are more spiritual: 'There is no tribe that is so stupefied that one cannot distinguish the two sides of its instinct: the material side and the moral side. The degree of intensity of the one or the other gives rise to the first and most important difference between the races.'[67]

Gobineau then reviews various groups, the Dahomeys, the Samoyeds, and others, in order to show which peoples favoured the material things of life and which other groups, closely related to them and very similar to them in every other way, favoured the moral element:

> In some [groups], physical needs greatly dominate; others on the contrary are carried away in contemplation. Thus the base hordes of the yellow race seem to be dominated by material sensation, although to be absolutely deprived of even a glimpse of spirituality would be sub-human. On the contrary, with most of the corresponding negro tribes the way of life is more agitated than thoughtful, and imagination puts a higher price on the unseen than on the tangible.[68]

As each group of whites or yellows masters (in the case of the materialists) or rises above (in the case of the more morally directed) their baser material needs, they take others under their power and mix their blood with them.

But Gobineau then finds a simpler way to put it—material cultures are masculine and moral cultures are feminine:

Here one can apply the Hindu symbolism, and represent what I have called the intellectual current with Prakriti, the female principle, and the material current with Parusha, the male principle—with the understanding that we take these words to imply a reciprocal fertilization, with no praise for one or blame for the other.[69]

Gobineau admits that any civilization, as it absorbs different strains of blood, will oscillate to some extent between the physical and spiritual, the masculine and the feminine. But he believes that the particular balance between the two principles is characteristic for each civilization.

At the head of the male category I put the Chinese; and as the prototype of the opposite class I choose the Hindus.

For those that follow the Chinese on the list I would set down most of the people of ancient Italy, the Romans of the early Republic, and the Germanic tribes. In the opposite camp I see the nations of Egypt and Assyria. They take their place behind the men of Hindustan.[70]

The Hindus lived with a few pieces of cloth and some rice—not because of the warm climate, but because they are more feminine and spiritual than masculine and material. Thus the Tibetans in the cold climate follow the Hindu pattern, with vast buildings for the monks and nothing for the common people.[71]

Gobineau is discussing the abstract ideal gender of whole societies. He is not discussing the position of real men and real women vis-à-vis one another at any one time in any specific society. The characteristic gender balance of each place is far more ethereal a matter than all that. But this abstract balance between the masculine and the feminine is real enough, Gobineau thinks. Over the course of several volumes, he uses it to explain the course of each civilization through history, as the Aryan bloodline at the heart of each civilization is joined by the blood of the conquered people in whom the male and female principles have combined in a somewhat different way. Thus, the Northern Chinese, who were entirely masculine, were joined by the feminine bloodline of Yunnan. The Northern Europeans started materialistic and masculine, and were confirmed in this by the influx of Celtic and Slavic blood, although the further south one goes, the less true this was and the more moral rather then material—the more feminine—things get. However, there are pockets of masculinity making up industrious groups in Piedmont and in Northern Spain.[72]

Thus it seems that Gobineau has an amazingly precise knowledge of the underlying psychosexual nature of different peoples across many centuries. And yet nowhere, as yet, has he explained *how* he knows the ultimate cultural gender balance of Yunnan, the Piedmont, or what have you. Is that all there is to him—making up labels? It begins to seem that way. Gobineau is bringing up historical groups only long enough to label them as masculine or feminine.

And that is the way that he continues to use evidence in succeeding pages, where he assigns various blood-genderings to the different dynasties of France, as the country began to be ruled more and more by feminized and decadent southerners. And he continues to proffer evidence of this kind for the remaining four volumes of his book, where he presents potted history after potted history of the ten civilizations that he believes the world has seen. Each time he discusses the varying gender proportions of its bloodline as its population expanded, conquered, and merged with others. During all of these analyses, Gobineau claims that he is being specific and scientific—pronouncing on the masculinity or femininity of nations, royal families, and even languages.

*   *   *

Here is his conclusion:

> Human history is like an immense tapestry. . . . The two inferior varieties of the human species, the black race and the yellow race, are the course foundation, the cotton and the wool, which the secondary families of the white race make supple by the mingling of their silk, while the Aryan group, intertwining its slender thread through noble generations, applies to the surface a dazzling masterpiece in arabesques of silver and gold.[73]

And yet except for flashes like these Gobineau is the bearer of a sombre faith. With no more sufficiently pure Aryans to ride in and save the day, the future is one of 'nations—no, human herds—crushed by a mournful somnambulance, living benumbed in their own in nullity like buffalo ruminating in the stagnant ponds of the Pontine marshes'.[74] This highly wrought picture surely stands as a parody of the Tocquevillean idea of the coming world-historical age of equality. For Gobineau, the racially mixed world of the future will be so decadent that there will soon be a fall in population, a fall that will continue until the human race becomes extinct. Gobineau's own era lay about nine thousand years along a timeline that would end with human extinction only three to five thousand years away.[75]

It was with several more of these flights of pessimism that Gobineau ended his great work.

TOCQUEVILLE'S REACTION

In his letters to Gobineau, Tocqueville's most frequent objection to all of this was to its determinism; Tocqueville would always reject determinism, insisting on the real importance of moral choices that we make.[76] Gobineau made his human categories into permanent *things* that determined human life. Tocqueville objected to applying 'fatalism not only to individuals but to those collections of individuals called *races*'.[77]

Of course, Tocqueville was appalled not only by Gobineau's materialism and racism, but also by the intellectual methods on view in Gobineau's work:

> Were it to be a matter of human families that were different in some profound and permanent manner in their external form, which could be distinctly recognized in the succession of ages, and call to mind a different scheme of creation, your doctrine, without being in my opinion any more true, would be less improbable and easier to get hold of. But if applied within one of these great families, such as that of the white race for example, the thread of reasoning disappears and escapes each time. What is more uncertain in this world than the question of learning from either history or tradition when, how, and in what proportions peoples were blended together who retain no visible trace of their origins?

Tocqueville has cut through to the meaninglessness of Gobineau's labels. He adds that Gobineau has thrown away all pretence of scholarly rigour:

> Do you believe that by trying taking up this line of explaining the destiny of different peoples that you have much clarified history, and that the science of man gains in certainty by abandoning the path travelled since the beginning of time by so many great minds who have searched for the causes of the events of this world in the influence of certain men, certain sentiments, certain ideas, certain beliefs?[78]

So Gobineau has thrown out all semblance of the tradition of careful, evidence-based scholarship. And this is not merely a procedural or technical fault. Tocqueville asks Gobineau, '[d]on't you see how your doctrine leads to all the evils that permanent inequality brings forth: pride, violence, contempt for one's fellows, tyranny and abjection in all their forms?'[79]

Gobineau's philosophical and moral failures were as glaring as his lack of evidence. If, as Tocqueville stated in another letter, the people of the eighteenth century had been too confident about the ability of man to understand and reshape the world, Tocqueville believed that those of the nineteenth century were too prone to give up in the face of some great deterministic principle; Gobineau's assurance that humanity was well on its way to an inevitable extinction certainly counted as one of these unhelpful doctrines of determinism.[80] So, Gobineau's thoughts add up to a great contraction or even the total abolition of human liberty. Thus I confess to you that having read your book I remain as before, fixed in extreme opposition to your doctrines. I believe they are very likely false and quite certainly pernicious.[81]

Tocqueville had already announced his opposition to Gobineau's central ideas in a letter written when he had yet to finish reading the book.[82] And even before receiving his copy of the first volume, he had shown his disapproval of the direction that Gobineau was going in. Tocqueville told Gobineau that he had gone to the trouble of reading a book about Buffon so that he could quote to Gobineau an Enlightenment source on the unity of mankind.[83]

Gobineau could not fail to understand Tocqueville's criticisms, but of course he rejected them.[84] Down through the years he would always maintain his ground: '. . . something else once again torments me, which is your incessant reproach that I am lulling to sleep already sleepy peoples.' Writing during the Crimean War, Gobineau added that far from sleeping, Europeans might still go out and conquer the Chinese, 'finish off the Turks', and 'drag the Persians to their inevitable fate'—but that despite all this, the processes that lead to enervation continue to operate, the level of enervation continues to get worse and worse, and the ultimate degeneration of humanity must follow. No one could do anything about it.[85]

In the meantime, Gobineau himself would be active enough in helping to project European power, serving in the French legation to Persia. The people and buildings that surrounded him there confirmed for him the role of the Aryans in history, as he described to Tocqueville as some length.[86] But he did not find Tocqueville sufficiently appreciative of these theories; finally, Gobineau wrote that he no longer wished to correspond on the matter, and while their personal correspondence continued unabated, they did not discuss Gobineau's great theory any further.[87]

In the last letter on race that Tocqueville would address to Gobineau, he simply pointed out that Gobineau's ideas were incompatible with Christianity, except for the version of it practiced by the American slave owners who had taken such comfort from his young friend's work.[88] For Tocqueville, Christianity meant a widening of the human sphere from the Jewish people to everyone, without distinction. Christianity could not be reconciled with setting up *new* distinctions between peoples. Nor did Genesis support the idea of the separate creation of races.[89] Meanwhile, Gobineau had bragged of his followers and translators in the American South.[90] Tocqueville responded that he recognized their names—they were ardent anti-abolitionists who would use the book for their own ends.[91] Gobineau was not just wrong; he was wrong in an important and terrible way.

Gobineau's ideas were to resonate in France, and even more so in Germany.[92] What about in England?

4 The Common Sense of Walter Bagehot

In the late 1860s, Walter Bagehot propounded a theory of history, of race, and of Aryanism that, point by point, matched the earlier thinking of Arthur de Gobineau. Working independently, and it seems without ever having heard of Gobineau, Bagehot was facing the same questions that Gobineau faced, and he arrived at the same conclusions. He reproduced the same intellectual mistakes for which Tocqueville had taken Gobineau to task. Bagehot wound up turning English racial thought in the direction of the physical heritability of cultural characteristics, the inevitability of racial conflict, and the central importance of the Aryans.

In this chapter, I will examine the anti-racist opinions that Bagehot began with. In the next chapter, I will turn to how close Bagehot's thinking came to Gobineau's.

RACE IN ENGLAND

In the introduction of this book I argued that French thinkers, in general, believed in physical races throughout the first half of the nineteenth century; that some thinkers in the northern United States also came to believe in heritable colour-races after 1840; and that English opinion came around to looking at humanity in this way only after 1850. After 1850, England's Prichardian, monogenist Christian orthodoxy was first broken by Robert Knox. At the same time, there was much speculation about Aryan language groups as markers of separate physical inheritances, but as yet there was no consensus.[1] Meanwhile, James Hunt, a speech therapist with no medical training, undertook a salacious campaign for racism through the Anthropological Society of London in the 1860s. Among other things, Hunt maintained that blacks had arms reaching down to the knee.[2] Hunt made a belief in physical races so odious by his advocacy of it that only in the later 1860s did the idea become firmly established among scientists and anthropologists/ethnologists. Only Hunt's death in 1869 finally removed the source of the controversy.[3]

That is the picture of the growth of racism in science.[4] And as Douglas Lorimer has shown in *Colour, Class, and the Victorians*, popular racism came about at the same time, in the 1850s and 1860s, as the music-hall performers and the missionaries, for their own very different reasons, portrayed blacks as degraded.[5] But if the scientists and the mass populace adopted ideas of separate physical-*cum*-moral races only well after 1850, what about the more perspicacious *non*-scientists?[6] Might the major writers and sages of the time have begun, for their own reasons, to sort the peoples of the world by physical and moral colour? Perhaps it will be among these more well-known *non*-scientific writers—people whose business it was to characterize the world for the ever-increasing hordes of middle-class readers—that we would find the supposedly natural belief in black and white and yellow and such.

Meanwhile, it will be worthwhile to keep in mind the point stressed by Georgios Varouxakis: Many Englishmen in the mid-nineteenth century discussed 'race'—by which they only meant groups of people.[7] The question here is who came to use 'race' to mean heritable physical and moral character.

THOMAS ARNOLD ON NATION AND RACE

In his introductory lecture upon becoming Regius Professor of Modern History at Oxford in 1841, the educator and famous headmaster of Rugby School, Thomas Arnold (1795–1842), argued that for England—'this great English nation, whose race and language are now overrunning the globe from one end of it to the other'[8]—there were four unifying, defining national characteristics running back to the period of the disappearance of Roman power: 'our blood, our language, the name and actual divisions of our country, [and] the beginnings of some of our institutions'.[9] Slightly later in the same essay, Arnold argues that 'the great elements of nationality' in the modern era are 'race, language, institutions, and religion'—which is a different list than he had before. One change is the substitution of 'race' for 'blood'. Both words seem to mean as much a superfamily sharing a common descent (the old sense of 'race' in the West) as anything else. If Arnold means race in the skin-colour-*cum*-inner-character sense, he is not stopping to say so.

Arnold goes on to argue that nowhere in Europe until sometime after the fall of Rome were all four of these markers of modern nationalities (again, 'race, language, institutions, and religion'), much less a fifth characteristic, 'sameness of place', to be found working together with each other, forging the identity of a nation. He admits that the first two of these national characteristics, race and language, might well be found associated with each other before 476. But 'it is better not to admit national identity til the two elements of institutions and religion, or at any rate one of them, be added to those of blood and language'. Putting the four together produces 'the national personality'.[10]

So, the 'national personality' is not, in his view, a matter of race or blood alone. He points out that England has inherited the cultures of Israel and Rome without inheriting their blood.[11]

And yet there is another part of Arnold's 'Introductory Lecture' that must be looked at in order to examine what 'race' meant at the time. Arnold goes on to discuss the special mission of the German race as such. To the possible surprise of the post-Nazi reader, in Arnold's view the world-encompassing, world-influencing Germans include the people of Latin America. German 'blood', the German language, and German institutions were communicated—through the various barbarian tribes who dismembered the Roman Empire—to a rather wide area:

> Germany, the Low Countries, Switzerland for the most part, Denmark, Norway, and Sweden, are all in language, and blood, and institutions, German most decidedly. But all South America is peopled with Spaniards and Portuguese, all North American and Australia with Englishmen. I say nothing of the prospects of the German race in Africa and India. . . . [12]

Arnold concludes with a discussion of how the German (or modern) phase of history is the latest creative step in a sequence of creative steps (Greek, then Roman, then Christian) that have made the world what it is. In each step the 'gifted' creative 'races' are the only creative elements, other cultures of the world being utterly remoulded by them or disappearing.[13] All this seems to anticipate Gobineau. But there the similarities end. Arnold's races are not physical. Nor does he assign a colour to each group, as Gobineau would do, nor identify all the creative races as 'Aryan'. For Arnold, Germans are indeed the most recent of the creative races, but the earlier creative races were *not* German.

In his earlier works, Arnold himself had argued against colour-racism and the whole way of thinking that stands behind it. In an 1835 essay on Thucydides, Arnold explained that in the ancient world,

> Citizenship was derived from race, but distinctions of race were not of the odious and fantastic character which they have borne in modern times; they implied real differences often of the most important kind, religious and moral. Particular races worshipped particular Gods, and in a particular manner.[14]

As Richard K. Barksdale showed in an article published in 1957,[15] Arnold rejected colour-racism on a number of occasions as un-Christian and incompatible with the belief in a common ancestry through Adam. Citing race prejudices in the American north, Arnold recognized (in an 1830 essay) that the colour and cultural differences which had grown up among people could be very difficult to breach.[16] There could also be 'a real difference of military prowess or wisdom', as in the superiority that the Europeans currently enjoyed over the 'Hottentots or the natives of New South Wales'. But he described the idea that such differences were permanent as a 'falsehood'. Racial differences had not been proved 'indestructible', and probably could be removed or 'infinitely lessened' if the 'superior race' showed 'half as much eagerness in elevating and enlightening the inferior, as they have generally done in degrading them'.[17] Arnold also maintained that the mixture of races—by which he meant cultural and moral characteristics—was required for human progress. But would not that process of mixing produce frictions between peoples? If so, a general belief in Christ should restore social peace. (While Arnold was not a colour-racist, he was anti-Semitic. Jews could not resolve their differences from everyone else through Christ—so they could never be citizens, only 'sojourners', and any state that allowed them citizenship would lose its essence and become hollow.[18])

Thomas Arnold's ideas about the cultural achievements of the various races had some influence, not least on the thinking of his son, the Victorian poet, literary critic, and cultural prophet Matthew Arnold.[19] But there was nothing in even the younger man's thought to suggest a turn toward biological or physical racism before the general English turn toward that way of thinking in the 1860s. By then Thomas Arnold was long dead.

Matthew Arnold would indeed make the turn to racism when it came. He adopted a biologically racialist position by the time of the publication of his *On the Study of Celtic Literature* in 1867. Large parts of the book seem to have been appropriated from the racist tradition of the Thierrys and Edwards in France. In his December 1871 essay 'A Persian Passion Play', Matthew Arnold even drew on some of Gobineau's later writings on Central Asia, and commended Gobineau's ethnology generally.[20] His father's view that permanent racial differences are a 'falsehood' did not seem to appeal to him.

ROBERT KNOX

Despite what some modern inventories of nineteenth-century racism say about Thomas Arnold and his 'Introductory Lecture',[21] we have seen that what he was looking at was what we would call civilizations, not races. He was not talking about a physical type that determines the epiphenomena of culture.[22] And it is the reinvention of racism in that sense—a way of dividing up the world into heritable colour-coded categories that predict culture, mentality, and human worth—that we are exploring.

The person who began to define the subject in that way in England was Robert Knox, who published *The Races of Man* in 1850.[23] He achieved great fame, but just how influential was he?

By the time Knox began writing on race, his career had already taken some strange turns. He was a teacher of anatomy at Edinburgh. By the 1830s, he was at the forefront of the anti-Cuvier school. Knox and others believed that the biology of different organisms proceeded according to analogous natural patterns and underlying archetypes, rather than because of the will of God or conditions of the environment. But then Knox's career in Edinburgh was ruined in a famous scandal over the procurement of the cadavers used for anatomical demonstrations. It seems that the supply of cadavers was being secured by murdering people. Although Knox himself did not kill anyone, his position was destroyed through his association with the scandal. After spending the 1840s in increasingly embittered isolation, and enduring the death of his wife, Knox moved to London. There he supported himself by giving public addresses on race.[24]

In arguing for the existence of physically separate races, Robert Knox differed profoundly and vocally from what would become Gobineau's position on key questions. He differed just as profoundly from the positions later adopted by Bagehot, Darwin, and everyone else in England. Knox insisted—perhaps under the influence of his friend and sometime guest in England, the French physician and racist W.F. Edwards[25]—that the varieties of man found by Cuvier (of whom Knox now seemed to approve) were quite separate. They could never cross, never hybridize successfully beyond one or two generations. Indeed, no strains of animals could ever hybridize successfully. (This would be news to Darwin with his many years of observing the various crossings carried out by cattle, horse, and pigeon breeders.) Nor could there be mixed-raced peoples.[26]

The belief that the human groups could not produce fertile offspring together had appeared in odd places in France. It had been stressed by Edward Long in Jamaica a half century before Knox. But the idea ran counter to what was still a near unanimous opinion.[27] In *English Traits*, an 1856 work widely read on both sides of the Atlantic, the American Ralph Waldo Emerson pointed out that Knox nowhere established, in evidence or logic, that the races that he talked about really existed. To refute Knox and his oversimplifications, Emerson stressed that every group shades off into everyone else; and that environment and custom can change the faces and characters of peoples. On the question of hybridity: 'Moreover, though we flatter the self-love of men and nations by the legend of pure races, all our experience is of the gradation and resolution of races, and strange resemblances meet us every where [sic]. It need not puzzle us that Malay and Papuan, Celt and Roman, Saxon and Tartar should mix . . . '[28]

So mixture was very well-known, especially to someone like Emerson, who came from a country where the skin-colour groups interbred all of the time. Knox's own insistence that the colour-races cannot mix is the most surprising point. He had also been an army doctor in South Africa. The evidence for racial mixing was walking all around him. What could Knox possibly mean by insisting that racial crossing and a stable mixed-race population was impossible? He explained that people might cross for a brief time, but no mixed-race group could be formed that would last.[29] Mixed peoples did not and could not exist. Where one group of people had bred with another, the new groups and their characteristics would soon disappear: 'The weakness might be numerical or innate'. Either way, as he explained, he had been assured that almost all traces of the European element in Mexico were gone. Soon the entire population would be exactly what they had been before 1492. The same was true of Peru and the rest of Latin America.[30]

More than that: All traces of the Spanish and the Portuguese would have disappeared from Latin America in any case, even if there had been no indigenous race to absorb them. Each race was created to be in a particular place. It could not live elsewhere. There were no examples of racial movement or of 'the pretended amalgamation of the races' on view in the history of Greece and Rome, or indeed anywhere in the modern world from the Russian Far East to Ireland to the English colonies in North America and Australia.[31] In both the United States and Australia, the European stocks were weakening and would soon be gone—save for new immigrants, but they could not keep arriving forever.

This idea that physical races could not live outside their original areas of the world, even where the climate was similar to where they had come from, meant that for Knox the colonists in Australia and elsewhere were dying out in the face of resurgent natives.[32] At the time, many Europeans believed that *natives* were dying out as the European populations around the world grew larger.[33] The idea that white settlement in Australia would soon disappear before the ascendant tide of Australian Aborigines, and that North America itself would soon be lost to the biologically ascendant American Indians,[34] may have had some French antecedents, as Robert J.C. Young has argued.[35] But it set Knox apart from every other notable thinker in England from then on (although the idea would be taken up by the American polygenists[36]). Knox stressed biological race, but not in the way that most British racial thinkers could believe in, a fact that Peter Mandler has pointed out.[37]

Nor could Knox's views be mistaken for Gobineau's. Rather than arguing that peoples are improved in being conquered by the Aryans, Knox believed that races could not change at all, much less be improved. And the word 'Aryan' had no meaning for him. He argued that the Germans were not the race that everyone thought them to be, but a small regional group sandwiched between the Saxons and the 'Slavonians'. For Knox, these modern Germans had come to be mistaken for the Germans whom the Romans knew. The truly superior race is Saxon, which for Knox meant Scandinavian.[38]

This was the Knox who went on to influence James Hunt—he of the Anthropological Society, with its outrageous ideas on race and its scandalous focus on sex, which repulsed the London of the 1860s, as we have seen. But as Mandler has argued, Knox did not influence very many others beyond Hunt's Anthropological Society.

THE MORE LIKELY SOURCES FOR BAGEHOT'S IDEAS

Still, if he was unlikely to have been influenced by Knox or Hunt, there were other far more acceptable intellectual strands to which Walter Bagehot might have been paying attention. James Cowles Prichard, who as we shall see was Bagehot's teacher, had used the word 'Aryan' (or 'Arian') by 1843.[39] Racialist ideas of an Aryan language-cum-ethnic group became notable in England after 1846, when the philologist Baron Bunsen, as Prussian ambassador, introduced Friedrich Max Müller to the country. Max Müller (as he is known) became a professor at Oxford and began spreading the word of the Aryan language family. He denied that a language family was the same as an ethnicity or a set of blood relations, but many people took his work on the Aryans in a more racialist sense.[40]

The idea of the Aryans bringing their language to India and Eastern Europe but losing their colour in a few generations, and merging physically into the conquered populations, does appear from time to time, as it did in the work of John Crawfurd.[41] It appears again in Charles Lyell's book *The Geological Evidences of the Antiquity of Man* (1863). But Lyell did not maintain or even discuss Gobineau's view that an infusion of Aryans was the reason for all cultural advances at all times and at all places in history. Nor did he posit a scheme of degeneration.[42] And in any case, Bagehot never cites Lyell. Nor, for that matter, does he ever in any of his writings (including his journalism) cite any of the French racial theorists. Nor does he cite the phrenologists Combe and Spurzheim, nor the Confederate agents and other characters in Hunt's Anthropological Society of London, such as Henry Hotze. Nor indeed does a computerized search of the corpus of Bagehot's writing show that he ever cited or even mentioned Knox or Hunt or Richard Burton themselves.

Bagehot does cite a number of major anthropological writers who had come to prominence in the 1860s: Edward Burnett Tylor, Sir Henry Sumner Maine, Henry Maudsley, John M'Clennon, Thomas Henry Huxley, and John Lubbock, plus Herbert Spencer, who had come before the public eye a decade earlier than the others. Huxley, Lubbock, and Spencer were Bagehot's colleagues in the Metaphysical Society, a debating club that began to meet in 1869. The first paper read at the Society was by Bagehot's friend, colleague, and later literary executor and biographer, R.H. Hutton. It was called 'On Mr. Herbert Spencer's Theory of the Gradual Transformation of the Utilitarian in Intuitive Morality by Hereditary Descent'.[43] The paper centred on the inheritance of socially acquired characteristics—but this address came more than a year after Bagehot had expounded that idea in the first parts of what would become *Physics and Politics*.

None of the men whom Bagehot cites had mentioned Gobineau. Only one—Tylor—had used 'Aryan' in a racial as opposed to a linguistic sense. Two others *had* used it linguistically. Identifying an 'Aryan' heritage in law was important in Henry Sumner Maine's work, for one example; but as a part of his Indo-European 'race', Maine included the dark peoples of India as well as the light peoples of Europe. James Hunt, colour-racist *extraordinaire*, excoriated the philologists for trying to mix colours in exactly the way Maine was doing. The other example of someone like Henry Sumner Maine is John M'Clennon. In his *Primitive Marriage* (1865) he uses the term 'Aryan' for a people and their laws, but he does not assign to this group any physical or biologically inheritable characteristics.[44]

Once again, the one man whom Bagehot cites who did use 'Aryan' ethnically rather than linguistically was Edward Burnett Tylor. In *Anahuac; or, Mexico and the Mexicans Ancient and Modern* (1861), Tylor mentions 'Aryan' folktales—but he uses the word only once, in an appendix. *Anahuac* is notable for its anti-Catholicism and not for its biological racism. In his more famous *Researches into the Early History of Mankind* (1865), Tylor goes much further, discussing 'our Aryan race', 'our own Aryan race', 'our Aryan fathers', and even 'the great Aryan race'. Tylor looks at the gestures, words, pictures, and myths of different peoples and 'races' of the world in order to find evidence of what he takes for the standard stages of cultural development. As George Stocking has pointed out, Tylor used the loose language of the time, indiscriminately describing the blood or race of these different groups (in an 1871 work).[45] But at bottom Tylor was not foregrounding or extending the concept of biological races, whether Aryan or otherwise, and certainly not in his earliest works. His 1865 book is regarded as one of the foundational texts of British cultural anthropology. Tylor's analysis of cultural signs has nothing to do with Gobineau's way of looking at the world, beyond an overarching assumption of European cultural superiority—which Gobineau did not always share. And again Tylor was the only author whom Bagehot cited who used the word 'Aryan' to describe the ethnicity of a (culturally) superior Europe.

John Lubbock and Herbert Spencer, whom Bagehot knew personally, did not use the word 'Aryan' at all in this period. Lubbock, in his *The Origin of Civilization and the Primitive Condition of Man* (1870), would later refer to the Aryans as a religious group, and at other times to Aryan languages; but the word 'Aryan' does not appear at all in his first book, *Prehistoric Times* (1865), published early enough to have influenced Bagehot. Spencer's earlier works do not mention Aryans.[46]

It was still possible in 1859 for an acolyte of Prichard, Robert Latham, to publish a two-volume 'descriptive ethnology' of the Old World that did not refer to or privilege 'Aryans' under that name or any other, and that was organized according to entirely different principles.[47] Nor did Latham discuss any other supposed race. He resisted the idea of doing so. In an

1853 article, 'On the Subjectivity of Certain Classes in Ethnology', he had explained that human populations

> when submitted to arrangement and classification, will not come out in any definite and well-marked groups, like the groups that constitute what is currently called species. On the contrary, they will run into each other, with equivocal points of contact, and indirect lines of demarcation, so that discrimination will be difficult, if not impracticable. If practical, however, it will be effected by having recourse to certain typical forms, around which such as approximate most closely can most accurately and conveniently be grouped. When this is done, the more distant outliers will be distributed over the debateable ground of an equivocal frontier.[48]

On the next page, Latham rejected the 'new and lax term—*race*'.[49] For Latham at least, 'type' was merely a generalization, approached though countless hours of linguistic analysis over the years, constructing comparative tables of nouns, pronouns, and verb formations. Type meant a fuzzy-edged generalization for describing a reality too complicated to be really captured by it. Type was brought to the evidence by the researcher. It was not present in the bodies of the observed. It was not neat, it was not racial, it was not Aryan racial.[50] Latham regretted arguing years before that the more primitive tribes of Malaya were the darker ones. That would be reifying 'type', taking it beyond the evidence in a way that the record of human groups shading off into one another could not support.[51]

ANOTHER GENERAL THINKER WITH NO CLEAR IDEA OF RACE—THE YOUNGER WALTER BAGEHOT

As the great editor of *The Economist*, Walter Bagehot was famous for dividing seemingly every subject and every group of people that he examined into contrasting types. He was always setting up types. But all the same for much of his life his position on human groupings reflected the commonsense views of his time. His 'types' were not physical races, and he rejected the idea of racial theorizing.

Yet as we will see, as Bagehot grew more intellectually ambitious, moving from journalism to treatise-writing, races would bloom in his mind.

*   *   *

Walter Bagehot was born in 1826 in Langport, in Somerset, into a well-educated and well-connected family of local notables and bankers. Although his mother raised him an Anglican, his father was Unitarian, and so at thirteen Bagehot went off to Bristol College. It had been founded the decade before to give a fixed home to the previously less formal schooling arrangements for the well-to-do young nonconformists of Somerset and Gloucestershire. The young Bagehot remained there for three years.

One of Bagehot's more important teachers at Bristol was his mother's brother-in-law, James Cowles Prichard, the very same man whose books dominated British anthropological thinking in the first half of the nineteenth century, not least providing the framework for Latham's nonracist work.[52]

As George Stocking has shown, Prichard's views on measuring bones and on the question of racial differentiation developed in complex ways over the years. But Prichard always argued for monogenesis. And he came to believe in the great importance of environmental factors, minimizing the role of inheritance in the shaping of human groups. By the 1830s and 1840s, the period of his life when he taught Bagehot, Prichard stressed linguistic and cultural groups rather than groups based upon physical traits.[53] For Prichard, writing in 1843, 'none of the [physical] differences in question exceed the limits of individual variety, or are greater than the diversities found within one nation or family'. That we are one species that undergoes superficial changes to fit different climates and modes of living was the position for which Prichard was long famous in popular circles, in part because of Latham's lecture tours after Prichard's death.[54]

For Bagehot especially, Prichard's influence extended beyond the classroom. While at school in Bristol, Bagehot spent most Sunday evenings in Prichard's house, apparently imbibing theories of progress and, it would seem, enjoying the household discussions of anthropological specimens and world handicrafts. As a young man Bagehot was proud of his knowledge of skulls; on one occasion he seems to have gone out to borrow one so that he could better follow some of Prichard's lectures in school.

While in Bristol, Bagehot also picked up an acquaintance with science—chemistry, zoology, physiology, and medicine were also a part of the curriculum—while he nonetheless concentrated his attention on classics, Hebrew, German, and mathematics. The ethnological part of his education was not to be completely forgotten in later years. In 1847 he would attend the addresses of Prichard, Latham, and Baron Bunsen before the Ethnological section of the British Association. Latham's address, Bagehot thought, had confused and bored Prince Albert.[55]

By then, Bagehot was reading politics and economics at University College, London, where Latham, a medical doctor, was professor of English language and literature. Latham and Bagehot do not seem to have maintained an acquaintance.

Walter Bagehot took his M.A. in 1848 (the year that Prichard died) and began to read for the bar. Meanwhile, the young Bagehot began to publish serious journalism. Then after a few years of trying to pursue both journalism and the bar, he fled his legal studies and went to France for a vacation late in 1851. Bagehot happened to be there when Prince-President Louis-Napoleon Bonaparte carried out his coup-de-état in December. The prince-president's term was close to expiring. He avoided the need for re-election by making himself president for life. It was a heady time.

BAGEHOT'S COUP AND THE NATIONAL CHARACTER OF THE FRENCH

The series of articles that Bagehot wrote on French politics in January and February 1852 confirmed the maturing young man, then turning twenty-six, in his desire to be a journalist. It is not clear how many people read these articles, for they were published in a Unitarian journal, but they showed to anyone who was looking that he could write with wit and grace on serious topics. Indeed, one of Bagehot's saving graces would always be the humour that he took in his own very human limits as an observer. He joked that as a young correspondent newly arrived in Paris, if he had his shoes shined and his hair cut, then in the London press a few days later he could cite the bootblack as his 'intelligent *ouvrier*' and the hairdresser as 'a person in rather a superior station'.[56]

The articles that he wrote from France would have surprised their audience not only with their gracious style but also with their view of French events. Although Bagehot was a liberal in economics and in his general outlook, he supported Louis-Napoleon's coup of December 1851. Why? Everyone in France had expected, Bagehot explained, that the French economy would crash when the prince-president's term expired in May 1852. Now Louis-Napoleon had given himself a life term (the title 'Emperor of the French' would come a year later). Commerce flourished. The New Year's fairs were like never before.[57]

Of course, the young Walter Bagehot would never have seen these fairs before, as he admits. He had just arrived in France. So how could he compare the fairs that he saw with those of earlier years? Bagehot claims that he saw things better than legions of Louis-Napoleon's critics who were not in the country.[58] He *had* seen the lean, craggy Montagnards setting up their barricades.[59] Plainly, such men needed to be stopped and commerce secured. It was not that democracy was unimportant but that commerce was vital: 'The first duty of society is the preservation of society'. Somehow over the course of six thousand years of civilization, people had come up with places to go to work, even if their products of their labour—as in the main industries of Lyon—were nothing more than tinsel and gewgaws. Gewgaws were important because people needed to leave their houses and go to work to make them.[60]

The whole social system had to be preserved and the dangerous classes kept under control; there were bad people about in France. Bagehot was sceptical about physical types. He said that he did not want to read 'in their feature the characters of such men', but the Montagnard who waved him away from a barricade fit the type too well.[61]

Yet otherwise Bagehot kept to his scepticism about bodily types. He refrained from the physical description of groups. What he described instead was what he called the French *'national character'* (italics in the original)—something like Thomas Arnold's 'national personality', minus the heritable elements. Bagehot's 'national character', explained why the French had such back luck with their democracies, and why Louis-Napoleon was right to preserve commerce at the cost of democracy.[62]

So what was the French character? The French were not sceptical enough. They kept spinning theories. They were too disputatious and impractical, just as the Greeks had been, and too ready to pursue every last logical deduction of whatever came into their heads. By contrast the British, like the Romans, had the cardinal virtue of stupidity, Bagehot said. They did not take up new ideas too easily. The English did not all of them individually insist on starting from first principles when discussing each and every question to come before a representative body. Bagehot spent some time illustrating how the French loved above all else overgeneralizing from first principles. They would not take the time for the patient accumulation of facts. They wanted to reach and teach their generalizations immediately, not study facts slowly over the years.[63]

NATIONAL CHARACTERISTICS

Where do different national characters come from? As Stefan Collini has pointed out, this was a frequent question in Bagehot's thought, from these short pieces of early journalism right into the more deliberately philosophical *Physics and Politics*, the book that we will explore in the next chapter.[64] In the third of his articles on the coup in France (there were seven articles in all), Bagehot asked openly, directly, what the sources of national character might be.[65]

The characteristics that he focused on were never physical, save for the short comments on the looks of the Montagnards of the barricades. Nor were these characteristics moral; as Bagehot observed in later years, French politicians under Napoleon III took bribes because that is what one did when so much power over the economy was concentrated in the hands of ministers, and when there was no effective parliament or free press to stop them.[66] So moral turpitude was not inborn, but a matter of opportunity and habit.

As we have seen, for Bagehot the social groups were neither physical nor moral, but psychological. What mattered about the French, the thing that made them 'French', was the way they thought. The French reasoned deductively and kept flitting from subject to subject while the English plodded along with their inductive common sense.[67]

But why do these *intellectual* national groups exist? 'The subtle system of obscure causes' by which children resembled their great-great-grandparents 'may very likely be destined to be very inscrutable.'[68]

But groups do exist, Bagehot insists. There is a French national character, and Bagehot simply ends this part of the discussion by saying that he did not think that his readers needed any more convincing on the point.

For Bagehot, the different national characters called for different institutions. The events of 1848 showed that not every European people was suited to parliamentary life.[69] And the wider world, too, showed that not everybody needed a parliament. Institutions have to be adapted to 'sense and circumstances'. Bagehot ridiculed the idea of a Dyak having a vote in a hypothetical Polynesian parliament.[70]

Indeed, this image marked an interesting turn in his argument. In giving this example of how politically different the different peoples of the world are—and in turning to the Dyaks for their exoticism and otherness—Bagehot has manoeuvred himself into broaching the physical aspect of 'race'. And it is now that he begins using the word 'race' itself: ' "Races and their varieties", says the historian, "seem to have been created with an inward *nisus* diminishing with the age of the world".' Indeed,

> The Jews of today are the face and form of the Jews of Egyptian sculptures; in character they are the Jews of Moses—the negro is the negro of a thousand years—the Chinese, by his own account, is the mummy of a million. . . . The people of the South are yet the people of the South, fierce and angry as their summer sun—the people of the North are still cold and stubborn like their own north wind—the people of the East 'mark not, but are still'—the people of the West 'are going through the ends of the earth, and walking up and down in it'. The fact is certain, the cause beyond us.[71]

This passage says a little less than it might, for while it links body and environment and character, it does so most strongly for the Jews, who have no one environment; and it links character to climate more by poetic fallacy than by serious speculation—for to what extent is the southern sun angry as opposed to stubborn, the northern wind stubborn as opposed to angry? Perhaps Bagehot means to include this element of mystery; it helps him make his case that really understanding such things seems impossible. And yet he does illustrate the point with what seems like heritable body-and-character racism:

> There are breeds in the animal man just as in the animal dog. When you hunt with greyhounds and course with beagles, then, and not till then, may you expect the inbred habits of a thousand years to pass away, that Hindoos can be free, or that Englishmen will be slaves.[72]

And yet even after all of this there is no reference to colour, no scheme of major races that the world is divided into—there are 'negros' and 'Chinese', but the latter are more of a nation, and there are no corresponding whites, browns, or yellows. And everything is originally more a matter of environment than of heredity. There is no idea of stock, or of polygenesis, or of one kind of people crossing with or mixing with another, with whatever degree of fertility in the next generation. There are elements of physical racism in Bagehot's comments, but they are set within an environmentally determinist worldview, where the environment in question is more psychological and political than anything else.

So, in terms of the methodology of identifying and characterizing human groups, what is going on here? For Bagehot, Englishmen who read journalism and modern history know what they are about; they know the different groups of people in the world, and where stable governments come from.[73] Their thought is sound because it is tied to old ideas (so different than the changeable thought of France).

> [P]eople of 'large roundabout common sense' will (as a rule) somehow get on in life . . . , while the more eminently gifted national character will but be a source and germ for endless and disastrous national failure . . . if it be deficient . . . in these plain, solid, and essential requisites.[74]

Perhaps Bagehot *himself* accepts the commonsense categories that everyone has heard of as more legitimate than what he could invent on his own. In any case they are the simplest way to communicate with other Englishmen.

In staying so close to common sense, Bagehot does not even allude to anything he learned about ethnology from Prichard. The only sign of Prichardian ethnology is how very explicitly Bagehot asked the question of why one group comes to differ in its way of thinking from another. Bagehot does drop the occasional hint about physical differences, or the possibility of the persistence of intellectual characteristics when people move to other social environments.[75] Yet these hints of physical race are only hints. Some of his references to 'race' are merely matters of verbal convenience in order to refer to groups or generations in modern Europe or among the different kinds of English-derived North Americans.[76]

For Bagehot, all these aspects of heritability fit within an environmentalist and monogenist way of looking at the world.[77] 'Races' are not foregrounded. Further, in Bagehot's case there is the humour. If he stresses a national characteristic of the French or the English here or there, or drops in the word 'race' in referring to the Belgians, he is being arch and funny, and writing with the freshness of a sometimes changing perspective, the freshness of the telling word. That telling word is not always meant as though he were writing a scientific treatise.[78] Indeed, Bagehot says that if too many people were thinking out of their own heads and setting up their own treatises upon these abstract questions, there would be no decent society—no Parliament, just someone like Louis-Napoleon imposing order upon a nation of babbling sophists. For Bagehot, the main weakness of the French was their habit of overgeneralization in want of real facts.[79] So the prince-president's silencing of the overexcitable French press in December 1851 was no bad thing.[80] Accordingly, Bagehot tries to avoid producing too much overgeneralization himself, too many new and untried thoughts, too much in the way of carefully defined races.

In England, Bagehot noted in 1860, no one had the patience to discuss all the scholastic subtleties of every question. (These subtleties were taken up by Mr. Gladstone but by very few others.[81]) Instead, as Bagehot would argue (in 1864), the very real problem of delineating and defining groups for all the infinitely diverse individuals of the world is solved merely by accepting the categories that one finds in common use, or at least in common use among the greatest writers:

> There are an infinite number of classes of human beings, but in each of these classes there is a distinctive type, which if we could expand on it in words, would define the class. We cannot expand it in formal terms any more than a landscape, or a species of landscape; but we have an art, an art of words, which can draw it. Travellers often bring home, in addition to their long journals . . . a pen-and-ink sketch, rudely done very likely, but which . . . gives a distinct notion, an emphatic edge, to all who see it. . . . True literature does the same. It describes sorts, varieties, and permutations, by delineating the type of each sort, the ideal of each variety, the central, the marking trait of each permutation.[82]

Good journalism, then, was they key to the most perspicacious and down-to-earth way of dealing with the complicated question of 'the infinite number of classes of human beings'. Indeed, all journalism, good and bad, played its role. With its free press, England was a noisy place, so that most people were rendered deaf to careful thought. Thus the English mind was inductive and down-to-earth, and largely immune to the danger of erecting new theories and categories.[83]

BAGEHOT AND SOCIAL EVOLUTIONISM

And that is the position that Bagehot, as a journalist, long held about whether to derive new categories for the peoples of the earth, and whether to question old ones. But in the later 1860s the scale of his intellectual ambition changed. For almost two decades by that point, he had been writing short pieces, such as the letters we have been looking at and his contributions to the *Economist* (of which he became editor in 1861, having been *de facto* editor since 1859); also, he had been writing articles ten to twenty times longer for the great quarterlies. Now he wanted to write on a bigger scale and link several of his larger articles together into books.

In writing a linked set of quarterly articles on the workings of the British government (1865–1867), and then republishing them together as *The English Constitution* in 1867, Bagehot produced a treatise.

With *Physics and Politics* and *Lombard Street* (1873), Bagehot went on to complete a trilogy of treatises in a very short time, the first on politics, the second and most abstract on the origins of the racial and political character of different nations, and the third on the workings of finance. The three books differed in character. *The English Constitution* was grounded in what particular people did in the course of their day in the Palace of Westminster, and *Lombard Street* in what people did in the eponymous street in the City of London. But *Physics and Politics* dealt with the more remote origins of modern life. It was far more theoretical. Bagehot ranged through history and across the world to look at the creation of national character wherever he could find it. *Physics and Politics* was Bagehot's main attempt to generalize, to move into world-encompassing categorization.

It may have had other sources, too, besides Bagehot's embrace of abstraction and worldwide comparison. In 1866, Bagehot had begun visiting and having long discussions with John Lubbock, whose first major book (*Pre-Historic Times as Illustrated by Ancient Remains*) came out in 1865, and who would become a pioneer in social evolutionist anthropology with the publication of *The Origin of Civilization and the Primitive Condition of Man* in 1870.[84] The social evolutionism of which Lubbock and soon Bagehot were pioneers held that different societies in the world illustrated different stages in the evolution of the more advanced European countries that were the culmination of history. As Jennifer Pitts has argued, this way of looking at other cultures as little more than way stations on the road to modern Britishness was very different from the view held by Adam Smith and other thinkers in the Scottish Enlightenment. Their typological classification of human cultures into nomadic, farming, and capitalistic stages might seem similar to social evolutionism, but the Scottish thinkers did not assume that any one people at any one stage was less brilliant, less carefully and thoughtfully adapted to its circumstances, less cultured, less intelligent, or less humane, than were the people of eighteenth-century Scotland.[85] The new social evolutionism would be far more teleological and far more judgmental. Highly developed European cultures were more accomplished and were composed of better people than all the other cultures of the world. Cultures at earlier stages were not so smart, not so cultured, and not so humane as the modern Europeans.

Some of the racialism that appears in *Physics and Politics* began to appear in Bagehot's occasional articles in the mid-1860s, with a hint or two of it earlier yet. For example, Bagehot wrote that Governor Eyre ought to have been especially kind to the Jamaican blacks, in their inferiority, rather than being especially harsh with them.[86] Meanwhile, one can't expect 'Orientals' to tell the truth to the taxman the way most Englishmen do; so Bagehot pointed out in 1860.[87] Tribal peoples (at what Lubbock would come to say were the earlier stages of social development) were worse yet: Bagehot claimed in 1862 that savages have no morals and no intellectual attainments. Culture only comes at the higher levels of civilization, and mainly to the elites. In the modern world, the elites of the different cultures are indeed coming to share the same cultivated beliefs about key things.[88]

In 1864 Bagehot wrote an article on the policies of Napoleon III called 'The Meaning and the Value of the Limits of the Principle of Nationalities'. It foreshadows the focus on racial conquest in *Physics and Politics*. Bagehot asserted that different human races do feel mutual antipathies, and do like to conquer one another. They are only welded together as nations through arms and then artifice.

But although this focus on race and conquest will appear in *Physics and Politics*, as we will see, in this short article Bagehot does not stress the importance of race to nearly the same degree. Indeed, he denied its significance. He argues that races such as the Welsh and the Cornish, 'alien in blood and language', plus the English race who conquered them, had come together as the English nation, losing their salience as races. In less successful, less fully integrated states, race might still matter:

> Between a great national history like that of Rome or England and the unelevated lives of an equal number of human beings—suppose of South Sea islanders or Esquimaux wanderers—there is as great a discrepancy as between the organized world of nature and the unorganized.

Racial identity no longer matters in advanced countries; nor should it be emphasized in any successful modern state. 'The doctrine of nationalities is not a good in itself, a dogma of superstition to be pursued at all times blindly. . . .'[89]

Behind this article there was a particular idea of progress that might have been influenced by Bagehot's friend Herbert Spencer. Spencer's main works, stressing pre-Darwinian arguments for progress and evolutionary change, had begun to appear—in what would become a huge series of linked and overly abstract volumes—in 1851, while Spencer was subeditor at *The Economist*. But I do not think that the urbane and clever Bagehot had to draw his ideas of progress from Spencer, for Bagehot at this time was very wary of Spencerian abstraction. Spencer was self-taught, and for a great Victorian sage he did not read very much. And that is an understatement. He did not like having books about, and those he had he kept behind curtains so, as he explained, he could 'be free of the sense of complexity which they yield'. Spencer claimed that he had read almost no serious books, and not many recreational ones. He said that when he was writing he would mine books and articles for facts to support his own generalizations, but he was not interested in reading anyone else's generalizations. Where did Spencer's own generalizations come from, then? The voluminous works that he produced proceeded mostly from his own first principles.[90] That is, they were ungrounded and overly deductive exercises in overgeneralizing from limited facts—exactly the kind of thing that Bagehot had repeatedly blamed on the French.[91]

But that was indeed the kind of *a priori* generalizing that Bagehot would have to indulge in when writing *Physics and Politics*. In foregrounding the subject of the origin of races in a work that was designed to transcend journalism, he would have to set down what 'races' really were. In stretching for science, Bagehot would achieve racism.

5   Bagehot Rewrites Gobineau

As he was writing *The English Constitution* (1867), Bagehot was also asking himself whether Darwinian thought (bared to the world with *The Origin of Species* in 1859) might help to clarify the deeper structures of society. *Physics and Politics* was based upon the idea that it could:

> [A]s every great scientific conception tends to advance its boundaries and be of use in solving problems not thought of when it was started, so here, what was put forward for mere animal history may, with a change in form, but an identical essence, be applied to human history.[1]

His own task in *Physics and Politics*, Bagehot announced, was to use evolution not to explain the development of the human species—which had already been done—but to explain the origin and development of human cultures. Bagehot applied evolution to the unit of culture rather than to biological species. Cultures competed with each other just as biological species did. With humans, rather than frogs or lilies, the innovations that led to success could be acquired through cultural learning rather than biological accident alone.

In *The English Constitution*, Bagehot had used Darwin as his example of a great modern thinker. There Bagehot contrasted Darwin's careful, evidence-based work with the deductive flights of Frenchmen like Descartes. Darwin had spent years gathering evidence rather than spinning abstractions.[2] But in his next book, Bagehot decided to spin them himself. *Physics and Politics* takes for granted its categories, including its 'races'. Here Bagehot takes races not as expedient generalizations but rather as discreet phenomena that really exist in the world. Instead of questioning his categories, he wanted to show that he knew how to apply them ever more widely.

THE DARWINIAN BACKGROUND

Was Bagehot's attempt to apply natural selection to human culture really new? Darwin himself had been applying evolution to humanity for a long time, if only in his private notes. Indeed, human examples were central to his original conception of natural selection in the late 1830s, as his note-books show.[3] And Darwin's thinking about humanity was further stimulated by an 1864 essay by Alfred Russel Wallace.

For Wallace, humanity had stopped its physical evolution when the process of cultural evolution took over. The physical differences between races had been frozen at that point, reflecting evolutionary adaptation to geographical environment. But everything mental and moral about humanity had come *after* cultural evolution had taken over from natural selection. The human races had separated before they became fully human. In the end, Wallace expected that whites would replace the evolutionarily inferior cultures of nonwhites the world over.

In this essay, whose general approach Darwin highly approved of,[4] Wallace differed from the thinking of Gobineau and Bagehot in key ways: Wallace had no truck with the idea of the physical evolution of acquired characteristics; he did not discuss the interbreeding of human groups, much less a process of human advancement through the spread of superior or Aryan blood; and he did not posit or contemplate any necessary hostility between human groups.[5]

Darwin did. He told Wallace that he had already been thinking of natural selection as operating through the violent conflict between groups of people.[6] Darwin had indeed opened himself to the examination of human societies in the 1830s, extending his thoughts into the human realm even before starting his notebook 'M' on the subject of man in 1838.[7] In 1868 he was full of praise for the first articles of the later *Physics and Politics*, recommending them to Wallace and others. (The series of articles that was to be republished as *Physics and Politics* had begun to appear in the *Fortnightly Review* in 1867. Because of Bagehot's health the last article and the book itself were not finished until 1872.) As we shall see in the next chapter, the earlier essays of what was to become *Physics and Politics* were to influence Darwin's own book on humanity, *The Descent of Man* (1871), in which Darwin credited Bagehot explicitly.[8]

Some amount of agreement between Bagehot and Darwin might have been understandable. Darwin, after all, had no idea of the principles of inheritance out of which came the variations upon which natural selection worked. Therefore he was as willing as Bagehot was to embrace at least the possibility of a Lamarckian inheritance of acquired characteristics. Thus, individuals will develop new traits—bigger muscles acquired through exercise, new behaviours developed to open nuts—and these new traits will be passed down physically to any offspring. Darwin stressed that this phenomenon was not the main cause behind the evolution of species—the main cause was natural selection operating through the 'struggle for existence'. Yet for all his years of careful research among livestock and pigeon breeders, the Darwin of *The Origin of Species* could not rule out the acquisition of acquired characteristics as one possible source of variation.[9]

The possibility of such a thing is now a difficult concept for us to grasp. We understand that the genetic heritage is set from conception. A woman's or a man's genetic contribution to the next generation is fixed before that person's own birth. We no longer imagine that the reproductive organs have some way of polling the adult body to check on degrees of use and disuse[10]—so that if an individual uses her biceps, the genetic material in her eggs will somehow be reprogrammed to make bigger biceps in the next generation. For Charles Darwin, this indeed happened. His view was that every part of the adult body is constantly sending out reproductive 'gemmules' that pool in the gonads. He called the process 'pangenesis'.[11]

For Bagehot, the unknown stuff of inheritance, whatever it might be, did indeed poll or at least respond to changes in the body. And he did no violence to Darwin's thoughts by placing the emphasis, at the outset of *Physics and Politics*, on how inheritance reflected not only the use and disuse of muscles but the use and disuse of the nervous system:

> Our mind in some strange way acts on our nerves, and our nerves in some equally strange way store up the consequences, and somehow the result, as a rule and commonly enough, goes down to our descendants; these primitive facts all theories admit, and all of them labour to explain.[12]

He was not sure how it worked. But he presented several pages of extracts from Thomas Henry Huxley, exploring the development of habits, and Henry Maudsley, establishing the physical heritability of even newly acquired habits.[13] So,

> [t]he special laws of inheritance are indeed as yet unknown. All which is clear, and all which is to my purpose, is that there is a tendency, a probability, greater or less according to circumstances, but always considerable, that the descendants of cultivated parents will have by born nervous organization, a greater aptitude of cultivation than the descendants of such as are not cultivated; and that this tendency augments, in some enhanced ratio, for many generations.[14]

INHERITANCE AND RACE

And establishing that point made all the difference for social analysis, truly allowing Bagehot to take Darwinian thought in a new direction. Bagehot, who opposed extending the franchise, had always thought that people from the upper classes were more fit to rule, because they were more cultured, better educated, more disinterested.[15] Now, the higher classes were physically better as well, because their cultural advantage in one generation makes them physically better in the next. The effect is cumulative, with certain groups getting better and better down through the generations. Each generation will start with better physical material in their nervous systems, and thus it will be able to attain new cultural heights—and in turn this new level of cultural achievement becomes a higher level of physical development and a higher starting point in the nervous systems of the next generation. And so human groups become very different from one another:

> Again, as to race, another authority teaches: 'Man's life truly represents a progressive development of the nervous system, none the less so because it takes place out of the womb instead of in it. . . . Power that has been laboriously built up as statical [*sic*] in one generation manifestly in such case becomes the inborn faculty of the next; and the development takes place in accordance with that law of increasing specialty and complexity of adaptation to external nature which is traceable throughout the animal kingdom. . . . [16]

And with this process of ramification in mind, 'a science of history is possible, as Mr. Buckle said—a science to teach the laws of tendencies—created by the mind, and transmitted by the body—which act upon and incline the will of man from age to age'.[17] The different human lines or cultures are composed of different biologically transmissible nervous endowments. And so out of the inheritance of acquired characteristics comes the idea of separate and unequal human races, and the possibility of understanding history as the story of these races.

GOBINEAU AGAIN

Writing in France in the late 1850s, just before the publication of *The Origin of Species* in 1859, Gobineau did not think so deeply as all this about the nature of heritability. He just assumed that it existed. He assumed that the most abstract cultural tendencies could be traced back and forth through inheritance lines, back and forth through the millennia.

Again, his main views were that there was a period of rapidly changing climates out of which humans emerged, but that as global conditions stabilized, humanity stabilized into a single species, with three permanent racial types: blacks, whites, and yellows. These groups hated one another. The better groups had a permanent need to conquer. The best group—the Aryan subset of the whites—continually came to rule others, mixing with them to form, in turn, each of the creative combinations that were the civilizations of history. In each fusion, the Aryans played the male, aggressive, competent, and energetic part, and the other races the female, civilizing part. Eventually the female element sapped the energy of the Aryan element, and led to the decadence and decline of the civilization. When any civilization reached the final stage of feminization and cosmopolitan decadence, it was doomed to be conquered in its turn by other, purer, not yet feminized Aryans. And this would mean the foundation of yet another new civilization. The new civilization would then expand until it, too, underwent the same cosmopolitan feminization and decline.

This process of racial conquest, crossing, and decline had produced several stages of ever less pure, ever more attenuated Aryans; there were no pure races left. The least pure races, such as the Polynesians, were fourth-generation crosses. Back in Europe, race crosses of stage three were coming to their period of decadence and disappearance. There was enough Aryan blood left to create one more civilization, but it would be the last, and it would fall in due course. With no sufficiently pure Aryans left to create a new stage of productive crossings, humanity was doomed to die out.

BAGEHOT'S MAJOR ARGUMENTS

In Bagehot's view, the races had differentiated before the dawn of history. They had become fundamental categories. Environment could 'no more make a Negro out of a Brahmin, or a red man out of an Englishman, than washing would change the spots of a leopard or the colour of an Ethiopian'.[18] Merely national characteristics can change, but history and ancient art show that what a 'red man' or a 'Negro' means never has changed and never will. How did the major racial types arise?:

> [T]here are but two explanations; *one*, that these great types were originally separate creations, as they stand—that the Negro was made so, and the Greek made so. . . . What the other explanation is I cannot pretend to say. . . . But by far the most plausible suggestion is that of Mr. Wallace, that these race-marks are the living records of a time when the intellect of man was not as able as it is now to adapt his life and habits to change of region. . . . [19]

It was then that there occurred

> Some strange preliminary process by which the main races of men were formed; they began to exist very early, and except by intermixture no new ones have been formed since. It was a process singularly active in the early ages, and singularly quiescent in later ages. Such differences as exist between the Aryan, the Turanian, the Negro, the red man, and the Australian are differences greater altogether than any causes now active are capable of creating in present men, at least in any way explicable by us.[20]

This passage deserves some parsing. First, throughout it there is the methodological and evidentiary similarity to Gobineau: Nothing is tested against any kind of evidence. The method of each author is to drop the names of different human groups into the argument, on the assumption that because the groups have different names they profoundly differ in reality.

And then there is the step-by-step similarity that Bagehot's view of the stages of history shares with Gobineau's: First came a stage when some major degree of human malleability—mysterious malleability, for Bagehot, climatic adaptation for Gobineau—created all the basic racial types, and these types have not changed to this day. The period of human change-ability has ended, and ever since—namely, for all of history and sometime before—new races have emerged only from the 'intermixture' (Bagehot's word) of the older and more basic ones. Not being afraid of scandalizing opinion in Roman Catholic France, Bagehot does not have to insist (as Gobineau did) upon an adherence to the doctrine of monogenism, so he can specify that this early creation of the human races came before the creation of 'the nature of men, especially before the mind and the adaptive nature of men, had taken their existing constitution'.[21] The picture, for Bagehot, was really one of polygenism. The races were quite different. As George W. Stocking has shown, *The Origin of Species* did not kill off polygenism, because for some nineteenth-century thinkers, the separate 'races' could have branched off from each other before any one of them had achieved sapience or full humanity.[22]

For Bagehot, there were two 'condition[s] precedent to civilization'. The first was the pre-existence of the races, and the second is the fact that men exist 'in something like families; that is, in groups, avowedly connected ... and gregarious, under a leader more or less fixed'.[23] Bagehot's ideas about the pre-existence of family feeling correspond nicely to Gobineau's postulate that there is a basic human tendency to self-love within small social groups and an even more striking mutual repellence between them. This within-group love and without-group hatred is the motor behind the process of conquest and racial mixing that is central to Gobineau's views. Bagehot will eventually stress and overstress the question of racial conflict and conquest.

Having set up the two postulates of the pre-existence of races and of family groups, Bagehot has got himself to the point where he feels that he is ready to explain the origin and development of civilization. And according to the inner logic of his account of how civilizations are formed, they soon reach a stasis that can only be broken by conquering or being conquered.

Stasis—a 'cake of custom' that hardens like mud around a people, form-ing a rigid shell—is reached this way: Early in a culture's development, Bagehot thinks, any action that someone takes may become associated with some other event that happened to take place at about the same time. The smarter people in the society will notice the coincidence, and their overactive minds will interpret the association as causation. A totem or a taboo will be erected.[24] The shaping of each culture's psychology is guided by the gifted (if overly superstitious) *individuals* who notice these things.

Bagehot does admit that things might get more complicated later on, and totems or taboos might be erected based on a theory of the likes or dislikes of the gods rather than upon direct association. By that point the whole society is marked by the 'contagious fancy', the 'dread of the powers of nature' that marked the ancient Athenians, among others.[25] This falling off from an earlier and higher level of perspicacity and individual freedom is one element of social degeneration. There are others.

Indeed, another formative process at work in this prehistoric period is what one might call *nonassociationalist* custom—custom that simply preserves the first ways things were done, from shoemaking to government, with no taboos involved.[26] This force is so important that in British India, Bagehot relates, new irrigation schemes have to be cloaked with the fiction of tradition, '[s]o difficult does this ancient race—like, probably, in this respect so much of the ancient world—find it to imagine a rule which is obligatory, but not traditional'.[27] Change and improvement, if any, would come from the British conquerors.

Indeed, the most important factor behind social improvement is the power of conquest and race mixture, as it was for Gobineau. In Bagehot's view, the other factors 'would not have been enough but for those continual wars of which I have spoken at such length in my essay on "The Use of Conflict". . . . '[28] (Here Bagehot is referring back to the article that would become the second chapter of the book.) No other factors can break the stasis; conquest and war are required for social advance.

Bagehot does seem to differ from the unnamed, unhinted-at Gobineau over how much racial conflict there was before people started to move around the world in the early stages of history. Bagehot suggests that closely related neighbours would not hate each other[29]—although he will change his mind about this later in the book. But for Bagehot as for Gobineau, racial mixture through conquest is the key to civilizational advance, as one society conquers another; and without this process of conquest, the only possible result is stultification and decline—the cake of custom (for Bagehot) or (for Gobineau) the decline that comes from the outright degeneration or feminization of the blood of what had been the leading sector of society. Custom becomes ever more stultifying and abstracted from the real needs of the people.[30] Sometimes even being conquered is not enough to arrest the decline:

> The experience of the English in India shows—if it shows anything—that a highly civilized race may fail in producing a rapidly excellent effect on a less civilized race, because it is too good and too different. The two are not *en rapport* together . . . the manner-language of the one is not the manner-language of the other.[31]

In looking at Bagehot's thinking about conflict, Paul Crook has suggested that his focus on the inheritability of social change owes something to Henry Maudsley. Maudsley argued that a kind of stored-up energy was built up and passed from one generation to another, in some way physically.[32] That may be one element in Bagehot's mind. Another element may have come from the work of Edward Burnett Tylor, in whose early terminology Stocking detects a confusion between cultural group and the colour gradients of 'races'.[33] As for the rest of Bagehot's complicated picture, little seems to have come from his own teacher Robert Cowles Prichard or from Robert Knox's newly influential, if idiosyncratic, work on race; nor does much if anything come from the American skull measurers, or the loose and mostly environmentally determinist ideas of 'race' expressed by Thomas Arnold. But while Bagehot's work did not stem from Gobineau, it matches his conclusions.

GOBINEAU'S DOPPELGÄNGER?

The first chapter of *Physics and Politics* ('The Preliminary Age', published as 'The Pre-Economic Age' in November 1867) covers the heritability of acquired racial characteristics. In the second chapter, 'The Use of Conflict' (April 1868), Bagehot looks in greater depth at the question of the emergence of biological race, the related question of polygenism or monogenism, and—for page after page—at the central role of racial conquest in the history of humanity: 'Early in history the continual mixtures by conquest were just so many experiments in mixing races as are going on in South America now. New races wandered into new districts, and half killed, half mixed with the old races.'[34] These 'races' conquered each other and created new mixtures of blood:

> The *mixture of races* was often an advantage, too. Much as the old world believed in pure blood, it had very little of it. Most historic nations conquered prehistoric nations, and though they massacred many, they did not massacre all. They enslaved the subject men, and they married the subject women.[35]

A mixture of races that were too dissimilar would produce untrustworthy half-castes who are 'between moralities', adhering to the essential morality of neither original race.[36] But if 'the two races were so near that their morals united as well as their breeds, if one race by its great numbers and prepotent organization so presided over the other as to take it up and assimilate it, *then* the admixture was invaluable'.[37]

In passage after passage and discussion after discussion, Bagehot reiterates these points. He multiplies unresearched examples—brief examples, mere assertions—about different peoples or different historical situations. For Bagehot as for Gobineau, climate does not determine history or make nations; race does.[38] 'Blood' tells. And war between these racialized groups was for Gobineau and for Bagehot alike the key to progress, at least since the beginning of recorded history:

> Every intellectual gain, so to speak, was in the earliest times made use of—was *invested* and taken out—in war; all else perished. Each nation tried constantly to be the stronger and so made or copied the best weapons; by conscious or unconscious imitation each nation formed a type of character suitable to war and conquest. Conquest improved mankind. . . . [M]any of these advantages can be imparted to subjugated races, or imitated by competing races; and . . . the energy of civilization grows by the coalescence of strengths and by the combination of strengths.[39]

And what race has been the most productive, has conquered most widely, and has formed the most progressive crosses? Which race, then, is the key to history? Bagehot has the same people in mind and the same name for them that Gobineau had used: the 'common Aryan stock' of 'the Teutons, Greeks and Romans'.[40]

There are some small differences between Bagehot's views and Gobineau's. After paralleling Gobineau's argument in the first two chapters of *Physics and Politics*, Bagehot moves, in his third chapter ('Nation-Making', part 1, published in July 1869), to the subject of how custom works in the changing literary styles of recent centuries. Citing the recent work of Lubbock (among others) on primitive men, Bagehot examines the world of eighteenth- and nineteenth-century English literary fads. He further explores the issue of custom in his fourth chapter ('Nation-Making', part 2, not published until December 1871), which is on the conquest of a people with one set of customs by a people with another. Then Bagehot returns to his Gobineau-like analysis of cultural inheritance and racial superiority (extending into his fifth and final long chapter, 'The Age of Discussion', published as an article in January 1872; Bagehot would also add a short conclusion to the collected book later that year).

Unlike Gobineau, Bagehot is not oblivious to reasonable objections—at least in those parts of *Physics and Politics* published after *The Descent of Man*. Bagehot admits that the idea that Aryan-led race mixture is the foundation of all free societies has some problems:

> [A]ll the so called Aryan race certainly is not free. The Eastern Aryans—those, for example, who speak languages derived from the Sanscrit—are amongst the most slavish divisions of mankind. You offer the Bengalee a free constitution, and to expect them to work one, would be the maximum of human folly. There must then be something else then besides Aryan descent which is necessary to fit men for discussion and train them for liberty; and . . . some non-Aryan races have been capable of freedom. Carthage, for example, was a Semitic republic. . . . So that

the theory which would make government by discussion the exclusive patrimony of a single race of mankind is on the face of it untenable.[41]

But Bagehot is so wedded to his idea of physically inherited Aryan cultural superiority that he says that he cannot resolve this difficulty. He asserts that there must be a substantial hereditary element in a culture's success, and that this element is Aryan—while a people with another, non-Aryan inheritance, especially a Semitic inheritance, can sometimes rise above their lack of Aryan-ness.[42]

In any case, he has shown, he says, that once a people has its vigour, it will prevail over others and gain further vigour. But what the initial spark of vigour was he is sure that he does not know. A people's initial spark does not come from climate (whose influence over the recent and even the more recoverable parts of the prehistoric past Gobineau strongly denied)—for, as Bagehot also points out towards the end of the book, similar climates have sheltered dissimilar peoples. All that he does know is that what is inherited matters more for a people than what is experienced.[43] The gaps between different peoples are heritable and they are widening. Bagehot quotes Herbert Spencer:

> Already the brain of the civilized man is larger by nearly thirty per cent. than the brain of the savage. Already, too it presents an increased heterogeneity—especially in the distribution of its convolutions. And further changes like these which have taken place under the discipline of civilized life, we infer will continue to take place.[44]

So the races are physically very different from one another in ways central to their mental capacity and human worth.[45] There is—in a further key parallel with Gobineau—the cloud of degeneration on the horizon. The more civilized peoples have moved away from the enlivening principles of conflict and conquest. For Gobineau, it will be remembered, there were no true Aryans left to reconquer and revivify overly cosmopolitan Europe; with no new source of Aryan vigour, the human species would soon become extinct.

Bagehot sees the same potential problem, but he also a solution for it:

> There is only a certain *quantum* of power in each of our race; if it goes one way it is spent, and cannot go in another. The intellectual atmosphere abstracts strength to intellectual matters; it tends to divert that strength which the circumstances of early society directed to the multiplication of numbers. . . . [46]

The solution is *English* free discussion, an *'animated moderation'* that strikes the right balance. And so, at great length, Bagehot's two final chapters discuss the origin of argumentative civilization out of customary civilization. In a way that recalls John Stuart Mill,[47] they assert that in England the world of discussion will prevent people's energy from being entirely dissipated by civilized life. Thus Bagehot reaches a different conclusion than Gobineau. Gobineau predicts degeneration and rapid human extinction. But for Bagehot, this liberty and energy of discussion make all the difference in many aspects of life:

> Upon plausible grounds—looking, for example to the position of Locke and Newton in the science of the last century, and to that of Darwin in our own—it may be argued that there is some quality in English thought which makes them strike out as many, if not more, first-rate and original suggestions as nations of greater scientific culture and more diffused scientific interest.[48]

English stoutness and good sense beat Continental sophistication any day. And with less energy siphoned off for overly fancy thinking, the English will have more babies, Bagehot says; the factors that make civilized men 'effeminate' and weak do not apply in England.[49] If Bagehot does not stop and label each civilization down through history as male or female, as Gobineau did, he does at least make clear that the English are more manly than the voluble French, or indeed anyone else. Among 'the agreed-on superiorities of the English' is an 'internal' and heritable superiority of body and mind, resulting in the Englishman having—among other things—better self-control than other men, a manly virtue if ever there was one.[50]

HOW TO CONSTRUCT A THEORY OF GOBINEAU/BAGEHOT RACISM

Now that we have been through all that, what does it mean that Bagehot has erected practically the same intellectual structure as Gobineau? The main differences between what the two men created are Gobineau's extra volumes of specious historical examples, plus the three sections particular to Bagehot: (1) On English literary fashion as an example of the workings of custom; (2) on the decline of the old customs and the growth of the different newer, rather different custom of free debate in England; and (3) on how the free spirit of discussion will keep the English from turning epicene and going extinct. But the two men share far more. For both of them, the basic *subject* of history, namely races, is the same; *what the three original and unchanging races are* is the same; the *rejection of climatic determinism* for racial or national change is the same; the *inevitability of racial conflict* is the same; the *heroes* of the story are the same, in that the Aryans make up the strong element in all racial mixtures; the *importance of these Aryan conquests* in all cultural achievements in history is the same; the *danger of stasis or degeneration* is the same, or very similar; the *diagnosis of modern life,* namely the vitiating or feminizing effect of cosmopolitanism, and of a civilization that removes Aryans from the need to conquer, is the same; and the *methodology,* simply citing the names of racial groups, as if that proved their differences with no further checking, is the same. Even the confusing *crossing and re-crossing of races in history* is very similar between the two authors. Each man even admits that the picture of racial crossing is confusing—Gobineau outright, and Bagehot in mentioning that he cannot understand the origins of the major races, or how a Semitic people could have been democratic. Short of deliberately copying Gobineau, Bagehot could hardly have come out with a closer version of his thinking, despite the sections that he added to celebrate free discussion in England. Some of the elements in Bagehot's thinking on the subject of degeneration had already been formulated by B.A. Morel and Philippe Buchez in France, writing in the 1850s,[51] and other elements regarding the conflict between races recall even the views of the disreputable Knox. But these facts do not really signify, for there is no evidence that Bagehot drew from such sources. He never discussed them in print, he never cited them, and he never corresponded with the French thinkers themselves or mentioned them to anyone with whom he did correspond.

There is no evidence that Bagehot drew his thinking from Gobineau, either, but the two men wound up with essentially the same theory. Whatever dribs and drabs the editor of the *Economist* might have picked up about French degeneration theory; and whatever ideas about Aryans that he might have picked up from reading Edward Burnett Tylor or, one supposes, hearing Friedrich Max Müller discussed over dinner; and whatever he remembered about Cuvier and Blumenbach from his education under James Cowles Prichard, this much can be said: In the end the ideas that appealed most to Walter Bagehot—and many of these ideas involving inheritance, degeneration, and social conflict seem to have been generated in his own mind, and not borrowed—were very like Gobineau's ideas.

Thus Gobineau and Bagehot were thinking in parallel about the multiplicity of cultures in the world, the 'races' that undergirded those cultures, and what it all meant. How is that possible? How is the whole laundry list of similarities between the two books to be explained? The first step in the construction of their thoughts on race seems to have been trying to understand why some nineteenth-century peoples were powerful and others were not, why some of the myriad social groups that they could think of were on top and others were falling behind. This is indeed the main point of *Physics and Politics*—at least as Bagehot looked back on it in the brief conclusion (the sixth chapter).[52] For his part, Gobineau despaired over the loss of power by the French aristocracy and the rise of bourgeois civilization. For Bagehot and for Gobineau alike, the prerequisite for a society that will know success in the modern world is a racial character that combines civility and good government with sufficient energy.[53] Both men consider themselves part of a technologically and economically superior European civilization that had run up against an unprecedented number of other cultures around the world.

So the second ingredient creeps in—and it occupies most of the first four chapters of Bagehot's book. This was the idea that the proper unit of analysis in such a world is in fact race—races as both large and small biological units of humanity, with some of the smaller races nested inside larger ones. The assumption is one of racial common purpose, common struggle, common striving along a single path of socioeconomic development.[54] It is not hard to see the influence of the Romantic preoccupation with national identity and national history.

For the construction of the Gobineau-Bagehot idea of race, in any case, the next ingredient is the element of conflict or struggle between these racial groups.[55]

Next we need to add the element of heredity: the idea that any advantage gained in the struggle between peoples accrues back to the racial victors in the form of *heritable* physical, mental, or spiritual superiority. For Gobineau the degenerationist, this element of growing Aryan superiority down through history was not present in the way that it was for Bagehot. According to Gobineau, with each crossing the Aryan blood became weaker. But Gobineau did believe that the admixture of Aryan blood and cultural attainment did secure a hereditary advantage for a conquered people. The Aryan influence made them better.

With something of this element of heritable improvement secured, and with a nod to its inverse—the idea of racial degeneration or decline—then to almost complete the picture one simply needs to identify one's own inherited race as the most victorious, and following the linguists to call it 'Aryan'.

If one can go this far, then why not trace out how race and racial conflict sit behind all the achievements and changes of human history? This is especially easy to do if one accepts that the continuous existence of the different biological races, large and small, can be demonstrated solely from the fact that historical peoples have their particular names. That is, different groups have their own names and therefore they are very different from one another.

One can develop a world-historical (and prehistorical) story of the founding and unfolding of different human races in competition among themselves, with the victorious, blood-leavening Aryans chief among them. 'I assume', Bagehot says

> A world of marked varieties of man, and only want to show how less marked contrasts would probably and naturally arise in each. Given large homogenous populations, some Negro, some Mongolian, some Aryan, I have tried to prove how small contrasting groups would certainly spring up within each—some to last and some to perish. There are eddies in each race stream ... sure to last till some new force

changes the current. These minor varieties, too, would be infinitely compounded, not only with those of the same race, but with those of others. . . . And then on the fresh mass the old forces of composition and elimination again begin to act, and create over the new surface of another world.[56]

And here we have Gobineau's several generations of racial crossing and re-crossing. Bagehot did not have to copy Gobineau. The world situation of Europe in the mid-nineteenth century was one that very well might lead social analysts to reify their category words into the sovereign races that we have been examining.

One objection to doing so—one of Tocqueville's objections—would be the total lack of carefully considered evidence for the races themselves, for how they cross, or for examples of racial crossings at different times. Another objection might come from the realization, with Tocqueville but also with the Darwin of *The Origins of Species*, that there are no real divisions between races; there can be no pure races. That is, races are only temporary conveniences in describing groups of individuals who merge seamlessly into one another; as categories they will not stand much logic chopping or system building. But as we shall see in next chapter, even Darwin would come around to the new way of thinking, reifying race.

BAGEHOTIAN AFTERTHOUGHTS

And yet Bagehot himself may have been on the cusp of abandoning this theory when he died in 1877. By then he had begun to write a more ambitious work of social theory.[57] He was also beginning to think more deeply about how our common ways of characterizing and grouping people can go wrong, and how specific methodological steps are needed to put our thinking right.

In December 1870, the ethnological portions of *Physics and Politics* had already appeared in the *Fortnightly Review*. Bagehot was moving on to the later sections on the importance of free discussion in advanced societies. In that month he gave an address to the Metaphysical Society. It was later reprinted in the *Contemporary Review* under the title 'On the Emotion of Conviction'. Here Bagehot questioned how it is that we know what we think we know. He concluded that we need to think carefully about evidence. We need to have degrees of conviction based upon what we think of the evidence; and while we are gathering our evidence, we ought to employ tentative hypotheses to help us along, forming our convictions only when the evidence is sufficient.[58] This method begins to suggest the care in asking questions and assembling evidence that Tocqueville maintained,[59] although in preparing *Physics and Politics* for publication in volume form some time afterward Bagehot did not use this methodology to re-examine his ways of categorizing the peoples of the world in his original articles.

Bagehot's thinking on methodological questions continued to develop after *Physics and Politics* was completed. In his early articles on France, Bagehot had been sceptical about the way people make up abstract categories. Now he seemed to be returning to that scepticism. In 1874, in another address to the Metaphysical Society, printed as 'The Metaphysical Basis of Toleration', Bagehot argued that many of our everyday evaluations of human character are wrong. Character is very complex, and yet each of us has only so much evidence about the real character of anyone else. How then can we form valid judgments about what people are like? Bagehot's answer is that in discussions with our friends we share our *data* (Bagehot's word and Bagehot's italics) on the characters of different people, and thus we form 'a rough summary. . . . In no other way is it possible to arrive at the truth of the matter. Without discussion each mind is dependent upon its own partial observation.'[60]

Without discussion, indeed, all our ideas about people are unexamined stereotypes. This is unacceptable: 'None of these [images of other people] must be stereotypes; all must be compared. To prohibit discussion is to prohibit the corrective process.' So discussion is key. But there are also some first principles that we should use in our judgments of people, principles that precede and remain more basic than what we learn though discussion: our ideas of taste, of beauty.[61] We must measure our characterizations against these standards, too. So, was Bagehot really about to reject stereotypes (again, his own word)—perhaps rejecting among these stereotypes his own prejudices against different colours or races—in favour of a methodology that recalls Tocqueville? He died too soon for us to know. His last extended statement on the issue of characterizing people by race had been *Physics and Politics* itself.

CONCLUSION

In writing *Physics and Politics,* Walter Bagehot wanted to draw his ideas together in a more connected and more profound way than he could in the two or more short essays that he produced each week for the *Economist,* or in his many longer essays on politics and literature for the monthlies and quarterlies.[62] And yet while he wanted to write more grandly, it seems that he did not want to leave his journalistic audience behind through methodological rigour. He did not want to rewrite the works of Prichard or Latham. Bagehot (like Gobineau) was a humanist, not a skull measurer or a philologist. Indeed, he once joked that 'Some people are unfortunately born scientific'—interested in the details of nature.[63]

And so in *Physics and Politics* Bagehot proceeded without methodological rigour, and without properly questioning his generalizations about people against the available evidence. In order to say something profound, he left his scepticism about categorization behind. He reified his ideas about national or cultural character into ideas of biological race.

Aspects of the new idea of race were also visible elsewhere in England in the 1860s, from the blackface minstrels to some of the writings of Anthony Trollope and Matthew Arnold. Yet Bagehot had developed his way of classifying humanity for his own reasons, elaborating on his ideas of race in a great many ways that recall Gobineau. And as a very serious popular writer, Bagehot helped give shape to the new ideas of race and racial conflict and to propel them forward. Charles Darwin would not be the only person whom *Physics and Politics* would influence.[64] Of course Darwin had his own measure of influence, to say the least. We turn to him next.

6   Darwin and Race

In a sense, Charles Darwin's humanitarianism made him an unlikely convert to racism. His mother, Sussanah, was born a Wedgwood. She was the daughter of the industrialist and abolitionist Josiah Wedgwood. She died when her son Charles was eight, but he was raised among the Wedgwoods as well as the Darwins, and thus he grew up at the centre of the British anti-slavery movement. Abolitionist values ran deep in him. Accordingly, during his voyage on the *Beagle* (1831–6) when he was in his twenties, Darwin bridled at the pro-slavery opinions of Captain Fitzroy. Furthermore he saw the effects of slavery for himself,[1] finding Brazil a land of 'moral debasement'.[2] Darwin recalled that before leaving England he had been told that seeing slaves would make him less of an abolitionist. Once he *had* seen the slaves he wrote that 'the only alteration I am aware of forming is a much higher estimate of the Negros [*sic*] character'.[3] Yet the fact that Darwin would always hate slavery does not mean that he would reject the idea of physically separate races, as we will see.[4] Humanitarians can be racists, too.

On the *Beagle*, Darwin could see the contrast between the colour of his own skin and the skin of the Brazilians, the Fuegians, the Pacific Islanders, and so forth. His journey through the southern oceans showed him markedly different peoples, eliding all the shades of skin and custom in between. It is by those intermediate shades that we can see that we are unified into one multidimensional continuum of skin colour and humanity. Since the first Portuguese explorations in the Eastern Atlantic in the fourteenth and fifteenth centuries, this experience of colour-contrast-through-elision has led Westerners to build racial theories.[5] Indeed, seeing two differently coloured groups of people next to each other in the Cape of Good Hope left Darwin speculating that were it not for racial blending and forced migration, the blacks of that region might have become a distinct species 'in 10,000 years'.[6] The characteristics of the inhabitants of Tierra del Fuego fascinated him. Darwin called the groups that he saw 'races' (and mixes of them 'breeds'), although he could still refer to Chilean miners as 'a peculiar race of men', using the older, looser meaning of 'race'.[7]

Seeing the contrast between different peoples was a formative experience for Darwin. Once back in London in 1836, he kept detailed notebooks on human varieties.[8] In the notebooks from his great creative period back in England the 1830s and early 1840s, he continued to employ racial categories.[9] In 'common language', he observed, blacks and whites already were two 'species', although mixed-race populations in South Africa seemed to belie this common parlance.[10] When considering these questions, Darwin thought about using evidence from Lawrence, Blumenbach, and Prichard.[11] But during the many years of further work that followed these early notebooks, as Darwin continued to gather his own evidence on natural selection, he moved *away* from the perspectives of his time with Fitzroy and the Fuegians. Even by the time that he published his first version of *The Voyage of the Beagle* late in 1839, his idea of a unified tree of life was already beginning to eclipse the colour-contrast perspective.[12]

TREES AND RACES

Darwin was moving away from an idea of ultimately separate races and toward another old idea in Western thought—that we are all cousins of one degree or another, in a huge family tree going back to Adam.[13] Of course tracing everyone's genealogy to Adam, so that we all share different degrees of cousinage, is central to the genealogy of nations in the book of Genesis. In the English language, the phrase 'family tree' goes back to the thirteenth century or before; and illustrations of the tree as a living tree of human ancestors, the tree coming complete with bark and foliage, appear frequently, as in the first painting in Hogarth's *Marriage à la Mode* in 1743. In the mid-nineteenth century, the image of the tree was in the ascendant in linguistics after Sir William Jones's demonstration of the branching off of the different languages of what came to be known as the 'Aryan' (and ultimately the 'Indo-European') language family. The family-tree diagram itself, or *Stammbaum*, with its labelled branches for different groups of languages, was first used for the evolution of species by Lamarck in 1809.[14] From that point forward it was much in use in treatments of race that relied on linguistic evidence for unity of descent.[15]

Darwin's attitude toward the genealogical tree that makes us all cousins was very complex. In *The Origin*, Darwin would refer to a 'genealogical arrangement of the races of man' that might explain the distributions and relationships of human languages. But this was merely to make clear his ideas about how branching works; Darwin did not think that enough was known about the extinct languages and their speakers for the racial/linguistic tree ever to be drawn up.[16]

Even if more evidence were discovered about the human branches of the tree of life, there would still be a problem with interpreting the picture. Whether one was looking at humans or at the animals or plants, there was the question of which branchings should mark the separation of full species and which should mark only the races within a species. Darwin was quite explicit in *The Origin* that there is no good criterion for distinguishing between whether two related populations are different species or whether they are merely separate races. Whether adjacent branches represented two races, two species, two genera or orders or what have you, would depend in part on an accidental factor: how many of the intermediate kinds of organisms had died out, widening the apparent gap.[17] It was also a matter of taste. The races of one species could be called entirely different species if one wished, or different adjacent species could be demoted to the level of the races of one overarching species. At least in *The Origin*, the words 'race' and 'species' (or for that matter 'genus', 'family', and so on) signified no predictable or constant degree of affinity or difference.[18]

But what about interbreeding? Doesn't the ability to produce fertile offspring form a simple and clear test of which varieties make up separate species and which are merely the different races of one species? No, and the question was much discussed in the nineteenth century. Any cattle-like species can interbreed with any other. They may not frequently do it, because they would not have occasion to—a North American bison would not naturally have the occasion to breed with a Central Asian yak or a champion Holstein. But a bull of one species and a cow of another, if they are put together in the same pen at the right time, will produce offspring that are mostly fertile. Clearly a bison and a yak and a Texas Longhorn are different 'species'—according to how most people normally use the term. But if producing fertile offspring is the test, then there is only one species of cattle in the world.

With horses and the other horse-like animals, the picture gets murkier still, for different degrees of fertility exist in the offspring of different crosses. There is no clear place to draw the same species/other species, fertility/infertility line. The cross between a horse and a donkey is usually infertile, but some of the offspring *are* fertile—if only for one more generation. Interfertility becomes a range of probabilities and degrees, with no clear way to distinguish between species and race.[19]

Against this background of scepticism about race in *The Origin of Species*, Darwin's abolitionist sympathies ran free in the 1860s. Darwin was revolted by the openly racist violence of Governor Eyre in Jamaica. Eyre's ideas reminded him of Captain Fitzroy's, and in 1866 Darwin joined the committee to have Governor Eyre prosecuted.[20] He certainly noticed the newly fashionable racism of the 1860s, as this passage from his *Variation of Plants and Animals under Domestication* (1868) makes clear:

> Thus the noble-hearted Humboldt, who felt none of that prejudice against the inferior races now so current in England, speaks in strong terms of the bad and savage disposition of the Zambos, or half-castes

between Indians and Negroes, and this conclusion has been arrived at by various observers.[21]

Darwin is telling us that there is racism and that he does not share it. Soon he would.

THE DESCENT OF MAN AND ITS CONTRADICTIONS

Darwin's book on humanity, *The Descent of Man, and Selection in Relation to Sex* appeared in 1871. From the outset of the book, Darwin cites reams of small details to show that humanity is closely related to apes and other mammals. Humanity has not emerged from animal life without preserving many telling but no longer functional animal characteristics.

What is important for us is that in bringing in some of his evidence about humanity, Darwin often refers to the physical characteristics of different 'races' as they have been reported by various scientific writers. Those working on the continent of Europe, in the United States, and in the possessions of the various European empires often sorted their data by skin colour, or by the racial theories that pertained in each location. Darwin says that he can draw upon this body of previous work in pursuing his own aims:

> The sole object of this book is to consider, firstly, whether man, like every other species, is descended from some pre-existing form; secondly, the manner of his development; and thirdly the value of the differences between the so-called races of man. As I shall confine myself to these points, it will not be necessary to describe in detail the differences between the several races—an enormous subject which has been described in detail in many valuable works.[22]

And in these words he is assuming that there *are* races. But in practice Darwin seems—if only at the outset of the book—too careful to accept, unexamined, the racial categories that ran though so many of his sources. And he is too sensitive to possible criticism to do so. He well knows that his explanation for the origins of humanity, down to the level of explaining the origins of human religious belief and the human love of beauty, will be controversial.[23] He does not want to attract even more criticism by seeming to propound the inhumane racialist beliefs of men like Knox or the Americans Nott and Glidden. On occasion he does cite them for anatomical points.[24] He even cites the racist William Lawrence, whom he may have known personally.[25] But he does not draw from these authors as much as he does from the richer and more anatomically detailed—and less consistently racist—works of Prichard. The first time he cites Nott, Glidden, and Knox is to show that they contradict one another on whether Egyptian sculptures look African (Nott and Glidden) or Jewish (Knox). He then undercuts their conclusions further by suggesting that more work is still necessary.[26] (Darwin is less chary of citing the Frenchmen Quatrefages and Broca, whose work he approves of less reservedly.)[27]

In a famous passage from his chapter on race, Darwin explicitly rejects all the schemes of races that had been proposed since the Enlightenment. The races could not be very distinct if no one could agree on how many there were:

> [T]he most weighty of all the arguments against treating the races of man as distinct species, is that they graduate into each other, independently in many cases, as far as we can tell, of their having intercrossed. Man has been studied more carefully than any other organic being, and yet there is the greatest possible diversity amongst capable judges whether he should be classed as a single species or race, or as two (Virey), as three (Jacquinot), as four (Kant), five (Blumenbach), six (Buffon), seven (Hunter), eight (Agassiz), eleven (Pickering), fifteen (Bory St. Vincent), sixteen (Desmoulins), twenty-two (Morton), sixty (Crawfurd), or as sixty-three, according to Burke.[28]

This passage comes as the culmination of the chapter that Darwin devotes entirely to the question of whether human races exist.

But we need to look rather more at *The Descent of Man*'s early chapter on race. It is organized around a thought experiment: Darwin imagines a hypothetical naturalist who had never looked at humanity before. What would such an observer coming to the subject afresh be likely to say about the existence of human races?[29]

Darwin begins with the arguments that the naturalist would consider *in favour of* the existence of human races. He even includes claims (which he ultimately rejects) that the human races are not completely interfertile. Darwin also rejects the idea that interfertility ought to be a test of speciation, since many clearly separate species can breed together.[30]

Turning to the evidence that the hypothetical naturalist might see as counting *against* the idea that humanity is divided racially, Darwin first discusses the degree of hybridization between different human groups, which is very high, telling against their separation.[31] So, ultimately, does the fact that there is great variety among the individuals within each supposed racial group.[32] And finally there are the many accidental (that is, non-survival-enhancing) similarities between the races, including many independently arrived at commonalities of culture and basic technology.[33] Therefore, Darwin concludes, humanity is highly variable at the individual level. We are *not* therefore a 'racial' species, for we are in a different biological category—we are a 'protean or polymorphic' species, with a high level of individual variation.[34] That is Darwin's conclusion in the one chapter that he dedicates to exploring the issue of human race. We do not have races. The human continuum does not clump up in that way.

And yet all the way through this section—and indeed all through the ten chapters that Darwin will dedicate to humanity in *The Descent of Man*—he continues to talk as though races do exist in human biology. When he is discussing a species of monkey, Darwin is not above crude racist humour: 'The resemblance of *Pithicia satanas* with his jet black skin, white rolling eyeballs, and hair parted on the top of the head, to a negro in miniature, is almost ludicrous'.[35] Darwin also assumes that physical race correlates with cultural levels. He repeatedly contrasts the 'civilized nations' with the 'lower races'.[36] He finds it extraordinary that black people think black skin attractive.[37] And, '[a]s bearing on the subject of imitation, the strong tendency in our nearest allies, the monkeys, in microcephalous idiots, and in the barbarous races of mankind, to imitate whatever they hear deserves notice.'[38]

In passages like this, it certainly seems that Darwin believes in human races, and that he believes in *unequal* human races. Throughout the human-centred half of *The Descent of Man* (ten chapters out of twenty-one), Darwin puts the races in a hierarchy, with blacks as the lowest part of humanity.[39] They are the race closest to the gorilla. Moreover, they will be exterminated—that is Darwin's word for what Caucasians will do to blacks, leading to an era of advancement for Caucasians themselves:

> At some future period, not very distant as measured by centuries, the civilized races of man will almost certainly exterminate and replace throughout the world the savage races. At the same time, the anthropomorphous apes, as Prof. Schaffenhausen has remarked, will no doubt be exterminated. The break will then be rendered wider, for it will intervene between man in a more civilized state, as we may hope, than the Caucasian, and some ape as low as a baboon; instead of as at present between the negro of Australia and the gorilla.[40]

And yet for all of his references to a hierarchy of human races in the text of *The Descent of Man*, in the chapter on whether human races exist Darwin had argued that they do not.[41]

THE MYSTERY

What was happening here? Darwin was consistently slipping between an analytical rejection of race and a demotic employment of the term. It has been pointed out by others that Darwin often used his terms very loosely. He frequently used anthropomorphic language to suggest that animals 'want' when really he meant to imply no such volition on their part.[42] But with these references to 'race' in *The Descent of Man* there seems to be more going on than a loose style. Darwin alternates between maintaining that races are real and stable across generations, and that blacks are at the bottom of a racial hierarchy, and maintaining on the other hand that races do not exist in human biology.[43] And I do not mean that he is moving back and forth in the section of the race chapter that we already looked at, where he was deliberately setting out the thinking of his hypothetical non-biased naturalist, examining first the evidence for human races and then the evidence against them. I mean that in the rest of the human-centred chapters of the book, written in his own voice, Darwin alternates between both sides of the question, never himself acknowledging the contradiction between his positions:

> [N]ot one of the external differences between the races of man are of any direct or special service to him. The intellectual and moral or social faculties must of course be excepted from this remark; but differences in these faculties can have had little or no difference on external characters. The variability of all the characteristic differences between the races, before referred to, likewise indicates that these differences cannot be of much importance; for, had they been important, they would long ago either have been fixed or preserved, or eliminated.[44]

And here we have the paradox: Races do not make coherent groups, given all the variability—but in the same breath the races are different physically, mentally, and even morally. The variety and lack of predictive power within the groups belie the groups, but Darwin keeps using the groups anyway. Sometimes this contradiction comes in the space of a very few words: 'If the greater hairiness of certain races be the result of reversion, unchecked by any form of selection, the extreme variability of this character, even within the limits of the same race, ceases to be remarkable.'[45] That is, certain races are of course hairier—except that the races vary so much internally that they have no predictive power for this characteristic. The assumption is that the races are divided by some consistent set of differences, making the races useful categories—except that those differences melt into the air whenever they are examined directly.

It would seem that in relation to race, Darwin lacked the courage of his methodology. Darwin was as careful with his classified notebooks and his massive and carefully organized sets of research data as Tocqueville was.[46] But at bottom Darwin will not stick to the conclusion of his own chapter on race. He will not take the Tocquevillean step of believing in the groupings that his own sorting of the evidence had produced, and of disbelieving in the names and categories that his evidence had disproven. In pursuing his main theme of the role of natural and sexual selection in human origins, Darwin will not abandon racial categorization, or consistently take the time to correct it, even when his own most careful sorting of the evidence—in a full chapter on the subject—has proven that human races do not exist. Darwin continues to use 'race' anyway, rejecting it only when he is thinking about it, but the rest of the time throwing his more careful use of the term to the winds.

DARWIN ON THE CULTURAL CONSTRUCTION OF RACE

And to some degree he must have known what he was doing. One clue that may help us to unravel how Darwin can deny racial categories yet rely on them anyway is what happens when, on occasion, he seems for a moment to acknowledge that racial distinctions are indeed a matter of cultural learning. Early on, for example, Darwin admits that the observations in the scientific literature that makes up the bulk of his evidence on human groups may contain bias. Thus, at the outset of the sections setting out the evidence for and against human races, he says that

> In regard to the amount of difference between the races, we must make some allowance for our nice powers of discrimination gained by the long habit of observing ourselves. In India, as Elphinstone remarks, although a newly arrived European cannot at first distinguish the different native races, yet soon they appear to him extremely dissimilar. . . . [47]

'Hindoos' went through the same process in learning to distinguish between Europeans.

So racial distinctions are to an important extent something that we learn rather than something we derive from real physical evidence. Further, '[e]ven the most distinct races of man, with the exception of certain negro tribes, are much more like each other in form than at first would be supposed'.[48] But Darwin quickly undercuts these suggestions of the cultural construction of difference by putting things back into a physical context:

> [t]here is, however, no doubt that the various races, when carefully compared and measured, differ much from each other,—as in the texture of the hair, the relative proportions of all parts of the body, the capacity of the lungs, the form and capacity of the skull, and even in the convolutions of the brain.[49]

And then:

> Their mental characteristics are likewise very distinct; chiefly as it would appear in their emotional but partly in their intellectual faculties. Everyone who has had the opportunity of comparison, must have been struck with the taciturn, even morose, aborigines of S. [*sic*] America and the light-hearted, talkative negroes.[50]

Might there be cultural factors behind these alleged differences, so that nurture and not nature is the reason for them? Darwin does not ask. The context suggests that the differences have more to do with the brain and its convolutions.

I believe that it is very significant that Darwin allows apparently cultural differences, when he broaches them, to merge back into the realm of physical difference. Here is another example: Darwin points to the photographic evidence assembled by the French racialists. The fact that all but certain blacks can be quite similar

> is well shown by the French photographs in the Collection Anthropologique du Muséum de Paris of the men belonging to various races, the greater number of which, as many persons to whom I have shown them have remarked, might pass for Europeans. Nevertheless, these men if seen alive would undoubtedly appear very distinct, so that we are clearly much influenced in our judgment by the mere colour of the skin and hair, by slight differences in the features, and by expression.[51]

So, 'slight differences' quite invisible in the photographs themselves would 'undoubtedly' mark the 'very different' races. Darwin will not accept the conclusion that his criticism of the photographic evidence would seem to point to: That there is something artificial about the racial categories that people are trying to use; that they are to some large degree cultural rather than biological. Rather, Darwin moves the question of cultural difference that the passage raises back into the realm of physical racial distinctions, however dubious they might be.

THE DECISIVE FACTOR: THE INHERITANCE OF ACQUIRED CHARACTERISTICS AND THE ROLE OF BAGEHOT

Why did Darwin come to believe that cultural differences can become physical differences? One factor was his shock at what he saw of the condition of the 'barbarous inhabitants of Tierra del Fuego'. He frequently refers to them.[52] They were very low on the scale of humanity but still human.[53] Dividing humanity into different physical races allowed Darwin to put some distance between his own culture and that of the Fuegians.

But there was something deeper at work. For Darwin, the cultural construction of race that he really does understand, as we have just seen, is no reason to abandon the concept of physically different human races: For cultural difference *leads* to physical difference, through the mechanism of the physical inheritance of acquired mental characteristics. Cultural differences can become physical differences.

Darwin's belief in the physical inheritance of acquired cultural characteristics is not in doubt. Darwin asserts the inheritance of acquired characteristics many times in *The Descent of Man*. As Michael Ruse has put it, ' . . . Darwin was always a Lamarckian. He was one before he discovered natural selection, he remained one after he discovered natural selection, and the mechanism appeared throughout his published work, including the *Descent of Man*.[54] For Darwin, then, externally produced changes in the shape of the skull can be inherited.[55] And then there were the internally produced changes that came from use and disuse: 'use-inheritance'. So when civilized people take to a softer diet, their jaws do not grow as long (leading to problems with wisdom teeth), and this effect is passed on to their children.[56] And newly acquired *mental* characteristics or achievements can be inherited, too.[57]

This idea of the inheritance of acquired *ideas* is an old one. It can be traced back to Darwin's grandfather Erasmus Darwin. (Indeed, perhaps Darwin inherited the idea.) Idea inheritance was one way to explain the origin of instincts.[58] For his part, Charles Darwin had considered the inheritance of acquired ideas and habits in the 1830s, but he had dismissed the notion for a time when he wrote *The Origin of Species*, where he tells us that he wished to emphasize natural selection above all else. Now, in *The Descent of Man*, Darwin wants to rebalance the picture by exploring other factors behind species change, chief among them sexual selection and use-inheritance.[59]

In *The Descent of Man*, Darwin sometimes introduces doubts that physical inheritance extends to acquired habits, but at other times he seems quite sure.[60] New mental characteristics and habits can directly effect one's offspring biologically, not merely through the young imitating the old. These changes stand apart from any inheritance of temperament that might be due to sexual selection down through the generations.[61] Therefore Darwin reifies, as Bagehot did, our cultural differences into inherited biological racial difference.

And thus Darwin's argument fell into line with Bagehot's. Bagehot's articles caught Darwin's attention as soon as they came out (as John C. Greene has explored).[62] So, citing Bagehot's 'remarkable series of articles on Physics and Politics in the "Fortnightly Review"', Darwin embraced the theory that humans competed with each other as races rather than as individuals. This was quite new, and it recalls nothing in Malthus, for whom individuals died in such numbers that the survival of the fittest and the strengthening of one stock of a species against another was not a factor. The idea of a struggle between races or groups can be traced back into the eighteenth century, but as for both Thomas Malthus and Erasmus Darwin in more recent times, there was no struggle for existence, for natural struggles take place against the background of providential accommodation; species or groups within them do not struggle *for existence*, as existence is guaranteed by the self-regulating mechanisms of nature.[63] But now Darwin had a different view, a view of competing animal and human races.

Further, Darwin pointed out that conformity and cultural cohesion were vital during the long early stages of the human racial struggle, 'as Mr. Bagehot has well shewn'.[64] For Darwin now, as for Bagehot, when natural selection works on human social and mental characteristics, it operates on the group within which people are like one another, or the larger group in which the tribes come together into nations. Between the tribes (or later the nations) there is the inevitable enmity.[65] Enmity occurs first at the level of tribes and later at the level of nations.

The hardships of life usually kept tribal populations under control, Darwin explains. But when hardships were not hard enough, 'and when one of two adjoining tribes becomes more numerous and more powerful than the other, the contest is soon settled by war, slaughter, cannibalism, slavery, and absorption.'[66] Thus, 'When civilized nations come into conflict with barbarians, the struggle is short, except where a deadly climate gives its aid to the native race.'[67] And '[e]xtinction follows chiefly from the conflict of tribe with tribe and race with race.'[68]

But, as Darwin credits Bagehot for pointing out, extinction before the coming civilized race is a modern phenomena; the ancient empires did not see their barbarian enemies melting away to disease or primitive habits.[69] Conquerors absorbed and transformed the conquered. In another Bagehotian note, the 'civilized races' or Europeans are described two pages later as Aryans.[70] Further, most of history is the record of stronger (that is, smarter) races conquering weaker ones, just as it is for Bagehot. 'In Europe the men of the Bronze period were supplanted by a more powerful and, judging from their sword-handles, larger-handed race; but their success was probably due in a much higher degree to their superiority in the arts.'[71]

Throughout the book Darwin uses current survivals to show how things must have been for more primitive humans. That is, he uses currently extant groups to show the developmental stages through which European man has passed. In other words, Darwin is using the social evolutionism of Lubbock and Bagehot. The difference is that Darwin is able to rely on more than only human evidence, for all the evidence that he cites of the developmental stages of European culture from William M'Lennon, E.B. Tylor, and others. But Darwin was at the centre of the network of biological research. He could also use his knowledge of current survivals in the *animal* world to show even earlier stages along the path to humanity. In including these biological examples alongside what he believed current primitive tribes illustrated about the dim mists of the European past, Darwin was practicing social evolutionism writ large. His social evolutionism used biological as well as social examples of how the more 'primitive' groups in today's world show how 'we' came to be.

This form of social evolutionism fell into line with what Darwin said were his three main goals in writing *The Descent of Man*: First, showing animal-like evolution in people; second, broadening the mechanism of evolution from natural selection to include sexual selection; and third, exploring the question of human races.[72] It is no wonder that Darwin admired the way Alfred Russel Wallace had tried to extend the principle of natural selection to humanity in his short essay of 1864.[73] But Darwin had disagreed with Wallace's argument that natural selection and physical change stopped when cultural evolution started, long ago.[74] Now, following

Bagehot, Darwin has argued that humans undergo physical changes in response to culture and they inherit these changes. Darwin, still following Bagehot, therefore concludes, it would seem, that the different cultural levels in the world, especially when they are different colours, are potentially different races. Darwin concludes this even though he had previously determined in his race chapter that the races are more diverse internally than they could be if they were now or ever had been coherent biological groups. The races do not exist in biology, but they soon will. At present the races are culturally different—and thus, for Darwin as for Bagehot, they are *now* becoming physically different, and in heritable ways.

And so are the classes within European society. Classes also become physically separate, heritably. Near the end of the book, Darwin expresses his hope that most people in his society will become cultivated enough to pass on a decent level of cultivation to their children, 'educating and stimulating in all possible ways the intellectual faculties of every human being'.[75] But without each class becoming educated enough to raise their children properly, the different classes will inherit different characteristics. Darwin is explicit about this differential inheritance of cultural factors between different countries or 'races'. Indeed, that is how he explains the moral influence of religion in Europe: 'It is not improbable that virtuous tendencies may through long practice be inherited. With the more civilised races, the conviction of the existence of an all-seeing Deity has had a potent influence on the advancement of morality'.[76] As for differential inheritance within English society, Darwin cites his younger kinsman Francis Galton—the founder of eugenics—on the problem of the best people choosing to have the fewest children: '[A]ll ought to refrain from marriage who cannot avoid abject poverty for their children'. But it will do no good, indeed, it will do great harm, if the most conscientious people avoid marriage when they can't afford it 'whilst the reckless marry': 'the inferior members will tend to supplant the better members of society'.[77]

So by the conclusion of *The Descent of Man*, Darwin's views have travelled a great distance from the argument of his human-races-do-not-exist chapter. But even at the conclusion of the chapter on race, Darwin seemed to think that the worst classes, like the worst races, are barely human. 'The taste for the beautiful differs widely in the different races of man', he announces. And so

> [j]udging from the hideous ornament and the equally hideous music admired by most savages, it might be urged that their aesthetic faculty was not so highly developed as in certain animals, for instance, in birds. Obviously no animal would be capable of admiring such scenes as the heavens at night, a beautiful landscape, or refined music; but such tastes, depending as they do on culture and complex associations, are not enjoyed by barbarians or by uneducated persons.[78]

Darwin's words in this passage show that he had a higher view of birds and a lower view of people than one of his scientific correspondents had demonstrated in a speech at Dumfries in 1866. Australian bowerbirds, the man had said, 'in their appreciation of beauty', had tastes 'as was to be expected—more similar to those of savages and apes & children in the objects of their selection than to those of civilized men'.[79] For Darwin, some birds had a *higher* aesthetic sense than whole 'races' of humanity.

White men have the best of the inherited differences, racially and sexually. On the sexual side: 'Man is more creative, pugnacious, and energetic than woman, and has more inventive genius.'[80] On the racial side, all doubt should be dismissed: The hairiness of creative European men does *not* mean that they are primitive, merely subject to individual reversion.[81] One is left with the inference that whites are smarter, especially those creative, pugnacious, and energetic men.

* * *

And so the human tree keeps on branching. Darwin can now accept race formation as a continuing process of ramification—even if the current 'races' do not cohere very well. Because of his belief in the inheritance of acquired cultural characteristics, as Robert Kenny has noticed, Darwin seems to regard racial divergence as a real phenomenon, and the human 'races' as useful categories[82]—even if the most careful treatment of the question in *The Descent of Man* shows that the races do not exist, at present. That is how Darwin could rely so heavily upon the concept and the vocabulary of race while nonetheless reaching the conclusion of his main racial chapter: that humans are one of those 'protean or polymorphic' species that are so variable that they do not have races.[83] This is our heritage from the past. For Darwin, even the social classes within England were *now* diverging into physically different inheritance races.

Near the end of *The Descent of Man*, then, Darwin could say that mankind has 'diverged into distinct races, or . . . sub-species'. Some races, 'for instance the negro and the European, are so distinct that, if specimens had been brought to a naturalist without any further information, they would undoubtedly have been considered by him as good and true species'. But still he goes on to say that the 'races' are similar in so many details, both physical and mental, that they clearly share a common descent from an ancestor who already 'would probably deserve to rank as man'.[84] The evidence against races is so strong that Darwin cannot escape it; however, he refuses to let the racist categories go.[85]

CONCLUSION

As Darwin saw, the human races of the present day make no sense if one tries to count them, to identify just what they are supposed to be and where they are in the world, or to map one set of varying characteristics against another. But he turns away from these detailed questions and uses racial terms anyway in a careful biological discussion. Apparently, the physical inheritance of cultural characteristics can be used to understand and define human races that remain unclear, even disproved, by one's most careful biological work. If races do not exist now, they soon will, through the process that Darwin found in Bagehot—the physical inheritance of acquired cultural characteristics. The result is the picture that Darwin took from Bagehot—a world of human races in mutual conflict, with the Aryan races on top of the game.

One might think that if the different cultures of the world were going to turn into different biological races, they might already have done so, after several thousand years of cultural divergence—so that when Darwin so carefully demonstrated the lack of current races in the human species, he might have seen through Bagehot's argument. Perhaps, then, for Darwin the human races were simply basic, as they are for some thinkers in the early twenty-first century. Darwin's frequent use of 'race' despite the problems that he has demonstrated with identifying any particular races may illustrate what Kwame Anthony Appiah calls 'intrinsic' racism; the races simply are different in character. They are an unquestioned part of our received set of language categories, and they require no appeal to evidence.[86] That is, races are out there in the world, even though every careful search for them fails. Apparently it just stands to reason that each big, continental group of people has diverged into a single race with covarying characteristics. Therefore, each continent naturally has a race. And each race has its look and its colour.

So, in the twenty-first century, this idea of natural, obvious race may still seem to 'simply stand to reason'. And so it seems obvious that something called the black race lives in Africa—until one remembers that tropical Africa, the most genetically diverse place on earth, has populations that look vastly different from each other, from Pygmies to the Bantu next door—except for the accident of sharing a colour appropriate to the environment. And that colour is shared with Melanesians, who are genetically the furthest people on earth from any African group.[87] The human groups in Africa are wildly different from each other, more so than elsewhere; there is no 'black race'.

Darwin may well have been an intrinsic racist, or he would not have found social evolutionism and Bagehot's brand of racism so appealing. He would not have seen such a gap between white men and others. It is that gap that informs his arguments. He well knew that human beings do not fall into biological racial categories, for he had explored the subject carefully in the appropriate chapter of *The Descent of Man*. And yet elsewhere in the same book he used those very categories—reifying them, and assigning negative characteristics to non-European 'races'. As we will see in the next chapter, the Duke of Argyll had already called Darwin's attention to the shortcomings of racialist thinking. Darwin even cites Argyll in *The Descent of Man*. Argyll had already pointed out the hollowness and the lack of scientific rigour behind some of the assumptions that Darwin would incorporate into the book—namely, the idea that primitive peoples were indeed primitive, rather than fully rational; the idea that groups of people biologically modify themselves (unconsciously, of course) instead of passing their cultural innovations through education; and the idea that this biological modification leads to distinct races. But while Darwin knew of Argyll's criticisms, his faith in the idea of racial progress was now too strong for him to listen.[88] In the best Tocquevillean tradition, Argyll was questioning the categories used in contemporary discourse. Darwin did not go as far as Argyll in this direction.

7 Argyll, Race, and Degeneration

The contemporary view seems to be that life has improved down through history: At least in terms of material comfort there has been a great deal of progress, and our more remote ancestors did not live as well as we do. But the founders of social evolutionism went further, adding three elements that would find less than unanimous support today: That there is an inevitable course of progress against which cultures can be judged; that all cultures developed through fixed stages, from Stone Age to Bronze Age to Iron Age to, ultimately, the Victorian Age; and that the earlier the culture in this cycle, the less imagination, intelligence, artistic sophistication, and sheer human worth its people were born with. Full humanity was hard-won. It took breeding.

Resisting this Victorian triumphalism were the degenerationists. The main proponent of the more extreme version of the theory of degeneration was the Archbishop of Dublin, Richard Whately (1787–1863). From our perspective, his beliefs may seem quaint: The diversity of world cultures did not come from the their varying degrees of progress out of a primitive state. Instead, cultures have degenerated to different degrees from the high standards of the book of Genesis.[1]

Degeneration seemed quaint to some of the Victorians, too. One man who rejected it was Sir John Lubbock. A friend of Walter Bagehot and an established banker, Lubbock had brought out his first book on anthropology in 1865.[2] In an 1867 address to the meeting of the British Association at Dundee,[3] he repudiated Whately's belief that God himself had created the first civilization, and that man could never progress to the civilized state on his own account. Lubbock argued that on the contrary, primitive peoples had many times developed into civilized ones.

And if that was all that Lubbock had said, it would have been hard to disagree with him. Although the Duke of Argyll was already a committed degenerationist, even he concurred with Lubbock that civilization had developed by degrees, in contrast to Whately's insistence that civilization had sprung fully formed from the head of Jehovah.[4] Yet Argyll saw what he thought were even deeper flaws in Lubbock's argument than in the late Archbishop's.[5] Lubbock did not stop at arguing the case for historical progress. He went on to insist that before that progress had taken place early humanity was a very sorry spectacle. Here Argyll rebelled. For him, early humanity may not have begun fully cultured but it did begin fully human. Indeed, early peoples were brilliant. They deserved the credit for creating the key building blocks of civilization—such as fire and agriculture.[6] Modern peoples do not have to be so inventive. Indeed, they can sink into decadence and ignorance.

That is what degeneration meant to Argyll. He recognized that we do have bigger buildings and better science than the ancients did. He did *not* think that we suffer from any kind of biological or inbred inferiority in comparison to our ancestors. But as the leading proponent of degeneration after Whately's death, he believed that because of our less challenging environment we may not always come up to the level of survival skills or moral strength of those who came before us. As individuals or as cultures, we may have fallen away from their high standard.

And with this view of the basic human worth of so-called primitive peoples, Argyll would bristle at the new picture of heritable and unequal human races, and what he thought was the shoddy thinking behind it.

ONE HUMAN RACE, BLENDING TOGETHER

Within a month of joining Gladstone's Cabinet as Indian Secretary in 1868, Argyll published a short book, *Primeval Man: An Examination of Some Recent Speculations*, setting down his thoughts on human development and where John Lubbock had gone wrong.[7] It was in this book that Argyll made his point that even our earliest human ancestors had full mental and moral lives. They did not have primitive souls to match their primitive tools—for as Peter Bowler has noted, Argyll saw no reason to suppose a relationship between one and the other.[8]

For Argyll, that was indeed all that Lubbock was doing—supposing things. John Lubbock had no real evidence by which to convict all early humanity of moral turpitude. Lubbock could not have the prehistoric world his own way—nasty and brutish, if not short—merely for saying so.

Argyll also questioned the evidence behind another of Lubbock's key assertions: that each culture with its different natural resources would go through the same stages of development—a Stone Age, Bronze Age, an Iron Age (Lubbock had invented these terms, apart from the use of 'Iron Age' in a very different sense by the Ancient Greeks). Argyll asked what proof there was for these stages.[9]

Most seriously of all, Lubbock misused what evidence he had. He assumed that any barbarous traits within a culture were *ipso facto* of earlier origin than its more civilized features.[10] But Argyll pointed out that the worst things are not always the oldest. They do not necessarily show the original conditions of society 'any more than the traces of Feudalism in the laws of modern Europe prove that feudal principles were born with the Human Race'.[11] Things could get worse as well as better; progress was not inevitable. Argyll believed that local climatic and other conditions could dramatically set back moral and civilizational achievements, and so could man's tendency to turn away from what is good. He cited Darwin on how far the Fuegians had degenerated. Darwin had been right, Argyll insisted, to point out that the Fuegians did not suffer from some original, inborn inferiority, but from a brutalizing environment.[12]

And this brings us to the heart of the matter. For Lubbock, primitive peoples and nonwhites—'these miserable beings', as he referred to them— were not only different but remarkably inferior to the nineteenth-century European norm.[13] Argyll disagreed; he did not divide the peoples of the world into large, intellectually unequal colour groups. He maintained that the human 'Races' were not so different as was often said, although long-established differences did exist between these 'varieties'.[14] Egyptian tomb paintings show that blacks have looked black, and were subservient to the Egyptians, for thousands of years. Argyll included a fold-out line illustration of one of these paintings.[15] But his argument in discussing the Egyptian paintings is that colour changes slowly, so mankind has been diverging from its 'single stock' for a period of time longer than what is allowed by the account in Genesis.[16] And in a key passage, he explains that colour is the only real difference between peoples:

> Strongly marked as the varieties of man now are, the variation is strongest in respect to colour, which in all organisms is notoriously the most liable to modification and change. And in this feature of colour it is remarkable that we have every possible variety of tint from the fairest to the blackest races, so that one extreme passes into the other by small and insensible gradations.[17]

Again, one colour passes gradually into another, without the sharp breaks there would be if the human 'varieties' were really different from each other. Everyone passes into everyone else 'by small and insensible gradations'. So there are no real racial groups, whether judged by colour or achievement. All modern peoples, even the 'savage races', can create works 'highly ingenious' and 'eminently beautiful'.[18]

*   *   *

Darwin's response will be the more significant for us, but first we should look at Lubbock's. His answer to Argyll came in an address to the British Association in 1869, an address that Lubbock would expand into an appendix to his book *The Origins of Civilization* in the following year.[19] Lubbock quickly dismissed Argyll's objection to the way he had used modern examples of cruelty as evidence of what things used to be like—rather than what things might have degenerated into.[20] And he did not address the arguments that Argyll put forward to show that savages are both intelligent and moral. Although Lubbock himself went out of his way to demonstrate Eskimo intelligence—in an attempt to refute Argyll's belief that Eskimo populations had fallen especially far from civilization[21]—yet nonetheless in other sections Lubbock would never admit that non-European groups share anything like his own mental level. He went so far as to say that if intelligence were the main criterion, the different races of mankind would be classed as different species, or even different genera.[22] This was quite a decided rejection of Argyll's central point that everyone merges into everyone else.

Perhaps Neal Gillespie is right to suggest that Lubbock's response to Argyll is full of deliberate 'bias and evasion'.[23] Or perhaps Lubbock was so sure of his picture of the stages of human progress, and of all the evidence that he had amassed for it, that he simply wanted to shout his argument all the louder so that people could apprehend its merits as well as they ought to. He would respond to minor objections but not to major ones.[24] In any case, the same key flaws that Argyll identified in Lubbock's earlier work still pervade *The Origin of Civilization* in 1870: Lubbock assumed the stupidity, the immorality, and at bottom the separate racial character of early peoples and most contemporary non-Europeans alike; he assumed a fixed set of stages through which societies pass; and most illogically he continued to assume that the more 'barbarous' surviving characteristics in a culture are in fact always the oldest parts of it.

Not everyone dismissed Argyll's views so easily. Alfred Russel Wallace, for one, was convinced by Argyll that early man was as moral as modern man. He announced his position publicly at the British Association in 1869.[25] (Darwin was perhaps less likely to listen to Wallace after his conversion to spiritualism over the preceding several years.) Another of Argyll's books, *The Reign of Law*,[26] which came out in 1866, had prompted serious comment for its discussion of specific biological details. Indeed, Argyll's argument that natural selection failed to explain the beautiful feathers of hummingbirds seems to have helped to goad Darwin into exploring the additional factor of sexual selection, and thus writing *The Descent of Man*.[27]

Argyll was a serious enough figure that he could not be completely ignored. He believed in deep geological time, and in the rise and extinction of myriad species in different geological ages.[28] He accepted natural selection as a method of species change.[29] He worked for many years on the anatomy of birds, and, as we will see, some of the greatest scientists of the day read his books. But there was a reason why certain thinkers did not take his arguments for degeneration very seriously. Argyll's works also featured abstract philosophical disquisitions on the meaning of such terms as 'supernatural', the 'Correlation of Forms', and 'Natural Law'—a theological terminology that left the scientific vernacular behind. Argyll wore his Christianity openly. For him, the world had been created for man, with God providing the varieties through which natural selection might operate. The rich detail of the world showed God's underlying plan.

And part of that plan was a single humanity. Whatever the different levels of technological progress among modern peoples, the gap between what God had created as human and what He did not was unbridgeable; all humans made in His image, His archetype, were fully moral, fully mentally capable beings. Colour-races do not come into the picture.

So, was Argyll's belief in a universal human nature and his rejection of race purely a matter of his Christian faith? Or did he perhaps share some methodological concerns or habits of mind with Tocqueville, or the early and more sceptical Walter Bagehot? Before we look at Darwin's reaction to Argyll, we need to get to know Argyll's thinking rather better.

ARGYLL AND METHODOLOGY

George Douglas Campbell, who was born in 1823, was 8th Duke of Argyll, Marquess and Earl of Argyll, Marquess of Lorne and Kintyre, Earl of Campbell and Cowal, Viscount of Lochow and Glenilla, Lord of Inverary, Mull, Morvern, and Tiry, all in the peerage of Scotland; Baron Sundridge and Baron Hamilton in the peerage of Great Britain; Hereditary Master of the Queen's Household in Scotland, and Keeper of the Great Seal of Scotland; Admiral of the Western Isles; Hereditary Sheriff of County Argyll; and Mac-Cailein-Mòr ('Son of the Great Colin', that is, Chief of Clan Campbell—but he preferred being addressed in the Gaelic form). He was a Fellow of the Royal Society; Chancellor of the University of St. Andrews (1851–1900); Rector of Glasgow University (1854–6); and President of the Royal Society of Edinburgh (1860–4). He served in Liberal cabinets for twenty years (across a twenty-nine year span) as Lord Privy Seal (1852–5, 1859–65, 1880–1), Postmaster-General (1855–8), and Secretary of State for India (1868–74). He was the author of numerous books of science, economics, theology, poetry, and current affairs. He owned 175,000 acres of the Scottish Highlands. After the death of a brother and an uncle, he had become heir to the dukedom when he was fourteen; from that point the young man was known as the Marquess of Lorne. He did not have to worry too much about the prejudices, racial or otherwise, of the lower orders.

Inheriting the dukedom at age twenty-four, in 1847, Argyll took his seat in the Lords, and his liberal streak was soon apparent. He supported free trade and the government of Lord John Russell. In his maiden speech in 1848, Argyll argued for Jewish emancipation.

'The Radical Duke', as he was soon called, had scientific interests from his earliest days. He was elected a Fellow of the Royal Society in January 1851, at age twenty-seven, largely on the basis of talks and papers that he had given on a fossil-bearing shale from his estate. He loved learning. Indeed, having been educated at home, amusing himself with scientific experiments on his own land, he had a somewhat romanticized view of the university life that he had never experienced. When he was elected chancellor of the University of St. Andrews at age twenty-eight, he confessed to the convocation his regret at not having attended some great school or university dedicated to 'a wise tolerance of the idiosyncrasies of others and broad catholicity of sentiment.'[30] He was never known for his ability to open up to or influence his colleagues in the Cabinet.[31]

In London, the young Argyll was sociable enough to relish one charming custom of the day. Certain great men of learning—among them Bishop Wilberforce, Monckton Milnes, Henry Hallam, Macaulay, Lord Mahon, and Sir Charles Lyell, the geologist who wrote on Aryans—were in the habit of giving each other substantial breakfasts over which the conversation flowed. Monckton Milnes especially 'delighted in paradox' and 'geniality'. It was at Monckton Milnes's that Argyll met Herbert Spencer, who would so influence late-nineteenth-century evolutionary thinking.

At breakfast with Lord Mahon, Argyll met two men with whom he did not get a chance to speak, but who struck him 'as quite typical Frenchmen of the highest intellectual class'. They were Guizot and Tocqueville, 'author of the book on democracy, which then had an immense reputation in the world', or so the by then elderly Argyll recalled the matter at the turn of the twentieth century. On another occasion Argyll was not present, but his wife (Elizabeth, active in her own right in abolitionism[32]) talked at length with Tocqueville.[33] In the early 1860s, Argyll wrote that he found Tocqueville's correspondence 'a charming book'.[34] He does not say whether he learned anything from it. But this much is clear: Tocqueville's way of balancing detail with theory, testing each against the other, would have appealed to Argyll.

For Argyll explained in his own words an almost Tocquevillean concern for this proper dialogue between detail and theory. Someone else whom he got to know at those London breakfasts in the 1840s was indeed one of the hosts, Charles Lyell, author of *The Principles of Geology*. Argyll recalled that

> it was interesting to hear Lyell talk when he was full of some new fact in his special science, which bore on his favourite theory of the uniformity of geological causation from the earliest to the latest time. Of that theory I had always a profound distrust, except under such limitations of meaning as greatly affected the whole conception. But Lyell was always a man most faithful to facts, and his eagerness in gathering and recording them made his company to me a perpetual delight.[35]

Lyell's delight in facts made for a healthy balance between specificity and theory, even when Argyll did not like the theory. Argyll explained more about his methodological position and some of the scientific controversies this way:

> [Lyell] had a theory without being a mere theorist. That theory was never accepted on the Continent as it was to a great extent in England. But, however great may be the deductions to be made from its truth—and I think they are very large—he never was himself at all a dogmatist. He used his theory as scientific hypotheses ought always to be used—as a string of thought by which the gems of ascertained fact could be connected with each other. It was, moreover, a theory which was invaluable in leading me to watch and see how much is being done or prepared, even now, in the way of geological causation.[36]

So Argyll was already sure that uniformist explanations of the history of the natural world did not please him—for he preferred the catastrophic explanations—but he enjoyed learning facts on either side of the argument, testing hypotheses, looking for patterns. So did Lyell himself. Argyll had a great fondness for the fact-loving Lyell, whom he thought was 'almost in awe of the immensities of time and of the mysteries of creation with which his science dealt, and on which the new fact might be found to tell'.[37]

At the same time—and we are still looking at the 1840s, when Argyll was a young duke-about-town—he was also becoming very close to Richard Owen, whose lectures on palaeontology at the Hunterian Museum in Lincoln's Inn Square he attended. Argyll says that in Owen's

> lecture-room, long before the publication of Darwin's 'Origin of Species', which did not take place until 1859, I became familiar with the significant but mysterious fact of the gradual appearance in the course of time of our domesticable animals, that they had been late introductions before the advent of man, and that approaches to their peculiar structure could be traced through an advancing series of pre-existing forms, as if these were being gradually prepared. . . .

It would seem that farm stock was being put upon earth just in time for man to use it. Owen would not say why this had happened, but as Argyll listened to the lectures, and continued making his observations of fossils and birds, he increasingly felt himself ready to provide an explanation: 'These facts, however dim and vague in their details, delighted me, as indications of the same element of preparation and design for a future destiny which had been so long familiar to me in the growth of the elements out of which wings are made. . . . '[38]

Argyll was struggling toward an explanation of Owen's sequence of development. And he spent years at the task. Rather than adopting the old position of natural theology ready-made—that the world had been created by God to house man, who could read God's purposes in nature[39]—Argyll spent large amounts of time in the lecture room, in the thick of debate with Charles Lyell and Richard Owen.

* * *

In later years Argyll would retain this work ethic. And he would retain his focus on the careful formation of theory out of observable fact, even if, as these passages intimate, his thinking was specifically Christian in approach. Argyll was always deliberate and careful in using categories. He tested theories and categories philosophically and experientially, as he had tested Lubbock's assumptions about unilinear progress and the moral and intellectual inferiority of all nontechnological peoples. 'All classification is ideal', Argyll wrote, 'and depends on the relative value to be placed on facts that are themselves indisputable'.[40]

Argyll did not simply accept categorizations from the intellectual atmosphere of the time. On the controversial question of racial categorization, when it came in the 1860s, it was especially necessary that he should make up his mind for himself, for by then his two intellectual masters disagreed with each other. Richard Owen would make, as it would happen, a famous rejection of the mistakes in brain anatomy made by the new racists of the 1860s, such as Thomas Henry Huxley; Argyll's other master, Charles Lyell, would on the other hand write a great deal about how the people of different cultures can be told apart by the shape of their skulls.[41] Argyll's own view in *Primeval Man* was that if we defined our terms with proper care, we could see that a human mind of whatever supposed colour was an entirely different thing than a gorilla mind. We all have our full measure of human intelligence and no gorilla is our equal.[42]

So classifications of humanity mattered to Argyll. Great moral points turned on them. It was against this background that he decided, as we have seen, that Lubbock's categories of 'Stone Age', 'Bronze Age', and 'Iron Age', as applied to differently situated groups of people around the world without careful thought, simply did not make sense. He reflected that 'Archaeologists are using language on this subject, which, if not positively erroneous, requires more rigorous definitions and limitations of meaning . . . '.[43] As he would later tell the sympathetic Friedrich Max Müller, who had his own objections to sloppy anthropological thinking, 'I entirely agree [about] the fallacies promoted by, and often consisting in, the lax and confused use of words. . . . [L]anguage is infinitely too blunt for the purposes of really accurate thought. . . . I agree . . . specifically in the prodigious importance of verbal analysis as one of the most powerful instruments in the detection of errors and the discovery of truth.'[44]

Yet when Argyll turned from the task of questioning racial categories and championing the idea of a unified humanity, and fixed his attention instead on the categories of nonhuman biology, he would often take his insistence on properly framed verbal construction a bit too far, as some readers noticed at the time. George Henry Lewes, the literary critic, writer on popular science, and helpmate of George Eliot, reviewed Argyll's *Reign of Law* in 1868. According to Lewes, the book boiled down to this: Argyll saw patterns in biology, and not content to use the patterns or categorizations as a shorthand or as analogue, he erected them into concrete, pre-existing things, a divine plan being worked out according to God's intention and God's laws. As Lewes pointed out,

> because the *nexus formativus* of a vast animal group can be abstracted as the concept of a Vertebral Type, *i.e.* a plan according to which each part may be exhibited as correlated, there have been philosophers, from Plato downwards, who believed that this Type existed before animals were created, and that when animals were created they were constructed after this model.[45]

But for Darwin, a shared body type could well mean a shared ancestor.[46] As Richard Owen's biographer, Nicolaas Rupke, has put it,

> It had of course been obvious to Chambers and to Owen himself that unity of type was an indication of genetic relationship and thus evidence of descent and organic evolution; Darwin went one step further and connected unity of plan to the process of natural selection while turning the archetype with a click of his fingers into a primitive ancestor of flesh and bone.[47]

So it was Darwin that killed Plato. But Plato still lived for Argyll.

The wonder that Darwin saw in the gloriously diverse plants and insects and animals of an entangled bank, all being the product of a few fixed laws, Argyll saw, too; but for him, the wonder was in how all the diverse details reflected the working out of God's plan. While natural selection may have happened as a mechanism, it was God who provided the variations and, yes, the permanent archetypes upon which natural selection worked.[48] That is why we can see analogous bones in the hand, the flipper, and the wing. Similarity in structure is evidence of similarity in purpose—the purpose of the conscious artificer.[49]

DARWIN'S REACTION

While Darwin paid a good deal of attention to Argyll's writings, we have seen from *The Descent of Man* that he never seems to have fully confronted Argyll's quite careful refutation of the assumptions behind social evolutionism. Argyll's Christian Platonism may have been one reason why Darwin ignored Argyll's critique of social evolutionism and race, but we will see that Darwin had other reasons as well.

Yet Darwin was quite respectful of Argyll before the 1858 announcement of the theory of evolution by natural selection. Darwin thought the duke an excellent speaker as president of the British Association in 1855. In the early 1860s, when Argyll began to criticize *The Origin of Species* on the grounds that it failed to explain the origins of the variations upon which natural selection operated, Darwin was less appreciative, although he was grateful for the duke's liberal tone and the compliments about the book with which Argyll had sweetened his attacks.[50] Darwin seemed to take Argyll most seriously when writing to Argyll's own friend Charles Lyell in 1865. Darwin said that as always Argyll's writing was '*extremely* clever', but not in a way that could shake Darwin's own conclusions. The duke had totally ignored that what natural selection might not create, sexual selection could. Darwin thought that Argyll should be more careful on such points.[51]

When he was writing to others, Darwin was less complementary—this was when Argyll was attacking *The Origin* in early the 1860s. Darwin joked about an article 'smashing the Duke of A. which we liked', and he bristled when Argyll questioned a point of evidence in *The Origin*.[52] When he read *The Reign of Law* in 1867, Darwin of course had to disagree with Argyll's various criticisms of unaided natural selection—that it did not address the *origin* of variation and thus of species, only their success or failure.[53] Darwin praised Wallace for refuting the duke in *The Quarterly Journal of Science*. While he told Wallace 'I am glad you praise the Duke's book, for I was much struck with it', he wrote to Charles Kingsley that *The Reign of Law* was 'very well written, very interesting, honest & clever & very arrogant'—telling off even John Stuart Mill for being imprecise—while Argyll's own work had its weaknesses and misunderstandings.[54]

So whatever the Platonism behind Argyll's views, we can see from this last comment that Darwin did not think highly of Argyll's methodological concerns, or his way of questioning the categories that famous thinkers used in their work.[55] Or so Darwin said in his correspondence. In his published work, in *The Descent of Man* itself, Darwin mentioned Argyll a number of times, usually to disagree with him over the distance between what animals do and what people do.[56] Elsewhere too in *The Descent*, Darwin says that he preferred Lubbock's idea that we began in a very primitive state to the idea (Argyll's idea, in *Primeval Man*) that early peoples were already fully human mentally and emotionally.[57] But rather than treating Argyll's arguments on their merits, and questioning the social evolutionism that he had introduced in the *Descent*, Darwin tied Argyll to the more extreme wing of degenerationism:

> The arguments recently advanced by the Duke of Argyll, and formerly by Archbishop Whately, in favour of the belief that man came into the world as a civilized being and that all savages have since undergone degeneration, seems to me weak in comparison with those advanced on the other side.[58]

Darwin cannot think of any peoples who can be shown to have lapsed into barbarism, having once been civilized, certainly not the much-discussed Fuegians.

As we saw a moment ago, Darwin had rejected Argyll's way of critiquing the language formulations and categorizations of major thinkers. Here, Darwin is rejecting in one breath Argyll's idea of a unified human nature and Whately's view that the highest of human civilizations was the earliest, coming directly from God. At bottom, what was important to Argyll was being very careful about category words, and always being very careful about demonstrating universal human dignity. What is important to Darwin—in his context, at this time—is denying that humans are always so special. He wants there to be some groups of people or some stages in human development that can serve to connect us with animality.[59] He prefers the social evolutionist view, grounded in the idea of the inheritance of acquired cultural characteristics, over Argyll's more Platonic view of a single unchanging human nature for all extant human populations.[60] Thus Darwin agrees with Lubbock on the nature of primitive humanity, and he denies Argyll's idea of a highly functional primitive population. Darwin does admit in one footnote to *Primeval Man* that Argyll 'has some good remarks on the contest in man's nature between right and wrong'.[61] But he does not fully engage with Argyll's arguments on human uniformity, and he does not wish to engage with Argyll's refutation of Lubbock's key methodological idea, that the least attractive characteristics of a society are always survivals from an earlier stage, rather than (some of them) examples of later degeneration.

While Darwin often sides with Lubbock's social evolutionism against Argyll's views, he also goes on to take the part of Bagehot's version of social evolutionism against Lubbock's—on the question of the presence of social cohesiveness in savage peoples. Unlike Lubbock, Bagehot thought that small-group social cohesiveness is a basic characteristic of humanity. So does Darwin, whose notes show that he does seem to have taken the idea from Bagehot.[62] This point is central to the competition between the internally cohesive, externally hostile racial groups of Gobineau-Bagehot social evolutionism, and this indeed emerges as Darwin's view of humanity by the end of *The Descent of Man*.[63]

Argyll had a fundamentally different view. He rejected the idea of looking at the world through the lens of race and the competition between races. In *Primeval Man*, as we have seen, Argyll denied that humanity can be divided into racial groups, for one colour blends into another. In *The Reign of Law*, he noted that the 'Nations of Antiquity' might have fallen to conquerors, but '[t]he epoch of conquering Races destroying the Governments, and reconstructing the Populations of the World, is an epoch which has passed away'.[64]

* * *

In the 1890s, Argyll and Lubbock vied with each other over whose thinking deserved the mantle of the long-deceased Charles Darwin (back in 1882, both Lubbock and Argyll had served among his pallbearers[65]). Now Argyll claimed Darwinian orthodoxy for his argument that humanity was of one stock; Lubbock for his argument that the colour-races stemmed from different parents, the races having separated from each other before they achieved full humanity.[66]

In a sense they were both right to claim the Darwinian mantle, for there had been two sides to Darwin's thinking on the matter. Lubbock, in these later years, could ground his views of racial separation on Darwin's belief in the inheritance of acquired characteristics.[67] That indeed had been the Darwinian racialist position pervading *The Descent of Man*. Argyll responded with a view equally grounded in the Darwinian canon—but relying more on *The Origin of Species*. Argyll stressed the common descent of a humanity stemming from a single branch in a single unified tree of life, so that the question of which varieties constitute races fades into the background of shared affinity.[68]

Today, Argyll's insistence on the unity of mankind has outlasted the invidious racial distinctions and racial conflict fantasies that Darwin allowed himself in *The Descent* (see above, pp. 106–8). Darwin never properly addressed the question of the validity of racial groups in human history in the way that Argyll did in *The Reign of Law* and *Primeval Man*. Instead, Darwin followed Bagehot in setting up races and the competition between races as the central fact of human history. He did this even though in his examination of the biological basis of human race he found that there was no such thing. Argyll, with his carefulness about how people ought to be divided, has had the better side of the argument over Lubbock—and on the matter of race, over Darwin himself.

RESISTING RACISM AND DEGENERATION

Whatever Argyll's mistakes in biology—and from today's neo-Darwinian point of view he made quite a number—his scepticism about categorizing humanity so as to negate human unity served him well intellectually. Before we turn from him, we should also look at what Argyll *did* with his anti-racialist perspectives, and how they unfolded in relation to public affairs and his role in helping to govern the British Empire. To what degree was an opposition to racial classification still possible not in the study but out in the world, with a new racism beginning to permeate society?

The way Argyll treated the problem of racial categorization in the contemporary world first became apparent when he began applying a degenerationist analysis to the American Civil War. From the outbreak of the war in 1861, he had supported the Northern side. Long an opponent of slavery and a friend of Harriet Beecher Stowe, he rejected his friend William Ewart Gladstone's arguments for pacifism. Argyll replied that freedom had usually been won by force, both in England and in ancient history.[69] He made a similar point at a public dinner for Lord Palmerston in Edinburgh in April 1863:

> I, for one, have not learned to be ashamed of that ancient combination of the Bible and the sword. Let it be enough for us to pray and hope that the content whenever it may be brought to an end, shall bring with it that great blessing to the white race of the final freedom of the black.[70]

And what was that great blessing for the 'white race'? What the white race needed delivery from was moral decay. To Argyll, whose degenerationism focussed on the falling off of mental and moral qualities, slavery was quite literally 'rotting the very heart and conscience of the Whites—all over the Union—in direct proportion to their complicity with it'.[71]

So as it was for Tocqueville, the American problem was the presence of white racism, not the presence of the black race. To Argyll's way of looking at things, racism of that kind was the royal road to the degeneration of the racists themselves. Reacting to a more sudden event, namely Governor Eyre's execution of the Jamaican leader George William Gordon in 1865, Argyll exclaimed to Gladstone 'How bloody we are when we are frightened . . . and impelled by hatred of race!' The Jamaican whites, Argyll noted, hated British abolitionists, whom they thought were full of cant. In killing blacks they were trying to get back at the abolitionists. Argyll added that fighting cant was 'hardly a good reason for hanging a man'.[72] So Argyll knew about racism, and he resisted it.

*   *   *

For Argyll the whole world contained the same people, facing the same problems, that he knew from his estates in Scotland—colour made no difference. Degeneration was possible anywhere. And it had to be fought everywhere, through the improvement of Scottish Highlands and tropical Africa alike.

Accordingly, sometime in 1857 or 1858, Argyll suggested to David Livingstone that British emigrants should be sent to a new colony in the interior highlands of East Africa. Nothing would come of this plan. Argyll would never return to it. But in its original formulation the idea was that the emigrants would drive slavery before them, civilizing the local population.[73] At a dinner for Livingstone in March 1858, whose ancestral Isle of Ulva Argyll owned, the duke drew attention to 'that great cause with which [the public] is especially connected—that great cause to which their attention was roused by the eloquence of Wilberforce and his associates—the cause of the African Race'.[74] But having made his point about promoting 'the civilization of the people of Africa', Argyll turned to the question of civilizing the Scots. He pointed out that he and Livingstone came from the same part of the same country. It was at Iona where, to quote Argyll's paraphrase of Dr.

Johnson, 'roving tribes and nude Barbarians derived the benefits of knowledge & the blessings of religion'. If the Scots could be civilized, so could the Africans—here was Argyll's belief in a single humanity.

Indeed, to Argyll some of the Scots needed civilizing as much as some of the East Africans did. He once pointed out that many of his tenants on the island of Mull did not even know to save hay for the winter, so the cattle nearly starved. Nor did the people know anything of crop rotation. Nor indeed would anyone fertilize the soil for next year's crops; the system of land ownership was communal and the land that a family worked each year was chosen by lot, so fertilization would be to no one's direct benefit. Thus,

> Geographic isolation had kept the Hebrides behind the rest of Scotland in the progress of civilization. The inhabitants were steeped in an ancient hereditary ignorance of the very elements of agricultural industry. . . . The very idea of improvement was impossible. The individual mind, the source of all power, was kept down to the level of the stupidest, who had the right to object to any change.[75]

Therefore 'the progress of civilization' and 'improvement' had to be undertaken even within the British Isles, if people were to avoid this degeneration of '[t]he individual mind', as he put it—much less if they were to avoid starvation on what was still, in part, a wild landscape. The Argyll estates contained groups as close to death from starvation or exposure as many an isolated family out in the empire. The 'improvement' that one might hope for, whether at home or abroad—and whether as a Hebridean landlord or as secretary of state for India—meant a very concrete shift from inadequate to adequate food supplies. It meant learning to save hay for winter or learning to rotate crops. As Argyll saw it, the first obstacle to improvement was not inherited race but the social structure.[76] In Scotland, the Argylls (in alliance with the Crown) had been struggling against the local social structure for generations, for good or ill.

INDIA

Argyll's service as secretary of state for India from 1868 until 1874 brought him closer to a larger area of possible cultural degeneration. Argyll believed in the real possibility of people falling away from the proper standard. But what would this mean in practice, in India? Indeed, might 'races' slip into his thinking in relation to India, with one group of people degenerating so far that they took on a separate character?

As secretary of state, Argyll presided over several attempts at modernization in Indian landholding, food production, tax collection, and transportation. Argyll pressed as well for the reintroduction of the Indian

Archaeological Department, which had been abolished not long before by Argyll's friend Lord Lawrence when he was viceroy of India (1864–9).[77] So we can say this much: Argyll believed that progress was possible in the Indian present, and that there was something worth studying in the Indian past. On civil service recruitment, he seems to have adopted the position of the London bureaucrats that Indian candidates should be promoted only when they had worked their way up, and not for scoring highly on a test— which many of them could very well do. Argyll did not want too many Indians promoted too fast, not because he was a racist himself but because he feared that Indians might be racists, or perhaps castists; he worried that if too many lower-caste Hindus were promoted into positions of rule over higher-caste populations, Indian sensibilities might be offended.[78]

But the most significant issue for us will be his treatment of the question of the exercise of power by Indian rulers, for he thought that a good number of them were degenerate. In his 1865 book *India under Dalhousie and Canning*—for he had long been interested in India—he made clear his position on what had gone wrong with the Indian people, or rather with Indian sovereigns. Argyll quoted a number of sources asserting that the heirs to the Indian thrones were, in the words of one of these sources, the viceroy's late brother Sir Henry Lawrence, 'mere children in mind, and as children they should be treated'. Henry Lawrence had concluded that 'After a certain career of vice or contumacy, the offender should be set aside, and replaced by the nearest-of-kin who gives greater promise'.[79]

Note that it was not the Indian people as a whole who were childlike degenerates, but those individuals who themselves had sat for a time on the thrones of Indian states. Argyll pointed out that as far as these native rulers went, 'the dependent position to which they are reduced by our power in India does not contribute to make them better'.[80] Even the most carefully selected puppet, the rajah of Nagpore, selected and set up by the British when he was a child, could die young, after three decades of dissolution. To pay for his debaucheries he started wars, sold judicial verdicts, even plundered his own feudal dependents; and as an individual he kept on degenerating until his death.[81]

For Argyll, then, British rule brought about the degeneration of Indian princes. Poor administration of the law by the British had also corrupted the judicial officers.[82] But the Raj also brought great benefits to the common people: 'The history of the world presents no more splendid example of deserved success than the administration of the Punjaub [*sic*] under Lord Dalhousie', Argyll explained. 'It displayed the highest virtues of a conquering and ruling race'—the high personal character of remarkable men.[83] Railways were built to abolish famine; and there were the canals and other public works. The Ganges Canal alone, begun in 1854, had more miles of waterways, Argyll reported, than the whole of Lombardy. Plus there was the foundation of a new and easily expandable system for secondary and higher education befitting a people who 'had a language and a civilization older than our own—a literature dating back to a language which was the great forefather of all the tongues of Europe'—the Aryan language. This new modern system of education would replace schools and colleges 'whose whole scope of instruction was oriental, designed to conciliate old prejudices and to propagate old ideas'.[84] These old 'oriental' ideas were those of the Indian culture of recent centuries, not be confused with the great achievements of the more remote Indian past. Indian culture had degenerated, but the Indian people could reclaim their former glories.

And yet even after the modern education system had taken root and produced large numbers of graduates, democracy would still be inappropriate for India (just as Tocqueville would withhold self-government from the Algerians). Those Indians who would participate in democracy would be too Western, merely a rich minority:

> A Calcutta Legislature would be the Legislature of a class in its worst and most aggravated form. The 'public opinion' of India is virtually the opinion of the small but powerful European community. Its interests are mainly commercial, and its ideas of policy and of law are liable to the bias and insuperable temptations which commercial interests involve.[85]

So, while Indian literature was too Oriental, it would seem that for Argyll real degeneracy in moral outlook and mental acuity was confined to three narrowly defined groups: (1) The native rulers who inherited Indian states and had become corrupt through their dependence on the British; (2) natives judges in certain situations; and (3) the Englishmen and other Europeans who lived with the 'insuperable temptation' of commerce in cities like Calcutta—these were the men referred to in the passage just quoted. Degeneracy was not a slow process that had afflicted the Indian people generally; instead, it could happen quickly. It could afflict any *individual's* level of cultural or moral attainment, afflicting anyone—such as an Indian ruler or a Western businessman—who suffered sustained exposure to morally or intellectually corrupting circumstances.

Argyll was prejudiced against Indian princes and Western businessmen in India, and he was an imperialist, but he was not a colour-racist. In his way of thinking, 'degeneracy ' conjured up neither the modern idea of inbreeding nor race stereotyping. Far from it. His idea of degeneracy presupposed a common place of origin for everyone and everything—some fully human Adam appearing in the evolutionary sequence.[86] And that is the biological inheritance that we all share. Degeneration is cultural, not biological. Some cultures had fallen further from the common heritage than had others, and some individuals because of the choices that they had made in their lifetimes had fallen quite far indeed, but degeneracy was a matter of nurture and not of nature.[87] All modern peoples could share in the highest levels of culture if they were raised that way from birth—and if no one put them into some sloppily defined category of inferiority.

*   *   *

For Argyll, human colours were a continuum, not a set of discreet types, and he was explicit about that point, writing as we have seen 'that one extreme passes into the other by small and insensible gradations'.[88] Differences in colour did not correlate with differences of any other kind. Everyone was fully human. Every group could make great art. Every individual and every group could degenerate, as with the whites of the United States who had become corrupted because of their complicity in racism and slavery. One had to be careful of categories and language when grouping the peoples of the world.

8   Frederick Weld and the Unnamed Neighbours

Imperial officials, too, invented colour-races sometime around mid-century. Many of the officials of the empire—who typically were posted to a wider variety of places than earlier generations of officials had been[1]—faced a similar need to categorize the noticeably diverse peoples of the world. They too illustrate the connections between classification and the development of racism.

There is no room here to examine dozens of officials in enough depth; we cannot watch the development of the thinking of so many people in the same way that we have done with the figures in earlier chapters. But we can look at someone whose imperial experiences were legion, and who wrote more than enough down through the years to register the mid-nineteenth-century turn toward the idea of heritable colour-race groups—but who remained well outside the metropolitan intellectual circles that we have been examining.

Our test case will be Sir Frederick Aloysius Weld (1823–1891), a New Zealand colonist and prime minister who went on to become governor of Western Australia, Tasmania, and the Straits Settlements (Singapore and Malaya). Weld left England before the widespread adoption of racist thinking in English society in the 1850s and 1860s. He developed the habit of classifying peoples. Then he discovered everyone else's way of doing it—the new thinking about race that had developed in England during his absence.

WELD BEFORE THE INVENTION OF RACE

Frederick Weld had come from an old Roman Catholic family in Dorset. They were comfortable but not wealthy, and their Roman Catholicism did not open many doors in English society, so Weld was educated at Freiburg. At that time the University of Freiburg was a centre of German liberalism, although as a Roman Catholic expatriate Weld was unlikely to be much affected by the liberal atmosphere.[2]

Weld's family could not afford to buy him an army career, so in 1843, the year he turned twenty, he went off to New Zealand, following his cousin

Charles Clifford, who had emigrated earlier that year.[3] Weld and Clifford settled next to each other in the North Island, and together they helped found the New Zealand sheep industry.[4] And there Weld had some experience with the Maori. What might he have thought of them?

It will be remembered that the general background of racial opinion in the England that Weld grew up in was this: Of course upper-class Englishmen were on top, but what they were on top of was a big complicated world where there were races of Norfolk country folk and the race of the Irish and the races of different parts of Italy and the race of London chimney sweeps and the race of London cabmen and the Maori race, *ad infinitum*; what mattered was one's class and status, not one's skin colour. Only in the new world of the 1860s did all the minstrels and magazine editors and illustrators and missionaries and crusading abolitionists convince more people—but still by no means everyone—that large colour-based 'racial' groups existed and were of prime importance.[5]

But what about out in the empire? Compared to its rise in England, racist rhetoric came earlier in the nineteenth century in the West Indies and in the Cape. In such places, self-consciously European colonists had long oppressed those who seemed different from themselves.[6] Yet the New Zealand to which Weld and Clifford immigrated was no such place. The country had only been annexed by Great Britain three years before. Racist discourse in the new sense came later in New Zealand, as it did in Great Britain itself. While the idea of a more or less linguistically defined 'Anglo-Saxon' race was widespread and long-established in England by the time Weld left the mother country,[7] he would not have been accustomed to hearing about white *versus* nonwhite categorizations of humanity, either back at home or in his adopted land. The usual view was that any group of people under discussion was a 'race', meaning a group whose characteristics persisted from one generation to another, whether by nature or by nurture.

THE YOUNG SETTLER

The earliest published record of Weld's own thoughts about race and empire was his wonderfully titled 1851 pamphlet, *Hints to Intending Sheep-Farmers in New Zealand*. New Zealand, he wrote, was a wonderful country. The supply of pure water was unlimited. Wool prices there were constantly going up. The horses and cattle had no diseases; the sheep had scab but little else, and animal diseases would not spread if people took proper measures. One should 'harass the flock' as little as possible. Lambing should begin on the 20th of March.[8]

Of course, things would work out so well only if the farmer should pay attention to the wisdom of senior farmers like Weld himself. Also, the beginning farmer should 'secure a few good and trustworthy servants rather than many and indifferent ones. . . . As years pass by, he will . . .

feel an honest pride in having won himself an independence by his own exertions.'[9] Well, really, it would be an honest pride in the exertions *of the servants* that Weld had mentioned. But who were those servants? Weld does not say, and he does not mention them again.

The emigrant, Weld added, must be sure before embarking on what might be a solitary life 'that he should have resources within himself'. In point of fact Weld was not solitary; he was constantly with Clifford, his other friends, and the Scots hands who actually knew sheep.[10] Weld and Clifford were the largest sheep magnates in New Zealand, and they had frequent visitors.[11]

But even when there were no Europeans about, Weld's was a strange solitude. The only reference to the Maori in his sheep pamphlet is to point out that on the North Island 'waste land for pasturage has been held chiefly on lease from the natives'.[12] But that is all. There is no mention of what the natives might be called, nor any hint of how to approach them, deal with them, or think about them, when Weld had included so much practical advice on every other point. Yet from his first days in New Zealand seven years before *Hints to Intending Sheep-Farmers*, Weld had extensive contacts with the Maori. Because the land that he had purchased sight unseen turned out to be in the possession of a hostile tribe, he rented land from other 'native chiefs' for several pounds a year. He was buying the Maori's pigs and their potatoes and employing Maori labourers on his farm, paying them in tobacco. In his own words—from an 1844 letter to his father—he often had a cousin or an acquaintance with him, a European shepherd or two, a Maori houseboy of about age ten, and one or two Maori farmhands, with sometimes one or more European farmhands as well.[13] Also, as his journal from 1844 indicates (as Jeanine Graham has shown), he spent much time and attention on the everyday problems that the Maori system of collective land tenure had created for him, and on the hostility that he thought he perceived among individual Maori.[14] As he wrote to his sister, he sometimes had to stay inside his house all day to keep Maori visitors from stealing from it. He also told her about Maori trading habits and the details of Maori dress. *Pace* M.P.K. Sorrenson, Weld did indeed use 'Maori' (as well as 'native') for original population of New Zealand, of which he seemed far more aware in these letters from the mid-1840s than in his sheep pamphlet from a few years later.[15] In his private writings he discussed Maori groups and individuals long before he was ready to discuss the Maori as a whole in his published work.

As modern scholars of anthropology as a professional field have discovered, elements of the emotive or nostalgic may adhere to an anthropologist's private letters or field notes but get stripped out of more professional writings.[16] Weld developed his ideas about races and everything else in different levels of discourse.[17] The full man wrote privately, continually reassuring himself with examples of his own giving and humorous nature; the public man employed public categories and was stripped of some of this humanity. Early on, Weld did not have the vocabulary for addressing racial questions in his public voice. So he strangely excluded the Maori among whom he lived from his published (although not his private) works on colonial life.

Later, he managed to develop a set of racial categories that he could present in public. He presented them in a dry, matter-of-fact sort of way. Later, as a respected older man and speechmaker, he abandoned the ideas of human race that he invented for himself in favour of those which had become fashionable in England, regaling his audience with picturesque details from his own experience.

WELD CLAIMS EXPERTISE ON NEW ZEALAND AND NATIVES

In letters home to his sister in the years before he wrote *Hints*, the young Weld wrote in almost anthropological detail about his expeditions to see different Maori chiefs, including what was eaten in the *pahs* [Maori fortifications] that he visited, how the Maori children were raised, the forms of music and dance, and what he thought about Maori politics and the way Europeans would someday occupy Maori lands—a picturesque travel narrative:[18]

> In some places one might almost have imagined being in an English park, and in others where the road left the valley the scenery became even more beautiful and wilder, and one caught sight of the distant snow-clad ranges of the Porirua. These plains would be of great value if any means could be devised of getting the produce to a market, as someday no doubt there will be, when the country is opened out.

That strangely passive construction on opening out the country manages to exclude the Maori from current possession of the land. But after two sentences on the quality of the timber, the Maori are back, and Weld is back to anthropological description—albeit with a sense of the distrust properly felt between Maori and pakeha:

> Towards evening we approached a large pah, and our arrival was announced by firing the guns and pistols—a great waste, but one that is insisted on by our conductors. The inhabitants were all assembled at the entrance, but not one moved forward or offered to greet us, until we all formed in order and advance all together towards them. We were then welcomed by loud whining, and cries of 'Come, come', uttered by all the old women of the place. The Tangi then followed, which is a ceremony peculiar to the Maori, and is used to wail over a dead body, or, as on this occasion, as a sign of joy at the meeting of friends.[19]

Showing up with guns firing suggests that Weld and his party—whatever Weld's own aversion to wasting the ammunition—did not want latent European power to remain all that latent. And how did he know that it was really joy behind the funeral song and not grief?

His view was that as a settler he knew his stuff: 'It is very difficult to judge of a native unless you have lived with him as we do here.' What he had seen convinced him that the Maori believed in a superficial, Bible-centred Christianity, promising salvation even if they misbehaved.[20]

Weld discusses native policy explicitly in these private letters. He showed the settler's sense of his own on-the-ground expertise about the natives and a disgust for the metropolitan humanitarians who would have the natives treated better: 'It is very difficult to judge of a native unless you have lived with him as we do here. A savage, when his passions are dormant and he is treated as a companion and friend, is quite as safe—probably more so—than two-thirds of the Europeans you meet in the colonies.'[21]

Among the worst of the Europeans were the Governors Hobson and Fitzroy (formerly of the *Beagle*), who had mollycoddled the natives to please their allies in Exeter Hall. On the *Beagle*, Darwin had found Fitzroy an apologist for slavery in Brazil. Now, little more than a decade later, Fitzroy's treatment of the Maori made him seem like an abolitionist—from Weld's perspective. And Weld most decidedly did not like those who recommended humanitarian policies any more than he liked the governors who seemed to be carrying them out. The reference that Weld was making to 'Exeter Hall' refers to the only metropolitan racial thinkers that it seems Weld had heard of at the time. Exeter Hall was the famous London headquarters of missionary and anti-slavery organizations. To Weld, Governors Hobson and Fitzroy seemed too closely allied with metropolitan missionary ideas; they did not seem to understand the need to keep the Maori under control, or the native propensity for violence and outright warfare. Indeed, as Weld had heard (but not seen), 'The horrors—cannibalism in its most revolting forms—inflicted on the bodies of the slain were past belief.'[22]

'Cannibalism', 'savage'—these were common terms in early New Zealand discourse on the Maori, as Pat Maloney has shown. But despite all that Weld said about the Maori in his letters, he did not elaborate on the origins of the Maori, or their history, or their institutions, or their stage of civilization, or their prospects, as many colonial writers did at the time.[23] He had not worked out in his own mind what he thought the 'savages' represented. Much less had he anticipated future thinking and turned to colour-races. As we have seen, Weld did not go on to discuss the Maori or his journeys among them in *Hints to Intending Sheep-Farmers*—however much their omission would compromise the report as a practical guide for settlers.[24] Instead, he filled his pages with practical advice on sheep.

In *Hints*, he also devoted space to political issues arising from the current system of land-law, a system inspired by the thinking of the British imperial theorist Edward Gibbon Wakefield. Yet somehow Weld ignored the Maori even here. He ignored how they might serve Wakefield's design of preventing the overextension of colonial settlement. Wakefield had worried that Europeans settlers going too far up-country and settling too wide a wilderness would fail to develop a concentrated urban civilization. In Wakefield's view, the hostility of the North American Indians had bottled up the English settlers in the seventeenth and eighteenth centuries, to the lasting benefit of North American society.[25] But Weld ignored Wakefield on the bottling-up role of natives. (When Weld rented his first home from the Maori, he was in contravention of the Wakefieldian law putting land sales under the colonial government for the purpose of concentrating settlement.[26]) Weld focussed on Wakefield's larger point: Creating new colonial societies for the overcrowded population of England to move to.

Indeed, in Weld's mind there were grand imperial dreams: Englishmen like himself were, he wrote, 'engaged in what Lord Bacon calls the "heroic work of colonization"'—high language.[27] But he was not yet ready to discuss in print the 'Maoris', the 'natives' or the 'savages' about whom he had written so much in his private letters. He had yet to develop grand intellectual categories about the races and what he thought they were.

WELD DISCOVERS CATEGORIES

Of all the colonies whose foundation he had inspired around he world, Edward Gibbon Wakefield chose New Zealand to immigrate to in 1853. Weld was then able to work closely with him in the agitation for responsible government; they had met in England on one of Weld's visits home the year before. With that introduction to politics, Weld took office in 1854 as one of three ministers responsible to the legislature. The new government also included three ministers appointed by the governor. The ministers responsible to the House quickly resigned office in frustration.[28]

Then, after a personal falling out with Wakefield, Weld took the additional step of resigning his seat in the New Zealand House of Representatives. His stated intention was to raise a force to fight in the Crimean War, but in fact he went on another of his expeditions into the New Zealand wilderness. He discovered a valley of hot springs, and he carefully documented everything he saw.[29] He also spent the better part of a year back on his farm. Lastly he chartered a schooner, sailed to Hawaii, and conquered not the Crimea but Mauna Loa.

Weld went to Moana Loa to witness a major eruption of the mountain. He published his notes as a seven-page article in *The Quarterly Journal of the Geological Society of London* in 1857. In the article, he mentioned three natives and a grass hut, but otherwise he had nothing to say of the Hawaiian people.[30] Yet along the way he had indeed made some ethnological observations about the natives of Hawaii, and also of Tahiti, where he had stopped *en route*. This ethnological material he published in a short article for a Roman Catholic review in the same year.

For now he had developed enough categorizations and ideas about the natives of the Pacific that he was finally ready to talk about them in a published work. No longer were the natives the picturesque human scenery that he had described to his sister.[31] Nor were the Maori descended from either the Semites or the Aryans, as some New Zealanders thought—but if Weld knew of these views he did not acknowledge them.[32] No, instead Weld chose a different, more private set of terms and categories for the natives of the Pacific. Using his Roman Catholic identity as a starting point, he developed a very original theory about who among peoples of the Pacific would survive and who would not, based upon their religion.

Weld began innocently enough. He stressed for his readers how interesting the Maori were, and how good they were at do-it-yourself Bible-reading theology. Weld wrote that the Maori, like all Pacific Islanders, were eager to be Europeanized, but they had received the Bible too eagerly and without the guidance of Rome. Protestant missionaries were not up to the job of spreading civilized order, and their efforts could produce only a thin veneer of Christianity. Weld had been assured by a Protestant Maori that he, Weld the Roman Catholic, himself believed in the god Jupiter. Cannibalism was not yet unknown among the Maori, and the hand of European government was too light in the up-country.[33]

The result, Weld was confident, would be the extinction of the Maori in another hundred years. Weld does not say whether the Maori would die from fighting among themselves or die from the ill effects of their own loose morals. As Patrick Brantlinger shows, nineteenth-century extinction discourse often failed to distinguish between extinction-by-disease, extinction-by-primitivism, and extinction-by-genocide.[34] But for Weld, bad morals would seem to be the heart of it. And bad morals came from being out of communion with Rome. Protestant forgiveness came too easily. It encouraged native misbehaviour.

We saw hints of this criticism of Protestant missionary activity in Weld's early letters. But now he had gone public with it, and he had turned it into systematic critique.

So, in this article Roman Catholicism in itself became the test that Weld applied to peoples throughout the Pacific. The Tahitians, for their part, numbered even fewer Roman Catholics among them than did the Maori, despite the rather high-handed rule of France in Tahiti. Because the Tahitians were still looser in their morals than the Maori, they would become extinct even sooner. Roman Catholicism was doing much better in Hawaii—but, Weld concluded, all of the Pacific Islanders and Maori (with the exception of Catholic converts) were people of low character, for all their cleverness and attractiveness; and after the extinction of the Pacific peoples the historians of the future would not be able to say anything more generous about them than that.[35]

Some people had adopted Roman Catholicism (and decent behaviour) and some had not. For now, this—and not inherited biology—was Weld's key principle of ethnological classification.

*   *   *

After a period of further travel and his marriage in England to Filumena (Mena) Phillipps, Weld returned New Zealand in 1860 for what was to be his second long period of residence. He arrived in time for a war with the natives whose existence—as far as his published writings went—he had ignored in 1851 and whose demise he had predicted in 1857.

Back in Parliament, and after briefly serving as native affairs minister in 1861, he would begin a short but very significant premiership (November 1864 to October 1865). Maori policy was now to be the responsibility of a man whose published view was that the Maori would be among the first Pacific Islander peoples to die out, for they had the highest proportion of Protestants and were therefore sexually immoral.

RACIAL CATEGORIES IN NEW ZEALAND IN THE 1860S

Of course Weld's views were peculiar. There were far more common ways to characterize people in New Zealand at the time of Weld's government and the Maori wars. We can begin with the matter of terminology. Colonial government documents would often refer to the 'European population' and the 'Maori population', each in the singular.[36] When 'race' instead of 'population' was used, the 'European races' was the more common form, while the Maori 'race' remained monolithic.

Only seldom was this a physical concept, as indeed it was in one medical description of the terrible lack of light and air, the foul and filth, in the prison hulks where the Maori were kept. 'I believe the Maori are, as a race, predisposed to consumption, phthisis, and other tubercular affections', wrote an army doctor.[37]

The plural formulation of 'Europeans races' was sometimes adopted by the Maori themselves—or so the British-based translator for the Aborigines Protection Society would have it: As he rendered the language that had been sent to him by a group of Maori leaders: 'It was the European races who brought the Gospel to this barbarous Island, also the sword to kill; these they (*i.e.* the Missionaries) had instructed, and now they (the Maoris) have no wish to lift up the sword which kills the body, but they wish to have 'the sword of the spirit, which is the word of God' (emendations in the original).[38]

Another group of Maori chiefs referred to 'uniting in one the Nations created by God; for though their languages are diverse, God made them, though their skins differ in colour, God made them'.[39] Here, nationality and language come before a nonetheless immutable skin colour.

For Europeans, 'race' was one of many ways of referring to peoples whom a similar lifestyle might bring together; the European settlers and the landed Maori would one day converge, or so the members of the Wakefield family had assumed in the period leading to the British annexation of the islands in 1840.[40] Even twenty years later, 'race' was no fixed set of moral and physical traits.[41] Colonial governors such as Thomas Gore Brown and Sir George Grey seemed to use 'race', 'natives', 'population', 'Maoris', 'fellow subjects', and 'peaceable citizens, of whatever race' in just this loose way, especially in arguing for the protection of Maori as against European interests.[42] (At other times the duplicitous Grey planned the 'destruction' of the natives.[43])

But by the 1860s, 'race' was coming to the fore in New Zealand. As Governor Grey explained,

> It should also be remembered in reference to the two distinct populations in this country, that the native population who are the largest landed proprietors in the Northern island, are unrepresented in the General Assembly, the other population, the European one is the governing body. Necessarily in a civil war the feeling of race exercises some influence, and men's passions more or less lead them to adopt extreme views, and too hasty and often ill considered acts, in which they are sustained by a public opinion to which there is little or no counterpoise. . . . [44]

It was, he thought, especially hard for ministers facing 'almost universal suffrage' and a colonial legislature 'composed of one race engaged in a civil war with a race it is to govern'. The members of the colonial legislature represent constituencies 'more or less excited against another race' that is itself excluded from the legislature.[45]

Soon even Grey was writing that 'Kereopa, Patara and their murderous followers left Warea with the head of a soldier, on their way from the Taranaki country to the East Coast, to convert other tribes to their superstition, and to try to bring about the destruction of the European race'.[46] From about 1850, conflict with the Maori had led some of the European settlers in New Zealand to speculate about the nature of human groups, but as yet no vocabulary of separate and physically heritable race was consistently employed.[47] The outright warfare of the early to mid-1860s (the Taranaki War of 1860–1 and the Waikato War of 1863–4) hardened the rhetoric of the racial other, as Grey had predicted.

But still there was nothing like unanimity. By the 1860s, when Darwinian thought led to more speculation about the biology of human difference, racial thought in New Zealand ranged from the tendentious claims by the atheistic Charles Southwell in the *Auckland Examiner* in 1860 that the races were different and very unequal, with the Maori incapable of civilization and unable to feel or express morality or gratitude in any sphere, to the attempts by the bishops of the land and men such as William Martin to secure the Maori their rights as fellow subjects of Her Majesty.[48]

WELD IN CHARGE

To appreciate the way that Weld himself was thinking about the idea of racial difference by that time, we need to follow his policies in some detail. He imposed ideas of law and categories of race upon the Maori for his own purposes.

As prime minister in 1865, Weld promised that those Maori who had remained loyal in the recent conflicts would get their land back after the war—where possible; and those who put down their arms would get some land, somewhere. But other groups were guilty of 'revolting barbarities'.[49] They would get nothing. Yet what would it mean for the Maori to get any land at all? Weld manipulated the legal system so as to dispossess the Maori with maximum efficiency. He argued that the Maori's interests could not be administered through European land law, for the Maori could not understand European legal thinking. This was because the Maori could not systematize. Weld somehow knew that they could not think systematically even though he had once proclaimed in Parliament that he had not learned the Maori language, and had ridiculed the idea of doing so.[50]

In place of the European land law that Weld found so inappropriate, his government claimed to follow what they said was the law of the Maori. To enforce their own idea of what the 'Maori' law was, the government modified an already barely workable system of European-controlled land courts and officials. Land claims were already adjudicated according to the version of Maori legal principles improvised by each European judge, with a level of improvisation and randomness that critics such as William Martin carefully exposed at the time.[51] Under Weld, the Maori were made full citizens, and thus given both representation in the legislature (in which they would be outvoted)[52] and the ability, as individuals, to alienate their lands. Under the previous system, the Maori could use their system of collective ownership to block disadvantageous land sales; under Weld's new system any individual could sell land, or testify that he had sold it.

There lay the root of the problem. A feature of Maori land inheritance was that while title was fragmented among children, title to any one piece of land remained in abeyance for anyone not making a public example of occupying and working it. A claim that was in abeyance for some time would disappear.[53] This had been much discussed by Martin, the lawyer and critic of government native policy, in light of parallels with medieval European land tenure.[54] Weld's government chose to misunderstand the principle. Weld and his fellow ministers assumed that titles were perpetual, fragmentary, and overlapping, and that any Maori claiming some portion of a title could sell the land in question to a European. Before Weld's innovations, changes in land title were at least delayed and advertised, almost like the reading of the banns in an English parish church, and the ultimate purchase was effected through a public negotiation. At least that was the ideal. But under Weld's ministry the land courts would accept only European-style evidence, such as the newly purchased European land title, not Maori traditions about multiple ownership, nor even Maori depositions. The Maori therefore had no defence against fraudulent land claims except for expensive and largely futile litigation before European courts.[55] Maori could individually sell land that did not rightly belong to them. Here then was the supposedly humanitarian native policy of the Weld ministry. As Alan Ward has put it, 'The greater tragedy was not simply that the utter disruption of Maori social relations was deliberately initiated but that it was initiated through a system of land purchase that encouraged cupidity and unscrupulousness among Maori landholders. . . .'[56] Governor Grey had admitted as much in 1864.[57]

As Ward has noted, one of Weld's ministers put it this way: '[T]he settler was, quite properly, anxious to extend settlement, nor could his desire for land properly be called greed. It was not individual wealth he was grasping; he was indulging in the healthy wish for the spread of civilization.'[58]

Speaking in the legislature, the same minister had these thoughts on the purpose of the plan of the Weld government to turn the Maori into regularly enfranchised citizens of the colony:

> Deprived of the superficial gloss of which [sic] mere independence gives, the ordinary savage Maori would sink below the uncultivated European, whilst others possessed of more real force of character would rise to a higher level, from the great power of wealth which was put into their hands.[59]

Note—besides the element of hubris here—that not all Maori were the same.

Weld himself did not yet see the Maori as a homogenous mass. As native affairs commissioner in 1861, he believed that if elementary self-government was to be instituted among some of the Maori, it would be best to start with the Rarawas. But setting up such a government would cost money. Not least it will take money to induce people to take up and develop a career in politics and administration, especially the 'Natives' who must do so.[60] Already he is thinking about constituting the native authorities through whom the native populations might be ruled, as he would one day do in Malaya.

But as prime minister, Weld went further than this. He wanted a more thorough *military* conquest of the natives than the imperial government would ever countenance, given Great Britain's moral duties and treaty commitments to the Maori.[61] Weld therefore wanted the British troops to leave immediately. New Zealand should be free to fight its own war in its own way, as befit a self-governing people—a people who did not have to suffer imperial interference in their military conflict with the natives. Weld called for the removal of British troops as soon as possible, for the system of 'double government'—colonial officials and imperial military commanders working at cross purposes—had 'resulted in evil to both races of Her Majesty's subjects in New Zealand'.[62] The 'races' were getting simpler.

We would not expect to find Weld in the thick of metropolitan scientific discussion, much less an adherent of the very atypical polygenist school of James Hunt and the Anthropological Society of London. We have seen that he had his own views. He was pressing a war between what he saw as two races. He defined them in his own special way, now defining race based upon the land needs of the colony as he saw them rather than by religion, as before. He could reinvent his racial categories *ad hoc*, standing apart from any metropolitan tradition.

REPRESENTING NEW ZEALAND BEFORE THE BRITISH PUBLIC

The fighting in New Zealand dragged on, with continuing difficulties in paying for the imperial troops. Exhausted and careworn by all of this, Weld was soon out of office. His government was brought down in mid-1865 over their attempt to pay for the war by taxing the provinces. He returned to England in 1867.[64]

This was the year that Bagehot's *Physics and Politics* began appearing in the *Fortnightly Review*. The England that Weld returned to was full of discussion—on parliamentary reform, to be sure—but also on the racist and polygenist theories of Hunt, however disreputable they were, and the larger controversy over Governor Eyre's own race war in Jamaica.

In England, Weld had the time to restore his health. He did it by writing. In February 1869, he published *Notes on New Zealand Affairs*. Its aim was to bring the colonial viewpoint to a British audience, often thought to be unsympathetic to the way colonials treated their native populations.[65] Reusing the quotation from Bacon with which he had closed *Hints* eighteen years earlier, Weld predicted that a long time would pass before

> Englishmen in these islands will have lost all sympathy for those who, to use Lord Bacon's well-known words, are engaged in 'the heroic work of colonization'—a work still more difficult and still more heroic, when it is united, as in the case of New Zealand, with the attempt to civilize and preserve a native race.[66]

An attempt to civilize and preserve the native race! In 1851 he had not acknowledged the Maori at all. Now in addressing the British, his first strategy is to claim to have been trying to save them—when he confiscated their lands and tried to wage unrestricted war upon them, without the limiting influence of the imperial troops.

Weld argued that popular British criticism of the colonists had gone too far, supposing that 'all Colonists must be greedy, graspers of other men's land, cruel and bloodthirsty'.[67] The colonists should be forgiven their sometimes excited and unmeasured condemnation of natives. They had to face the danger of native attack. And they had to face the great question of—here it comes again—solving 'the great problem of civilizing and saving the native race'.[68] As a part of that endeavour, and if money were unlimited, the Maori military effort could be crushed. But Weld said that he was not in favour of that course, for 'it is quite beyond the means of the Colony; it would inevitably lead to a general war, in which neutrals would become our enemies, and it would destroy hopes which still exist, of saving a large portion of the native race'. So rather than an overall attack that would alienate the Maori and lead to their extinction,

> I should . . . hold myself ready to punish outrages with severity, I should treat them as locally as possible . . . ; I should gradually endeavour, by encouraging the natives without regard to their being friendly, or neutral, or ill-disposed, to have recourse to the land courts, to individualize their titles to the land, and to raise themselves out of communism. . . . [69]

This no-nonsense approach—in which Weld sticks to a hard line while denying that his policy is either harsh or inhuman, and in which he lumps together racially all of the Maori regardless of which side they had taken in the hostilities—is central to his self-presentation in the pamphlet. He is no sentimental traveller here, but the statesman.

Still, he does have to establish that he sees that the Maori are human; otherwise his no-nonsense policy for saving them will sound too hollow—or too Hunt-like for a British readership used to making fun of Hunt. So, New Zealand colonists might well say rough things, he wrote, but they understood that the Maori were 'not destitute of savage virtues, and even of higher qualities'.[70] The Maori are noble, and they are warlike: 'To anyone who has read the preceding narrative [Weld's own] of the wars of New Zealand it will be obvious, that the love of war, the love of excitement, the love of distinction, is inherent in the New Zealander. . . . '[71] And he thought that some Maori could play a part: 'The first and immediate duty of the Colonial Government is now to repress murder and outrage; they must form and keep up a defensive corps of both races; it will not do to rely on one race alone'.[72]

Differentiating between the Rarawas and other Maori groups was not appropriate when writing for the British public, so far from New Zealand. Instead, Weld writes of whole races. And in writing for the British, Weld portrays his countrymen in New Zealand as having been engaged in the more general, worldwide task of preserving native races of whatever kind. That generalized mission, and the equally generalized idea of nonwhite races that stands behind it, have both taken flight of any real evidence. Neither fit the truth very well.

GOVERNOR WELD

Weld's own ideas were still developing. In 1869, the year that he published *Notes on New Zealand Affairs*, the Gladstone government appointed him governor of Western Australia.

As Governor, Weld sent a number of expeditions into the interior to look for more pasturage of the kind on which he had built his first New Zealand home. And he went on some of these expeditions himself, writing the kind of letters and diaries that he liked to write, on the varieties of the fan palm, with their 'slim tall shaft and graceful fronds', and on how dry the land was, so that the English settlers of the future would be raising Arabian horses but not cattle.[73] His exhaustive and highly coloured minutes to the Colonial Office prompted R.W. Herbert, the permanent secretary, to note in 1874 that while Weld was honest and a gentleman, 'Mr Weld's mind and literary style are those of a promising lad of fifteen.'[74] But Herbert was seeing Weld's voluminous official arguments and reports. He was not seeing what Weld was writing for himself or for his close relations—the even more sentimental and even less self-censored scenes of the picturesque.

Meanwhile, as R.H.W. Reece has noted for eastern Australia, the settlers killed the kangaroos with abandon, the aborigines killed the sheep with equal abandon, and the settlers would then kill the aborigines for theft.[75] In the western part of the continent, Governor Weld worked hard to concentrate judicial violence into the hands of the state. He ordered that anyone who felt the need to execute an aborigine in a remote district should report the fact to the local magistrate afterward, or face suspicion as a murderer. Normally there would be no suspicion if the proper paperwork was done. Weld went so far as to dismiss a magistrate—with whom he had clashed politically on other issues—for being insufficiently zealous in prosecuting a well-connected young settler for the murder of an aborigine. The Colonial Office gave in to public pressure by reinstating the magistrate and reducing the settler's sentence from five years to one.[76] In commenting to his brother that the colonist ought to have served the full five-year sentence for manslaughter, Weld disparagingly invoked the spectre of the British humanitarian campaigners:

> What were the Aborigines Protection Society about? Had such a case occurred in New Zealand, Exeter Hall would have started indignation meetings and held up the colonial authorities, as well as the author of the deed and its abettors, to everlasting obloquy. Were the aborigines of Western Australia outside the pale of humanity? Had they not likewise souls?[77]

Perhaps Weld's categories for people were getting more general, if no less deadly. Weld once had a strong suspicion that two particular aborigines charged with killing settlers had been instead defending themselves against a likely 'execution'. Weld faced the question of whether he as governor should commute their sentences. Should he order an investigation? Instead he approved the death sentences. They were carried out.[78]

MALAYA AND THE NEW RACIAL THOUGHT

From 1875 to 1880, Weld served as governor of Tasmania. None of the Tasmanian natives survived and the colonists enjoyed self-government, leaving the governor with relatively little to do. Then Weld became governor of the Straits Settlements (Singapore and peninsular Malaya).

Weld spent much of his seven-year governorship—save a long visit to Europe—travelling Malaya and getting to know all the local princes. Indeed, he travelled so much that the British Residents who served under him in the different Malay states could not enjoy their full freedom of action. The Residency system could not really come into effect until, as one Colonial Office bureaucrat put it, 'Sir F. Weld retires, & we appoint a Governor ignorant of native affairs & too lazy to travel'.[79] Weld's travels meant that he could himself deal with the leaders of racial groups that he favoured, that he (literally) recognized, and that he helped to constitute.[80] As he moved about, he was fêted by the local leaders as their overlord—and as the guarantor of their own political ascendance over others.

He told the Royal Colonial Institute in London in 1884 that 'Personal government is . . . a necessity for Asiatics; it is the outcome of their religious systems, of their habits of thought, and of long centuries of custom.' An 'Asiatic' race exists, then, as the product of long-inherited custom. On the British side, 'I think that capacity for governing is a characteristic of our race. . . . ' And 'happy is the Colony which keeps free from little wars, successfully and noiselessly rules four or five different races' while carrying out public works and staying out of debt.[81]

This language reflects the new racial world of the 1880s. For Weld, what did the new picture entail?

As governor of the Straits, Weld laid great stress in the fact that he had ridden his horse the length of the Malayan Peninsula—he was the only man living who had done so.[82] His travels had shown him that '[t]he Malay race is one which no one can know without becoming attached to it'.[83] His (supposed) insight about the dependent nature of otherwise intelligent 'Asiatics' had allowed him to keep everything working very well, or so he thought. As he put it more simply: 'I imposed peace.'[84] Or so people told him: '"Why, if anybody hurt us nowadays, I should travel till I found a magistrate and your police, and wouldn't they just make an example of the evildoers!" '[85] The Sultan of Selangor asked Weld for the introduction of a British Resident, abolished slavery, and ever after chuckled to Weld over the peace that he, the sultan, then enjoyed, or so Weld said.[86] One wonders if Weld quite believed these characterizations of himself as a peacemaker when they were delivered by those over whom he exercised power. He certainly believed in his own power, even his own physical power. Weld reported that two Europeans (one of them Weld himself) and one Malay policeman were enough to keep order before hundreds of backcountry chiefs in 1881.[87]

Great things would come from Weld's power, from British power, as Weld said. Under British rule, the Malay peninsula would support millions of people, not the current several hundred thousand.[88] Most of these immigrants would come from China. This was a happy prospect, for the Chinese would magnify but in no way endanger British rule. Divided as they were among their many races and secret societies[89]—and here Weld was using 'race' in the old particular sense—the Chinese community in Malaya had known peace ever since Governor Clarke's system of imposing British residents had ended its internecine wars.[90] Thus the Chinese had come to see the British as natural rulers, the grooms to their racehorses, as Weld put it. The Chinese chased money and enjoyed the good things in life, while they left to the Europeans the mere business of government.[91]

So Weld not only knew the characteristics of the Chinese as such; he also knew that the Chinese understood the Europeans in a certain way. For him, now, everyone from England to China knew that the main divisions of the world were racial. Within Malaya, he could rank the native peoples by their colour, by which wave of ancient immigration he thought they represented, and by their degree of civilization—if no longer by their degree of Roman Catholicism. When Weld classified people, skin colour was now king; religion had been deposed. And so in the following passage there is an elaborate perception of physical types, centring on skin colour but extending also into other attributes of interest to late-Victorian anthropology, from physical build to the language associated with each physical type to their level of cultural development:

> There is another race in the Peninsula besides Malays, which may be termed the aborigines. The have more or less marked Negrito characteristics. As the Malays are closely akin to the Polynesian races, so are the Sakei, Simang, or Jukun tribes akin to the darker races of New Guinea, Australia, Fiji, and other islands; even in New Zealand and the Chatham Islands there are traces of this darker race. They have nevertheless affinities with the Malays, and probably represent an earlier wave of Asiatic immigration. They are very low indeed in the scale of civilization, but they are harmless, kind, cheerful, and very simple people.

Speaking before a metropolitan audience, Weld was employing the new metropolitan, anthropological view of classifiable physical races. Skin colour matters, and it predicts one's place in a scale of cultures that are named, mapped, and ruled by Europeans.

Weld both patronizes the people and takes their measure—down to the inch or so:

> Before starting down the river I distributed presents amongst about sixty Sakeis who had come to see me. They are the aboriginal tribe of the Peninsula, and live in the mountains. They do not resemble the Malays at all; the latter are supposed to have come from Sumatra and to have conquered the country in the eleventh or twelfth century. The Sakeis are small—about 4 feet 4 or 6 inches high, and active, and have light-coloured complexions, with low foreheads, and curly hair, and pleasant expressions. They seem cheerful and good-tempered. They said since we came the Malays no longer steal their children and carry their wives off to captivity.[92]

Weld identified many local groups, but also the overall category of 'Asiatics' that he could discuss before the Royal Colonial Institute.

And now he believed that this kind of anthropological, racial knowledge was vital for the proper administration of the empire. One could not rule by 'cut-and-dried codes or constitutional theories', assuming a universal human nature; imperial rule must be suited 'to the soil', and grow 'out of the heart and life of the people of the country'.[93] British rule ought to be 'congenial to the habits and feelings of the native races'.[94]

One had to see the races as he thought the races saw each other. Races were a basic category of the world. These races were both physical and cultural, stemming from the basic phenomenon of skin colour. Coming to understand these races as such was what had allowed Weld, in his own mind, to succeed so well as he moved about the empire. But truth be told, by this point in his life he had little more to add to what he thought everyone knew about the major races of the world. As a long-experienced governor speaking before a colonial interest group in London, he could simply add the local colour of his own colony, as it were, to the picture of global races that was already familiar to his audience.

Weld's idea of constituting groups by their degree of Roman Catholicism was long gone, but he did not try to hide his Roman Catholic sympathies from his listeners. He waxed sentimental over the old quarters where the first Roman Catholic missionaries at Malacca had first set foot, and he picturesquely described the ruins of the old Roman Catholic church destroyed by the Dutch. But he thought the attempt to spread Roman Catholicism to the Asians of Malaya and the local European element alike had been doomed. As Weld went on to say, St. Francis Xavier in the sixteenth century had shaken the dust of Malacca, the unconverted, off his sandals, a 'prediction' that 'does not appear likely to be reversed. The descendants of the Portuguese to whom he vainly preached are now chiefly poor fishermen, bearing many of them noble and historical names.'[95] Apparently they were not the race that could be converted to the true faith.

As late as 1857, Weld had not believed in such racial distinctions; he believed in Roman Catholicism for all. Now, racial distinctions were paramount.

In 1885 Weld retired to Dorset, and he was able to add a papal knighthood to the British knighthood awarded for his long career as a colonial governor. He died in 1891.

CONCLUSION

In *Hints to Intending Sheep-Farmers*, Weld had suppressed his daily conflicts with the Maori by suppressing any mention of them. His 1857 Roman Catholic review article was the beginning of a change. He had found a public voice on who the natives were and what should be done with them.

It did not matter what his categories were in 1857, but it mattered that he had them, a set of abstract categories to opine about in public. He might as well have been ranking the peoples of the Pacific by their ability to produce backgammon players or classical scholars as by their ability to produce Roman Catholics. He had developed the habit of developing categories.

Then, ruling over non-Europeans as a colonial governor, he further developed his ideas about the populations that he was governing. With the key emergence of 'race' as a category in England, Weld could let go of his particular racial vocabulary, based as it was on an odd ranking of the religious belief and sexual morality of whole peoples, or the land hunger of New Zealand settlers. Now he focused on the larger, more widely understood category of 'Asiatics', plus the peoples whom he now saw as subsets of that category. Such people he was now willing to sort by skin colour, and by the new light of late-nineteenth-century anthropology. It would seem that Weld adopted his new racial way of dividing up the world with no self-awareness at all of his methodology in doing so, and barely any thought about the adequacy or the lack thereof of the evidence that had come his way.

It must not be imagined that Weld was the only colonial governor to come to adopt the new-style colour-racist categories of the 1860s and after. Examples could be multiplied, from Eyre in Jamaica to William Denison in Australia and India.[96]

The older, smaller, more specific, more *ad hoc* ideas of 'race' began to change in the 1850s. Until this period there were no overall global colour groups. The groups of 'savages' or 'races' were small, and they were particular to individual colonies or groups of colonies. But these smaller, more *ad hoc* groupings were no longer in vogue by the period of the New Imperialism in the 1880s. Newer, bigger ideas of 'race' were there for the taking. Even Weld could pick up on them. The golden age of racism had begun.

9 By Way of a Conclusion
Arthur Gordon

In a sense no conclusion to a book on the reinvention of races is possible. Races can always be reinvented. We must always take care that in grouping people into one analytical category or another, we do not reify the categories that we choose, making them inheritable although we have no evidence that they are.

Etienne Balibar puts it this way:

> It would be quite futile to inquire whether racist theories have emanated chiefly from the elites or the masses, from the dominant or the dominated classes. It is however, quite clear that they are 'rationalized' by intellectuals. And it is of the utmost importance that we enquire into the function fulfilled by the theory-building of academic racism (the prototype of which is the evolutionist anthropology of 'biological races' developed at the end of the nineteenth century) in the crystallization of the community which forms around the signifier, 'race'. . . .
>
> [T]he theories of academic racism mimic scientific discursivity by basing themselves upon visible 'evidence' . . . or, more exactly, they mimic the way in which scientific discursivity articulates 'visible facts' to 'hidden causes' and thus connect up with a spontaneous process of theorization inherent in the racism of the masses.[1]

To put part of this in another way: Racial ideas can reverberate in many directions within society; not the least of them is when intellectuals invent or reinvent races in trying to classify and understand the peoples of the world. But given these reverberations, is race really an intellectual error at all, or is it entirely a moral error—a wilful failure to exercise a decent amount of intellectual care?

By way of a conclusion, then, there is one final person to examine—somewhat more briefly than we have looked at others.

Arthur Hamilton Gordon was a colonial governor and contemporary of Frederick Weld who resisted racial categorization intellectually, *in part* for moral reasons. He shows that a nonracial social science was possible in the later decades of the nineteenth century, even in imperial administration.

We started with someone who understood that races were not always the best categories into which to divide people—Tocqueville. We will also end with someone who understood the same thing. It was still possible in the 1870s and 1880s to resist the new racial categories—to float one's sub-divisions of humanity in the tide of the evidence, keeping these categories constantly in question.

GORDON, THEN

Born in 1829, Arthur Gordon (he preferred to drop his middle name of 'Hamilton') was the younger son of Lord Aberdeen. He was his father's private secretary when Lord Aberdeen was prime minister from 1853 to 1855 and for several years thereafter. As the prime minister's son and secretary, and for a time an M.P., the young Gordon was at the centre of world governance and world culture in his early to mid-twenties, helping to dole out ecclesiastical preferments, carrying on extensive correspondence with cabinet ministers twice his age, commenting on the intrigues of the Princess Lieven, dining out, enjoying the glittering table talk.[2] Gordon would come to believe that one reason that he did not get along with Edward Cardwell in later years, when Gordon himself was a humble colonial governor and Cardwell was colonial secretary and Gordon's chief, was that Cardwell could not forget that Gordon had been in a position of power in 10 Downing St. when Cardwell himself was merely a backbencher.[3]

In the glittering period of Gordon's youth, the idea of race had yet to reach its later prominence. Gordon must have seen that there was little time for anthropology or race in the best conversation of the day, and he did not seem to think that discussion of it was the most rewarding way to spend one's time in later decades, either. Frederick Weld was out of the country when Knox and Hunt spread their propaganda. Gordon was out of range socially.

But then his father died and he needed a career. After casting about, he chose colonial governance.

In his first colonial posting, as lieutenant governor of New Brunswick (1861–1866), he met and got to know many American Indians and a variety of settlers.[4] He employed none of the soon-to-be-dominant racial vocabulary in describing these early encounters. In the colonial governorships that he held next (Trinidad, which Gordon governed from 1866 to 1870, and Mauritius, 1870–1874), Gordon was unimpressed by the new meanings attached to the word 'race'. But by the end of the 1870s Gordon, now governor of Fiji, had learned that vocabulary. He learned it to fight the racist depredations carried out by European colonists.

GORDON IN TRINIDAD

The way Gordon saw things, one of his main tasks in Trinidad was to reconcile the interests of two 'races'—his word. But the racial groups that he was trying to reconcile were the Protestants and Roman Catholics, against whom the Protestant establishment had passed restrictive legislation.[5] Governor Gordon asked why the separation should exist of 'the children of English race from those of other origin', and 'Roman Catholic children from those of other religions'? Why should they not go to school together, since 'they play together in the streets of the village or neighbourhood'?[6]

'Race' could have other meanings, too. If the educational system were not improved and made equal to all faiths, he worried about superstition spreading

> in a colony where the balance of the population is of a race which when freed from the restraints of religious influences has often shown itself credulous . . . in immediate contact with a large and annually increasing number of Asiatic heathens, whose vices and idolatries are not altogether uncontagious.[7]

This statement may be biased, but at least on the surface it is not biased with the racism of heritable colour-races. Instead, Gordon seems to be using 'race' for cultural identities that can be passed on through learning—again, these 'vices and idolatries are not altogether uncontagious'. And in any case this statement is an example of Gordon trying to play on the sympathies of the secretary of state for the colonies to win support for educational reform and nonsectarian schooling.

Gordon's basic position was far less prejudiced than his use of the word 'Asiatics' would suggest. He freely discussed and promoted increased Chinese immigration, which he hoped would lead to more intermarriage and the creation of more 'creoles'. That the Chinese would intermarry was one reason to prefer them to the 'Hindoos' as immigrants. The first Chinese who came to Trinidad had been 'ill-selected', increasing prejudice against them. Later groups, especially the Hakka, were very good people[8] (so not all Chinese were alike—they had their own ethnicities). Those 'well-selected' Chinese who married with the locals or became Christians 'would become amalgamate [*sic*] with the population and a permanent gain to the colony'.[9] This was not a man who believed in sorting the world into separate or essential colour-races—if anything he believed in bringing them together. And as one did in the Trinidad of the time, Gordon referred frequently to 'coolies'. But through land grants and better treatment, Gordon wanted to turn the 'coolie' into 'a permanent colonist'.[10]

Note also that Gordon had mentioned 'the English race'. As opposed to what? Often enough, not people of another colour, but another language, another heritage. Again, playing together were 'boys of the English race and Protestant religion along with those of the French origin and Roman Catholic faith'.[11] Here, 'race' means cultural origin, just as in the eighteenth century. But resisting this camaraderie are the 'whites, who want to wrest control from the coloured population'.[12] Colour comes into Gordon's language because of the prejudice of the community politically opposed to him. Colour-racism entered Gordon's life from the direction of the colonial elites in Trinidad whose educational and tax privileges he fought.

Racial prejudice began coming in from England, too. An imperial directive in the summer of 1868 directed Gordon to count people by race in the registration of births, marriages, and deaths—reflecting it would seem the new racial sensibilities at home. Gordon was beside himself explain to the Colonial Office that to many Trinidadians it will be 'offensive'. '[W]hat is generally called the "coloured" population' cannot be so easily subdivided, he explained. Strong feelings would be stirred up, and the result would probably be 'worthless'.[13]

For Gordon, who-was-who was not a simple or a resolvable or a countable issue. Some months later, in answer to a different Colonial Office enquiry, he was finally moved to try to produce a pen-portrait of the 'diverse' population of Trinidad and its 'races'. He did not oversimplify it, and thus he undermined any idea of skin-colour groups.

Gordon began his account by laying out the Trinidadian population by religion, language, national origin, and local customs, showing that all these factors crossed each other in ways that would confound the collectors of racial statistics. Gordon took his readers on quite a tour. He moved through Trinidad's Spanish community, its British settlers who had fled the American Revolution, its French Corsicans who had fled after the fall of Napoleon, and eventually through another group that he called the 'old colonists' (the influential settlers from Britain). He then moved to the German immigrants, who were close to still other groups: The Spanish, the French, and the Italian creole Roman Catholics. This introduction of the word 'creole' in relation to the Italians was his first hint that the Spanish and French groups that he had already covered were not pure and unmixed in colour. Next Gordon brought in the apolitical Portuguese—and only then did he turn to the 'mixed' or 'coloured' 'race'.

This deliberately fissiparous picture of 'race' was Gordon's attempt to answer a question from the colonial secretary about whether the Trinidadians would support an attempt to annex the colony to the United States. Only when he had taken the Colonial Office through so much of Trinidadian society did Gordon come round to answering the question: What would the *mixed race* people do? 'Impulsive, fickle and profoundly treacherous in all social relations, it is impossible to trust them . . . ', Gordon said. But he did think they would remain loyal. They were split by language, religion, and national origin, just as the white community was. Many were propertied and conservative. Many were Roman Catholic and thus stood against any annexation to the United States. Besides, they had no sufficiently influential leaders.

And then Gordon got to the blacks, whom he called docile and far from treacherous. Like most of the other Catholics of Trinidad, they would not want to be annexed to the United States because they wanted the Roman Catholic Church to continue to be recognized and supported by the state.[14] And then there were the Chinese and the Indians—at least the first of whom, it will be remembered, gratified Gordon in that they were already creolizing with the other groups.

Up close, then, the people whom he was governing were not simply Trinidadians, or even white Trinidadians, mixed Trinidadians, and black Trinidadians. Categorization was far dicier than that. Gordon categorized people culturally, not racially, constituting his groups when he was in Trinidad as much by Protestantism or Roman Catholicism as in any other way. As we have seen, he had protested against the idea of counting everyone by race, and now a few months later he demonstrated the complexities of trying to do so. The Colonial Office got their answer about who was likely to remain loyal and who was not—but Gordon created this answer out of his own *ad hoc* classification of the population, not out of any supposedly precise census or registration data. Several weeks in Gordon's company in Trinidad in 1870 were enough to moderate Charles Kingsley's racist views, developed back in the days of the Governor Eyre controversy. Kingsley—who had been cured of stammering by none other than James Hunt, the racist author and speech therapist—no longer believed that blacks are inferior by nature. During his visit he plunged himself into the question of the education of blacks on the island.[15]

FROM TRINIDAD TO FIJI

In Gordon's next governorship, in Mauritius in the early 1870s, the social categories that he found were somewhat different. To describe social divisions in Mauritius, Gordon used the language of rich and poor, not the Protestant and Catholic terminology that he had employed in the Caribbean, although in Mauritius he also noted the various national origins and religious confessions. (Anti-Catholicism among the elite colonists was a source of contention in Mauritius as well as in Trinidad.) In Mauritius, Gordon found a glaring social split: The 'rich' had exempted themselves from most taxes while imposing a myriad of taxes on the formerly indentured workers. Gordon was astonished to find even a £1 per annum tax on casual labourers. He also found what the early twenty-first-century observer can only call an *apartheid*-style system of photographic passbooks, all of which had to be paid for again and again over the course of the year, with a new passbook being required after any change in job or address. And each time the paperwork was away being revised, the labourers were subject to fines and quite commonly imprisoned.[16]

Gordon's efforts at reform naturally caused friction with the rich. He disliked everything about Mauritius, including the climate, and he spent much of his posting trying to arrange a transfer, or on leave. Eventually Gordon escaped the spoiled Mauritius planters and went on to his next posting, Fiji, where he was governor from 1875 to 1880. This is the governorship that Gordon is justifiably the most famous for.

*   *   *

Gordon decided to rule Fiji indirectly, half creating and half preserving a system of chiefs and assemblies of chiefs. That is to say, Gordon set up a native-run parliamentary system in Fiji at a time when racism and imperialism were reaching their full stride in European culture. And in many other ways, too, Gordon tried to preserve much of Fiji's culture from the dangers it faced. He tried to counter the depredations caused by the cash economy of the European settlers, and he resisted European attempts at land-grabbing. He even created a tax system payable in native Fijian products, largely removing the need of the Fijians to work in the white-owned plantations. Without these measures, he believed that the Fijians would be enslaved or driven to extinction. Indeed, 40,000 of the 150,000 Fijians had been killed by the measles just before Gordon's arrival. As Martin Wiener has shown, Gordon also strove to make sure that justice was done to Europeans charged with physically assaulting Fijians.[17]

Gordon not only took steps to safeguard the Fijian population, he (rather embarrassingly, to some people at the time) adopted some Fijian customs, had himself made a chief, and began trying to learn what he could of native culture.[18] Gordon also arranged for himself to be appointed the first high commissioner of the Western Pacific, and also consul-general—positions that he retained for a time after he left Fiji. He was trying to protect all the natives he could.[19]

ARTHUR GORDON, ANTHROPOLOGIST?

It has been claimed by James Legge, Peter France, and (following their lead) George Stocking that when Gordon became the first governor of the newly annexed Fiji in 1875, he read Henry Sumner Maine on the nature of traditional societies. Therefore it is argued that contemporary anthropological writing helped to shape his system of indirect rule through local chiefs. But as Ian Heath has shown, this anthropological awareness on Gordon's part is doubtful and comes down to one disputable reference. Gordon did on one occasion refer to a book by Henry Sumner Maine, although whether Gordon read the book, read reviews of it, or merely heard it discussed is not clear. He owned a copy by 1880, because he passed it on to someone in that year—that he mentioned doing so was his one reference to the book. Yet in the same letter in which Gordon mentions it, he dismisses all the 'subtle explanations' for human behaviour that one would find in authors like Maine.[20] So he does not seem to have much confidence in contemporary theories about human groups. And even if he did, it would not have been Maine that he would have turned to for guidance. As George Stocking and John D. Kelly have both pointed out, Henry Sumner Maine was, of all the anthropological writers of the time, the man least interested in the racial questions that Darwin, John Lubbock, and Gordon's friend Argyll himself were working through. Maine was more interested in law.[21]

Perhaps Gordon had indeed heard something from his friend Argyll about the controversies over human development that we have been studying. And yet in the 1850s and 1860s they never wrote to each other about anthropology, evolution, or race, when Argyll was in the thick of these subjects.[22] Indeed, there is no evidence in his letters that Gordon paid attention to any of these issues.[23] Another of Gordon's intimate correspondents at the time, with whom he created what are now several bound volumes of correspondence, was Bishop Samuel Wilberforce. Wilberforce was in close contact with Gordon just after Wilberforce's famous Oxford debate with Thomas Henry Huxley on 30 June 1860. But in their ample correspondence on varied topics great and small, there is no mention of the debate, and no mention of the issues of human uniqueness that in Wilberforce's view lay behind the debate.[24] Perhaps they discussed these matters in person. Perhaps they did not.

After a long break in Gordon's correspondence with Wilberforce, which Gordon said was due to the pressure of work in his first years as governor of Trinidad, he did once ask the bishop to tell him about how the Duke of Argyll's work was received—this was when Argyll was publishing *Primeval Man*.[25] (Wilberforce replied that Argyll's work was thoughtful and contained good material, but that the old liked it more than the young[26].) From this period Gordon does make the occasional reference to whiteness, as with the largely white population of the very neat country of Venezuela.[27]

But there is no reason to think that he had changed his approach to categorizing people. He still had a sense of the ridiculous when it came to the identities that people take so seriously. On coming back to Fiji from leave in England in 1879, Gordon stepped off the boat wearing his new Oxford robes as a doctor of civil law—on top of his colonial governor's uniform.[28] More tellingly, perhaps (for that episode of the robes has been used as evidence that Gordon had no sense of humour, not that he had a good one), was an earlier incident. When Gordon and his family party went on a tour of Germany in 1868, they all wore Russian folk costumes and spoke only in French. That way they could see how they would be treated by middle-class British tourists. So indeed one night at an inn they overheard some British voices discussing what kind of meat was in the peasant dish that everyone was eating. It must be some kind of exotic local bird, people thought.

Another British tourist said that he had heard shooting that morning. Finally one of them decided to ask the name of the local game bird in the pie. He asked Gordon's sister, in French. In English she replied: 'Chicken'.[29] And it was Gordon who told this story. *Épater les bourgeois.*[30]

Apparently we can sum him up this way: Gordon is another example of someone whose consciousness of heritable colour-races was not born before mid-century. It was not part of his early life, and he did not take middle-class discussions of racial or national identities very seriously. Instead, his knowledge of 'race' came later, from the colour-racists in certain English colonies in the mid-1860s.[31] And when Gordon saw this new racial categorization, he resisted it.[32] Indeed, as Tocqueville did when he visited mixed societies, Gordon used *ad hoc* definitions of who was who—all the cultural and religious categories that he found in Trinidad, the categories of rich and poor in Mauritius, the traditional local institutions and groups through which he ruled in Fiji.

As we are about to see, Gordon, like his friend Argyll, operated on the assumption that at bottom all peoples have the same mental and moral sophistication.

GORDON AND THE MORAL QUESTION

By his time in Fiji in the late 1870s, Gordon could bring many colonial experiences to bear in understanding his new posting. As it happened, he wound up echoing Argyll in a number of ways. He echoed Argyll's degenerationism, as well as Argyll's belief in universal human intelligence and morality. So, when natives are pushed into the European economy and their lands are stolen, they do degenerate: '[At] best the natives, bewildered and depressed, . . . sink into indolence, apathy, and vice, and exposed almost without any safeguard to snares and temptations innumerable, they lose position, property, self-respect, health, and perish from off the face of the earth. . . . ' But this is because their spirit is broken, as anyone's would be: 'The moral sense of a semicivilized race is often very unlike our own, but is not on that account the less real. . . . '[33]

It must be admitted that Gordon was flawed, and he introduced the lash for petty crimes in Trinidad and Ceylon.[34] He introduced Indian labour into Fiji in order to isolate Fijians from plantation life. And in doing so he was motivated in part by the need to raise the money to administer Fiji by expanding its economy. His superiors in London in any case required him to move toward balancing the new colony's budget—colonies were expected to pay the costs of their own administration.[35] But admitting all this about Gordon and the lash and Gordon and economic development, I still think that he introduced a new level of concern for preserving the lives and interests of colonized peoples vis-à-vis the interests of European settlers, a level of concern that had not been seen since the days when James Stephen and other scions of the abolitionist Clapham Sect staffed the Colonial Office a generation before. As permanent secretary at the Colonial Office from 1836 to 1848, Stephen had fought against what he called 'the hatred with which the white man regards the black' in the colonies.[36]

Perhaps Gordon deserves the blame for so entrenching Fijian land rights that there would be a permanent divide between the Fijians and the East Indians whom Gordon brought to the country.[37] Gordon may ultimately be responsible for the division at the heart of Fijian society today. But it was later generations that kept all of this going. In his own time—and as Gordon himself frequently pointed out—his entrenching of Fijian land rights and political institutions was his way of saving the Fijian people from near slavery on European plantations, or from warfare with the European settlers on the scale of the Maori wars of New Zealand—or from something like the massacres, the dog unleashings, and the well poisonings that had long taken place in Australia.[38]

In Fiji, Gordon claimed that he was trying 'to secure the native race from oppression and fraud'.[39] To his confidant William Ewart Gladstone, the prime minister who had (reluctantly) annexed Fiji in order to stop the circum-Pacific kidnapping of natives to work on plantations, Gordon wrote that the people in Fiji, 'except for a few hundreds of heathen mountaineers', were in the state of civilization that our Scotch rural ancestors were in the fifteenth century. If treated like nineteenth-century British subjects and exposed to the full wrath of the planters, they would disappear, but if allowed twenty-five years to catch up they would create their own distinct 'civilization'. Gordon described the Fijian houses, their rooms, their curtains, their chests of drawers, their toilet tables. And he related the scene in one rural Fijian house when a wife had taken out the letters of her absent husband and read the governor some of her husband's long chatty accounts of rural politics. No whites had brought reading and writing here, but Fijian teachers had, Gordon stressed. And the kind of letter writing that so impressed Gordon sounds exactly like what Gordon himself was engaging in with Gladstone, which was his point. The state of civilization in Fiji, Gordon claimed, would surprise most people in England. He referred to an American who has asked him why he did not 'clear out these damn niggers'. Gordon did not see why he should, but he admitted than nine-tenths of the whites in the colony agreed with the American.[40]

GENERALIZING ABOUT THE VICTORIANS

Gordon was ruling non-English peoples in the Pacific, and, yes, having some of them flogged. So is the fact that he did not refer to races in the new racist way, and found it offensive, just a matter of language?[41] But that is all that the races of mankind and womankind are, just a matter of language. Of all the ways to divide people up into analytically manageable groups—by their degree of rurality or urbanity, their level of education, their participation in the cash economy, their language, their religion, their amount and kind of travel—their skin colour is by no mean the most interesting feature to pick. It does not predict the others. It does not form coherent groups, and it cuts across families. Using colour to subdivide people makes no more sense than using blood type. Yet in twenty-first-century Japan, blood type is thought to predict talents and temperament, so that Type O is the blood of warriors and baseball pitchers, and Type B the blood of hunters—people who are independent and creative.[42]

Using racial category words in that way, as predictives, is a very poor response to the problem of how to group people to see them in the round. As Gordon put it, the 'speedy sweeping away . . . of the native race' in the Pacific because of bad legislation and bad administration was due more to 'a want of imagination of the native, or the capacity to grasp an unfamiliar state of things,—not from any *intention* to do injustice'.[43] The creation of oversimplified colour-races in people's minds starts as a matter of semantics, 'the want of imagination' that Gordon identified, but it soon ramifies into a matter of how people treat one another.

Elsewhere I have made a case about the social and intellectual atmosphere of mid-nineteenth-century England. I have argued that such factors as steam-powered printing, the lowering of taxes on the burgeoning world of newspapers and periodicals, the laying of undersea-telegraph cables, the creation of larger webs of correspondence, and not least the growth of a larger and more specialized urban life in London, with more specialized social clubs and professional associations, all led to an increase in the flow of information that at least the more comfortable part of the British population had about the places and peoples of the world. Some British people responded by trying to escape the new complexity. They attempted to simplify the world by imposing ever larger, ever more general, and ever more imperial categories upon it. Sometime after 1850, and certainly by the later 1860s, these men had developed grand visions for a resurgent British Empire, visions that extended all the way into the tropics.[44]

In this book we have seen that in the 1860s, at the same time that a single overarching idea of British imperialism was being constructed by those men who chose to think about the subject, there was also constructed— and across a broader swathe of British society—an overarching idea of 'race'. 'Races' became much more biological and colour-centred, and more important as ways characterizing people. The methodological demurring of Tocqueville, Argyll, and Gordon notwithstanding, the immediate future belonged to the new racial characterizations of Gobineau, Bagehot, and Darwin. What had been a properly complex world had been reduced to (more or less) black, yellow, white, and Aryan.

The information explosion of the time has been examined in their different ways by other scholars.[45] Patricia Anderson has examined the new ubiquity of visual images in Britain at mid-century. Douglas Lorimer has looked at the rise of blackface minstrels in urban music halls, the fame of Harriet Beecher Stowe, the careers of various ex-slaves who toured England on speaking engagements, and the role of missionaries and abolitionists serving as publicists for the idea of racial difference. In this noisy urban world, it was easier to lump people together into races than to remember their differences, their specificity. Thinking about particulars gave way to thinking about big generalizations.

For his part, Robert M. Young has argued that the growth in printing and in the newly literate middle classes after 1850 led to a coarsening of thought in the mass media of the time. After 1870 or so, the public intellectual life of the nation retreated to newly specialized journals. The old, intellectually demanding generalist quarterlies declined. So did the general intellectual societies, such as the British Association. The world of the *Bridgewater Treatises* (1833–1840), an attempt to sum up and unite all knowledge and science into a Christian worldview, had passed. Instead, some writers became narrow specialists and vastly more became cheap popularizers.[46]

A similar process of fragmentation and popularization has been pointed out in Victorian thinking on the subject of how our minds work. For Sarah Winter, the old school of associationalist psychology, stemming from John Locke, held fast to the idea that people *learn* their personal and cultural identities. So there can be no heritable racial mentalities. Winter shows that the associationalist view was still alive and well in the work of Harriet Martineau. Martineau's social science methodological treatise, *How to Observe: Manners and Morals* (1838), counselled travel writers to avoid making cheap generalizations about the peoples of the world, and instead to explore cultures carefully as social constructions, using an explicit observational methodology.[47] In successive editions of his *System of Logic* (published from 1843 to 1872), John Stuart Mill would continue to call for a science of 'ethology' along these lines. He favoured the systematic exploration of the idea of culture. Social observers would first interrogate their own beliefs, as well as 'the recognised results of common experience' about the cultural groups they wanted to explore. Then, armed with philosophical rigour and a set of research questions to pursue, they would turn to detailed empirical evidence. This would be the beginning of a true science of society in which—as Mill stressed—generalization and specific evidence could be in continual dialog with one another.[48] But at the time little came of Mill's plans for this new science of culture. For the 'recognised results of common experience' on which he would found such a science were in fact changing in ways that he could not accept. Because he believed that 'the formation of national or collective character' is founded on the experiences and education of individuals, rather than on their colour or their blood, he was out of touch with the growing belief in race.[49] The nurture-not-nature school of Martineau and Mill seems to have broken up at about the same time that Robert Young's school of theologian/naturalists did—in the more fragmented world of the 1850s and 1860s.

With the passing of the early-Victorian theologians-*cum*-scientists and the shared intellectual world that they created, and the foundation of all the new more specialized professional associations, social clubs, and venues of publication, something else had passed as well, as Young argues. The old-style theologian-scientists could fit all of creation, material and spiritual, into a single comprehensive picture for their readers. But in the new age the specialists could no longer discuss universals, and the new generalists were not good with specifics—for now they were writers in the more down-market, middle-brow periodicals and no longer personally active at the forefront of science. So in the age of specialization in some forums and popularization in many more, the old, deeply learned, more balanced case for specific-peoples-within-universal-humanity could no longer be made.[50]

What seems to have disappeared was the idea that on one level human 'races' are numerous and fluid—while at the same time on another level, underneath all of that diversity, humanity is really one race united in dignity, all created in God's image (despite the subsequent degradation of some groups).[51] The heyday of Christian monogenism had passed. By mid-century, there was room for a multitude of opinions about what the human races might be. That is, there was room for people to generate new racial categories, scientific or otherwise. Douglas Lorimer stresses a movement from the Christian consensus to an exaltation of science, but I think the movement was toward a variety of exaltations, not all of them scientific.[52] That is, the new consensus was a lack of consensus about what to pay attention to. There was an overflow of information. Racism grew as one of the classifications developed to cope with this overflow.

Some thinkers thus began to employ a suspect methodology, as we have seen. They imposed hard-and-fast racial groupings upon the human continuum without adequate evidence tests. They imposed colour categories that did not stand up to close analysis. Once such thinkers—Gobineau, Bagehot, and Darwin—had their races, they set them in competition. They made the social factors that led to 'success' in this competition physically heritable. And once our thinkers had done that, they created a category for the race that had outcompeted and become superior to all the others; to name it they adopted the word 'Aryan'. Gobineau and Bagehot both did so, and Darwin followed Bagehot in this direction.

THOUGHTS, OR MORAL FEELING?

Very different was the case of Argyll. In arguing against Lubbock's social evolutionism, Argyll maintained that full human dignity was a characteristic of all human races and groups, ancient or modern. And that indeed is in every sense the heart of the matter: Argyll stayed true to his basic idea that anyone who looked human really was human. For all the scientific to-ings and fro-ings, Argyll would not let go of the conviction of universal human dignity and moral autonomy.

Tocqueville, like Argyll, had an essential moral grounding that left him sceptical of new 'discoveries' in racial science. He rejected Gobineau's hard and fast laws. For Tocqueville, Gobineau stripped people of their autonomy and freedom by telling them that they were bound to live and decay according to some racial nature. Tocqueville saw that any racial nature that existed, although surely not the one that Gobineau identified, was purely a social construction amenable to change through individual and group initiative.

Now we have seen that Argyll's friend, Governor Gordon, also worked from a basic moral grounding. He wanted to maintain the culture and the independent lives of the people he governed. As he frequently insisted, he was trying to save his charges from extinction. Gordon simply ignored the new ideas of race for as long as he could.[53] He worked for the equality of whatever social groups, not necessarily 'races', that he happened to find in the colonies that he governed. In the 1870s, when he could ignore racism no longer, he rejected it.[54]

Tocqueville, Argyll, and Gordon all evinced something of the older particularism-generalism—that is, a belief in a multitude of particular, changeable human groups, joined to an overall belief in a single universal humanity.

So was the racist mistake one of methodology or morality? Was it failing to see the artificiality of the headings under which people can be totted up in a table, and the failure to remake one's categories afresh in each new situation? Or was the failure a moral one, a failure to stay true to an idea of universal humanity? I think the alternative faced by each man was simultaneously methodological and moral: Use evidence carefully, remaking rather than assuming one's groups—or cut people apart into the two-dimensional figures in a table.

It is not surprising that when a monogenist consensus was breaking up in the mid-nineteenth century, some generalists—in setting out to bring order to their knowledge of the world—would reinvent heritable colour-races. For in another confusing age, our own, some people are still inventing races, even though the consensus in human biology has moved beyond race. Laura Tabili has put it very well:

> [I]n much scholarship, racial identities have been treated as objective qualities, innate attributes, unproblematically fixed essences, from which we can predict or extrapolate how people will behave or must have behaved with only occasional recourse to evidence.[55]

She also suggests a solution:

> [T]he naturalness of racial categories must automatically provoke the question: 'would such a simplistic formulation be tolerated if it applied

to gender or class?' Applying these tests and the lessons of class analysis to racial processes could enhance our ability to historicize race, understanding racial formation as on-going and ever-changing, a process thus susceptible to historical analysis.[56]

And yet today, when ideas of social evolutionism and heritable class inferiority have been defeated at the level of careful academic discourse, popular ideas of race can still seep into otherwise careful speech. Perhaps they have always done so.[57] That is what seemed to happen with Charles Darwin, who analyzed the concept of human races out of existence and then kept using them anyway—although at least he had the excuse of believing in the inheritance of acquired characteristics. Léon Poliakov has pointed out that E.B. Tylor also rejected racial categories while continuing to use the language of race nonetheless.[58]

But even if popular ideas of race are carefully avoided and refuted, the very fact of trying to analyze the world in a careful way still requires us to divide people into groups. Racial systems can be reinvented—and that is the danger.[59] We need to question and continually refashion the categories by which we divide and analyze humanity, as Tocqueville (usually) did—rather than letting our categories turn into the heritable races encoded in the racial terms of *The Descent of Man*.

Notes

NOTES TO CHAPTER 1

1. Roxann Wheeler, *The Complexion of Race: Categories of Difference in Eighteenth-Century British Culture* (Philadelphia: University of Pennsylvania Press, 2000), esp. pp. 300–2; Colin Kidd, *The Forging of Races: Race and Scripture in the Protestant Atlantic World, 1600–2000* (Cambridge University Press, 2006).
2. Christine Bolt, *Victorian Attitudes to Race* (London: Routledge and Kegan Paul; Toronto: University of Toronto Press, 1971), pp. x, 7. On at least one occasion in 1866 (10 April), as detailed in Bolt, pp. 87–8, the *Times* discussed blacks in Jamaica and the United States as being everywhere the same.
3. As attested in Bolt, *Victorian Attitudes to Race*, pp. 18–19, 24, 48, 151; Lorimer, *Colour, Class, and the Victorians: English Attitudes to the Negro in the Mid-Nineteenth Century* (Leicester: Leicester University Press, 1978), p. 138.
4. On Hunt's lack of a sympathetic audience, see Douglas Lorimer, 'Theoretical Racism in Late-Victorian Anthropology, 1870–1900', *Victorian Studies* 31, 3 (Spring 1988), pp. 405–30 at pp. 428–9.
5. He might have been borrowing the term 'black' from South Asian Britons who used the word to describe themselves in the 1980s as a way of identifying with Britons and Americans of African ancestry; but East Asian Britons do not seem to have used it in that way. See Avtar Brah, 'Difference, Diversity, and Differentiation', in James Donald and Ali Rattansi (eds), *'Race', Culture, and Difference* (London: Sage, 1992), pp. 126–45. In any case, a Chinese American would never use the term, either as self-description or as protest.
6. Bernard Lewis, *Race and Slavery in the Middle East: An Historical Enquiry* (New York: Oxford University Press, 1990), pp. 109–10, 110 n. 1. For the spread of the idea of a shared whiteness down through the class system, reaching the working class by the 1950s—by the way, it seems, of the working classes in the colonies of settlement—see Alastair Bonnett, 'How the Working Class Became "White": The Symbolic (Re)formation of Racialized Capitalism', *Journal of Historical Sociology* 11, 3 (September 1998), pp. 316–40; and Jonathan Hyslop, 'The Imperial Working Class Makes Itself White: White Labourism in Britain, Australia and South Africa Before the First World War', *Journal of Historical Sociology* 12, 4 (December 1999), pp. 398–421.
7. Henry Mayhew, *London Labour and the London Poor*, 4 vols ([1861–1862]; New York: Dover, 1968), I, pp. 1–3, 477, II, pp. 137–8, 364–7. On the interconnections between ideas of race, degrees of dirtiness, and degrees of Irishnesss, see Mary Poovey, *Making a Social Body: British Cultural Formation,*

1830–1864 (University of Chicago Press, 1995), pp. 57–72. For discussions of how Mayhew's class categories were informed by *imperial* colour distinctions, rather than (as Foucault would have it) class distinctions proceeding from pre-existing racial distinctions *within* Europe, see Ann Laura Stoler, *Race and the Education of Desire* (Durham, North Carolina: Duke University Press, 1995), pp. 123–30; and John Marriott, *The Other Empire: Metropolis, India, and Progress in the Colonial Imagination* (Manchester: Manchester University Press, 2003), pp. 114–20, 152–5.

8. *Spectator*, 13 July 1861, p. 750; as quoted in Bolt, *Victorian Attitudes to Race*, p. 60.

9. The idea that racial categories can derive their power from the way they simplify social and psychological analysis is nicely explored in Uday Singh Mehta, 'Essential Ambiguities of Race and Racism', in Davis (ed.), *Political Power and Social Theory,* pp. 234–46.

10. Jorge Luis Borges, 'Funes the Memorious', Anthony Kerrigan (trans.), in *Ficciones* (New York: Grove Weidenfeld, 1962), p. 115.

11. Vincent P. Pecora, 'Arnoldian Ethnology', *Victorian Studies* 41, 3 (Spring 1998), pp. 355–79 at pp. 372–4. Other interesting observations along these lines have been made by Lionel Trilling, in *Matthew Arnold* [1939], The Works of Lionel Trilling: Uniform Edition (New York: Harcourt Brace Jovanavich, 1977), pp. 235–6; and David Reisman, 'Psychological Types and National Character: An Informal Commentary', *American Quarterly* 5, 4 (Winter 1953), pp. 325–43.

12. George M. Fredrickson, *The Comparative Imagination: On the History of Racism, Nationalism, and Social Movements* (Berkeley and Los Angeles: University of California Press, 1997), pp. 84–5; Harry Louis Gates, Jr., 'Talkin' that Talk', in idem. (ed.),*"Race," Writing, and Difference* (Chicago: University of Chicago Press, 1986), pp. 402–9.

13. Cf. Stoler, 'Racial Histories and their Regimes of Truth', in Diane E. Davis (ed.), *Political Power and Social Theory* 11 (Greenwich, Connecticut: JAI Press, 1997), pp. 183–206, especially pp. 193–4.

14. Collette Guillaumin suggests that this was true of Tocqueville, Durkheim, Weber, and Boas—Guillaumin, 'The Idea of Race and its Elevation to Autonomous Scientific and Legal Status', in Guillaumin, *Racism, Sexism, Power, and Ideology*, Andrew Rothwell with Max Silverman (trans.) (London: Routledge, 1995), pp. 61–98 at p. 65.

15. George Wilson Pierson, *Tocqueville in America* ([*Tocqueville and Beaumont in America*, 1938]; Baltimore: Johns Hopkins University Press, 1996), pp. 158n–159n; Melvin Richter, 'The Uses of Theory: Tocqueville's Adaptation of Montesquieu' in idem. (ed.), *Essays in Theory and History: An Approach to the Social Sciences* (Cambridge: Massachusetts: Harvard University Press, 1970), pp. 90–1; James T. Schleifer, *The Making of Tocqueville's Democracy in America* (Chapel Hill: University of North Carolina Press, 1980), pp. 263–73.

16. Geoffrey Bowker and Susan Leigh Star, *Sorting Things Out: Classification and Its Consequences* (Cambridge, Massachusetts: MIT Press, 1999), pp. 285, 302–3, 307, 319–20, 235–6.

17. Deborah Posel, "What's in a Name?: Racial Categorisations under Apartheid and their Afterlife', *Transformation* 47 (2001), pp. 45–74.

18. For other turns through the subject of the nonexistence of biological races in the human species, see Daniel G. Blackburn, 'Why Race Is Not a Biological Concept', in *Race and Racism in Theory and Practice*, Berel Lang (ed.) (Lanham, Maryland: Rowman & Littlefield, 2000), pp. 3–26; Kidd, *The Forging of Races,* pp. 3–18.

19. Kwame Anthony Appiah, *In My Father's House: Africa in the Philosophy of Culture* (New York: Oxford University Press, 1992), pp. 32–9.
20. Luigi Luca Cavalli-Sforza and Francesco Cavalli-Sforza, *The Great Human Diasporas: The History of Diversity and Evolution*, Sarah Thorne (trans.) (Reading, Pennsylvania: Addison-Wesley, 1995), pp. 95–6, and 198, fig. 7.7; Rick Kittles, 'Nature, Origin, and Variation of Human Pigmentation', *Journal of Black Studies* 26, 1 (September 1995), pp. 36–61; Nina G. Jablonski and George Chaplin, 'The Evolution of Human Skin Coloration', *Journal of Human Evolution* 39, 1 (2000), pp. 57–106; Asta Juzeniene, Richard Setlow, Alina Porojnicu, Arnfinn Hykkerud Steindal, and Johan Moan, 'Development of Different Human Skin Colors: A Review Highlighting Photobiological and Photobiophysical Aspects', *Journal of Photochemistry and Photobiology B: Biology* 96 (2009), pp. 93–100.
21. Jeffrey C. Long and Rick A. Kittles, 'Human Genetic Diversity and the Nonexistence of Biological Races', *Human Biology* 75, 4 (August 2003), pp. 449–71.
22. Jablonski and Chaplin, 'Evolution of Human Skin Coloration', pp. 78–9.
23. Ivan Hannaford, *Race: The History of an Idea in the West* (Washington, DC: Woodrow Wilson Center Press/Baltimore: Johns Hopkins University Press, 1996).
24. Carl H. Nightingale, 'Before Race Mattered: Geographies of the Color Line in Early Colonial Madras and New York', *American Historical Review* 113, 1 (February 2008), pp. 48–71—esp. pp. 51 and 67–70; Wheeler, *The Complexion of Race*, pp. 5–7, 31.
25. See John D. Garrigus, 'Sons of the Same Father: Gender, Race, and Citizenship in French Saint-Domingue, 1760–1792', in Christine Adams, Jack R. Censer, and Lisa Jane Graham (eds), *Visions and Revisions of Eighteenth-Century France* (University Park, Pennsylvania: Pennsylvania State University Press, 1997), pp. 137–53; Guillaumin, 'The Specific Characteristics of Racist Ideology', pp. 31–5, 55–6.
26. On Hume: Richard H. Popkin, 'The Philosophical Bases of Modern Racism', in Craig Walton and John P. Anton (eds), *Philosophy and the Civilizing Arts: Essays Presented to Herbert W. Schneider* (Athens, Ohio: Ohio University Press, 1974), pp. 126–65—'Appendix on Hume', pp. 154–65; Emmanuel C. Eze, 'Hume, Race, and Human Nature', *Journal of the History of Ideas* 61, 3 (July 2000), pp. 691–8. On Long: Edward Long, *The History of Jamaica*, 3 vols (London: T. Lowndes, 1774; New York: Arno Press, 1972), II, pp. 351–485; Anthony J. Barker, *The African Link: British Attitudes to the Negro in the Era of the Atlantic Slave Trade, 1550–1807* (London: Frank Cass, 1978), pp. 45–55, 160–1; Wheeler, *The Complexion of Race*, pp. 209–33.
27. On Jefferson, and the earlier interpretation of him by Winthrop Jordan in the 1960s: Alexander O. Boulton, 'The American Paradox: Jeffersonian Equality and Racial Science', *American Quarterly* 47, 3 (September 1995), pp. 467–92; Peter S. Onuf, '"To Declare Them a Free and Independent People": Race, Slavery, and National Identity in Jefferson's Thought', *Journal of the Early Republic* 18, 1 (Spring 1998), pp. 1–46; and Bruce Dain, *A Hideous Monster of the Mind: American Race Theory in the Early Republic* (Cambridge, Massachusetts: Harvard University Press, 2002), pp. 1–3, 26–39. On Kames: William C. Lehmann, *Henry Home, Lord Kames, and the Scottish Enlightenment: A Study in National Character and in the History of Ideas* (The Hague: Martinus Nijhoff, 1971), pp. 253–4; Kidd, *The Forging of Races*, pp. 95–9, 111–14; Wheeler, *The Complexion of Race*, pp. 187–8; and Kames himself—Henry Home, Lord Kames, *Sketches of the History of Man* [1788], James Harris (ed.), 3 vols (Indianapolis, Indiana: Liberty

Fund, 2007), I, 'Preliminary Discourse'. On Kant: Mark Larrimore, 'Race, Freedom, and the Fall in Steffens and Kant', pp. 91–120, in Sara Eigen and Mark Larrimore (eds), *The German Invention of Race* (Albany: State University of New York Press, 2006); Robert Bernasconi, 'Who Invented the Concept of Race?: Kant's Role in the Enlightenment Construction of Race', in idem. (ed.), *Race* (Malden, Massachusetts: Blackwell, 2001), pp. 11–36; Hannaford, *Race*, pp. 218–24.

28. Richard H. Popkin, *Isaac La Peyrère (1596–1676): His Life, Work, and Influence* (Leiden: E. J. Brill, 1987), pp. 115–65; David N. Livingstone, *Adam's Ancestors: Race, Religion, and the Politics of Human Origins* (Baltimore, Maryland: Johns Hopkins University Press, 2008) Chapters 1–2.

29. Popkin, 'Philosophical Basis of Modern Racism'; Michael Banton, *Racial Theories*, 2nd edn (Cambridge University Press, 1998), pp. 30–2, 44–8; Joyce E. Chaplin, 'Natural Philosophy and an Early Racial Idiom in North America: Comparing English and Indian Bodies', *William and Mary Quarterly* (January 1997), pp. 229–52; Karen Ordahl Kupperman, 'Presentment of Civility: English Reading of American Self-Presentation in the Early Years of Colonization', *William and Mary Quarterly* (January 1997), pp. 193–228.

30. Kathleen Brown, 'Native Americans and Early Modern Concepts of Race', in Martin Daunton and Rick Halpern (eds), *Empire and Others: British Encounters with Indigenous Peoples, 1600–1850* (Philadelphia: University of Pennsylvania Press, 1999), pp. 79–100; Nightingale, 'Before Race Mattered', pp. 50–1; Wheeler, *The Complexion of Race*, pp. 9–11.

31. For some comments on the state of mind which insists that everyone must fit into a few supposedly 'obvious' skin-colour categories, despite all the people who don't, see Collette Guillaumin, 'Race and Nature: The System of Marks', in Guillaumin, *Racism, Sexism, Power, and Ideology*, pp. 133–52 at pp. 134–5.

32. Nicholas Hudson, 'From "Nation" to "Race": The Origin of Racial Classification in Eighteenth-Century Thought', *Eighteenth-Century Studies* 29, 3 (1996), pp. 247–64; idem., '"Hottentots" and the Evolution of European Racism', *Journal of European Studies* 34, 4 (December 2004), pp. 308–32; Banton, *Racial Theories*, pp. 25–9; Reginald Horsman, *Race and Manifest Destiny: The Origins of American Racial Anglo-Saxonism* (Cambridge, Massachusetts: Harvard University Press, 1981), pp. 31–52; Michael Adas, *Machines as the Measure of Men* (Ithaca, New York: Cornell University Press, 1989), pp. 64–8; Wheeler, *The Complexion of Race*, pp. 14–21. Somewhat more racist were the views developing among certain circles in America: Joyce E. Chaplin, "Race", in David Armitage and Michael J. Braddick (eds), *The British Atlantic World, 1500–1800* (Basingstoke: Palgrave Macmillan, 2002), pp. 154–72. Philip D. Morgan points out that societies dominated by slavery developed more extreme views of African slaves than societies where slavery was rare, as in England—Morgan, "British Encounters with Africans and African-Americans, circa 1600–1780", in Bernard Bailyn and Philip D. Morgan (eds), *Strangers within the Realm: Cultural Margins of the First British Empire* (Chapel Hill: University of North Carolina Press, 1991), pp. 157–219, esp. 166–7, 193–4, 213–17.

33. Theodore W. Allen, *The Invention of the White Race*, vol. 1, *Racial Oppression and Social Control* (London: Verso, 2004), pp. 21–3; Shruti Kapila, 'Race Matters: Orientalism and Religion, India and Beyond, c. 1770–1880', *Modern Asian Studies* 41, 3 (May 2007), pp. 471–513. As Kapila's evidence shows, fixed racial categories date from closer to the middle of the nineteenth century (p. 500).

34. Ladelle McWhorter, 'Sex, Race, and Power: A Foucauldian Genealogy', *Hypatia* 19, 3 (Summer 2004), pp. 38–62 at p. 49.

35. Tzvetan Todorov, '"Race," Writing, and Culture', in Harry Louis Gates, Jr. (ed.), *"Race," Writing, and Difference* (Chicago: University of Chicago Press, 1986), pp. 370–80 at p. 372.

36. The turn-of-the-century period of speculation over questions of race and character, coupled with curiosity about tales of African travel and the exhibition of Saartjie Baartman (the 'Hottentot' Venus), is brought to life in H. L. Malchow, 'Frankenstein's Monster and Images of Race in Nineteenth-Century Britain, *Past and Present* 139 (May 1993), pp. 90–130; see also Peter J. Kitson, *Romantic Literature, Race, and the Colonial Encounter* (New York: Palgrave Macmillan, 2007), Chapters 1–2.

37. James Cowles Prichard, *Researches into the Physical History of Mankind*, 3rd edn, 5 vols (London: Sherwood, Gilbert, and Piper, 1836); George Stocking, *Race, Culture, and Evolution: Essays in the History of Anthropology* (New York: Free Press, 1968), pp. 13–41; Nancy Stepan, *The Idea of Race in Science: Great Britain, 1800–1960* (New York: Archon Books, 1982), pp. xii–xiv, 2–5, 13–16, 38–9; Stocking, *Victorian Anthropology* (New York: The Free Press, 1987), pp. 48–53, 68; idem., introduction to James Cowles Prichard, *Researches into the Physical History of Man* [1813], George Stocking (ed.), (Chicago: University of Chicago Press, 1973), pp. li–lviii, lxxi–xc; Wheeler, *The Complexion of Race*, 291–7.

38. Although Kitson's conclusion in *Romantic Literature, Race, and the Colonial Encounter* is that races of some kind did become established in English thought in the Romantic period through the work of Kant and Lawrence (pp. 45–49), his evidence supports my contention that fixed heritable races did not exist in English minds in the early nineteenth century, even when someone wrote on colour and human difference. See Kitson's discussion of Thomas de Quincey (pp. 203–13). The racist exception was William Cobbett—see Kitson, pp. 39, 96, quoting Cobbett, *Political Register*, 4 August 1821. But Cobbett had spent a number of years in America.

39. Lewis, *Race and Slavery in the Middle East*, pp. 22–6, 40–53; James H. Sweet, 'The Iberian Roots of American Racist Thought', *William and Mary Quarterly* 54, 1 (January 1997), pp. 143–66.

40. B. Netanyahu, *The Origins of the Inquisition in Fifteenth Century Spain* (New York: Random House, 1995), pp. 978–97. Netanyahu's monumental book is controversial for reasons that cannot be explored here; see the review article by John Edwards, 'Was the Spanish Inquisition Truthful?', *Jewish Quarterly Review*, new series 87:3/4 (January 1997), pp. 351–66. Nonetheless, Netanyahu establishes that the *conversos* suffered racial and not merely religious persecution. On this point, see also Stafford Poole, 'The Politics of Limpieza de Sangre: Juan de Ovando and His Circle in the Reign of Philip II', *Americas* 55, 3 (1999), pp. 359–89; and Miriam Bodian, '"Men of the Nation": The Shaping of Converso Identity in Early Modern Europe', *Past and Present* 143 (May 1994), pp. 48–76.

41. D. Nirenberg, 'Mass Conversion and Genealogical Mentalities: Jews and Christians in Fifteenth Century Spain', *Past & Present* 174 (February 2002), pp. 3–41; idem., 'Race and the Middle Ages: The Case of Spain and Its Jews', in Margaret R. Green, Walter D. Mignolo, and Maureen Quilligan (eds), *Rereading the Black Legend: The Discourses of Religious and Racial Difference in the Renaissance Empires* (Chicago: University of Chicago Press, 2007), pp. 71–87—see also the other essays in that volume.

42. Ilona Katzew, *Casta Painting* (New Haven, Connecticut: Yale University Press, 2004); M. Carrera Magali, *Imagining Identity in New Spain: Race,*

Lineage, and the Colonial Body in Portraiture and Casta Paintings (Austin: University of Texas Press, 2003), pp. 5, 9–15, 36–7, 53–68; María Elena Martínez, *Genealogical Fictions: Limpieza de Sangre, Religion, and Gender in Colonial Mexico* (Stanford, California: Stanford University Press, 2008); idem., 'The Language, Genealogy, and Classification of "Race" in Colonial Mexico', in Ilona Katzew and Susan Deans-Smith (eds), *Race and Classification: The Case of Mexican America* (Stanford, California: Stanford University Press, 2009), pp. 25–42.

43. Bruce A. Castleman, 'Social Climbers in a Mexican City: Individual Mobility within the *Sistema de Castas* in Orizaba, 1777–1791', *Colonial Latin American Review* 10, 2 (2001), pp. 229–49.

44. Guillaume Aubert, '"The Blood of France": Race and Purity of Blood in the French Atlantic World', *William and Mary Quarterly* 61, 3 (July 2004), pp. 439–78.

45. Sue Peabody, '*There Are No Slaves in France': The Political Culture of Race and Slavery in the Ancien Régime* (New York: Oxford University Press, 1996), pp. 60–9; Todorov, '"Race," Writing, and Culture', pp. 371–2; Martin S. Staum, *Labeling People: French Scholars on Society, Race, and Empire, 1815–1848* (Montreal and Kingston: McGill-Queen's University Press, 2003); Seymour Drescher, 'The Ending of the Slave Trade and the Evolution of European Scientific Racism', *Social Science History* 14, 3 (Autumn 1990), pp. 415–50.

46. For more examples of the reinvention of race, see Jonathon Glassman, 'Slower than a Massacre: The Multiple Sources for Racial Thought in Colonial Africa', *American Historical Review* 109, 3 (June 2004), pp. 720–54 at p. 726 n. 30. On race as modern classification and something continuingly reinvented, see also two essays in Robert Ross (ed.), *Racism and Colonialism: Essays in Ideology and Social Structure* (The Hague: Martinus Nijhoff, 1981): D. Van Arkel, 'Racism in Europe', pp. 11–31; and Ernst van den Boogaart, 'Colour Prejudice and the Yardstick of Civility: The Initial Dutch Confrontation with Black Africans, 1590–1635', pp. 33–54.

47. Stoler, 'Racial Histories and Their Regimes of Truth', p. 189.

48. Wilson, *The Island Race: Englishness, Empire, and Gender in the Eighteenth Century* (London: Routledge, 2003), p. 11.

49. See many of the essays in Karim Murji and John Solomos (eds), *Racialization: Studies in Theory and Practice* (Oxford: Oxford University Press, 2005).

50. Society of Fraternal Democrats [George Julian Harney], 'Declaration of Principles' [1846], given in G.D.H. Cole and A.W. Filson, *British Working Class Movements: Select Documents, 1789–1875* (London: Macmillan; New York: St. Martin's, 1965), pp. 402–3. The lack of racism in the Chartist movement (the Chartists flourished from 1838 to 1848) has struck Dorothy Thompson. See Thompson, *Outsiders: Class, Gender, and Nation* (London: Verso, 1993), p. 41—cf. the Chartist awareness of national and religious difference, pp. 126–7. Kelly J. Mays reaches a conclusion similar to Thompson's in 'Slaves in Heaven, Laborers in Hell: Chartist Poets' Ambivalent Identification with the (Black) Slave', *Victorian Poetry* 39, 2 (Summer 2001), pp. 137–63.

51. Winthrop Jordan, *White over Black: American Attitudes toward the Negro, 1550–1812* (Chapel Hill: University of North Carolina Press, 1968; New York: Pelican Books, 1969), pp. 304–8 (Book 3, Chapter 6, Part 7), 525–41 (Book 5, Chapter 6, Parts 5–8); Mark M. Smith, *How Race Is Made: Slavery, Segregation, and the Senses* (Chapel Hill: University of North Carolina Press, 2006), Chapter 2; Michael O'Brien, *Conjectures of Order: Intellectual Life in the American South, 1810–1860*, 2 vols (Chapel Hill: University of North Carolina Press, 2004), Chapter 18; Harold B. Tallant, *Evil Necessity:*

Slavery and Political Culture in Antebellum Kentucky (Lexington, Kentucky: University Press of Kentucky, 2003), pp. 3–7, 73–8.

52. Eva Sheppard Wolf, *Race and Liberty in the New Nation: Emancipation in Virginia from the Revolution to Nat Turner's Rebellion* (Baton Rouge: Louisiana State University Press, 2006), pp. 17–20, 151–2.

53. Kidd, *The Forging of Races*, pp. 143–8; O'Brien, *Conjectures of Order*, chapter 5.

54. William Stanton, *The Leopard's Spots: Scientific Attitudes toward Race in America, 1815–59* (Chicago: University of Chicago Press, 1960); George M. Fredrickson, *The Black Image in the White Mind: The Debate on Afro-American Character and Destiny, 1817–1914* (1971; Middletown, Connecticut: Wesleyan University Press, 1987), Chapters 2–3; Adam Dewbury, 'The American School and Scientific Racism in Early American Anthropology, *Histories of Anthropology Annual* 3 (2007), pp. 121–47; Dain, *Hideous Monster*, pp. 197–236; Banton, *Racial Theories*, pp. 53–62.

55. Another Englishman writing along these lines was the autodidact John Bigland, in the apparently little noted *An Historical Display of the Effects of Physical and Moral Causes on the Character and Circumstances of the Ancients and the Moderns in Regard to their Intellectual and Social State* (London, 1816), as given in Hannah Franziska Augstein (ed.), *Race: The Origins of an Idea* (Bristol: Thommes Press, 1996), pp. 68–80.

56. James Brewer Stewart, 'The Emergence of Racial Modernity and the Rise of the White North, 1790–1840', *Journal of the Early Republic* 18, 2 (Summer 1998), pp. 181–217.

57. Josiah Nott, writing in Nott and George Glidden, *Types of Mankind* (Philadelphia: Lippincott, Grambo, 1854; Miami, Florida: Mnemosyne, 1969), pp. 50–2.

58. Lorimer, *Colour, Class*, pp. 15–16, 22, 31. On the continued existence of slavery itself within the British Isles until 1833, see p. 28.

59. Ibid., pp. 45–57, 137–9, 158–9.

60. Mark Francis, 'The "Civilizing" of Indigenous People in Nineteenth-Century Canada', *Journal of World History* 9, 1(1998), pp. 51–87 at pp. 56, 60–3. Thomas C. Holt has explored the French vs. English 'racial' question in the aftermath of the Canadian Rebellions of 1837–8, and how the Canadian-derived idea of race-as-colonial-faction took on black-vs.-white overtones among British officials in dealing with Jamaica after 1850—Holt, *The Problem of Freedom: Race, Labor, and Politics in Jamaica and Britain, 1832–1938* (Baltimore, Maryland: Johns Hopkins University Press, 1992), pp. 236–43.

61. Bolt, *Victorian Attitudes to Race*, pp. 2, 7–9, 13–19; Lorimer, *Colour, Class*, pp. 134–40; Stocking, *Victorian Anthropology*, pp. 63–9; Stepan, *The Idea of Race in Science*, pp. 44–6; Kidd, *Forging Races*.

62. Patricia Anderson, *The Printed Image and the Transformation of Popular Culture, 1790–1860* (Oxford: Clarendon Press, 1991). Illustrations of the empire from older and more expensive books were reprinted for a mass audience and sold cheaply in the thirty-six numbers of the *Imperial Gazetteer*, whose first edition came out from 1850 to 1855—see Michael Hancher, 'An Imagined World: *The Imperial Gazetteer*', in Julie F. Codell (ed.), *Imperial Cohistories: National Identities and the British and Colonial Press* (Madison, New Jersey: Fairleigh Dickenson University Press, 2003), pp. 45–67. On those earlier images themselves, see Kay Dian Kriz, *Slavery, Sugar, and the Culture of Refinement: Picturing the British West Indies, 1700–1840* (New Haven, Connecticut: Yale University Press, 2008).

63. Marcus Wood, *Blind Memory: Visual Representation of Slavery in England and America, 1780–1865* (London: Routledge, 2000), pp. 162–83.

64. Richard Burton, *The Lake Regions of Central Africa: A Picture of Exploration*, 2 vols (1860; New York: Horizon Press, 1961), I, p. 304, II, pp. 20, 278, 324–8.

65. Patrick Brantlinger, 'Victorians and Africans: The Genealogy of the Myth of the Dark Continent', *Critical Inquiry* 12:1 (Autumn 1985), pp. 166–203; Andrew Porter, *Religion Versus Empire?: British Protestant Missionaries and Overseas Expansion, 1700–1914* (Manchester: Manchester University Press, 2004), pp. 157–9; Philip D. Curtin, *The Image of Africa: British Ideas and Action, 1780–1850* (Madison: University of Wisconsin Press, 1964), pp. 324–8.

66. Lorimer, *Colour, Class*, pp. 67–70, 75–6, 81–90; Christine Bolt, 'Race and the Victorians', in C.C. Eldridge (ed.), *The British Empire in the Nineteenth Century* (Houndsmills, Basingstoke, England: Macmillan, 1984), pp. 126–47; Ellingson, *The Myth of the Noble Savage*, pp. 243–7; Richard Altick, *The Shows of London: A Panoramic History of Exhibitions, 1600–1862* (Cambridge, Massachusetts: Belknap Press, 1978), pp. 268–87; Kathryn Castle, 'The Representation of Africa in Mid-Victorian Children's Magazines', pp. 145–58, in Gretchen Holbrooke Gerzina (ed.), *Black Victorians/Black Victoriana* (New Brunswick, New Jersey: Rutgers University Press, 2003); Catherine Hall, *Civilising Subjects: Metropole and Colony in the English Imagination, 1830–1867* (Chicago: University of Chicago Press, 2002), pp. 203–4, 216, 273–84, 320–2, 332–3, 354–8; Zine Magubane, *Bringing the Empire Home: Race, Class, and Gender in Colonial South Africa* (Chicago: University of Chicago Press, 2004), Chapter 3; Judie Newman, 'The Afterlife of *Dred* on the British Stage', in Denise Kohn, Sarah Meer, and Emily B. Todd (eds), *Transatlantic Stowe: Harriet Beecher Stowe and European Culture* (Iowa City: University of Iowa Press, 2006), pp. 208–24, especially p. 210. An older tradition of black characters on the London stage, in which they were portrayed more nobly, was in decline by the 1830s—Felicity A. Nussbaum, 'The Theatre of Empire: Racial Counterfeit, Racial Realism', in Kathleen Wilson (ed.), *A New Imperial History: Culture, Identity, and Modernity in Britain and the Empire, 1660–1840* (Cambridge: Cambridge University Press, 2004), pp. 71–90; Hazel Waters, *Racism on the Victorian Stage: Representation of Slavery and the Black Character* (Cambridge: Cambridge University Press, 1977), pp. 43, 98–118, 125–9. For the rise of blackfaced minstrel buskers starting in the late 1840s, see George F. Rehin, 'Blackface Street Minstrels in Victorian London and Its Resorts: Popular Culture and Its Racial Implications as Revealed in Polite Opinion', *Journal of Popular Culture* 15, 1 (Summer 1981), pp. 19–38, esp. p. 22.

67. Lorimer, *Colour, Class*, pp. 112–13; Catherine Hall, 'The Nation Within and Without', in Catherine Hall, Keith McClelland, and Jane Rendall, *Defining the Victorian Nation: Class, Race, Gender, and the Reform Act of 1867* (Cambridge: Cambridge University Press, 2000), pp. 179–233. See also Hugh A. MacDougall, *Racial Myth in English History: Trojans, Teutons, and Anglo-Saxons* (Montreal: Harvest House, 1982); Bernard Semmel, 'The Issue of "Race" in the British Reaction to the Morant Bay Uprising of 1865', *Caribbean Studies* 2, 3 (October 1962), pp. 3–15 at p. 14. For the later career of Anglo-Saxondom as a political as well as a racial concept, see Duncan Bell, *The Idea of Greater Britain: Empire and the Future of World Order, 1860–1900* (Princeton, New Jersey: Princeton University Press, 2007), especially pp. 113–19.

68. Peter Mandler, '"Race" and "Nation" in Mid-Victorian Thought', in Stefan Collini, Richard Whatmore, and Brian Young (eds), *History, Religion, and*

Culture: British Intellectual History, 1750–1950 (Cambridge: Cambridge University Press, 2000), pp. 222–44 at pp. 226–9.

69. Hall, *Civilising Subjects*, pp. 210–21, 349–53, 358–62, 374, 385.
70. David Livingstone, *Travels and Researches in South Africa* (Philadelphia: J.W. Bradley, 1858).
71. Anthony Trollope, *The West Indies and the Spanish Main*, 2nd edn (London: Chapman and Hall, 1860; facsimile edn, London: Frank Cass, 1968), pp. 59, 61–2.
72. Stepan, *The Idea of Race in Science*, pp. 45–6.
73. For the officials, see Edward Beasley, *Mid-Victorian Imperialists: British Gentlemen and the Empire of the Mind* (London: Routledge, 2005), pp. 76–80, 82–8, 145; for the writers, the scholarly literature is huge, but one précis is Michael Banton, *The Idea of Race* (London: Tavistock, 1977), pp. 18–26. For popular ideas of whether the Irish were a race in the physical sense, which seem to have come well after 1850, see D.G. Paz, 'Anti-Catholicism, Anti-Irish Stereotyping, and Anti-Celtic Racism in Mid-Victorian Working-Class Periodicals', *Albion* 18, 4 (Winter 1986), pp. 601–16 at pp. 613–16.
74. David Arnold, 'Race, Place and Bodily Difference in Early Nineteenth-Century British India', *Historical Research* 77, 196 (May 2004), pp. 254–75; see also Mark Harrison, *Climates and Constitutions: Health, Race, Environment and British Imperialism in India, 1600–1850* (Oxford: Oxford University Press, 1999), pp. 104–112; Susan Bayly, 'Caste and "Race" in the Colonial Ethnography of India', in Peter Robb (ed.), *The Concept of Race in South Asia* (Delhi: Oxford University Press, 1995), pp. 165–218; Crispin Bate, 'Race, Caste, and Tribe in Central India: The Early Origins of Indian Anthropometry', in Robb (ed.), *The Concept of Race in South Asia*, pp. 219–251; Francis Hutchins, *The Illusion of Permanence: British Imperialism in India* (Princeton, New Jersey: Princeton University Press, 1970), pp. 61–73; Uday Singh Mehta, *Liberalism and Empire: A Study in Nineteenth-Century British Liberal Thought* (Chicago: University of Chicago Press, 1999), pp. 15–16; Hall, *Civilising Subjects*, p. 371; Marriott, *The Other Empire*, p. 160.
75. Alan Lester, 'British Settler Discourse and the Circuits of Empire', *History Workshop Journal* 54 (Autumn 2002), pp. 24–48. On recent work on the development of local sets of knowledge and local ways of categorizing the world in different colonial situations, see Tony Ballantyne, 'Empire, Knowledge, and Culture: From Proto-Globalization to Modern Globalization', in A.G. Hopkins (ed.), *Globalization in World History* (New York: W.W. Norton, 2002), pp. 116–40 at pp. 130–3.
76. Henry Reynolds, 'Racial Thought in Early Colonial Australia', *Australian Journal of Politics and History* 20, 1 (1974), pp. 25–53.
77. Clifton Crais, *White Supremacy and Black Resistance in Pre-Industrial South Africa, 1770–1865* (Cambridge University Press, 1992), pp. 126–8; Andrew Bank, 'Losing Faith in the Civilizing Mission: The Premature Decline of Humanitarian Liberalism at the Cape, 1840–1860', in Daunton and Halpern (eds), *Empire and Others*, pp. 364–83; Richard Price, *Making Empire: Colonial Encounters and the Creation of Imperial Rule in Nineteenth-Century South Africa* (Cambridge University Press, 2008), pp. 127–9, 155–6. David Livingstone, for one, resisted this harder idea of race in Southern Africa, as shown in Christopher Petrusic, 'Violence as Masculinity: David Livingstone's Radical Racial Politics in the Cape Colony and the Transvaal, 1845–1852', *International History Review* 26, 1 (March 2004), pp. 20–55. For the disillusioned missionaries of Jamaica rethinking their flocks, see Hall, *Civilising Subjects*, pp. 98, 245–52, 375, and for an earlier example, from 1847, see pp. 343–5. For the racism of missionary disappointment beyond Southern

Africa and Jamaica, see Alison Twells, *The Civilising Mission and the English Middle Class, 1792–1850* (Basingstoke: Palgrave Macmillan, 2009), pp. 13–15, 203–5.
78. Stocking, *Victorian Anthropology*, pp. 63–8; Lorimer, *Colour, Class*, p. 135; Bolt, *Victorian Attitudes to Race*, pp. 11–14.
79. Young, *Colonial Desire*, p. 136.
80. C.F. Beckingham, 'A History of the Royal Asiatic Society, 1823–1973', in Stuart Simmonds and Simon Digby (eds), *The Royal Asiatic Society: Its History and Treasures* (Leiden and London: E.J. Brill, 1979), pp. 1–77 at pp. 65–6.
81. Hall, *Civilising Subjects*, pp. 399–400.
82. Stocking, *Victorian Anthropology*, pp. 246–53; idem., 'What's in a Name?: The Origins of the Royal Anthropological Institute, 1837–71', *Man*, new series, 6, 3 (September 1971), pp. 369–90; Ronald Rainger, 'Race, Politics, and Science: The Anthropological Society of London in the 1860s', *Victorian Studies* 22, 1 (Autumn 1978), pp. 51–70.
83. [Richard Burton], *Wanderings in West Africa from Liverpool to Fernando Po* (2 vols, London: Tinsley Brothers, 1863; facsimile edn in one volume, New York: Dover, 1991), I, pp. 176–9, 208–9; Dane Kennedy, *The Highly Civilized Man: Richard Burton and the Victorian World* (Cambridge, Massachusetts: Harvard University Press, 2005), pp. 48–51, 115–16, 131–7, and 140–60.
84. Ter Ellingson, *Myth of the Noble Savage* (Berkeley and Los Angeles: University of California Press, 2001), pp. 253–6; Robert J.C. Young, *Colonial Desire: Hybridity in Race, Theory, and Culture* (London: Routledge, 1995), pp. 125–6, 133–9; Robert E. Bonner, 'Slavery, Confederate Diplomacy, and the Racialist Mission of Henry Hotze', *Civil War History* 51, 3 (2005), pp. 218–316. Bonner notes that Josiah Nott commissioned the young Swiss immigrant to translate Gobineau, when Hotze was working as a tutor on an Alabama plantation.
85. Earl de Grey and Ripon [George Frederick Samuel Robinson], 'Address to the Royal Geographical Society of London', *Proceedings of the Royal Geographical Society of London* 4, 4 (28 May 1860), pp. 117–209 at pp. 186–7.
86. Semmel, 'The Issue of "Race" in the British Reaction to the Morant Bay Uprising of 1865', pp. 5–6; Hall, *Civilising Subjects*, pp. 407–12; Gad Heuman, *The Killing Time: The Morant Bay Rebellion in Jamaica* (Knoxville, Tennessee: University of Tennessee Press, 1994), pp. 118–28.
87. Charles Darwin, *The Origin of Species by Means of Natural Selection, or the Preservation of Favoured Races in the Struggle for Life* (London: John Murray, 1869), pp. 489–90. Prichard had believed the same thing, at least part of the time: Stocking, Introduction to Prichard's *Researches*, p. lxxix.
88. Peter Nichols, *Evolution's Captain* (New York: Perennial, 2004), pp. 95, 221.
89. Paz, 'Anti-Catholicism', p. 614. Mainstream phrenologists rejected the idea that the head could be reshaped in this way, but phrenology had no central authority to enforce mainstream opinion. Phrenological ideas of various stripes percolated through society—leading to early speculation (as early as the 1840s, which was early for England) about racial typologies based upon alleged shapes of the skull. See David de Giustino, *Conquest of Mind: Phrenology and Victorian Social Thought* (London: Croom Helm; Totowa, New Jersey: Rowman and Littlefield, 1975), pp. 21–3, 69–71, 78–80, 88–91, 185; Paul Turnbull, 'British Anatomists, Phrenologists, and the Construction

of the Aboriginal Race, c. 1790–1830', *History Compass* 5, 1 (2007), pp. 26–50.
90. Hall, *Civilising Subjects*, p. 354.
91. [Robert Chambers], *Vestiges of the Natural History of Creation* (London: John Churchill, 1844; photographic reprint, Leicester: Leicester University Press, 1969), pp. 277–84, 294–7, 305–10. Later editions cite Prichard explicitly: Robert Chambers, *Vestiges of the Natural History of Creation, with a Sequel* (New York: Harper and Brothers, [1857]), pp. 142–6, 151–2, 158–60. For the book's wide sale, see James A. Secord, *Victorian Sensation: The Extraordinary Publication, Reception, and Secret Authorship of 'Vestiges of the Natural History of Creation'* (Chicago: University of Chicago Press, 2000), pp. 123–32 and subsequent chapters.
92. Charles Dilke, *Greater Britain: A Record of Travel in English-Speaking Countries*, 2 vols (London: Macmillan, 1868), I, pp. 124, 130, 135, II, p. 114; for the easier-to-find one-volume edition, Charles Dilke, *Greater Britain: A Record of Travel in English-Speaking Countries*, 7th edn (London: Macmillan, 1880), pp. 84, 88, 92, 369.
93. David N. Livingstone, 'Human Acclimatization: Perspectives on a Contested Field of Enquiry in Science, Medicine, and Geography', *History of Science* 25 (1987), pp. 359–94; and Peter Bowler, *The Eclipse of Darwinism* (Baltimore: Johns Hopkins University Press, 1983), pp. 58–98.
94. Beyond the issue of the separateness and stability of human races, there were still differences in national approach. See Staum, *Labeling People*, pp. 165–7, 178–86; Andrew Zimmerman, *Anthropology and Antihumanism in Imperial Germany* (Chicago: University of Chicago Press, 2001), pp. 66–70, 136–46.
95. Lorimer, *Colour, Class*, pp. 140–1, 173, 202–3; Young, *Colonial Desire*, pp. 118–23. For some thoughts on the way colonial racism came home to roost in British metropolitan racial attitudes in the second half of the nineteenth century, see Douglas Lorimer, 'Reconstructing Victorian Racial Discourse', in Gerzina (ed.), *Black Victorians/Black Victoriana*, pp. 187–207, especially pp. 190, 194.
96. Heather Streets, *Martial Races: The Military, Race, and Masculinity in British Imperial Culture, 1857–1914* (Manchester: Manchester University Press, 2004).
97. For the Archbishop of Dublin, Richard Whately, the Peruvians had probably been civilized by a white man from the east—Whately, 'Of the Origins of Civilization', in *Lectures Delivered before the Young Men's Christian Association in Exeter Hall*, vol. 10, *1854–1855* (London: James Nisbet, 1855), pp. 3–36 at p. 13.
98. For Africa, where even the city of Great Zimbabwe was thought to have been built by Caucasians from the far north: Edith R. Sanders, 'The Hamitic Hypothesis: Its Origin and Functions in Time Perspective', *Journal of African History* 10, 4 (1969), pp. 521–32; Philip S. Zachernuk, 'Of Origins and Colonial Order: Southern Nigerian Historians and the "Hamitic Hypothesis" c. 1870–1970', *Journal of African History* 35, 3 (1994), pp. 427–55; V.Y. Mudimbe, *The Invention of Africa: Gnosis, Philosophy, and the Order of Knowledge* (Bloomington and Indianapolis: Indiana University Press; London: James Currey, 1988), pp. 13–14; Ole Bjørn Rekdal, 'When Hypothesis Becomes Myth: The Iraqi Origin of the Iraqw', *Ethnology* 37, 1 (Winter 1998), pp. 17–38; Curtin, *Image of Africa*, pp. 256–8. For India: Thomas R. Trautmann, *Aryans and British India* (Berkeley and Los Angeles: University of California Press, 1997), pp. 194, 199–215; Ronald Inden, *Imagining India* (Oxford: Blackwell, 1990), pp. 59–65; Romila Thapar, 'The Theory of

Aryan Race and India: History and Politics', *Social Scientist* 24, 1–3 (January-March 1996), pp. 3–29; Peter Heehs, 'Shades of Orientalism: Paradoxes and Problems in Indian Historiography', *History and Theory* 20, 3 (1986), pp. 169–75 at pp. 172, 175, 184–7. For Europe, an Indo-European movement into Greece is accepted among scholars today. Yet the idea originated in the nineteenth century, before any archaeological evidence for it had been found. And in its earlier forms, the theory posited a 'white' race coming into Greece from the north: Robert Drews, *The Coming of the Greeks: Indo-European Conquests in the Aegean and Near East* (Princeton, New Jersey: Princeton University Press, 1988), pp. 3–10, 25–8; J.P. Mallory, 'A Short History of the Indo-European Problem', *Journal of Indo-European Studies* 1 (1973), pp. 21–65 at pp. 30–9.

99. As with the work of A.H. Keane and A.C. Haddon—see Lorimer, 'Theoretical Racism', pp. 425–8.

100. William Denison, 'On Permanence of Type in the Human Race', *Journal of the Ethnological Society of London* (23 March 1869), pp. 194–8.

101. See, for example, certain articles by Edward Freeman in 1877, as discussed in George Watson, *The English Ideology: Studies in the Language of Victorian Politics* (London: Allen Lane, 1973), pp. 198, 204. For anti-'race' writers and agitators in the 1890s, see Lorimer, 'Theoretical Racism', pp. 200–1.

102. For a discussion of how the continuum of humanity was forced, after 1860, into a few 'pure' races and the supposedly quantifiable degrees of hybridization between them, see Nancy Lys Stepan, *Picturing Tropical Nature* (London: Reaktion Books, 2001), pp. 85–94, 111–17, 139–42.

103. Stocking, *Race, Culture, and Evolution*, pp. 57–63; Stepan, *The Idea of Race in Science*, pp. 96–104; Stephen Jay Gould, *The Mismeasure of Man* (New York: W.W. Norton, 1981), pp. 73–107; Lorimer, 'Theoretical Racism in Late Victorian Anthropology', pp. 418–26.

104. Luigi Luca Cavalli-Sforza, *Genes, Peoples, and Languages*, Mark Seielstad (trans.) (Berkeley and Los Angeles: University of California Press, 2000), pp. 12–31.

105. Snait B. Gissis, 'When Is "Race" a Race? 1946–2003', *Studies in History and Philosophy of Science Part C: Studies in History and Philosophy of Biological and Biomedical Sciences* 39, 4 (December 2008), pp. 437–450.

106. Joseph. L Graves, Jr., *The Emperor's New Clothes: Biological Theories of Race at the Millennium* (New Brunswick, New Jersey: Rutgers University Press, 2001), pp. 173–92; James Kingsland, 'Colour-Coded Cures', *New Scientist* 186, 2503 (11 June 2005), pp. 42–7; Guido Barbujani and Elise M.S. Belle, 'Genomic Boundaries between Human Populations', *Human Heredity* 61 (2006), pp. 15–21; Jonathan Kahn, 'Race in a Bottle', *Scientific American* 297, 2 (August 2007), pp. 40–5; Lundy Braun, Anne Fausto-Sterling, Duana Fullwiley, Evelynn M. Hammonds, Alondra Nelson, William Quivers, Susan M. Reverby, and Alexandra E. Shields, 'Racial Categories in Medical Practice: How Useful Are They?', *PLoS Medicine* 4, 9 (September 2007), pp. 1423–8. The opposite case, that races are good enough for clinical use in predicting drug interference—and that because people are different in some ways race has some biological basis—is made in Stephanie Malia Fullerton, 'On the Absence of Biology in Philosophical Considerations of Race', in Shannon Sullivan and Nancy Tuana (eds), *Race and Epistemologies of Ignorance* (Albany: State University of New York Press, 2007), pp. 241–58. But as Gissis shows in his 2008 study, the data are more meaningfully grouped and they show greater clumping when people are sorted by socioeconomic class or environmental conditions, as in the United Kingdom. Gissis also explains *why* the American data are sorted by race; rather than this way of classifying

people coming out of American science, racial categories were mandated by the National Institutes of Health for political reasons—Gissis, 'When is "Race" a Race? 1946–2003'. See also Duana Fullwiley, 'The Molecularization of Race: U.S. Health Institutions, Pharmacogenetics Practice, and Public Science after the Genome', in Barbara A. Koenig, Sandra Soo-Jin Lee, and Sarah S. Richardson (eds), *Revisiting Race in a Genomic Age* (New Brunswick, New Jersey: Rutgers University Press, 2008), pp. 149–71.

107. Amy Harmon, 'In DNA Age, New Worries about Prejudice', *New York Times*, 11 November 2007. In his review of the 2004 book *Race: The Reality of Human Differences*, by Vincent Sarich and Frank Miele, the anthropologist Mark Nathan Cohen points out that the authors are so enamoured of the idea of continental racial groups that they ignore their own strong evidence, within their own book, showing that continental racial coherence is precisely *not* what they have found, whether for Africa or anywhere else. See Cohen, 'Race and IQ Again', *Evolutionary Psychology* 3 (2005), pp. 255–262. For a detailed critique of the practice of deriving continentalist conclusions from the genetic data fed into contemporary statistical software, see Deborah A. Bolnick, 'Individual Ancestry Inference and the Reification of Race as a Biological Phenomenon', in Koenig, Lee, and Richardson (eds), *Revisiting Race in a Genomic Age*, pp. 70–85.

108. Tracie Matysik, 'International Activism and Global Civil Society at the High Point of Nationalism: The Paradox of the Universal Races Congress, 1911', in A.G. Hopkins (ed.), *Global History: Interactions between the Universal and the Local* (New York: Palgrave Macmillan, 2006), pp. 131–59; Michelle Brattain, 'Race, Racism, and Anti-Racism: UNESCO and the Politics of Presenting Science to the Post-War Public', *American Historical Review* 112, 5 (December 2007), pp. 1386–1413; Elazar Barkan, 'The Politics of the Science of Race: Ashley Montagu and UNESCO's Anti-Racist Declarations', in Larry T. Reynolds and Leonard Lieberman (eds), *Race and Other Misadventures: Essays in Honor of Ashley Montagu in His Ninetieth Year* (Dix Hills, New York: General Hall, 1996), pp. 96–105; idem., *The Retreat of Scientific Racism: Changing Concepts of Race in Britain and the United States between the World Wars* (Cambridge University Press, 1992), pp. 76–95.

109. W.E.B. DuBois, *Dusk to Dawn* [1940], in *W.E.B. DuBois: Writings*, Nathan Huggins (ed.) (New York: Library of America, 1986), pp. 549–802 at pp. 625–7, 639–40—quotation at p. 627. See also idem., 'The Conservation of Races', American Negro Academy Occasional Papers no. 2, 1897, in the same volume, at pp. 815–26; in this piece DuBois reflects the acceptance of physical racial difference typical of the late nineteenth century.

110. DuBois, *Dusk to Dawn*, pp. 665–6; Anthony Appiah, 'The Uncompleted Argument: DuBois and the Illusion of Race', in Gates (ed.), *"Race," Writing, and Difference*, pp. 21–37; Tommy Lott, 'DuBois's Anthropological Notion of Race', in Bernasconi (ed.), *Race*, pp. 59–83; Daniel G. Williams, *Ethnicity and Cultural Authority from Arnold to DuBois* (Edinburgh: Edinburgh University Press, 2006), Chapter 4, especially pp. 204–7. For the racist ideas that DuBois faced in the late nineteenth and early twentieth centuries, and the humanity of his response to these inhuman categorizations, see Edward J. Blum, *W.E.B. DuBois: American Prophet* (Philadelphia: University of Pennsylvania Press, 2007), pp. 51, 70–81, 123.

111. Jordan, *White over Black*, pp. 592–5 ('Note on the Concept of Race'); for a slightly later example, Watson, *The English Ideology*, p. 199. For Philip Curtin in *The Image of Africa* [1964], races are natural and obvious categories that really exist: 'there is the simple and unavoidable fact that major racial differences are recognizable. In every racially mixed society, in every

contact between people who differ in physical appearance, there has always been instant recognition of race: it was the first determinant of intergroup relations' (p. 28; see also pp. 227–8; cf. p. 84 n. 58 for modern science giving him some pause in his views). When his eighteenth- and early nineteenth-century Englishmen do not seem to notice the obviously key fact of race, he faults them for it (pp. 52–6, 115–16, cf. p. 243). Or he bridges the gaps in what *should be* the unbroken history of the idea of physical 'race' in England by (1) shifting over to French and German anatomists (Cuvier and his followers) and the very different tradition of French racism (pp. 230–1) when his English story runs dry; (2) shifting over to the American school of Samuel Morton (pp. 367–8, 371–2); (3) back in England, putting too much emphasis on the unusual opinions of Edward Long (pp. 43–6) and William Lawrence (pp. 231–2, 239–40) as though they were as influential as Prichard; and (4) reading W.F. Edwards as more or less English (pp. 235, 363) when he Franco-Belgian by education and career (p. 332).

112. Although the opposite of '*negro*' in the richly worked-out system of Colonial Spanish 'racial' categories' in their New World colonies was '*español*', not '*blanco*', as Nightingale has pointed out—Nightingale, 'Before Race Mattered', p. 62; Katzew, *Casta Painting.*

NOTES TO CHAPTER 2

1. Curtis Stokes, 'Tocqueville and the Problem of Racial Inequality', *Journal of Negro History* 75, 1/2 (Winter/Spring, 1990), pp. 1–15; August Nimtz, *Marx, Tocqueville, and Race in America: The 'Absolute Democracy' or 'Defiled Republic'* (Lanham, Maryland: Lexington Books, 2003), pp. 18–19. As Zetterbaum points out, Tocqueville sometimes records what his American informants thought about race, but he does so only to tear apart the very views that he is reporting—Marvin Zetterbaum, *Tocqueville and the Problem of Democracy* (Stanford, California: Stanford University Press, 1967), p. 26 n. 1. Zetterbaum was defending Tocqueville from the charges in Richard Resh, 'Alexis de Tocqueville and the Negro: *Democracy in America* Reconsidered', *Journal of Negro History* 48, 4 (October 1963), pp. 251–9.

2. David Reisman, 'Psychological Types and National Character: An Informal Commentary', *American Quarterly* 5, 4 (Winter 1953), pp. 325–43.

3. Tzvetan Todorov, *Nous et les autres: La réflexion française sur la diversité humaine* (Paris: Éditions du Seuil, 1989), pp. 219–34; idem., 'Introduction: Tocqueville et la doctrine coloniale', in Alexis de Tocqueville, *De la Colonie en Algérie* (Paris: Éditions Complexe, 1988), pp. 9–34; George M. Frederickson, in *The Comparative Imagination: On the History of Racism, Nationalism, and Social Movements* (Berkeley and Los Angeles: University of California Press, 1997), pp. 98–116; Cheryl B. Welch, 'Colonial Violence and the Rhetoric of Evasion: Tocqueville on Algeria', *Political Theory* 31, 2 (April 2003), pp. 235–64; Jennifer Pitts, *A Turn to Empire: The Rise of Imperial Liberalism in Britain and France* (Princeton, New Jersey: Princeton University Press, 2005), pp. 189–239.

4. Harry Liebersohn, *Aristocratic Encounters: European Travelers and North American Indians* (Cambridge: Cambridge University Press, 1998), pp. 102–6.

5. Ivan Hannaford, *Race: The History of an Idea in the West* (Washington, DC: Woodrow Wilson Center Press; and Baltimore: Johns Hopkins University Press, 1996), pp. 222–76; Michael Banton, *Racial Theories*, 2nd edn (Cambridge: Cambridge University Press, 1998), pp. 1–116.

6. Stokes, 'Tocqueville and the Problem of Racial Equality', pp. 5–6.
7. Frederickson, *The Comparative Imagination*, pp. 106, 108–111; Pitts, *A Turn to Empire*, pp. 9–11; and Melvin Richter, 'Tocqueville on Algeria', *The Review of Politics* 25, 3 (July 1963), pp. 362–98.
8. Richter, 'Tocqueville on Algeria', p. 372; Pitts, *A Turn to Empire*, pp. 196–8, 232; Jennifer Pitts, 'Empire and Democracy: Tocqueville and the Algeria Question', *Journal of Political Philosophy* 8, 3 (September 2000), pp. 295–318.
9. This narrative of a divergence between physiological racism in France and environmentalist ethnology in England owes much to Seymour Drescher, 'The Ending of the Slave Trade and the Evolution of European Scientific Racism', *Social Science History* 14, 3 (Autumn 1990), pp. 415–50 at pp. 425–31. See also idem., 'British Way, French Way: Opinion Building and Revolution in the Second French Slave Emancipation', *American Historical Review* 96, 3 (June 1991), pp. 709–34.
10. Alyssa Goldstein Sepinwall, *The Abbé Grégoire and the French Revolution: The Making of Modern Universalism* (Berkeley and Los Angeles: University of California Press, 2005), pp. 150–4, 172–4, 181–96.
11. Drescher, 'The Ending of the Slave Trade and the Evolution of European Scientific Racism', pp. 432–40; Philip Curtin, *The British Image of Africa: British Ideas and Action, 1780–1850* (Madison: University of Wisconsin Press, 1964); Martin S. Staum, *Labeling People: French Scholars on Society, Race, and Empire, 1815–1848* (Montreal and Kingston: McGill-Queen's University Press, 2003), pp. 136–50; William B. Cohen, *The French Encounter with Africans: White Response to Blacks, 1530–1880* (Bloomington, Indiana: Indiana University Press, 1980), pp. 181–94, 212–16; Sue Peabody, *'There are No Slaves in France': The Political Culture of Race and Slavery in the Ancien Régime* (New York: Oxford University Press, 1996), pp. 4, 60–9, 117–19, 122–3, 134–5.
12. Charles-Louis de Secondat, Baron de Montesquieu, *The Spirit of the Laws,* Anne M. Cohler, Basia Carolyn Miller, and Harold Samuel Stone (trans and eds) (Cambridge: Cambridge University Press, 1989), pp. 241–2 (Book XIV, sects. 12–13). Tocqueville read Montesquieu but surpassed him: Melvin Richter, 'The Uses of Theory: Tocqueville's Adaptation of Montesquieu' in idem. (ed.), *Essays in Theory and History: An Approach to the Social Sciences* (Cambridge, Massachusetts: Harvard University Press, 1970), pp. 74–102; Jean-Claude Lamberti, *Tocqueville and the Two Americas*, Arthur Goldhammer (trans.) (Cambridge, Massachusetts: Harvard University Press, 1989), pp. 14–19.
13. Tocqueville to Beaumont, 5 October 1828, in Tocqueville, *Ouevres Completes*, VIII, 1, pp. 47–71 at pp. 51–2.
14. Jardin, *Tocqueville*, p. 95; Schleifer, *The Making of Tocqueville's Democracy in America*, pp. 40, 78; Liebersohn, *Aristocratic Encounters*.
15. Ter Ellingson, *The Myth of the Noble Savage* (Berkeley and Los Angeles: University of California Press, 2001), pp. 111–17.
16. Tocqueville to Gobineau, 15 May 1852, in Alexis de Tocqueville, *The European Revolution and Correspondence with Gobineau*, John Lukacs (ed. and trans.) (Garden City, New York: Doubleday Anchor Books, 1959), p. 221.
17. On the nineteenth-century tradition of racism in France, see Henri Peyre, 'Three Nineteenth-Century Myths: Race, Nation, Revolution', in idem., *Historical and Critical Essays* (Lincoln, Nebraska: University of Nebraska Press, 1968), pp. 24–61 at pp. 25–34; Cohen, *The French Encounter with Africans*, pp. 218–38; Claude Blanckaert, 'On the Origins of French Ethnology: William Edwards and the Doctrine of Race', Susan Paulson and George W.

Stocking, Jr. (trans.), in Stocking (ed.), 'Bones, Bodies and Behavior Essays in Biological Anthropology', *History of Anthropology 5* (Madison, Wisconsin: University of Wisconsin Press, 1988), pp. 18–55; Elizabeth A. Williams, *The Physical and the Moral: Anthropology, Physiology, and Philosophical Medicine in France, 1750–1850* (Cambridge: Cambridge University Press, 1994), pp. 224–32; Staum, *Labeling People*. According to Françoise Mélonio, the young Tocqueville had read Augustin de Thierry on the subject of French Revolution—Mélonio, *Tocqueville and the French*, Beth G. Raps (trans.) (1993; Charlottesville, Virginia: University Press of Virginia, 1998), p. 8. For Tocqueville's passing references to some of the other members of the Académie, see Tocqueville to Beaumont, 1 July 1841, in Tocqueville, *Ouevres Completes*, VIII, 1, pp. 433–7 at pp. 435–6 and p. 435 n. 6.

18. Alexis de Tocqueville, *Writings on Empire and Slavery*, Jennifer Pitts (ed. and trans.) (Baltimore, Maryland: Johns Hopkins University Press, 2001), pp. xxix–xxxii, 198–226; Tocqueville, 'Report on Abolition to the Chamber of Deputies, 6 June 1839', given in Seymour Drescher (ed.), *Tocqueville and Beaumont on Social Reform* (New York: Harper & Row, 1968), pp. 98–136; and idem., 'On the Emancipation of Slaves', articles from *Le Siècle*, 1843, given in Drescher (ed.), *Tocqueville and Beaumont on Social Reform*, pp. 136–73; Cohen, *French Encounter with Africans*, pp. 194–9.

19. Alexis de Tocqueville, *De la démocratie en Amérique*, 2 vols (Paris: Librarie de Médicis, 1951), II, p. 3, author's translation [compare Alexis de Tocqueville, *Democracy in America*, Arthur Goldhammer (trans.) (New York: Library Classics of the United States, 2004), p. 483].

20. George Wilson Pierson, *Tocqueville in America* ([*Tocqueville and Beaumont in America*. 1938]; Baltimore: Johns Hopkins University Press, 1996), pp. 49, 78–80, 112–13, 401–2, 720–1, 727, 742–6; André Jardin, *Tocqueville: A Biography*, Lydia Davis with Robert Hemenway (trans.) (London: Peter Halban, 1988), pp. 200–1; Saguiv A. Hadari, *Theory in Practice in Tocqueville's New Science of Politics* (Stanford, California: Stanford University Press, 1989), pp. 86–8; Edward T. Gargan, 'Tocqueville and the Problem of Historical Prognosis', *American Historical Review* 68, 2 (January 1963), pp. 332–45.

21. Jardin, *Tocqueville*, pp. 178–9. A similar process of constructing questions, notebooks, and journals before travelling, using them in certain ways while travelling, and setting to work to make generalizations from the results once one is back home, is described in Harriet Martineau, *How to Observe Manners and Morals* [1838] (New Brunswick, New Jersey: Transaction, 1989), Chapter 6.

22. Seymour Drescher, 'Tocqueville and England', *Harvard Historical Monographs 55* (Cambridge, Massachusetts: Harvard University Press, 1964), pp. 13–14.

23. Drescher, *Tocqueville and England*, pp. 25–7; James T. Schleifer, *The Making of Tocqueville's Democracy in America* (Chapel Hill: University of North Carolina Press, 1980), pp. 62–9, 309 notes 15, 18.

24. Luigi Luca Cavalli-Sforza and Francesco Cavalli-Sforza, *The Great Human Diasporas: The History of Diversity and Evolution*, Susan Thorne (trans.) (Reading, Massachusetts: Helix Books, 1995), esp. pp. 106–25 and 226–44.

25. Tocqueville, *Démocratie*, II, pp. 23–4 [Goldhammer edn, p. 494].

26. Ibid., II, p. 26 [Goldhammer edn, p. 497].

27. Ibid., II, p. 27 [Goldhammer edn, p. 497].

28. Ibid., I, pp. 38–40 [Goldhammer edn, pp. 32–3].

29. Given in J.P. Mayer, *Alexis de Tocqueville: A Biographical Essay in Political Science*, M.M. Bozman and C. Hahn (trans.) (New York: Viking Press, 1940), p. 112.
30. Schleifer, *The Making of Tocqueville's Democracy in America*, pp. 66, 72, and 309 n 19.
31. Tocqueville, *Démocratie*, I, p. 483 [Goldhammer edn, pp. 366–7].
32. Ibid, I, pp. 485–7, 489–93 [Goldhammer edn, pp. 368–9, 371–4]. See also André Jardin, 'Alexis de Tocqueville, Gustave de Beaumont, et le problème de l'inégalité des races', in Pierre Guiral and Émile Temime (eds), *L'idee de race dans la pensée politique française contemporaine* (Paris: Centre National de la Recherche Scientifique, 1977), pp. 199–219.
33. Tocqueville, *Démocratie*, I, p. 530 [Goldhammer edn, p. 406].
34. Ibid., I, pp. 43, 563–5 [Goldhammer edn, pp. 35, 432–4].
35. Ibid., I, pp. 541, 563, II, p. 308 [Goldhammer edn, pp. 415–16, 432, 720].
36. Ibid., I, pp. 515, 536, 545–6 [Goldhammer edn, pp. 394, 411, 418–19].
37. Ibid., pp. 484–5 [Goldhammer edn, p. 367].
38. Nimtz, *Marx, Tocqueville, and Race in America*, p. 18.
39. Tocqueville, *Démocratie*, I, pp. 467–8, 484–5, 511, 530, 563–6, II, pp. 302–3 [Goldhammer edn, pp. 353, 367, 391, 406, 432–5, 715].
40. Pitts, *A Turn to Empire*, pp. 169–73, 199–200; George Stocking, *Victorian Anthropology* (New York: The Free Press, 1987), pp. 169–71.
41. Liebersohn, *Aristocratic Encounters*, p. 17.
42. Tocqueville, *Démocratie*, I, p. 498–9 [Goldhammer edn, p. 379].
43. Ibid., II, p. 455 [Goldhammer edn, p. 834].
44. Ibid., I, pp. 496–8 [Goldhammer edn, pp. 376–8].
45. Liebersohn, *Aristocratic Encounters*, pp. 4, 94.
46. Tocqueville, *Démocratie*, I, p. 496 [Goldhammer edn, p. 377].
47. Ibid., I, p. 501 [Goldhammer edn, pp. 381–2].
48. Ibid., I, pp. 514–15, 534–5 [Goldhammer edn, pp. 393–4, 410–11].
49. Ibid., I, p. 516 [Goldhammer edn, p. 394].
50. Ibid.
51. Margaret Kohn (like Lauren Janara) suggests that Tocqueville's racial views are clear only when one considers them in the context of Beaumont's novel *Marie, or Slavery in the United States*—Kohn, 'The Other America: Tocqueville and Beaumont on Race and Slavery', *Polity* 35, 2 (Winter 2002), pp. 169–93; Lauren Janara, 'Brothers and Others: Tocqueville and Beaumont, U.S. Genealogy, and Racism', *Political Theory* 32, 6 (December 2004), pp. 773–800. We have seen that *Democracy in America* itself makes a clear statement about race: That the racial prejudices of the *demos* had real and horrible effects on the outcome of the American democratic experiment.
52. Tocqueville, *Démocratie*, I, pp. 534–5 [Goldhammer edn, p. 410].
53. Michael J. Heffernan and Keith Sutton, 'The Landscape of Colonialism: The Impact of French Colonial Rule on the Algerian Rural Settlement Pattern, 1830–1987', in Chris Dixon and Michael Heffernan (eds), *Colonialism and Development in the Contemporary World* (London: Mansell, 1991) pp. 121–52 at pp. 123–7.
54. Michael J. Heffernan, 'The Parisian Poor and the Colonization of Algeria in the Second Republic', *French History* 3, 4 (December 1989), pp. 377–403 at pp. 380–2.
55. Jardin, *Tocqueville*, pp. 318–38.
56. From a Marxist position, one that finds fault with Tocqueville for his failure to support class revolution, the argument can be made that Tocquevillean liberalism was in any case no more than an ideology of disdain for the proletariat, so that Tocqueville's disdain for the Algerian proletariat should

not be surprising—Nimtz, *Marx, Tocqueville, and Race in America*, pp. 45, 59–60, 198. It is the liberals who feel most strongly the incongruity of Tocqueville's Algerian illiberalism—Mark Reinhardt, *The Art of Being Free: Taking Liberties with Tocqueville, Marx, and Arendt* (Ithaca, New York: Cornell University Press, 1997), pp. 87–8.

57. Stéphane Dion, 'Durham et Tocqueville sur la colonisation libérale', *Revue d'études canadiennes/Journal of Canadian Studies* 25, 1 (Spring 1990), pp. 60–77; David Clinton, *Tocqueville, Lieber, Bagehot: Liberalism Confronts the World* (New York: Palgrave Macmillan, 2003), pp. 31–2.

58. Frederickson, *The Comparative Imagination*, pp. 113–15.

59. Jardin, *Tocqueville*, pp. 62–3, 528.

60. Melvin Richter, 'Tocqueville on Algeria', *Review of Politics* 25, 3 (July 1963), pp. 362–98.

61. Roger Boesche, 'The Dark Side of Tocqueville: On War and Empire', *Review of Politics* 67, 4 (Fall 2005), pp. 737–52.

62. Richard Boyd, 'Tocqueville's Algeria', *Society* 38, 6 (September/October 2001), pp. 65–70.

63. Aurelian Craiutu, 'Tocqueville's Paradoxical Moderation', *Review of Politics* 67, 4 (Fall 2005), pp. 599–629 at pp. 604–5; idem., *Liberalism under Siege: The Political Thought of the French Doctrinaires* (Lanham, Maryland: Lexington Books, 2003), pp. 287–8; Alan S. Kahan, *Aristocratic Liberalism: The Social and Political Thought of Jacob Burckhardt, John Stuart Mill, and Alexis de Tocqueville* (New York: Oxford University Press, 1992).

64. Richard Boyd, *Uncivil Society: The Perils of Pluralism and the Making of Modern Liberalism* (Lanham, Maryland: Lexington Books, 2004), pp. 208–34.

65. Mourad Ali-Khodja, 'Tocqueville Orientaliste?: Jalons pour une réinterpretation de ses écrits et de son engagement en faveur de la colonisation française en Algérie', *French Colonial History* 7 (2006), pp. 77–96.

66. Michael Hereth, *Alexis de Tocqueville: Threats to Freedom in Democracy*, George Bogardus (trans.) (Durham, North Carolina: Duke University Press, 1986), pp. 161–3.

67. Welch, 'Colonial Violence and the Rhetoric of Evasion'.

68. Tocqueville, *Démocratie*, I, pp. 495–6, 536–47 [Goldhammer edn, pp. 376–7, 412–19].

69. Liebersohn, *Aristocratic Encounters*, p. 87. As Irving M. Zeitlin put it in a book designed for students, 'To Tocqueville, the races appeared "distinct" not so much as a result of their outward characteristics as of their education and culture'—Zeitlin, *Liberty, Equality, and Revolution in Alexis de Tocqueville* (Boston: Little, Brown, and Co., 1971) pp. 26–7.

70. Jennifer Pitts, 'Introduction', in Alexis de Tocqueville, *Alexis de Tocqueville: Writings on Empire and Slavery*, Jennifer Pitts (ed. and trans.) (Baltimore, Maryland: Johns Hopkins University Press, 2001), pp. xxxii, 5.

71. Kergolay's letters to Tocqueville from Algeria in the summer of 1830, given in Alexis de Tocqueville, *Oeuvres Complètes*, J.P. Mayer et al. (eds), 18 vols (Paris: Gallimard, 1952–2003), XIII, pp. 189–209.

72. Alexis de Tocqueville, 'First Letter on Algeria (23 June 1837)', in Tocqueville, *Alexis de Tocqueville: Writings on Empire and Slavery*, Pitts (ed.), pp. 5–13 at p. 6.

73. Ibid.

74. Ibid., pp. 7–8.

75. Ibid., p. 8.

76. Ibid., p. 9.

77. Ibid., pp. 10–13.

78. Tocqueville, 'First Letter on Algeria', p. 8.
79. Alexis de Tocqueville, 'Second Letter on Algeria (22 August 1837)', in Tocqueville, *Alexis de Tocqueville: Writings on Empire and Slavery*, Pitts (ed.), pp. 14–26 at p. 25.
80. Alexis de Tocqueville, 'Essay on Algeria (October 1841)', in Alexis de Tocqueville, *Alexis de Tocqueville: Writings on Empire and Slavery*, Pitts (ed.), pp. 59–116 at p. 59.
81. Boyd, 'Tocqueville's Algeria'.
82. Tocqueville, 'Essay on Algeria', pp. 70–3.
83. Welch, 'Colonial Violence and the Rhetoric of Evasion', pp. 236–7.
84. Alexis de Tocqueville, 'Travail sur l'Algérie (octobre 1841)', in Tocqueville, *Oeuvres*, vol. 1, André Jardin, Françoise Mélonio, and Lise Queffélec (eds) (Paris: Gallimard, 1992), pp. 691–759 at p. 752, translation by the author [Pitts edn: Tocqueville, 'Essay on Algeria', p. 111].
85. Alexis de Tocqueville, 'Notes to the Voyage to Algeria in 1841', given in Tocqueville, *Alexis de Tocqueville: Writings on Empire and Slavery*, Pitts (ed.), pp. 36–58 at p. 36.
86. Ibid., p. 37.
87. Ibid., pp. 39, 41, 52, 55.
88. Ibid., pp. 51–4.
89. Tocqueville, 'Essay on Algeria', p. 62.
90. Tocqueville, 'Notes to the Voyage to Algeria in 1841', p. 56.
91. Ali-Khodja, 'Tocqueville Orientaliste', p. 86.
92. Tocqueville, 'Essay on Algeria', p. 75 n.
93. Ibid., p. 76 n.
94. Ibid., pp. 72–3; Tocqueville, 'Travail sur l'Algérie', p. 707.
95. Tocqueville, 'Essay on Algeria', p. 61.
96. Ibid., pp. 59, 70–3, 83.
97. Todorov, *Nous et les autres*, p. 234; idem., 'Introduction: Tocqueville et la doctrine coloniale', pp. 33–4.
98. Craiutu, 'Tocqueville's Paradoxical Moderation', pp. 620–621; Mayer, *Alexis de Tocqueville*, pp. 145–7.
99. Tocqueville, 'Travail sur l'Algérie', p. 719 [Pitts edn: Tocqueville, 'Essay on Algeria', p. 83].
100. Hadari, *Theory in Practice*, 6–8; Robert T. Gannett, *Tocqueville Unveiled: The Historian and His Sources for the Old Regime and the Revolution* (Chicago: University of Chicago Press, 2003); Alan S. Kahan, 'Tocqueville and the French Revolution', *History & Theory* 45, 3 (October 2006), pp. 424–35 at pp. 428–30.
101. Alexis de Tocqueville, 'The Emancipation of the Slaves' [1843], given in Tocqueville, *Alexis de Tocqueville: Writings on Empire and Slavery*, Pitts (ed.), pp. 199–226 at p. 211.
102. Ibid., p. 213.
103. Ibid., pp. 212, 215.
104. Ibid., p. 199.
105. Ibid., pp. 201, 207.
106. I do not agree with Seymour Drescher's argument that Tocqueville was a racialist—Drescher, *Dilemmas of Democracy: Tocqueville and Modernization* (Pittsburgh: University of Pittsburgh Press, 1968), p. 276. When Tocqueville was looking for the sources of national character in *The Old Régime and the French Revolution* (1856), he continued to look through or around any stable, colour-based, or predictive idea of race—Alexis de Tocqueville, *L'Ancien Régime et la Révolution Française* [1856], J.P Mayer (ed.) (Paris: Gallimard, 1967), pp. 14, 133–4, 147–8, 157; Alexis de Tocqueville, *The*

Old Régime and the French Revolution, Stuart Gilbert (trans.) (New York: Anchor Books, 1955), pp. 72, 221, 241, 252–3.
107. Tocqueville, *Oeuvres Complètes*, Mayer edn, III, pp. 163–212.

NOTES TO CHAPTER 3

1. Arnold Rowbotham, *The Literary of Works of Count de Gobineau* (Paris: Librarie Ancienne Honoré Champion, 1929), p. 26.
2. Michael D. Biddiss, *Father of Racist Ideology: The Social and Political Thought of Count Gobineau* (New York: Weybright and Talley, 1970), pp. 12–16, 19; Rowbotham, *Literary Works of Gobineau*, pp. 4–9.
3. Biddiss, *Father of Racist Ideology*, pp. 19–43, 175–7, 268.
4. Ibid., pp. 51, 96–8.
5. André Jardin, *Tocqueville: A Biography*, Lydia Davis with Robert Hemenway (trans.) (London: Peter Halban, 1988), pp. 391, 431–2; Seymour Drescher, *Dilemmas of Democracy: Tocqueville and Modernization* (University of Pittsburgh Press, 1968), pp. 203–4; Biddiss, *Father of Racist Ideology*, p. 57.
6. Biddiss, *Father of Racist Ideology*, pp. 62–3, 82, 91, 111; Arthur de Gobineau, *Essai sur la inégalité des races humaines*, 5 vols (Paris: Firmin-Didot, 1853–5).
7. Arthur de Gobineau, *Essai sur la inégalité des races humaines* [1853–5], 2 vols (Paris: Firmin-Didot, 1940), II, p. 550—author's translation. The 1856 translation by Henry Hotze is unfaithful, twisting Gobineau into an apologist for the slave-owning class of the American South—whose society Gobineau thought just as degenerate as anyone else's. See Robert E. Bonner, 'Slavery, Confederate Diplomacy, and the Racialist Mission of Henry Hotze', *Civil War History* 51, 3 (2005), pp. 218–316 at pp. 291–4. The 1915 translation of Gobineau's *Essai* by Adrian Collins, which has been consulted by the present author, is of inconsistent quality, and it covers only the first volume of the original: Arthur de Gobineau, *The Inequality of Human Races*, Adrian Collins (trans.), (New York: G.P. Putnam's Sons, 1915). The Collins translation has been reprinted along with some newly translated fragments of Gobineau's last volume, in Arthur de Gobineau, *Selected Political Writings*, Michael D. Biddiss (ed.), Adrian Collins and Brian Nelson (trans.) (London: Jonathan Cape, 1970). Biddiss has changed Gobineau's chapter titles.
8. Ibid., I, p. v.
9. Ibid., I, pp. iii–iv; Alexis de Tocqueville, *De la démocratie en Amérique*, 2 vols (Paris: Librarie de Médicis, 1951), I, p. 38 [see also Alexis de Tocqueville, *Democracy in America*, Arthur Goldhammer (trans.) (New York: Library Classics of the United States, 2004), p. 32].
10. Gobineau, *Essai*, pp. iii–iv.
11. Ibid., I, p. iii.
12. Ibid., I, p. vi.
13. Ibid.
14. Ibid., I, p. vii.
15. Ibid.
16. Ibid., II, pp. 492–525, (Book VI, Chapter 7). For some of these speculations Gobineau cites the American, Morton. Some years later, certain native Americans in Newfoundland reminded Gobineau of the Aryan element among the population of Tehran (Gobineau had served as a diplomat in both Newfoundland and Iran)—Arthur de Gobineau, *Voyage à Terre-Neuve* [1861], *Literature des voyage* (Paris: Aux amateur des livres, 1989), IV, pp. 60–3.

After Gobineau had published his *Essay*, there arose in New Zealand an apparently independent school of thought holding that the Maori were Aryan and their religion Vedic. An earlier New Zealand tradition had connected the Maori to the Semites. See Tony Ballantyne, *Orientalism and Race: Aryanism and the British Empire* (Basingstoke: Palgrave, 2002), Chapters 2 and 4. Certain Maori nationalist leaders responded to the Maori-Aryan hypothesis with the belief that they were indeed Israelites, not Aryans—Ballantyne, Chapter 5, pp. 164–7.

17. Gobineau, *Essai*, I, pp. 222–3. For a discussion of Gobineau's tripartite racial scheme and his ideas on the mixing of 'blood', see Robert J.C. Young, *Colonial Desire: Hybridity in Race, Theory, and Culture* (London: Routledge, 1995), pp. 103–8. I would add that for Gobineau, racial mixing comes not only because whites are attracted to nonwhites, but because whites conquer nonwhites; and the larger the conquest empire, the more nonwhites there are to mix with. So whereas hybridity is a key concept for Gobineau, a key locus for him is the large empire, in which there is the normal, cosmopolitan range of sexual unions.

18. Gobineau, *Essai*, II, pp. 560–2.

19. Drescher, *Dilemmas of Democracy*, pp. 157–8, 171–4.

20. William B. Cohen, *The French Encounter with Africans: White Response to Blacks, 1530–1880* (Bloomington, Indiana: Indiana University Press, 1980), pp. 216–18, 238; Michael Banton, *The Idea of Race* (London: Tavistock, 1977), p. 41; Jean Boissel, *Gobineau (1816–1882): Un Don Quichote Tragique* (Paris: Hachette, 1981), p. 214.

21. Biddiss, *Father of Racist Ideology*, p. 99.

22. Martin S. Staum, *Labeling People: French Scholars on Society, Race, and Empire, 1815–1848* (Montreal and Kingston: McGill-Queen's University Press, 2003), pp. 101, 135–6, 148, 202–12; Biddiss, *Father of Racist Ideology*, pp. 106–7.

23. Drescher, 'The Ending of the Slave Trade and the Evolution of European Scientific Racism', pp. 432–40; Staum, *Labeling People*, pp. 136–50.

24. Claude Blanckaert, 'On the Origins of French Ethnology: William Edwards and the Doctrine of Race', Susan Paulson and George W. Stocking, Jr. (trans.), in Stocking (ed.), *Bones, Bodies and Behavior: Essays in Biological Anthropology*, History of Anthropology 5 (Madison, Wisconsin: University of Wisconsin Press, 1988), pp. 18–55.

25. Blanckaert, 'On the Origins of French Ethnology', pp. 25–6, 34–5, 45; Staum, *Labeling People*, pp. 129–30; Biddiss, *Father of Racist Ideology*, pp. 105–6; Léon Poliakov, *The Aryan Myth: A History of Racist and Nationalist Ideas in Europe*, Edmund Howard (trans.) (London: Chatto Heinemann, 1974), pp. 228–9, 233.

26. Gobineau, *Essai*, I, 106–22, 144–5; on Carus and others as possible precursors of Gobineau, see Banton, *Idea of Race*, pp. 36–44; Poliakov, *The Aryan Myth*, pp. 217–29.

27. Janine Buenzod, *La formation de le pensée de Gobineau et l'*Essai sur l'inégalité des races humaines (Paris: Librarie A.-G. Nizet, 1967), pp. 288–9, 327, 332, 339, 405, 601–9. Gobineau and Augustin Thierry were friends.

28. Gobineau, *Essai*, I, p. 8. Gobineau cites Prichard on this point. He also seems to say, elsewhere, that the propensity to kill people is a racial characteristic; one of his examples is the long-time habit of the Celtic peoples of descending on shipwrecked sailors—p. 44.

29. Ibid., I, pp. 18–21.

30. Ibid., I, p. 72 n., and see p. 21.

31. Ibid., I, p. 77.

32. Ibid., II, pp. 489–90.
33. Ibid., II, p. 492.
34. Ibid., II, pp. 530–2.
35. Ibid., II, p. 536.
36. Ibid., I, pp. 35–53 (Book I, Chapter 5).
37. Ibid., I, p. 35.
38. Ibid., I, p. 36.
39. Ibid., I, p. 36.
40. Ibid., I, p. 37.
41. Ibid., II, pp. 37–8.
42. Ibid., I, pp. 46–7. Elsewhere, Gobineau reiterated the idea that missionaries could civilize their charges—apart from mixing with them racially, p. 70.
43. Ibid., I, pp. 47–9.
44. Ibid., I, p. 22.
45. Ibid., I, pp. 23–4.
46. Ibid., I, pp. 158–67.
47. Ibid., I, pp. 88–9, 93–104.
48. Ibid., I, p. 184.
49. Ibid., I, pp. 185–6.
50. Ibid., I, p. 108.
51. Ibid., I, pp. 112–14.
52. Ibid., I, pp. 119–23, 137.
53. Ibid., I, pp. 112–20.
54. Ibid., I, pp. 115, 122n., 129–30, 134–5.
55. Ibid., I, p. 140.
56. Ibid., I, p. 149.
57. Ibid., I, pp. 123–4, 139.
58. Ibid., I, pp. 142–4, 149–50.
59. Ibid., I, p. 141.
60. Ibid., I, p. 153.
61. Ibid., I, p. 153 n. 2.
62. Ibid., I, pp. 153–4.
63. Ibid., I, p. 146, and pp. 150–5 *passim.*
64. Ibid., I, pp. 203–4, 212–13.
65. Ibid., I, p. 25.
66. Ibid., I, p. 86.
67. Ibid., I, p. 84.
68. Ibid., I, pp. 84–5.
69. Ibid., I, p. 86. That Gobineau assigns the male or female principle to different races is briefly discussed in Young, *Colonial Desire*, pp. 111–13.
70. Gobineau, *Essai*, I, p. 87.
71. Ibid., I, p. 90–1.
72. Ibid., I, pp. 88–92.
73. Ibid., II, p. 538.
74. Ibid., II, p. 561.
75. Ibid., II, pp. 562–3.
76. Jack Lively, *The Social and Political Thought of Alexis de Tocqueville* (Oxford: Oxford University Press, 1962), pp. 32–41, 64–5; Edward T. Gargan, 'Tocqueville and the Problem of Historical Prognosis', *American Historical Review* 68, 2 (January 1963), pp. 332–45; Saguiv A. Hadari, *Theory in Practice: Tocqueville's New Science of Politics* (Stanford, California: Stanford University Press, 1989), pp. 28–9, 46–50; Cheryl B. Welch, 'Tocqueville's Resistance to the Social', *History of European Ideas* 20 (2004), 83–107. For Tocqueville's impassioned justification of

the idea of the human freedom and the moral agency of adults, as opposed to Gobineau's idea that people are childish and must be manipulated, see Tocqueville to Gobineau, 24 January 1857, as discussed in Hugh Brogan, *Alexis de Tocqueville: A Life* (New Haven, Connecticut: Yale University Press, 2006), pp. 593–5.

77. Tocqueville to Gobineau, 11 October 1853, in Alexis de Tocqueville, *Oeuvres Complètes,* J.P. Mayer (ed.), (Paris: Gallimard, 1980), IX, pp. 199–201, translation the author's. A précis of the racial disagreement between Tocqueville and Gobineau in the 1850s is André Jardin, 'Alexis de Tocqueville, Gustave de Beaumont, et le problème de l'inégalité des races', in Pierre Guiral and Émile Temime, *L'idee de race dans la pensée politique française contemporaine* (Paris: Centre National de la Recherche Scientifique, 1977), pp. 199–219. An earlier exploration was Melvin Richter, 'The Study of Man—A Debate on Race: The Tocqueville-Gobineau Correspondence', *Commentary* 25, 2 (February 1958), pp. 151–60. An involved but less historically well-grounded treatment is James W. Ceaser, *Reconstructing America; The Symbol of America in Modern Thought* (New Haven, Connecticut: Yale University Press, 1997), pp. 87–105, 136–49—where the attempt to set up Gobineau as the proponent of a well worked-out (albeit unfortunate) form of political science renders the Frenchman's work in an overly modern, overly intellectual, and overly technical vocabulary. Ceaser also assumes that Gobineau was the first racist theorist, and fails to note or explore the inadequacies in Gobineau's use of evidence.

78. Tocqueville to Gobineau, 17 November 1853, in Tocqueville, *Oeuvres Complètes,* IX, pp. 201–4.

79. Ibid.

80. Tocqueville to Gobineau, 20 December 1853, in ibid., pp. 205–6.

81. Ibid., 17 November 1853, p. 202.

82. Ibid., 11 October 1853, pp. 199–201.

83. Ibid., 15 May 1852, pp. 197–8. The book that Tocqueville specifies is Pierre Flourens, *Histoire des travaux et des idées de Buffon* (1850).

84. See Michael D. Biddiss, 'History as Destiny: Gobineau, H.S. Chamberlain, and Spengler', *Transactions of the Royal Historical Society,* sixth series, 7 (1997), pp. 73–100.

85. Gobineau to Tocqueville, 20 March 1856, in Tocqueville, *Oeuvres Complètes,* pp. 257–62 at pp. 258–9.

86. Gobineau to Tocqueville, 15 January 1856, in ibid., pp. 246–57.

87. Ibid., 20 May 1857, pp. 281–4.

88. Tocqueville to Gobineau, in ibid., 24 January 1857, pp. 276–81. For explorations of Tocqueville and Gobineau's disagreement in the mid-1840s on the value of Christian morality for social progress, see Michael D. Biddiss, 'Prophecy and Pragmatism: Gobineau's Confrontation with Tocqueville', *Historical Journal* 13, 4 (1970), pp. 611–33; and Aristide Tessitore, 'Tocqueville and Gobineau on the Nature of Modern Politics', *Review of Politics* 67, 4 (Fall 2005), 631–57.

89. Tocqueville to Gobineau, 24 January 1857, in Tocqueville, *Oeuvres Complètes,* p. 276–8.

90. Gobineau to Tocqueville, 1 May 1856, in ibid., pp. 262–4.

91. Tocqueville to Gobineau, 30 July 1856, in ibid., pp. 265–9 at pp. 267–8.

92. Henri Peyre, 'Three Nineteenth-Century Myths: Race, Nation, Revolution', in idem., *Historical and Critical Essays* (Lincoln, Nebraska: University of Nebraska Press, 1968), pp. 24–61 at 34–6; Jacques Barzun, *Race: A Study in Superstition,* rev. edn (1937; New York: Harper and Row, 1965), pp. 61–2, 66–77.

NOTES TO CHAPTER 4

1. John Leopold, 'British Applications of the Aryan Theory of Race to India, 1850–1880', *English Historical Review* 89, 352 (July 1974), pp. 578–603; Thomas R. Trautmann, *Aryans and British India* (Berkeley and Los Angeles: University of California Press, 1997), pp. 168–86; Tony Ballantyne, *Orientalism and Race: Aryanism and the British Empire* (Basingstoke: Palgrave, 2002), Chapter 1.

2. Anonymous, 'Discussion of "On the Negro's Place in Nature"', by James Hunt', *Journal of the Anthropological Society of London* 2 (1864), pp. xv–lvi at pp. xv–xvi. Even some of his audience balked at some of his wilder points, and at the morality behind them—pp. xix–xxi.

3. George Stocking, *Victorian Anthropology* (New York: The Free Press, 1987), pp. 247–57; Ronald Rainger, 'Race, Politics, and Science: The Anthropological Society of London in the 1860s', *Victorian Studies* 22, 1 (Autumn 1978), pp. 51–70, at pp. 58–66. Hunt had been trained in speech therapy by his father, a tenant farmer. In 1856 the younger Hunt purchased a doctorate from the University of Geissen and opened a practice in speech therapy and breathing exercises. Among his clients were Charles Kingsley and Charles Dodgson—*Oxford Dictionary of National Biography*.

4. Nancy Stepan, *The Idea of Race in Science: Great Britain, 1800–1960* (New York: Archon Books, 1982), Chapter 2; George Stocking, 'What's in a Name?: The Origins of the Royal Anthropological Institute, 1837–71', *Man*, new series, 6, 3 (September 1971), pp. 369–90 at pp. 374–5.

5. Douglas Lorimer, *Colour, Class, and the Victorians: English Attitudes to the Negro in the Mid-Nineteenth Century* (Leicester: Leicester University Press, 1978), pp. 215–23. Lorimer's points about the presence and agency of people of African ancestry in Great Britain are reinforced in Ian Duffield, 'Skilled Workers or Marginalized Poor?: The African Population of the United Kingdom, 1812–52', *Immigrants and Minorities* 12, 3 (November 1993), pp. 49–87; and, for a slightly earlier period, Norma Myers, *Reconstructing the Black Past: Blacks in Britain, c. 1780–1830* (London: Frank Cass, 1996).

6. George Watson argued that the racial turn in major novels came in the 1860s—Watson, *The English Ideology: Studies in the Language of Victorian Politics* (London: Allen Lane, 1973), pp. 204–7.

7. Georgios Varouxakis, *Victorian Political Thought on France and the French* (Basingstoke: Palgrave, 2002), pp. 104–5. Varouxakis's reading of Bagehot on race—namely that Bagehot's early articles featured rigid ideas of race while his later work *Physics and Politics* denied them (pp. 117–18)—is quite the opposite of what I am arguing about Bagehot in this chapter and the next. Bagehot moved to race, not from it.

8. Thomas Arnold, *Introductory Lectures on Modern History* [1842], Henry Reed (ed.) (New York: D. Appleton, 1880), pp. 41–2.

9. Ibid.

10. Ibid., pp. 43–4.

11. Ibid. Robert J.C. Young focuses on the importance to Arnold of a blood tie between England and the ancient Romans, a blood tie that I believe Arnold explicitly denies—Young, *The Idea of English Ethnicity* (Malden, Massachusetts: Blackwell, 2008) pp. 26–7, 51.

12. Arnold, *Introductory Lectures*, pp. 45–6.

13. Ibid., pp. 46–8. For the importance of civilizational categories in Thomas Arnold's thought, see Sue Zemka, 'Spiritual Authority and the Life of Thomas Arnold', *Victorian Studies* 38, 3 (Spring 1995), pp. 429–62. Zemka

traces Arnold's idea of national character or 'race' to Barthold Niebuhr and the German idea of *bildung*—p. 440.

14. Thomas Arnold, 'Preface to the Third Volume of the Edition of Thucydides' [1835], given in *The Miscellaneous Works of Thomas Arnold, D.D.* (London: B. Fellowes, 1845; Farnborough, England: Gregg International Publishers, 1971), pp. 381–99 at p. 393.

15. Richard K. Barksdale, 'Thomas Arnold's Attitude toward Race', *Phylon Quarterly* 18:2 (1957), pp. 174–80.

16. Thomas Arnold, 'On the Social Progress of States' [1830], given in *The Miscellaneous Works of Thomas Arnold, D.D.* (London: B. Fellowes, 1845; Farnborough, England: Gregg International Publishers, 1971), pp. 81–111 at p. 106.

17. Ibid, 89–90.

18. Arnold, *Thucydides*, p. 396.

19. L.P. Curtis, Jr., *Anglo-Saxons and Celts: A Study of Anti-Irish Prejudice in Victorian England* (Bridgeport, Connecticut: Conference on British Studies at the University of Bridgeport, 1968), pp. 41–5.

20. For a discussion of these issues and the scholarly literature on them, see Vincent P. Pecora, 'Arnoldian Ethnology', *Victorian Studies* 41:3 (Spring 1998), pp. 355–79; see also Varouxakis, *Victorian Political Thought on France and the French*, pp. 106–11; and the pioneering analysis by Frederic Faverty, *Matthew Arnold the Ethnologist* (Evanston, Illinois: Northwestern University Press, 1951)—esp. pp. 35–7; Robert J.C. Young, *Colonial Desire: Hybridity in Race, Theory, and Culture* (London: Routledge, 1995), pp. 59–64, 82–9; idem., *The Idea of English Ethnicity*, pp. 140–55; and Matthew Arnold, 'A Persian Passion Play', *Cornhill Magazine* 24 (December 1861), pp. 668–87. The historian E.A. Freeman also began with a Thomas Arnoldian position and then developed a virulent colour-racism between the 1860s and the 1880s. He also took some of his racial thinking from Thierry, as Matthew Arnold did—C.J.W. Parker, 'The Failure of Liberal Racialism: The Racial Ideas of E.A. Freeman', *Historical Journal* 24, 4 (December 1981), pp. 825–46.

21. Philip D. Curtin, *The Image of Africa: British Ideas and Action, 1780–1850* (Madison: University of Wisconsin Press, 1964), pp. 375–6; Reginald Horsman, *Race and Manifest Destiny: The Origins of American Racial Antagonism* (Cambridge, Massachusetts: Harvard University Press, 1981), pp. 65–6.

22. For another believer in cultural races, the Birmingham Baptist preacher George Dawson, see Catherine Hall, *Civilising Subjects: Metropole and Colony in the English Imagination, 1830–1867* (Chicago: University of Chicago Press, 2002), pp. 365–70. As Hall shows, Dawson took his belief in the Romantic national 'races' of Europe from the revolutions of 1848 and from what Carlyle wrote on cultural groups before his infamous essay of 1849.

23. Robert Knox, *The Races of Man: A Fragment* (Philadelphia: Lea and Blanchard, 1850; Miami, Florida: Mnemosyne Publishing Company, 1969).

24. Philip F. Rehbock, *The Philosophical Naturalists: Themes in Early Nineteenth-Century British Biology* (Madison: University of Wisconsin Press, 1983), Chapter 2; Evelleen Richards, 'The "Moral Anatomy" of Robert Knox: The Interplay between Biological and Social Thought in Victorian Scientific Naturalism', *Journal of the History of Biology* 22, 3 (Fall 1989), pp. 373–436.

25. Young, *Colonial Desire*, pp. 75–80.

26. Knox, *Races of Men*, pp. 14, 52–3.

27. The idea that different human groups or races are indeed interfertile, thus confirming a shared humanity, was attested in the work of Prichard and was noted by his readers: [William Grove], 'Natural History of Man', *Blackwood's Edinburgh Magazine* 56 (September 1844), pp. 312–30 at pp. 313–14, 322–3. Young argues that the matter was brought up with some frequency from the 1840s: Young, *Colonial Desire*, pp. 6–18. The idea of interracial infertility was to be popularized after mid-century by Morton and Nott in the American north (starting in 1847) and Paul Broca in France (from 1856), although Broca admitted that he did not have enough evidence to be sure about it. Blanckaert, 'Of Monstrous Métis?: Hybridity, Fear of Miscegenation, and Patriotism from Buffon to Paul Broca', in Sue Peabody and Tyler Stovall (eds), *The Color of Liberty: Histories of Race in France* (Durham, North Carolina: Duke University Press, 2003), pp. 42–70 at pp. 46–50; George W. Stocking, Jr., *Race, Culture, and Evolution: Essays in the History of Anthropology* (New York: The Free Press, 1968), pp. 48–9; Cohen, *The French Encounter with Africans*, pp. 233–5.

28. Ralph Waldo Emerson, *English Traits* [1856], in *Emerson: Essays and Lectures*, Joel Porte (ed.) (New York: Library of America, 1983), pp. 763–936 at pp. 790–4—quotation at p. 793; Richard Altick, *The English Common Reader: A Social History of the Mass Reading Public, 1800–1900* (Chicago: University of Chicago Press, 1957), p. 204; Susan Castillo, ' "The Best of Nations?": Race and Imperial Destinies in Emerson's "English Traits" ', *Yearbook of English Studies* 34 (2004), pp. 100–111.

29. Knox, *Races of Men*, p. 66–9.

30. Ibid., p. 53, 78–9.

31. Ibid., pp. 53–5.

32. Ibid., pp. 52–3, 75–7, 95–9. Knox's focus on this point is one reason why I cannot agree with others, such as Robert J.C. Young (in *The Idea of English Ethnicity*, pp. 47–8, 71–86), that Knox was anywhere close to the mainstream of English writing on race. Young does note these aspects of Knox's thinking—p. 79.

33. Patrick Brantlinger, *Dark Vanishings: Discourse on the Extinction of Primitive Races, 1800–1930* (Ithaca, New York: Cornell University Press, 2003).

34. Knox, *Races of Men*, pp. 56–7.

35. Young, *The Idea of English Ethnicity*, pp. 87–93.

36. Young, *Colonial Desire*, pp. 126–33.

37. Peter Mandler, *The English National Character: The History of an Idea from Edmund Burke to Tony Blair* (New Haven, Connecticut: Yale University Press, 2006), pp. 74, 85. Mandler has a different reading than I will present here of the importance of race for Bagehot. Mandler minimizes how, in Bagehot's view, the 'cake of custom' and the inheritance of acquired characteristics lead to heritable racial differences (pp. 77–81). Robert J.C. Young, in *The Idea of English Ethnicity* (pp. 46–9), briefly corrects Mandler about Bagehot's focus on race. But then Young goes on to ridicule Mandler. Young says that Mandler's refusal to say that Knox's views were typical of English opinion proves that all that Mandler will admit is a '*soupçon*' of English racism (Young, p. 49). I stand with Mandler here; Knox was atypical of British opinion, which was nonetheless moving in a racist direction.

38. Knox, *Races of Men*, pp. 15–16, 228–35. The three-way splitting of the Germans was Knox's closest approach to orthodoxy. A similar idea, a two-way German-Slavonian split, in which the German identity reached north to include the Scandinavians, while the Slavonians were the different, darker people of southern Germany, was one of the favourite ideas of Prichard's disciple Robert Latham, and Latham credited Prichard for it: Robert Latham,

The Ethnology of the British Colonies and Dependencies (London: John van Voost, 1851), pp. 6–7. Latham nonetheless carefully rejected erecting racial categories; he also stressed that philological evidence about groups is limited by the way people have adopted the languages of others. He seems to be deliberately rejecting Knox: Latham, *The Germania of Tacitus, with Ethnological Dissertations and Notes* (London: Taylor, Walton, and Maberly, 1851), frontispiece map, and prolegomena, especially pp. i–ii, ix–xi, xvi, xxxvi–xxxviii. As the years went by, Latham was careful to reject any idea of a Germanic mind, or any other type of ethnic or racial mind: idem., *The Nationalities of Europe*, 2 vols (London: William H. Allen, 1863), pp. I, vi–viii, II, 304–5.

39. Prichard, quoted in [Grove], 'Natural History of Man', p. 324.

40. J.W. Burrow, *Evolution and Society: A Study in Victorian Social Theory* (Cambridge University Press, 1966) , pp. 149–52; Thomas R. Trautmann, *Aryans and British India* (Berkeley and Los Angeles: University of California Press, 1997), pp. 171–83, 194–7; Stocking, *Victorian Anthropology*, pp. 58–61.

41. John Crawfurd, 'On the Aryan or Indo-Germanic Theory', *Transactions of the Ethnological Society of London* 1 (1861), pp. 268–86 at p. 269.

42. (London: John Murray, 1863), pp. 455–7, 469, 505–6. See also Stephen Jay Gould, *Time's Arrow, Time's Cycle: Myth and Metaphor in the Discovery of Geological Time* (Cambridge, Massachusetts: Harvard University Press, 1987), Chapter 4.

43. Other members included Gladstone, who learned the word 'metaphysics' there, Lord Tennyson, and Cardinal Manning. William Irvine, *Apes, Angels, and Victorians: The Story of Darwin, Huxley, and Evolution* (New York: McGraw-Hill, 1955), pp. 251–8; Mrs. Russell Barrington, *The Works and Life of Walter Bagehot*, vol. 10, *The Life* (London: Longmans, Green, and Co., 1915), pp. 421–2; Alan Willard Brown, *The Metaphysical Society: Victorian Minds in Crisis, 1869–1880* (New York: Columbia University Press, 1947; New York: Octagon Books, 1973).

44. Henry Sumner Maine, *Ancient Law*, 2nd edn (London: John Murray, 1863); Burrow, *Evolution and Society*, pp. 161–4; John F. M'Clennon, *Primitive Marriage* (Edinburgh: Adam and Charles Black, 1865), pp. 7–8, 218, 308–11. And then there were the writings of the men who did *not* use the word. For Maudsley: Henry Maudsley, *The Physiology of Mind*, 2nd edn (London: Macmillan, 1868); idem., *Body and Mind* (London: Macmillan, 1870). For Huxley: Thomas Henry Huxley, *Evidence as to Man's Place in Nature* (New York: D. Appleton, 1863); idem., *On Our Knowledge of the Causes of the Phenomena of Organic Nature* (London: Robert Hardwicke, 1863); idem., *Lessons in Elementary Physiology*, 2nd edn (London: Macmillan, 1868); idem. and William Jay Youmans, *The Elements of Physiology and Hygiene* (New York: D. Appleton, 1868).

45. Edward Burnett Tylor, *Anahuac; or, Mexico and the Mexicans Ancient and Modern* (London: Longman, Green, Longman, and Roberts, 1861), p. 339; idem., *Researches into the Early History of Mankind* (London: John Murray, 1865), pp. 47, 68, 135, 223, 297, 326, for Aryans, and p. 3 for his program of cultural analysis; Stocking, *Victorian Anthropology*, pp. 235, 299–301; Frédéric Regard, 'The Catholic Mule: E.B. Tylor's Chimeric Perception of Otherness', *Journal of Victorian Culture* 12, 2 (2007), pp. 225–37.

46. John Lubbock, *The Origin of Civilization and the Primitive Condition of Man* (London: Longmans, Green, 1870; Chicago: University of Chicago Press, 1978), pp. 219–20; idem., *Primitive Man* (London: Williams and Norgate, 1865); Herbert Spencer, *Social Statics* (London: John Chapman, 1851); idem., *Principles of Psychology* (London: Longman, Brown, Green,

and Longmans, 1855); idem., *Principles of Psychology,* 2nd edn (London: Williams and Norgate, 1870); idem., *Education: Intellectual, Moral, Physical* (1860; London: G. Manwaring, 1861); idem., *Education: Intellectual, Moral, Physical* (1860; New York: D. Appleton, 1866); idem., *First Principles* (London: Williams and Norgate, 1862); idem., *First Principles,* 2nd edn (London: Williams and Norgate, 1867); idem., *First Principles,* 3rd edn (London: Williams and Norgate, 1870); idem., *Principles of Sociology,* 2nd edn (London: Williams and Norgate, 1877), 24 (§16), 46 (§24), 314 (§150), 319 (§151), 377 (§178), 593 (§262), 667 (§293n), 712 (§316), 730 (§319), 732 (§319), 760 (§327), 773 (§333), Appendix A, pp. l–m.

47. Robert Latham, *Descriptive Ethnology* [1859], reprinted as *Tribes and Races: A Descriptive Ethnology of Asia, Africa, & Europe,* 2 vols (Delhi: Cultural Publishing House, 1983). See especially vol. II, Chapters 4, 7, and 48. The book does show cultural racism—see vol. I, Chapter 1. Yet Latham explicitly rejected the idea of human biological races, and he explained that he therefore avoided the term 'race', as in his 1863 two-volume work *The Nationalities of Europe,* I, pp. vii–viii. This book, too, had no room in its structure or its discussion for Aryanism.

48. Robert Latham, 'On the Subjectivity of Certain Classes in Ethnology' [1853], reprinted in idem., *Opuscula: Essays Chiefly Philological and Ethnological* (London: Williams & Norgate, 1860), pp. 138–42.

49. He had made a similar point in *Man and His Migrations* (London: John van Voost, 1851), pp. 61–2.

50. In 1862 Latham would propose that the Indo-European languages did not originate in India and move north, but rather that they originated in Lithuania and moved south. That this idea would later come up among Aryan theorists in the 1880s, and then in Nazi Germany, does not in my view mean that Latham indulged in Aryanism—Robert Latham, *Elements of Comparative Philology* (London: Walton and Maberly, 1862), pp. 610–12; cf. Young, *The Idea of English Ethnicity,* pp. 76–7. Indeed, Latham was so resistant to Aryanism that with John Crawfurd he led the resistance to Friedrich Max Müller's Aryan theories in linguistics; perhaps Latham was wary of Aryanism because of Robert Knox's work. See Trautmann, *Aryans and British India,* pp. 178–80.

51. Latham, 'On the Subjectivity of Certain Classes in Ethnology', p. 140; idem., *Opuscula,* p. 190.

52. Alastair Buchan, *The Spare Chancellor: The Life of Walter Bagehot* (East Lansing, Michigan: Michigan State University Press, 1960), pp. 26–8.

53. George Stocking, introduction to James Cowles Prichard, *Researches into the Physical History of Man* [1813], George Stocking (ed.) (Chicago: University of Chicago Press, 1973), pp. lviii–xc; Hannah Augstein, *James Cowles Prichard's Anthropology: Remaking the Science of Man in Early Nineteenth-Century Britain* (Amsterdam: Editions Rodopi, 1999).

54. Quoted in [Grove], 'Natural History of Man', p. 322—see generally pp. 313–14, 320–3; Hall, *Civilising Subjects,* pp. 277–9; Stocking, *Victorian Anthropology,* pp. 50–3.

55. Barrington, *The Works and Life of Walter Bagehot,* vol. 10, *The Life,* pp. 84, 97–100, 178–180; Bagehot to T.W. Bagehot, 26 April 1842, given in Norman St. John-Stevas (ed.), *The Collected Works of Walter Bagehot,* 15 vols (London: The Economist, 1965–1986), XII, pp. 147–8; Buchan, *The Spare Chancellor,* p. 28.

56. Walter Bagehot, 'Letters on the French Coup de État of 1851', Letter 1, 'The Dictatorship' [8 January 1852, published in *Inquirer,* 10 January 1852], in *Collected Works,* IV, pp. 29–34 at p. 29.

57. Bagehot, 'Letters on the French Coup de État of 1851', Letter 1, 'The Dictatorship', IV, p. 33.
58. Ibid., pp. 30–1; Walter Bagehot, 'Letters on the French Coup de État of 1851', Letter 3, 'On the New Constitution of France and the Aptitude of the French Character for National Freedom' [20 January 1852, published in *Inquirer*, 24 January 1852], *Collected Works*, IV, pp. 45–53 at p. 47.
59. Bagehot, 'Letters on the French Coup de État of 1851', Letter 1, 'The Dictatorship', IV, pp. 32–3.
60. Walter Bagehot, 'Letters on the French Coup de État of 1851', Letter 2, 'The Morality of the Coup de État' [15 January 1852, published in *Inquirer*, 17 January 1852], *Collected Works*, IV, pp. 35–44 at pp. 35–6.
61. Bagehot, 'Letters on the French Coup de État of 1851', Letter 1, 'The Dictatorship', IV, pp. 32–3.
62. For background on the political rather than the racial sense of 'national character', see Roberto Romani, *National Character and Public Spirit in Britain and France, 1750–1914* (Cambridge: Cambridge University Press, 2002).
63. Walter Bagehot, 'Letters on the French Coup de État of 1851', Letter 4, 'On the Aptitude of the French Character for National Freedom' [29 January 1852, published in *Inquirer*, 31 January 1852], *Collected Works*, IV, pp. 54–62 at pp. 55–61.
64. Stefan Collini, 'Sense and Circumstances: Bagehot and the Nature of Political Understanding', in Stefan Collini, Donald Winch, and John Burrow, *That Noble Science of Politics: A Study in Nineteenth-Century Intellectual History* (Cambridge University Press, 1983), pp. 163–81 at pp. 164–5.
65. Bagehot, 'Letters on the French Coup de État of 1851', Letter 3, 'On the New Constitution of France and the Aptitude of the French Character for National Freedom', IV, pp. 49–50.
66. Walter Bagehot, 'Caesareanism as It Now Exists' [*The Economist*, 4 March 1865), *Collected Works*, IV, pp. 111–16 at pp. 114–15.
67. Walter Bagehot, 'Letters on the French Coup de État of 1851', Letter 4, 'On the Aptitude of the French Character for National Self-Government', IV, pp. 55–61.
68. Bagehot, 'Letters on the French Coup de État of 1851', Letter 3, 'On the New Constitution of France and the Aptitude of the French Character for National Freedom', IV, p. 50.
69. Ibid., p. 49.
70. Ibid., p. 48.
71. Ibid., p. 50.
72. Ibid.
73. Walter Bagehot, 'Letters on the French Coup de État of 1851', Letter 5, 'On the Constitution of the Prince-President' [undated, published in *Inquirer*, 7 February 1852], *Collected Works*, IV, pp. 63–70 at pp. 63–4.
74. Bagehot, 'Letters on the French Coup de État of 1851', Letter 3, 'On the New Constitution of France and the Aptitude of the French Character for National Freedom', IV, p. 49.
75. Walter Bagehot, 'The American Constitution at the Present Crisis' [*National Review*, October 1861], *Collected Works*, IV, pp. 283–313 at pp. 284–5.
76. Ibid., p. 295; Bagehot, 'Letters on the French Coup de État of 1851', Letter 5, 'On the Constitution of the Prince-President', IV, p. 66, Bagehot, 'Caesareanism as It Now Exists', IV, p. 113.
77. Bagehot, 'The American Constitution at the Present Crisis', IV, pp. 293–6.
78. See Collini, 'Bagehot and the Nature of Political Understanding', pp. 170–1.
79. Bagehot, 'Letters on the French Coup de État of 1851', Letter 4, 'On the Aptitude of the French Character for National Self-Government', IV, pp. 57–8.

80. Walter Bagehot, 'Letters on the French Coup de État of 1851', Letter 6, 'The French Newspaper Press' [10 February 1852, published in *Inquirer*, 14 February 1852], *Collected Works*, IV, pp. 71–6.

81. Walter Bagehot, 'Mr. Gladstone' [*National Review*, July 1860], *Collected Works*, III, pp. 414–40 at pp. 426–9.

82. Walter Bagehot, 'Wordsworth, Tennyson, and Browning: or, Pure, Ornate, and Grotesque Art in English Poetry' [*National Review*, November 1864], *Collected Works*, II, pp. 321–66 at p. 326. Norman St. John-Stevas suggests of this passage that Bagehot is deriving some of his concern for types from Hazlitt—St. John-Stevas, *Walter Bagehot* (London: Longmans, Green, and Co., 1963), pp. 34–5.

83. Bagehot, 'Caesareanism as It Now Exists', IV, pp. 113–14.

84. Barrington, *The Works and Life of Walter Bagehot*, vol. 10, *The Life*, p. 389.

85. Jennifer Pitts, *A Turn to Empire: The Rise of Radical Liberalism in Britain and France* (Princeton, New Jersey: Princeton University Press, 2005), Chapter 2.

86. Walter Bagehot, 'Mr. Carlyle on Mr. Eyre' [*The Economist*, 15 September 1866], *Collected Works*, III, pp. 563–5.

87. Walter Bagehot, 'Memoir of the Right Hon. James Wilson' [*The Economist*, 17 November 1860], *Collected Works*, III, pp. 323–64 at pp. 354–5.

88. Walter Bagehot, 'The Ignorance of Man' [*National Review*, April 1862], in *Collected Works*, XIV, pp. 93–115 at pp. 112–13.

89. Walter Bagehot, 'The Meaning and the Value of the Limits of the Principle of Nationalities' [*The Economist*, 18 June 1864], *Collected Works*, VIII, pp. 149–53.

90. Spencer to F. Howard Collins, 3 December 1855, given in David Duncan, *The Life and Letters of Herbert Spencer*, 2 vols (New York: D. Appleton, 1908), II, p. 117; Spencer to Leslie Stephen, 2 July 1899, given in Duncan, II, pp. 145–8; F.J.C. Hearnshaw, 'Herbert Spencer and the Individualists', in idem. (ed.), *The Social and Political Ideas of Some Representative Thinkers of the Victorian Age* (London: George E. Harrap, 1933), pp. 53–83; Burrow, *Evolution and Society*, pp. 185–95.

91. For another encomium to patient English fact gathering, see Bagehot's 'The Tribute at Hereford to Sir G.C. Lewis' [*The Economist*, 10 September 1864], in *Collected Works*, III, pp. 401–3 as discussed in Watson, *The English Ideology*, p. 53.

NOTES TO CHAPTER 5

1. Walter Bagehot, *Physics and Politics*, in Norman St. John-Stevas (ed.), *The Collected Works of Walter Bagehot*, 15 vols (London: The Economist, 1965–1986), VII, pp. 15–144 at p. 42.

2. On this see Mohammed Abdul-Muizz Nasr, *Walter Bagehot: A Study in Victorian Ideas*, Faculty of Arts Publication no. 9 (Alexandria, Egypt: Alexandria University Press, 1959), pp. 136–9; Walter Bagehot, *The English Constitution* [1867], 2nd edn [1872], in *Collected Works*, V, pp. 165–409 at pp. 363–5.

3. For Darwin's early reliance on Adam Smith and other writers on human culture for ideas about variability and the competition between individuals, see Sylvan Schweber, 'The Origins of the *Origin* Revisited', *Journal of the History of Biology*, 10, 2 (Fall 1977), pp. 229–316 at pp. 232–3, 274–93.

4. John C. Greene, 'Darwin as a Social Evolutionist', *Journal of the History of Biology* 10 (1977), pp. 1–27, reprinted in idem., *Science, Ideology, and World View: Essays in the History of Evolutionary Ideas* (Berkeley and Los Angeles: University of California Press, 1981), pp. 95–127, at pp. 103–4.

5. Alfred Russel Wallace, 'The Origin of Human Races and the Antiquity of Man Deduced from the Theory of "Natural Selection" ', *Journal of the Anthropological Society* 2 (1864), pp. clviii–clxx.

6. Darwin to Wallace, 28 [May 1864], given in Frederick Burckhardt, Duncan M. Porter, Sheila Ann Dean, Paul S. White, Sarah Wilmot, Samantha Evans, and Alison M. Pearn (eds), *The Correspondence of Charles Darwin*, vol. 12, *1864* (Cambridge: Cambridge University Press, 2001), pp. 216–17.

7. Paul H. Barrett, Peter J. Gautrey, Sandra Herbert, David Kohn, and Sydney Smith (eds), *Charles Darwin's Notebooks, 1836–1844: Geology, Transmutation of Species, Metaphysical Enquiries* (London: British Museum [Natural History], and Ithaca, New York: Cornell University Press, 1987), pp. 517–19; Greene, 'Darwin as a Social Evolutionist'; Robert M. Young, 'Darwinism *Is* Social', in David Kohn (ed.), *The Darwinian Heritage* (Princeton, New Jersey: Princeton University Press, 1985), pp. 609–38 at pp. 618–20; and Barry W. Butcher, 'Darwinism, Social Darwinism, and the Australian Aborigines', in Roy MacLeod and Philip H. Rehbock (eds), *Darwin's Laboratory: Evolutionary Theory and Natural History in the Pacific* (Honolulu: University of Hawaii Press, 1994), pp. 371–94 at pp. 371–81. For comments on the reluctance to find Social Darwinism in Darwin's work, see Steven Shapin and Barry Barnes, 'Darwin and Social Darwinism: Purity in History', in Barry Barnes and Steven Shapin (eds), *Natural Order: Historical Studies of Scientific Culture* (Beverly Hills, California: Sage, 1979), pp. 125–42. For an example of that reluctance, see James Allen Rogers, 'Darwinism and Social Darwinism', *Journal of the History of Ideas* 33, 2 (April–June 1972), pp. 265–80. In this article Rogers describes and quotes Darwin's Social Darwinist views at some length (pp. 271–6)—but then in his concluding paragraph Rogers absolves Darwin and his thinking of having any connection to Social Darwinism.

8. Two of the classic statements of the opposite position—that Bagehot's Social Darwinism was untrue to Darwin's thought, and that Darwin himself was no Social Darwinist—are C.H. Driver, 'Walter Bagehot and the Social Psychologists', in F.J.C. Hearnshaw (ed.), *The Social and Political Ideas of Some Representative Thinkers of the Victorian Age* (London: George E. Harrap, 1933), pp. 194–221 at pp. 215–16; and Gertrude Himmelfarb, *Darwin and the Darwinian Revolution* (New York: Doubleday, 1959), pp. 403–7. Arguing instead that Bagehot's thinking was indeed Darwinian are William Montgomery McGovern, *From Luther to Hitler: The History of Fascist-Nazi Political Philosophy* (Boston: Houghton Mifflin, 1941), pp. 465–73; and William Irvine, *Apes, Angels, and Victorians: The Story of Darwin, Huxley, and Evolution* (New York: McGraw-Hill, 1955), pp. 190–1, 332.

9. Charles Darwin, *On the Origin of Species by Means of Natural Selection, or the Preservation of Favoured Races in the Struggle for Life* (London: John Murray, 1859; reprinted in facsimile, with an introduction by Ernst Mayr, Cambridge, Massachusetts: Harvard University Press, 1964), pp. 29, 43, 489–90.

10. Except that little creatures are very complicated, and there are suggestions that some of them communicate from one generation to the next in one or another form of extranucleic heredity. See Otto E. Landman, 'Inheritance of Acquired Characteristics Revisited', *BioScience* 43, 10 (November 1993), pp. 696–705.

11. R.C. Olby, 'Charles Darwin's Manuscript of Pangenesis', *British Journal for the History of Science* 1, 3 (June 1963), pp. 251–63, especially p. 258; idem., *Origins of Mendelism* (New York: Schocken Books, 1966), pp. 55–62; Charles Darwin, *The Variation of Animals and Plants under Domestication*, 2 vols (London: John Murray, 1868), II, pp. 357–404 (Chapter 27); Gloria Robinson, *A Prelude to Genetics: Theories of a Material Substance of Heredity, Darwin to Weismann* (Lawrence, Kansas: Coronado Press, 1979), pp. 3–25, 32–41; James Schwartz, *In Pursuit of the Gene: From Darwin to DNA* (Cambridge, Massachusetts: Harvard University Press, 2008), pp. 1–4, 12–20.

12. Bagehot, *Physics and Politics*, in *Collected Works*, VII, p. 22.

13. Ibid., pp. 18–21. Bagehot's identification of instinct as the early form of knowing (one that gives way before either the civilized state of active reflection or the primitive state of multiple and overdetermined customs) is explored in Kathleen Frederickson, 'Liberalism and the Time of Instinct', *Victorian Studies* 49, 2 (Winter 2007), pp. 302–12.

14. Bagehot, *Physics and Politics*, in *Collected Works*, VII, p. 21.

15. Walter Bagehot, 'Parliamentary Reform' [*National Review*, January 1859], *Collected Works*, VI, pp. 187–235 at pp. 192, 202–4, 208–9.

16. Quoted from Maudsley's *Physiology and Pathology of the Mind*. Bagehot, *Physics and Politics*, in *Collected Works*, VII, p. 20.

17. Bagehot, *Physics and Politics*, in *Collected Works*, VII, pp. 22–3.

18. Ibid., VII, p. 78.

19. Ibid., pp. 78–9.

20. Ibid, p. 94.

21. Ibid.

22. George Stocking, 'The Persistence of Polygenist Thought in Post-Darwinian Anthropology', in idem., *Race, Culture, and Evolution: Essays in the History of Anthropology* (New York: The Free Press, 1968), pp. 42–68, especially p. 46.

23. Bagehot, *Physics and Politics*, in *Collected Works*, VII, pp. 94–5.

24. Ibid., pp. 95–7.

25. Ibid., p. 97.

26. Ibid.

27. Ibid., p. 98.

28. Ibid., p. 99.

29. Ibid.

30. On the last point, see Ibid., Bagehot, in *Collected Works*, VII, pp. 98–9.

31. Ibid.

32. Paul Crook, *Darwinism, War, and History: The Debate on the Biology of War from the 'Origin of Species' to the First World War* (Cambridge: Cambridge University Press, 1994), pp. 48–53.

33. George Stocking, *Victorian Anthropology* (New York: The Free Press, 1987), p. 235.

34. Bagehot, *Physics and Politics*, in *Collected Works*, VII, p. 57.

35. Ibid., p. 56.

36. Ibid., p. 58.

37. Ibid.

38. Ibid., pp. 47–8, 65–7, 139.

39. Ibid., pp. 45–6.

40. Ibid., p. 55.

41. Ibid., pp. 120–1.

42. I do not agree with Peter Mandler over the interpretation of *Physics and Politics*, VII, pp. 120–1. I think that Bagehot acknowledges these difficulties

to save his own rule, not to disprove it. See Mandler, ' "Race" and "Nation" in Mid-Victorian Thought', in Stefan Collini, Richard Whatmore, and Brian Young (eds), *History, Religion, and Culture: British Intellectual History 1750–1950* (Cambridge: Cambridge University Press, 2000), pp. 224–44 at pp. 234–5.

43. Ibid., p. 121.
44. Ibid., p. 129.
45. I cannot agree with Christopher Herbert: He claims that Bagehot's scientific passages in *Physics and Politics* show, in their very failure to convince us, a deliberate pattern on Bagehot's part of undermining and (yes) deconstructing ideas of hierarchy and racial grouping. I think on the contrary that when Bagehot said that people have been divided into heritable races since before the dawn of history, he meant it. When Bagehot talked about the characteristics of 'negros' and 'Asiatics', he thought that he was saying something real about physiologically and ethnologically verifiable groups. Cf. Herbert, *Culture and Anomie: Ethnographic Imagination in the Nineteenth Century* (University of Chicago Press, 1991), pp. 142–5.
46. Bagehot, *Physics and Politics*, in *Collected Works*, VII, p. 130.
47. Other examples of the spectre of Mill include pp. 50, 99–100, and 111.
48. Bagehot, *Physics and Politics*, in *Collected Works*, VII, pp. 132–3.
49. Ibid., pp. 44–5.
50. Ibid., pp. 91–2.
51. Martin S. Staum, *Labeling People: French Scholars on Society, Race, and Empire, 1815–1848* (Montreal and Kingston: McGill-Queen's University Press, 2003), pp. 163–5; Daniel Pick, *Faces of Degeneration: A European Disorder, c. 1848–c. 1918* (Cambridge: Cambridge University Press, 1989), pp. 44–67. There were hints of degeneration thinking in England in the 1860s, among those looking at the problem of urban poverty—José Harris, 'Between Civic Virtue and Social Darwinism: The Concept of the Residuum', in David Englander and Rosemary O'Day (eds), *Retrieved Riches: Social Investigation in Britain, 1840–1914* (Aldershot, England: Scolar Press, 1995), pp. 66–87 at p. 73.
52. Bagehot, *Physics and Politics*, in *Collected Works*, VII, p. 134.
53. Ibid., pp. 112, 137–8.
54. This, after some brief reflection, is the view of what progress is and how it should be measured that Bagehot opts for in his last chapter, which he calls 'Verifiable Progress'—Bagehot, *Physics and Politics*, in *Collected Works*, VII, pp. 135–6.
55. Ibid., pp. 139–40.
56. Ibid., pp. 79–80.
57. Mrs. Russell Barrington, *The Works and Life of Walter Bagehot*, vol. 10, *The Life* (London: Longmans, Green, and Co., 1915), pp. 446–9.
58. Walter Bagehot, 'On the Emotion of Conviction' [*Contemporary Review*, April 1871], *Collected Works*, XIV, pp. 46–56 at pp. 55–6.
59. Bagehot, who was wonderfully well read in modern history and French culture, never seems to have had much time for Tocqueville. He mentioned Tocqueville only on rare occasions, to dispute some technical point about America—see David Clinton, *Tocqueville, Lieber, and Bagehot: Liberalism Confronts the World* (New York: Palgrave Macmillan, 2003), pp. 8–9. As we have seen, Bagehot would not accept the coming of equality, nor the idea that the masses should be educated in self-government by being allowed to govern themselves at the local level—Bagehot, 'Letters on the French Coup de État of 1851,' Letter 7, 'Concluding Letter' [19 February 1852, in *Inquirer*, 6 March 1852], *Collected Works*, IV, pp. 77–84 at pp. 81–2.

60. Walter Bagehot, 'The Metaphysical Basis of Toleration' [*Contemporary Review*, April 1874], *Collected Works*, XIV, pp. 58–74 at p. 68.
61. Ibid.
62. Norman St. John-Stevas, in Bagehot, *Collected Works*, I, pp. 15–19.
63. Walter Bagehot, 'Mr. Macaulay' [*National Review*, April 1856], *Collected Works*, I, pp. 397–428 at p. 397.
64. H.S. Jones, *Victorian Political Thought* (Basingstoke: Macmillan, 2000), p. 67; Crane Brinton, *English Political Thought in the Nineteenth Century* [1933] (NY: Harper & Row, 1962), pp. 188–93.

NOTES TO CHAPTER 6

1. Darwin to J. Henslow, 18 May–16 June 1832, given in Frederick Burkhardt et al. (eds), *The Correspondence of Charles Darwin*, 32 vols [projected] (Cambridge: Cambridge University Press, 1985–), I, pp. 236–9 at p. 238; Charles Darwin, *The Autobiography of Charles Darwin, 1809–1882*, Nora Barlow (ed.) (1958; New York: Norton, 1969), p. 74.
2. Charles Darwin, *Journal of the Researches into the Geology and Natural History of the Countries Visited by H.M.S. Beagle* (1839; New York: Hafner, 1952), p. 592 (6 August 1836).
3. Darwin to Catherine Darwin, 22 May–14 July 1833, given in Burkhardt, *Correspondence of Charles Darwin*, I, pp. 311–15 at p. 312.
4. I cannot agree with Adrian Desmond and James Moore, *Darwin's Sacred Cause: How a Hatred of Slavery Shaped Darwin's Views on Human Evolution* (Boston: Harcourt Mifflin, 2009). In putting so much stress on Darwin's abolitionism, mainly before 1859, Desmond and Moore ignore the justly infamous racism of *The Descent of Man*. In the small part of their book that they devote to *The Descent*, Desmond and Moore mention its racism only in passing (pp. 358–9 and 364–75), saying merely that Darwin came to reflect the racism of the society around him (pp. 365 and 368).
5. Kenneth E. Bock, 'The Comparative Method in Anthropology', *Comparative Studies in Society and History* 8, 3 (April 1966), pp. 269–80 at pp. 270–1; J.W. Burrow, *Evolution and Society: A Study in Victorian Social Theory* (Cambridge: Cambridge University Press, 1966), pp. 11–12. The Westerners who sailed from place to place sometimes projected onto the people they met categories that cut across skin colour, such as when they classified peoples by whether they were wild or civilized—see Barry Alan Joyce, *The Shaping of American Ethnography: The Wilkes Exploring Expedition, 1838–1842* (Lincoln, Nebraska: University of Nebraska Press, 2001), pp. 117–22.
6. Paul H. Barrett, Peter J. Gautrey, Sandra Herbert, David Kohn, and Sydney Smith (eds), *Charles Darwin's Notebooks, 1836–1844: Geology, Transmutation of Species, Metaphysical Enquiries* (London: British Museum [Natural History], and Ithaca, New York: Cornell University Press, 1987), p. 343 (D38–39). In 1868, Darwin speculated on whether, if immigration were cut off, 'Anglo-Saxons' in the United States might 'be greatly modified in the course of two or three thousand years'—already they seemed to have longer, thicker necks and stiffer, lankier hair. See Charles Darwin, *The Variation of Plants and Animals under Domestication*, 2 vols (London: John Murray, 1868), II, p. 277. Ter Ellingson has argued that the Darwin of Tierra del Fuego was employing 'race' terminology for what were really different levels of cultural achievement. But Ellingson shows that Darwin also had breeding and other biologizing metaphors ready to hand on the *Beagle* voyage—Ellingson,

The Myth of the Noble Savage (Berkeley and Los Angeles: University of California Press, 2001), pp. 140–7.
7. Darwin, *Journal of the Researches*, pp. 83–4 (Chapter 4, 11 August 1833), p. 418 (4 May 1835).
8. Key explorations of them are Howard E. Gruber, *Darwin on Man: A Psychological Study of Scientific Creativity*, 2nd edn (Chicago: University of Chicago Press, 1981), pp. 178–85, and Sylvan Schweber, 'The Origins of the *Origin* Revisited', *Journal of the History of Biology* 10, 2 (Fall 1977), pp. 229–316.
9. Sandra Herbert, 'The Place of Man in the Development of Darwin's Theory of Transmutation, Part II', *Journal of the History of Biology* 10, 2 (Fall 1977), pp. 155–227 at pp. 196–7.
10. Barrett et al., *Darwin's Notebooks*, p. 179 (B34), p. 216 (B182).
11. Barrett et al., *Darwin's Notebooks*, p. 303 (C204).
12. Dov Ospovat, *The Development of Darwin's Theory: Natural History, Natural Theology, and Natural Selection, 1838–1859* (Cambridge: Cambridge University Press, 1981), pp. 108–10, 115–17, 165–19, 171, 174–6. I doubt Stephen G. Alter's point—which he himself calls a conjecture—that Darwin's 1840 and 1844 readings of Samuel Stanhope Smith's 1810 work, *An Essay in the Causes of the Variety of Complexion and Figure in the Human Species*, marked a new and transformative moment in Darwin's focus on both sexual selection and human racial identity. Darwin had already had his transformative experience of human varieties in South America. Cf. Alter, 'Separated at Birth: The Interlinked Origins of Darwin's Unconscious Selection Concept and the Application of Sexual Selection to Race', *Journal of the History of Biology* 40, 2 (Summer 2007), pp. 231–58 at pp. 232, 234–5, 246–51.
13. Barrett et al., *Darwin's Notebooks*, p. 286 (C154–155). Of course Darwin does mention Adam here.
14. Konrad Koerner, 'Schleicher and Trees', in Henry M. Hoenigswald and Linda F. Walker (eds), *Biological Metaphor and Cladistic Classification: An Interdisciplinary Perspective* (Philadelphia: University of Pennsylvania Press, 1987), pp. 109–13.
15. Stephen G. Alter, *Darwinism and the Linguistic Image: Language, Race, and Natural Theology in the Nineteenth Century* (Baltimore: Johns Hopkins University Press, 1999), especially pp. 28–34, 108–17; Thomas R. Trautmann, *Aryans and British India* (Berkeley and Los Angeles: University of California Press, 1997), pp. 6–11; Harriet Ritvo, 'Classification and Continuity in *The Origin of Species*', in David Amigoni and Jeff Wallace (eds), *Charles Darwin's The Origin of Species: New Interdisciplinary Essays* (Manchester: Manchester University Press, 1995), pp. 47–67; George Stocking, *Victorian Anthropology* (New York: The Free Press, 1987), pp. 52, 58.
16. Darwin, *The Origin of Species*, pp. 422–3.
17. Ospovat, *The Development of Darwin's Theory*, pp. 171–3, 177–9, 183, 187; Silvan S. Schweber, 'The Wider British Context in Darwin's Theorizing', in David Kohn (ed.), *The Darwinian Heritage* (Princeton, New Jersey: Princeton University Press, 1985), pp. 35–69 at pp. 61–2. Darwin's point was anticipated by Robert Latham, 'On the Subjectivity of Certain Classes in Ethnology' [1853], reprinted in idem., *Opuscula: Essays Chiefly Philological and Ethnological* (London: Williams & Norgate, 1860), pp. 138–42 at pp. 140–1.
18. Darwin, *The Origin of Species*, pp. 419–22; John Beatty, 'Speaking of Species: Darwin's Strategy', in Kohn (ed.), *The Darwinian Heritage*, pp. 265–81, especially pp. 276–8.

19. Harriet Ritvo, *The Platypus and the Mermaid, and Other Figments of the Classifying Imagination* (Cambridge, Massachusetts: Harvard University Press, 1987), pp. 85–107; Nancy Stepan, *The Idea of Race in Science: Great Britain, 1800–1960* (New York: Archon Books, 1982), pp. 33, 36–7. Darwin pointed out that he had seen the cross between a Canada Goose and a Penguin Duck from Bombay (the second bird is now called an Indian Runner Duck)—see Schweber, 'The Origin of the *Origin* Revisited', p. 258. For Darwin's own rejection of the idea that interfertility can define a species, see David N. Stamos, *Darwin and the Nature of Species* (Albany: State University of New York Press, 2007), pp. 68–9, 107–121.

20. Bernard Semmel, *The Governor Eyre Controversy* (London: MacGibbon and Kee, 1962), pp. 120–1.

21. Darwin, *Variation of Plants and Animals*, II, p. 47.

22. Charles Darwin, *The Descent of Man and Selection in Relation to Sex*, 2 vols (London: John Murray, 1871), I, pp. 2–3.

23. Ibid., II, pp. 394–6, 401–2.

24. Ibid., I, p. 243 n. 44, II, p. 352 n. 64.

25. Ibid., II, p. 352 n. 65; Gruber, *Darwin on Man*, p. 205.

26. Darwin, *Descent of Man*, I, pp. 217–18 n. 5, 218 n. 6.

27. For Quatrefages: Darwin, *Descent of Man*, I, pp. 225 n. 15, 242 n. 41, 243 n. 47, 246 n. 50, II, pp. 321 n. 14, 357. For Broca: I, pp. 146, 152, 220, 237, 240.

28. Ibid., I, p. 226.

29. Ibid., I, pp. 217–26.

30. Ibid., I, pp. 222–3.

31. Ibid., I, pp. 224–225. Victorian ideas of hybridity have attracted some attention: Robert J.C. Young, *Colonial Desire: Hybridity in Theory, Culture, and Race* (London: Routledge, 1995), especially pp. 6–17; Claude Blanckaert, 'Of Monstrous Métis?: Hybridity, Fear of Miscegenation, and Patriotism from Buffon to Paul Broca', in Sue Peabody and Tyler Stovall (eds), *The Color of Liberty: Histories of Race in France* (Durham, North Carolina: Duke University Press, 2003), pp. 42–70.

32. Darwin, *Descent of Man*, I, pp. 225–6, II, p. 388.

33. Ibid., I, pp. 231–4.

34. Ibid., I, p. 249.

35. Ibid., II, p. 382.

36. Ibid., I, pp. 169, 173.

37. Ibid., II, pp. 381–2.

38. Ibid., I, pp. 57–8.

39. See Stepan, *The Idea of Race in Science*, pp. 50–7.

40. Darwin, *Descent of Man*, I, p. 201. This passage has also been highlighted by Leila S. May, in 'Monkeys, Microcephalous Idiots, and the Barbarous Races of Mankind: Darwin's Dangerous Victorianism', *Victorian Newsletter* 102 (Fall 2002), pp. 20–7.

41. He says he prefers 'sub-species'; on this, see Michael T. Ghiselin, *The Triumph of the Darwinian Method* (Berkeley and Los Angeles: University of California Press, 1969; Chicago: University of Chicago Press, 1984), pp. 188–9. For the word 'race', see Darwin, *Descent of Man*, I, pp. 111–12, 229–30, 235, 237.

42. As Stanley Edgar Hyman pointed out, Darwin seems to have been less interested in animalizing humanity than in humanizing animals—Hyman, *The Tangled Bank: Darwin, Marx, Frazer, and Freud as Imaginative Writers* (1959; New York: Grosset & Dunlap, 1962), p. 50. For loose or anthropomorphic uses of 'struggle' in *The Origin of Species*, see Barry G. Gale,

'Darwin and the Concept of a Struggle for Existence: A Study in the Extra-scientific Origins of Scientific Ideas', *Isis* 63, 3 (September 1962), pp. 321–44 at pp. 323–4. See also Gillian Beer, *Darwin's Plots: Evolutionary Narrative in Darwin, George Eliot, and Nineteenth-Century Fiction* (London: Routledge and Kegan Paul, 1983), pp. 52–9. David Kohn discusses the looseness of Darwin's references to God: Kohn, 'Darwin's Ambiguity: The Secularization of Biological Meaning', *British Journal for the History of Science* 22, 2 (July 1989), pp. 215–39; and James Eli Adams considers Darwin's uses of a 'Nature' as an active and conscious force in 'Woman Red in Tooth and Claw: Nature and the Feminine in Tennyson and Darwin', *Victorian Studies* 33, 1 (Autumn 1989), pp. 7–27 at pp. 10–12.

43. Darwin, *Descent of Man*, I, pp. 246–7; Darwin's ambivalence on race has been noted by Paul Crook, *Darwinism, War, and History: The Debate on the Biology of War from the 'Origin of Species' to the First World War* (Cambridge: Cambridge University Press, 1994), pp. 25–7; and Stephen G. Alter, 'Race, Language, and Mental Evolution in Darwin's *Descent of Man*', *Journal of the History of the Behavioral Sciences* 43, 3 (Summer 2007), pp. 239–55. Alter restricts his attention to what Darwin thought about racial differentiation in the remote past (p. 240). He leaves out the differentiation that arises from the physical inheritance of acquired cultural inequalities, as well as Darwin's focus on the confusion about how many races there are, and indeed Darwin's explicit statement that man is a polymorphic but nonracial species—Darwin, *Descent of Man*, I, p. 249.

44. Darwin, *Descent of Man*, I, pp. 248–9.

45. Ibid., II, p. 379.

46. Herbert, 'The Place of Man in the Development of Darwin's Theory of Transmutation', pp. 180–8; Gruber, *Darwin on Man*, pp. 20–3. Darwin read *Democracy in America* early in 1849, and thought it 'very good'—Burkhardt, *Correspondence of Charles Darwin*, IV, Appendix 4, p. 478; Darwin to Hooker, 24 December 1862, X, pp. 624–5.

47. Darwin, *Descent of Man*, I, p. 215.

48. Ibid., I, pp. 215–16.

49. Ibid.

50. Ibid.

51. Ibid., I, p. 216.

52. Ibid., I, pp. 67, 115, 136, 138, 156, 167, 181, 232, II, pp. 348, 348, 351 n. 62, 404. See Ruth Mayer, 'The Things of Civilization, the Matters of Empire: Representing Jemmy Button', *New Literary History* 39 (2008), pp. 193–215.

53. Darwin, *Descent of Man*, I, p. 34.

54. Ibid., I, pp. 18, 57–8, 115, 117, 143–4, 152–4, 246; Ruse, 'Social Darwinism: The Two Sources', *Albion* 12, 1 (Spring 1980), pp. 23–36 at p. 34.

55. Darwin, *Descent of Man*, II, p. 380 n. 23.

56. Ibid., I, pp. 117–18.

57. Ibid., I, p. 164, II, pp. 390, 394.

58. Robert J. Richards, 'The Emergence of Evolutionary Biology of Behaviour in the Early Nineteenth Century', *British Journal for the History of Science* 15, 3 (November 1982), pp. 241–80.

59. Gruber, *Darwin on Man*, pp. 30, 185–6, 190–2; Darwin, *Descent of Man*, I, pp. 152–3.

60. Darwin, *Descent of Man*, I, pp. 37–8, 97, 117, II, pp. 353–4.

61. Ibid., II, p. 329.

62. John C. Greene, 'Darwin as a Social Evolutionist', in idem., *Science, Ideology, and World View: Essays in the History of Evolutionary Ideas*

(Berkeley and Los Angeles: University of California Press, 1981), pp. 95–127—reference at pp. 109–12. Green also shows that Darwin would go on to read other articles on evolution in human society, although except for articles by Francis Galton on the inheritance of mental characteristics he does not seem to have been much influenced by them; Darwin noted major disagreements with each—pp. 104–14. Galton's articles and others also may have pushed Darwin in the direction of considering the question of whether altruism in civilized societies preserved the unfit, although this was also something that Scrooge had asserted in *A Christmas Carol* two decades before, following the controversy over the New Poor Law of 1834.

63. Darwin, *Descent of Man*, I, p. 155; Peter J. Bowler, 'Malthus, Darwin, and the Concept of Struggle', *Journal of the History of Ideas* 37, 4 (October–December 1976), pp. 631–50; Robert J. Richards, *Darwin and the Emergence of Evolutionary Theories of Mind and Behavior* (Chicago: University of Chicago Press, 1987), pp. 167–8; Barry G. Gale, 'Darwin and the Concept of a Struggle for Existence: A Study in the Extrascientific Origins of Scientific Ideas'.

64. Darwin, *Descent of Man*, I, pp. 162–3 and 162 n. 5. Darwin is citing the first three articles of what would become Bagehot's book—those parts which had been published up to July 1869. He first cites these 'able' articles at I, p. 93 n. 23.

65. Ibid., I, p. 100.

66. Ibid., I, p. 238.

67. Ibid.

68. Ibid.

69. Ibid., I, p. 239.

70. Ibid., I, p. 240.

71. Ibid., I, pp. 159–60.

72. And so Darwin himself says: Ibid., I, pp. 1–2, 152–3, II, p. 402.

73. Alfred Russel Wallace, 'The Origin of Human Races and the Antiquity of Man Deduced from the Theory of "Natural Selection" ', *Journal of the Anthropological Society* 2 (1864), pp. clviii–clxx; Darwin, *Descent of Man*, I, pp. 158–9; Darwin to J.D. Hooker, 22 May [1864], and Darwin to Asa Gray, 28 May [1864], both given in Burckhardt, *Correspondence of Charles Darwin*, XII, pp. 203–4, 211–12. Writing to Wallace himself, Darwin highlights Wallace's ideas on how 'the struggle between the races of man' is a mental one—Darwin to Wallace, 28 [May 1864], pp. 216–7. Wallace would later break from the Anthropological Society over the strength of its racism—Martin Fichman, *An Elusive Victorian: The Evolution of Alfred Russel Wallace* (Chicago: University of Chicago Press, 2004), p. 154.

74. Darwin, *Descent of Man*, I, pp. 137–8. By 1869, Wallace's conversion to spiritualism had led him to take man out of nature and, as it happened, to reify the special nature of each human 'race'; Darwin had not approved of these changes in Wallace's approach, and that may have led him to make his criticism in this passage of *The Descent of Man* the more pointed. See Stepan, *The Idea of Race in Science*, pp. 66–77; Malcolm Jay Kottler, 'Alfred Russel Wallace, the Origin of Man, and Spiritualism', *Isis* 65, 2 (June 1974), pp. 145–92; Fichman, *An Elusive Victorian*, Chapter 4.

75. Darwin, *Descent of Man*, II, p. 393.

76. Darwin, *Descent of Man*, II, p. 394.

77. Ibid., I, pp. 168–9, II, pp. 393–4, 403–4; see also Gregory Claeys, ' "The Survival of the Fittest" and the Origins of Social Darwinism', *Journal of the History of Ideas* 61, 2 (April 2000), pp. 223–40 at pp. 237–8.

78. Darwin, *Descent of Man*, I, p. 64.

79. Memorandum of a Meeting of the Natural History & Antiquarian Society, Dumfries, 6 February 1866, in James Shaw to Charles Darwin, [6–10 February 1866], given in Burkhardt et al. (eds), *Correspondence of Charles Darwin*, XIV, pp. 42–3.
80. Darwin, *Descent of Man*, II, pp. 316–17.
81. Ibid., II, p. 378.
82. Robert Kenny, 'From the Curse of Ham to the Curse of Nature: The Influence of Natural Selection on the Debate on Human Unity before the Publication of *The Descent of Man*', *British Journal for the History of Science* 40, 3 (September 2007), pp. 367–88 at 381–2.
83. Darwin, *Descent of Man*, I, p. 249.
84. Ibid., p. 388.
85. In the second edition of the book, Darwin would add some fascinating passages on race, but he would not resolve the contradiction between denying it in certain places and affirming it in his fundamental language—Charles Darwin, *The Descent of Man, and Selection in Relation to Sex*, 2nd edn (1874; New York: Hurst, n.d.), pp. 42–3, 142.
86. Kwame Anthony Appiah, *In My Father's House: Africa in the Philosophy of Culture* (1992), pp. 14–15.
87. Gary Stix, 'Human Origins: Traces of Distant Past', *Scientific American* 299, 1 (July 2008), pp. 56–63.
88. Hyman, *Tangled Bank*, pp. 56–57; Ospovat, *The Development of Darwin's Theory*, pp. 212–28; Michael T. Ghiselin, 'Darwin, Progress, and Economic Principles', *Evolution* 49, 6 (December 1995), pp. 1029–37.

NOTES TO CHAPTER 7

1. George Douglas Campbell, eighth Duke of Argyll, *Autobiography and Memoirs*, Dowager Duchess of Argyll [Ina Erskine Campbell] (ed.), 2 vols (London: John Murray, 1906), II, p. 58; Richard Whately, 'Of the Origins of Civilization', in *Lectures Delivered before the Young Men's Christian Association in Exeter Hall*, vol. 10, *1854–1855* (London: James Nisbet, 1855), pp. 3–36 at pp. 11, 17; John Harris, 'Social Organization', in *Lectures Delivered before the Young Men's Christian Association*, vol. 3, *1847–1848* (London: James Nisbet, 1878), pp. 37–63 at pp. 56–8.
2. John Lubbock, *Prehistoric Times* (London: Williams and Norgate, 1865).
3. Given in John Lubbock, *The Origin of Civilization and the Primitive Condition of Man* (London: Longmans, Green, 1870; Chicago: University of Chicago Press, 1978), pp. 325–37. Lubbock's *Prehistoric Times* had also attacked degeneration, in passing—pp. 337–8.
4. George Douglas Campbell, 8th Duke of Argyll, *Primeval Man: An Examination of Some Recent Speculations*, 3rd edn (London: Strahan & Co., 1870), pp. 29–33.
5. Ibid., pp. 5–6, 198–200.
6. Argyll, *Primeval Man*, pp. 152–4.
7. Ibid., pp. iv–v.
8. Argyll, *Primeval Man*, pp. 30–31, 130–3; Lubbock, *Origin of Civilization*, pp. 352–61; Peter J. Bowler, *The Invention of Progress* (Oxford: Basil Blackwell, 1989), pp. 81–2.
9. Argyll, *Primeval Man*, pp. 180–3.
10. See Lubbock, *Prehistoric Times*, Chapters 11, 12, and 13; idem., *Origin of Civilization*, pp. 1–2.
11. Argyll, *Primeval Man*, pp. 132–136; quotation at p. 133.

12. Ibid., pp. viii–ix, 172–6, 188.
13. Lubbock, *Prehistoric Times*, p. 338. See also pp. 354–6, 462–8.
14. Argyll, *Primeval Man*, p. 97.
15. Ibid., pp. 98–103 and frontispiece.
16. Ibid., pp. 103–7.
17. Ibid., pp. 107–8.
18. Ibid., pp. 150–2. For Lubbock's acknowledgement of the ingenuity of early inventors, and the rather different context in which he discusses the matter, see *Prehistoric Times*, Chapter 13.
19. Given in Lubbock, *Origin of Civilization*, pp. 337–62.
20. Ibid., pp. 340–2.
21. Ibid., pp. 343–4; Mark Patton, 'Science, Politics, and Business in the Work of Sir John Lubbock: A Man of Universal Mind' (Aldershot: Ashgate, 2007), pp. 82–3, 86.
22. Given in Lubbock, *Origin of Civilization*, p. 338.
23. Neal C. Gillespie, 'The Duke of Argyll, Evolutionary Anthropology, and the Art of Scientific Controversy', *Isis* 68 (1977), pp. 40–54 at p. 40; see also pp. 48–9.
24. Lubbock, *Origin of Civilization*, pp. 347–51.
25. Anonymous, 'Anthropology at the British Association, 1869', *Anthropological Review* 7, 27 (October 1869), pp. 414–42 at p. 420–1.
26. George Douglas Campbell, 8th Duke of Argyll, *The Reign of Law* [1866], 5th edn (New York: A.L. Burt, n.d.), pp. ii–iii.
27. Adrian Desmond and James Moore, *Darwin* (New York: Warner Books, 1991), pp. 545–7.
28. Argyll to Gladstone, 23 November 1860, GP vol. XIII, BL Add. MS 44098, fo. 339; Argyll to Gladstone, 23 November 1860, fos. 341–2; Argyll, *Primeval Man*, pp. 46, 113–26.
29. Argyll, *The Reign of Law*, p. 130.
30. *Dictionary of National Biography*.
31. Many years later Lord Kimberley recalled that Argyll had lacked any influence in politics. And '[a]s to his writings I must confess I never could esteem them highly. A smattering of metaphysics mixed with a narrow religious orthodoxy characterised most of them, and the confidency, or rather the "cocksureness" with which he laid down the law & confuted to his own satisfaction the most eminent scientific minds of the age struck me as almost ludicrous.' Kimberley's journal, 25 April 1900, in Angus Hawkins and John Powell (eds), *The Journal of John Wodehouse, First Earl of Kimberley, for 1862–1902*, Camden 5th ser., vol. 9 (London: Royal Historical Society, 1997), p. 475.
32. Argyll and his wife had a very happy marriage; she bore twelve children but then became ill—from exhaustion, as Queen Victoria pointed out when she was told about the duchess of Argyll's illness in 1870. Joan Perkin, *Women and Marriage in Nineteenth-Century England* (London: Routledge, 1989), p. 97.
33. Argyll, *Autobiography and Memoirs*, I, pp. 400–2. For notes on the Duchess, see Christine Bolt, *Victorian Attitudes to Race* (London: Routledge & Kegan Paul; Toronto: University of Toronto Press, 1971), pp. 61, 78, 90, 96; and Douglas Lorimer, *Colour, Class, and the Victorians: English Attitudes to the Negro in the Mid-Nineteenth Century* (Leicester: Leicester University Press, 1978), pp. 63, 83.
34. Argyll to Gladstone, 10 December 1861, GP vol. XIV, BL Add. MS 44099, fo. 98.
35. Argyll, *Autobiography and Memoirs*, I, p. 403.

36. Ibid.
37. Ibid., I, pp. 404.
38. Ibid., I, pp. 408–9.
39. Keith Thomson, *Before Darwin: Reconciling God and Nature* (New Haven, Connecticut: Yale University Press, 2005); [Robert Chambers], *Vestiges of the Natural History of Creation* (London: John Churchill, 1844; photographic reprint, Leicester: Leicester University Press, 1969).
40. Argyll, *Primeval Man*, p. 51.
41. Nicolaas A. Rupke, *Richard Owen: Victorian Naturalist* (Yale and London: Yale University Press, 1994), pp. 272–4, 279–80; Charles Lyell, *The Geological Evidences of the Antiquity of Man* (London: John Murray, 1863)—see much of the book, but especially pp. 387–8.
42. Argyll, *Primeval Man*, pp. 51–65.
43. Ibid., p. 180.
44. Argyll to Max Müller, 29 November 1888, given in Argyll, *Autobiography and Memoirs*, II, pp. 532–3.
45. George Henry Lewes, quoted in Rupke, *Richard Owen*, p. 209.
46. Howard E. Gruber, *Darwin on Man: A Psychological Study of Scientific Creativity*, 2nd edn (Chicago: University of Chicago Press, 1981), pp. 198–200.
47. Rupke, *Owen*, p. 209; for Rupke on Argyll, see pp. 213–14; Adrian Desmond, *Archetypes and Ancestors: Palaeontology in Victorian London, 1850–1875* (1982; Chicago: University of Chicago Press, 1984), pp. 49–54, 177–9.
48. For an exploration of Argyll's views on evolution, see Neal C. Gillespie, *Charles Darwin and the Problem of Creation* (Chicago: University of Chicago Press, 1979), pp. 93–103.
49. Argyll, *Reign of Law*, pp. 117–123, 157, 181–2.
50. Charles Darwin to T.H. Huxley, 1 April [1861], given in Frederick Burkhardt et al. (eds), *The Correspondence of Charles Darwin*, 32 vols [projected] (Cambridge University Press, 1985), IX, p. 77.
51. Darwin to Lyell, 22 January 1865, given in Burkhardt, *Correspondence of Charles Darwin*, XIII, pp. 34–5.
52. Darwin to Hooker, 29 [December 1862], and Darwin to Asa Gray, 26[–27] November [1862], both given in Burkhardt, *Correspondence of Charles Darwin*, X, pp. 640–1 and pp. 563–6 at p. 565. In a number of letters Hooker seems to have established the atmosphere of verbal attacks on Argyll, a lead that Darwin did not always follow. See, for example, Hooker to Darwin, 16 September 1862, pp. 410–11, and [15 and] 20 November [1862], pp. 527–8; and for an example of Darwin's quieter responses, Darwin to Hooker, [10–]12 November [1862], pp. 513–15. See also Darwin to Huxley, 1 April 1861, given in Burkhardt, *Correspondence of Charles Darwin*, IX, p. 77.
53. Argyll, *The Reign of Law*, pp. 129–31.
54. Darwin to Wallace, 12 and 13 October [1867], given in Burkhardt, XV, pp. 394–5. See also Darwin to Lyell, 1 June [1867], pp. 285–6. Darwin to Kingsley, 10 June [1867], pp. 297–9.
55. At several points in *The Reign of Law*, Argyll criticizes Mill for inaccurately using general or popular terms—Argyll, *Reign of Law*, pp. 172–188, and Appendix D.
56. Charles Darwin, *The Descent of Man and Selection in Relation to Sex*, 2 vols (London: John Murray, 1871), I, p. 62.
57. Darwin, *Descent of Man*, I, pp. 65, 155–6. Darwin also criticized W.H. Lecky for overestimating the mental and moral level of early peoples: Darwin, *Descent of Man*, I, p. 97 and 97 n. 31.

58. Darwin, *Descent of Man*, I, p. 181.
59. Ibid., I, p. 35. This strategy went back to Darwin's early notebooks, as Matthew Day has shown—Day, 'Godless Savages and Superstitious Dogs: Charles Darwin, Imperial Ethnography, and the Problem of Human Uniqueness', *Journal of the History of Ideas* 69, 1 (January 2008), pp. 49–70 at p. 59.
60. Paul Crook, 'Social Darwinism: The Concept', *History of European Ideas* 22, 4 (1996), pp. 261–74; Gregory Claeys, ' "The Survival of the Fittest" and the Origins of Social Darwinism', *Journal of the History of Ideas* 61, 2 (April 2000), pp. 223–40; Darwin, *Descent of Man*, II, p. 403; Peter Gay, *The Bourgeois Experience: Victoria to Freud*, III, *The Cultivation of Hatred* (New York: W.W. Norton, 1993), pp. 47 and 47 n., 54–5.
61. Darwin, *The Descent of Man*, I, p. 104 n. 38.
62. Greene, *Science, Ideology, and World View*, pp. 109–12. Greene's full demonstration of this point from Darwin's notes was anticipated by some perspicacious suggestions in Thomas Cowles, 'Malthus, Darwin, and Bagehot: A Study in the Transference of a Concept', *Isis* 26, 2 (March 1937), pp. 341–8 at p. 346.
63. Darwin, *The Descent of Man*, I, pp. 164–6, 178, 234.
64. Argyll, *Reign of Law*, p. 230.
65. Janet Browne, *Charles Darwin: The Power of Place*, 2 vols (New York: Alfred A. Knopf, 2002), II, p. 497.
66. Lubbock to Argyll, 10 March 1890, fol. 82, Avebury Papers, BL Add. MS 49654; Argyll to Lubbock, 10 March 1890, fos. 83–5.
67. Lubbock to Argyll, 13 March 1890, Avebury Papers, BL Add. MS 49654, fol. 86.
68. Argyll to Lubbock, 10 March 1890, Avebury Papers, BL Add. MS 49654; fos. 83–5.
69. Argyll, *Autobiography and Memoirs*, II, pp. 54–64, 195; Argyll to Gladstone, 25 Dec, 1860, GP vol. XIII, BL Add. MS 44098, fos. 351–4; Argyll to Gladstone, 29 April 1862 and 13 May 1862, given in Argyll, *Autobiography and Memoirs*, II, pp. 189–90.
70. Argyll, *Autobiography and Memoirs*, II, pp. 196–7.
71. Argyll to Gladstone, 2 September 1862, GP vol. XIV, BL Add. MS 44099, fos. 152–9. Gladstone and Argyll both went on to support the Freedmen's Aid Societies—Argyll to Gladstone, 31 January 1866, GP vol. XXV, BL Add. MS 41110, fos. 94–5.
72. Argyll to Gladstone, 29 December 1865, GP vol. XXV, BL Add. MS 41110, fos. 82–5.
73. Dorothy O. Helly, *Livingstone's Legacy: Horace Waller and Victorian Mythmaking* (Athens, Ohio: Ohio University Press, 1977), pp. 240–1, 243; Oliver Ransford, *David Livingstone: The Dark Interior* (New York: St. Martin's Press, 1978), p. 159.
74. Argyll to Murchison, 25 March [1858?], Murchison MSS, BL Add. MS. 46125, fos. 45–7, encl.
75. Argyll, *Autobiography and Memoirs*, I, pp. 282–3.
76. Ibid., I, pp. 283.
77. Argyll, *Autobiography and Memoirs*, II, pp. 272–3, 280–3; Malcolm C.C. Seton, *The India Office* (London and New York: G.P. Putman's Sons, 1926), pp. 114–15, 249; Argyll to Gladstone, 12 March 1869, GP vol. XVI, BL Add MS 44101, fos. 34–6.
78. B.B. Misra, *The Bureaucracy in India: An Historical Analysis of Development up to 1947* (Delhi: Oxford University Press, 1977), pp. 109–11.
79. George Douglas Campbell, 8th Duke of Argyll, *India under Dalhousie and Canning* (London: Longman, Green, Longman, Roberts, & Green, 1865), pp. 17, 34–5.
80. Ibid., p. 30.

81. Ibid., pp. 34–5. A similar point about the way British overlordship in India leads to the degeneracy of the native rulers features three years later in the nearly 30 percent of Charles Dilke's *Greater Britain* that is devoted to the subcontinent—Dilke, *Greater Britain: A Record of Travel in English-Speaking Countries*, 2 vols (London: Macmillan, 1868).
82. [George Douglas Campbell, 8th Duke of Argyll], 'The Administration of Justice in India', *National Review* 18 (1864), pp. 136–68 at p. 165.
83. Argyll, *India under Dalhousie and Canning*, p. 9.
84. Ibid., pp. 40–2, 63–4.
85. Ibid., p. 126.
86. He had been thinking about this issue for some time—Argyll to Gladstone, 23 November 1860, GP vol. XIII, BL Add. MS 44098, fos. 341–2.
87. He kept to this view. See George Douglas Campbell, 8th Duke of Argyll, *The Unity of Nature* (New York and London: G.P. Putnam's Sons, 1884), pp. 398–9, 406–7, 413, 429–32.
88. Argyll, *Primeval Man*, p. 108.

NOTES TO CHAPTER 8

1. David Lambert and Alan Lester (eds), *Colonial Lives across the British Empire: Imperial Careering in the Long Nineteenth Century* (Cambridge: Cambridge University Press, 2006).
2. Woodruff D. Smith, *Politics and the Sciences of Culture in Germany, 1840–1920* (New York: Oxford University Press, 1991), pp. 13–15.
3. Alice M. Fraser, Lady Lovat, *The Life of Sir Frederick Weld, GCMG, a Pioneer of Empire* (London: John Murray, 1914), pp. 11–12.
4. Lovat, *Weld*, p. 12; W.J. Gardner, 'A Colonial Economy', in Geoffrey W. Rice (ed.), *The Oxford History of New Zealand*, 2nd edn (Auckland: Oxford University Press, 1992), pp. 57–86 at p. 63.
5. Douglas Lorimer, *Colour, Class, and the Victorians: English Attitudes to the Negro in the Mid-Nineteenth Century* (Leicester: Leicester University Press, 1978), pp. 140–1, 173, 195, 202–3.
6. Clifton Crais, *White Supremacy and Black Resistance in Pre-Industrial South Africa, 1770–1865* (Cambridge University Press, 1992), pp. 126–8; Andrew Bank, 'Losing Faith in the Civilizing Mission: The Premature Decline of Humanitarian Liberalism at the Cape, 1840–1860', in Martin Daunton and Rick Halpern (eds), *Empire and Others: British Encounters with Indigenous Peoples, 1600–1850* (Philadelphia: University of Pennsylvania Press, 1999), pp. 364–83.
7. George Stocking, *Victorian Anthropology* (New York: Free Press, 1987), p. 62; Hugh A. MacDougall, *Racial Myth in English History: Trojans, Teutons, and Anglo-Saxons* (Montreal: Harvest House, 1982).
8. Frederick A. Weld, *Hints to Intending Sheep-Farmers in New Zealand* (London: Trelawny Saunders, 1851).
9. Ibid., p. 11.
10. Jeanine Graham, 'Pastoralist and Maoris: Frederick Weld at Wharekaka', *New Zealand Journal of History* 11, 1 (April 1977), pp. 28–53.
11. For one visit, see John Robert Godley to his father, 8 July 1850, Godley Papers, Canterbury Museum, given in W. David McIntyre and W.J. Gardner (eds), *Speeches and Documents on New Zealand History* (Oxford: Clarendon Press, 1971), pp. 26–8.
12. Weld, *Hints to Intending Sheep-Farmers*, p. 12.
13. Lovat, *Weld*, pp. 20–1; Weld to his father, no date given [1844], excerpted in Lovat, *Weld*, pp. 49–61.

14. Graham, 'Pastoralist and Maoris'.
15. Lovat, *Weld*, pp. 53, 56–9, 60–1; M.P.K. Sorrenson, *Maori Origins and Migrations* (Auckland, New Zealand: Auckland University Press, 1979), p. 59.
16. Renato Rosaldo, 'Imperialist Nostalgia', *Representations* 26 (Spring 1989), pp. 107–22 at pp. 117–19.
17. Scholars often examine the multiple images of Self and Other in any one example of colonial discourse, rather than the different registers that one person will employ in his or her different writings. For example, see Homi K. Bhabha, *The Location of Culture* (London: Routledge, 1994), especially the first parts of Chapter 2, 'Interrogating Identity: Frantz Fanon and the Postcolonial Prerogative', pp. 40–52.
18. Weld in a series of letters to his sister, no date given [1844], quoted in Lovat, *Weld*, pp. 51–63.
19. Lovat, *Weld*, p. 57.
20. Ibid., p. 61.
21. Ibid., p. 53.
22. Ibid., p. 63. Weld repeated this charge of cannibalism elsewhere, as in a 20 March 1865 memorandum that he wrote as New Zealand prime minister (still referred to as 'Colonial Secretary'): *Appendices to the Journal of the House of Representatives (AJHR)* 1865, A-1, p. 9, no. 9.
23. Pat Maloney, 'Savagery and Civilization: Early Victorian Notions', *New Zealand Journal of History* 35, 2 (October 2001), pp. 153–76.
24. Other writers had produced 'colonist's handbooks' that did indeed discuss the natives—Sorrenson, *Maori Origins and Migrations*, pp. 70–1.
25. Edward Gibbon Wakefield, *A Letter from Sydney* [1829] (London: J.M. Dent, 1929).
26. In 1847 he moved from Wharekaka in the North Island to the more open sheep country near Flaxbourne on the South Island. Weld to his father, no date given [1847], given in Lovat, *Weld*, p. 72.
27. Weld, *Hints to Intending Sheep-Farmers*, p. 12.
28. Richard Garnett, *Edward Gibbon Wakefield: The Colonization of South Australia and New Zealand* (New York: Longmans, Green, 1898), p. 330; Great Britain, Parliament (PP), *Copies of the Recent Correspondence between Her Majesty's Secretary of State for the Colonies and the Acting Governor of New Zealand on the Subject of Responsible Government*, No. 160 (1854–1855), pp. 10–11, 19.
29. Weld's travel journal, October 1853, given in Lovat, *Weld*, pp. 94–9.
30. Frederick Weld, 'On the Volcanic Eruption at Hawaii in 1855–56', *Quarterly Journal of the Geological Society of London* 13, 2 (No. 50, 1 May 1857), pp. 163–9.
31. Weld was interested in the detailed landscape *and* in his own feelings, so he cut across the 'objectivity' and 'sentimentality' schools of travel writing postulated by Mary Louise Pratt, *Imperial Eyes: Travel Writing and Transculturalization* (London: Routledge, 1992). Her categories are summarized in Gerry Kearns, 'The Imperial Subject: Geography and Travel in the Work of Mary Kingsley and Halford Mackinder', *Transactions of the Institute of British Geographers* new series 22 (1997), pp. 450–72 at 451–4.
32. Tony Ballantyne, *Orientalism and Race: Aryanism in the British Empire* (Basingstoke: Palgrave, 2002), Chapters 2 and 4; Sorrenson, *Maori Origins and Migrations*, pp. 4–16, 72–4.
33. Frederick A. Weld, 'Christianity in the Pacific', *The Rambler* n.s. 7 (1857), pp. 202–12.

34. Patrick Brantlinger, *Dark Vanishings: Discourse on the Extinction of Primitive Races, 1800–1930* (Ithaca, New York: Cornell University Press, 2003), pp. 6–9.
35. Weld, 'Christianity in the Pacific'. On the myth of the dying Maori, see James Belich, 'Myth, Race, and Identity in New Zealand', *New Zealand Journal of History* 31, 3 (April 1997), pp. 9–22.
36. *AJHR*, 1861, E-1 No. 1D, 'Further Papers relative to the Native Insurrections: A Memorandum of a Conversation between a Deputation of Representative of the Province of Wellington and His Excellency the Governor', p. 4. See also James Belich, 'Myth, Race, and Identity in New Zealand', *New Zealand Journal of History* 31, 1 (April 1997), pp. 9–22 at pp. 12–13.
37. William Mackinnon, Surgeon 57th Regiment, Sanitary Officer, Statement of 4 June 1864, *AJHR* 1864 E-5 enclosure, p. 12.
38. Maori Chiefs to the Aborigines Protection Society, 29 October 1864, *AJHR* 165 A-6 No. 25 sub-enclosure 2 to enclosure 1, 'Despatches from the Right Hon. The Secretary of State for the Colonies to the Governor of New Zealand', p. 23.
39. Ibid, sub-enclosure 1 to enclosure 1, 'Despatches from the Right Hon. the Secretary of State for the Colonies to the Governor of New Zealand', p. 22.
40. John Miller, *Early Victorian New Zealand: A Study of Racial Tension and Social Attitudes, 1839–1852* (London: Oxford University Press, 1958), pp. 8–10.
41. Maori Chiefs to the Aborigines Protection Society, 29 October 1864, 'Despatches from the Right Hon. The Secretary of State for the Colonies to the Governor of New Zealand', pp. 20–1, section 6, nos. 1, 3–4.
42. Grey to the Aborigines Protection Society, 7 April 1864, *AJHR* 1864 E-2, 'Papers Relating to Native Policy', no. 2; Grey to Cardwell, 7 February 1865, *AJHR* 1865 A-5 No. 15, 'Despatches from the Governor of New Zealand to the Secretary of State', p. 5. Grey to Newcastle, 6 January 1864, *AJHR* 1864 E-2 appendix, 'Confiscations of Native Lands: Despatches from the Governor', p. 11, quoting Gov. Gore Brown in April 1857, on the Maori 'desire for the amalgamation of the races . . . , to maintain a separate nationality, and . . . to have a chief of their own election. . . . ' In his early role of Australian explorer, Grey had defined races in the first instance by language, ignoring physical characteristics: George Grey, *Journals of Two Expeditions of Discovery in North-west and Western Australia, During the Years 1837, 38, and 39*, 2 vols (London: T. and W. Boone, 1841; facsimile reprint, Adelaide: Libraries Board of South Australia, 1964), II, pp. 207–8.
43. James Gump, 'The Imperialism of Cultural Assimilation: Sir George Grey's Encounter with the Maori and the Xhosa, 1845–1868', *Journal of World History* 9, 1 (Spring 1998), pp. 89–106 at pp. 90–1, 104–6; J.B. Peires, *The Dead Will Rise Again: Nongqawuse and the Great Xhosa Cattle-Killing Movement of 1856–7* (Johannesburg: Ravan Press, 1989), pp. 318–19; Leigh Dale, 'George Grey in Australia, New Zealand, and South Africa', in Peter Hulme and Russell McDougall (eds), *Writing, Travel, and Empire in the Margins of Anthropology* (London: I.B. Tauris, 2007), pp. 19–41.
44. Grey to Newcastle, 26 August 1864, *AJHR* 1864 E-5, p. 9.
45. Later, when Grey thought that the struggle really had become 'a war of races' rather than a question of how to treat 'subjects after a rebellion', he began to support the widespread confiscation of Maori land. Grey to the Duke of Newcastle, 6 January 1864, *AJHR*, 1864, D-6, 'Despatches from the Governor of New Zealand to the Right Honorable Secretary of State for the Colonies', no. 2. For some thoughts on the hardening of racialist attitudes among settlers who had grown up in New Zealand during the

Maori wars of the 1840s, see Miller, *Early Victorian New Zealand*, p. 77.

46. Grey to Cardwell, 27 April 1865, *AJHR* 1865 A-5 No. 34, 'Despatches from the Governor of New Zealand to the Secretary of State', p. 22.

47. Catherine Hall, *Civilising Subjects: Metropole and Colony in the English Imagination, 1830–1867* (Chicago: University of Chicago Press, 2002), pp. 287–8.

48. John Stenhouse, 'Imperialism, Atheism, and Race: Charles Southwell, Old Corruption, and the Maori', *Journal of British Studies* 44 (October 2005), pp. 754–74 at pp. 770–1; idem., 'The Darwinian Enlightenment and New Zealand Politics', in Roy MacLeod and Philip H. Rehbock (eds), *Darwin's Laboratory: Evolutionary Theory and Natural History in the Pacific* (Honolulu: University of Hawaii Press, 1994), pp. 395–425. As native affairs commissioner, Weld circulated the New Zealand government response to Martin: Memorandum by Weld, *AJHR*, 1861, E-2, 'Further Papers Relative to the Taranaki Question', No. 2, 'Notes on Sir William Martin's Pamphlet'—see pp. 41–2.

49. Weld as prime minister to Gov. Grey, 2 September 1865, *AJHR* 1865 A-1 No 40.

50. Weld in the NZ House of Representatives, 3 August 1860, given in PP, *Papers Relating to the Recent Disturbances in New Zealand, 1859–61*, No. 2798 (1861), p. 375, col. 2.

51. *AJHR*, 1861, E-2 No. 1, 'Copy of a Pamphlet by Sir William Martin, DCL', p. 2, nos. 5–7, and pp. 11–12, nos. 1–4. The accusation was repeated—in an attempt to answer Martin and the many witnesses he cited—in Gov. Gore Brown to Colonial Secretary the Duke of Newcastle, 14 December 1860, p. 7, no. 14, *AJHR*, 1861, E-1.

52. Certain Maori leaders had been asking to be able to speak for themselves in the Assembly—*AJHR*, 1864, E-15.

53. Ann R. Parsonson, 'The Expansion of a Competitive Society: A Study in Nineteenth-Century Maori Social History', in D.A. Hamer (ed.), *New Zealand Social History: Papers from the Turnbull Conference on New Zealand Social History, 1978* (Auckland, New Zealand: Auckland University Press, 1978), pp. 83–98 at p. 86.

54. *AJHR*, 1861, E-2 No. 1, 'Copy of a Pamphlet by Sir William Martin, DCL', pp. 1–2, nos. 1–9.

55. Alan Ward, *A Show of Justice: Racial 'Amalgamation' in Nineteenth Century New Zealand* (Toronto: University of Toronto Press, 1974), pp. 177–93; Stuart Banner, 'Conquest by Contract: Wealth Transfer and Land Market Structure in Colonial New Zealand', *Law & Society Review* 34, 1 (2000), pp. 47–96 at pp. 64–88; idem., 'Two Properties, One Land: Law and Space in Nineteenth-Century New Zealand', *Law & Social Inquiry* 24, 4 (Autumn 1999), pp. 807–52. For the earlier twistings and turnings in the European policy of using either European or Maori law as a way to get lands away from the Maori—half of New Zealand by 1853—see Michael Belgrave, 'Preemption, the Treaty of Waitangi, and the Politics of Crown Purchase', *New Zealand Journal of History* 31, 1 (April 1997), pp. 23–37; M.P.K. Sorrenson, 'Maori and Pakeha', in Rice (ed.), *Oxford History of New Zealand*, pp. 141–66 at pp. 147–8.

56. Ward, *A Show of Justice*, p. 187; on Maori land sales and social upheaval, see also Parsonson, 'The Expansion of a Competitive Society', pp. 94–5.

57. Memorandum by Grey, 6 January 1864, *AJHR*, 1864, Appendix to E-2, p. 8, no. 4.2.

58. J.C. Richmond in the *New Zealand Parliamentary Debates, 1864–1866,* 349, quoted in Ward, *A Show of Justice,* p. 187.

59. Ibid., 347, quoted in Ward, *A Show of Justice,* p. 187.

60. Weld (as native affairs commissioner) memo to Gov. Gore Brown, 22 May 1861, *AJHR,* 1861, E-3e, 'Further Papers Relative to Native Affairs. Correspondence Respective the Introduction of a Better System of Government Among the Rarawas', no. 2.

61. Susan H. Farnsworth, *The Evolution of British Imperial Policy During the Mid-Nineteenth Century: A Study of the Peelite Contribution, 1846–1874* (New York: Garland, 1992), pp. 129–30, 142, 157–8, 193–5, 209.

62. *AJHR,* 1864 A-2; repeated in Weld's memorandum of 20 March 1865, *AJHR,* 1865 A-4, p. 6.

63. James Belich, 'The Victorian Interpretation of Racial Conflict and the New Zealand Wars: An Approach to the Problem of One-sided Evidence', *Journal of Imperial and Commonwealth History* 15:2 (January 1987): pp. 123–47, especially after p. 131. See also idem., *The Victorian Interpretation of Racial Conflict: The Maori, the British, and the New Zealand Wars* (Montreal and Kingston, Ontario: McGill-Queen's University Press, 1986), pp. 321–30.

64. W.P. Morrell, *The Provincial System in New Zealand, 1852–1876,* 2nd edn (Christchurch, New Zealand: Whitcombe and Tombs, 1964), pp. 148–53, 159–62; B.J. Dalton, *War and Politics in New Zealand, 1855–1870* (Sydney: Sydney University Press, 1970), pp. 208–27, 237–9; Jeanine Graham, *Frederick Weld* (Auckland, New Zealand: Auckland University Press, 1983), pp. 102–8.

65. For this genre of writing, see Alan Lester, 'British Settler Discourse and the Circuits of Empire', *History Workshop Journal* 54 (Autumn 2002), pp. 24–48.

66. Frederick A. Weld, *Notes on New Zealand Affairs* (London: Edward Stanford, 1869), pp. 3–4.

67. Ibid., p. 78. Weld is referring to charges made against himself, his ministry, and Gov. Grey by the British commander in New Zealand, Lieu-Gen. Sir Duncan Cameron—Cameron to Grey, 28 January 1865, *AJHR* 1865, A-4, pp. 6–7, no. 19; see also the memoranda by Grey and Weld, 7–8 April 1865, *AJHR,* 1865, A-1, p. 10–11, nos. 11–12. Similar charges against the colonists were raised in the English press, especially when the Maori were winning: Colonial Treasurer Reader Wood to the Secretary of State for the Colonies, 13 and 19 July 1864, *AJHR,* 1864, B-2, pp. 32–33, nos. 18–19. Some of the charges that the war was being fought for the benefit of selfish colonists at the expense of British and Maori lives came from the letters home of British soldiers—*AJHR,* 1864, E-2a, pp. 3–4, no. 7.

68. Weld, *Notes on New Zealand Affairs,* p. 78.

69. Ibid., p. 72.

70. Ibid., p. 3.

71. Ibid., p. 73.

72. Ibid., p. 72.

73. Weld, 30 January 1872, given in Lovat, *Weld,* p. 205.

74. Quoted in Graham, *Frederick Weld,* p. 143.

75. R.H.W. Reece, *Aborigines and Colonists: Aborigines and Colonial Society in New South Wales in the 1830s and 1840s* (Sydney: Sydney University Press, 1974), pp. 213–15.

76. Weld openly specified his goal at least once at the beginning of his governorship, as quoted in Graham, *Frederick Weld,* pp. 125, 135–40; and see Paul Hasluck, *Black Australians: A Survey of Native Policy in Western Australia,*

1829–1897, 2nd edn (Melbourne: Melbourne University Press, 1970), pp. 64–7, 164.

77. Quoted in Lovat, *Weld*, p. 210.
78. C.M.H. Clark, *A History of Australia*, IV, *The Earth Abideth Forever, 1851–1888* (Melbourne: Melbourne University Press, 1978), pp. 216–17.
79. Permanent Undersecretary of State for the Colonies Sir Robert Herbert, n.d., in H. Low to the Colonial Office, 5 October 1886, CO 273/138, quoted in Ernest Chew, 'Sir Frank Swettenham and the Federation of Malay States', *Modern Asian Studies* 2, 1 (1968), pp. 51–69 at p. 57—see also pp. 54–6.
80. Graham, *Frederick Weld*, pp. 177–84.
81. Frederick Weld, 'The Straits Settlements and British Malaya', *Proceedings of the Royal Colonial Institute 1884*, reprinted in Paul H. Kratoska (ed.), *Honourable Intentions: Talks on the British Empire in South-East Asia Delivered at the Royal Colonial Institute 1874–1928* (Singapore: Oxford University Press, 1983), pp. 43–74. Quotations at p. 46.
82. Ibid., p. 71.
83. Ibid.
84. Weld, 'The Straits Settlements and British Malaya', p. 69.
85. Ibid., p. 74.
86. Ibid., p. 67.
87. Ibid., p. 70.
88. Ibid., p. 57.
89. Ibid., p. 46.
90. Ibid., p. 63.
91. Ibid., p. 47.
92. Weld's journal, 4 February to 10 March 1881, given in Lovat, *Weld*, pp. 331–3.
93. Lovat, *Weld*, p. 71.
94. Ibid., p. 366.
95. Frederick Weld, 'The Straits Settlements and British Malaya', pp. 53–4. Denison also developed racial stereotypes after, like Eyre, being strongly opposed to them in his earlier writings. See Edward Beasley, *Mid-Victorian Imperialists: British Gentlemen and the Empire of the Mind* (London: Routledge, 2005), Chapter 6.

NOTES TO CHAPTER 9

1. Etienne Balibar, 'Is There a Neo-Racism?', in Etienne Balibar and Immanuel Wallerstein, *Race, Nation, Class: Ambiguous Identities* (Etienne Balibar translated by Chris Turner) (1988; London: Verso, 1991), pp. 17–28 at p. 19.
2. Paul Knaplund (ed.), 'Gladstone-Gordon Correspondence, 1851–1896: Selections from the Private Correspondence of British Prime Minister and a Colonial Governor', *Transactions of the American Philosophical Society*, new series 51, 4 (1961), pp. 1–116—see Chapters 1 and 2.
3. Chapman, *The Career of Arthur Hamilton Gordon, First Lord Stanmore: 1829–1912* (Toronto: University of Toronto Press, 1964), pp. 36 and 36 n.
4. Arthur Gordon, *Wilderness Journeys in New Brunswick in 1862–3* (St. John, New Brunswick: J. & A. M'Millan, 1864), pp. 24–8, 36–9, 42–3, 51–3, 56–63.
5. Gordon also resisted Gladstone's anti-Catholic tirades after the proclamation of papal infallibility. Gordon to Gladstone 6 November [1874], given

in Knaplund (ed.), 'Gladstone-Gordon Correspondence', p. 61; see also the editorial note just above the letter.

6. Trinidad, Minutes of the Proceedings of the Legislative Council, 7 March 1870, Gordon Papers, New York Public Library [henceforth GP NYPL], Official Correspondence, III, Crown Lands and Immigration, April 1866–February 1871.

7. Gordon to Secretary of State for the Colonies the Duke of Buckingham and Chandos, 24 May 1867, GP NYPL, Official Correspondence, IV, Education, December 1866–June 1870, No. 56, Trinidad Legislative Council Papers, 19 November 1869, pp. 5–6.

8. Gordon to Buckingham and Chandos, 11 March 1867, GP NYPL, Drafts of Official Despatches, V, 1867–68, no. 37; and Gordon to Buckingham and Chandos, 12 April 1867, no. 39.

9. Gordon to Buckingham and Chandos, 22 April 1867, GP NYPL, Drafts of Official Despatches, V, 1867–68, no. 55.

10. Gordon to Kortwright, [?] June 1869, GP NYPL, Official Correspondence, III, Crown Lands and Immigration, April 1866–February 1871, n.p. [p. 15].

11. Gordon to Buckingham and Chandos, 8 January 1868, GP NYPL, Drafts of Official Despatches, V, 1867–68, no number, section 8.

12. Gordon to Buckingham and Chandos, 10 February 1868, GP NYPL, Drafts of Official Despatches, V, 1867–68, no. 20.

13. Draft of Gordon to Rogers, 3 September 1868, GP NYPL, Drafts of Official Despatches, VIII, September 1868—December 1870.

14. Gordon to Buckingham and Chandos, n.d. [early May 1869], GP NYPL, Drafts of Official Despatches, VIII, September 1868–December 1870.

15. Brenda Colloms, *Charles Kingsley: The Lion of Eversley* (London: Constable; New York: Barnes & Noble, 1975), pp. 293–6, 315–18; Bernard Semmel, *The Governor Eyre Controversy* (London: MacGibbon & Kee, 1962), pp. 92–4, 99–100; Michael Banton, *The Idea of Race* (London: Tavistock, 1977), Chapter 4, especially pp. 67, 73, 76–7; letter from Kingsley to James Hunt, March 1856, given in Hunt, *Stammering and Stuttering, Their Nature and Treatment* (1861; New York and London: Hafner, 1967), pp. 173–4; Donald Wood, *Trinidad in Transition* (London: Oxford University Press, 1968), pp. 229, 286–7. Kingsley's racist views of Ireland are also infamous— see L.P. Curtis, *Anglo-Saxons and Celts: A Study of Anti-Irish Prejudice in Victorian England* (Bridgeport, Connecticut: Conference on British Studies at the University of Bridgeport, 1968), p. 84; letter to Prof. Lorimer, 17 December 1866, given in Frances Kingsley, *Charles Kingsley: His Letters and Memories of his Life*, one vol. edn (London: Macmillan, 1883), pp. 277–80. In this letter, Kingsley took exception to 'de Tocqueville and his school' on political education (through experience of local government) being the *sine qua non* for stable democratic government; for Kingsley, the *sine qua non* was racial, which is why neither the Irish nor the French could ever govern themselves properly.

16. Gordon to Gladstone, 3 May 1871, given in Knaplund, 'Gladstone-Gordon Correspondence', pp. 56–7 at p. 56; Chapman, *Gordon*, pp. 129–32; Bridget Brereton, *Law, Justice, and Empire: The Colonial Career of John Gorrie, 1829–1892* (Mona, Jamaica: University of West Indies Press, 1997), pp. 88–94.

17. Martin J. Wiener, *An Empire on Trial: Race, Murder, and Justice under British Rule, 1870–1935* (Cambridge University Press, 2009), pp. 79–89.

18. Peter France, *The Charter of the Land: Custom and Colonization in Fiji* (Melbourne: Oxford University Press, 1969), Chapter 7; Chapman, *Gordon*,

Chapter 5; James Legge, *Britain in Fiji, 1858–1880* (London: Macmillan, 1958), Chapters 7–12, especially pp. 206–7.

19. Chapman, *Gordon*, Chapter 7; Deryck Scarr, *Fragments of Empire: A History of the Western Pacific High Commission, 1877–1914* (Canberra: Australian National University Press, 1967), pp. 28–9, 34–43, 51–6, 60–4, 90–3, 125–30, 177–80.

20. Ian Heath, 'Toward a Reassessment of Gordon in Fiji', *Journal of Pacific History* 9 (1974), pp. 81–92 at pp. 82–5.

21. George Stocking, *Victorian Anthropology* (New York: The Free Press, 1987), p. 236; John D. Kelly, 'Gordon Was No Amateur: Imperial Legal Strategies in the Colonization of Fiji', in Sally Engle Merry and Donald Brenneis (eds), *Law and Empire in the Pacific: Fiji and Hawai'i* (Santa Fe: School of American Research Press; Oxford: James Currey, 2003), pp. 61–100 at pp. 77–85.

22. George Douglas Campbell, 8th Duke of Argyll, *Autobiography and Memoirs*, ed. by the Dowager Duchess of Argyll, 2 vols (London: John Murray, 1906), I, p. 373. Gordon is less prominent in Argyll's memoirs than he might have been; he had estranged himself from the Argylls in 1893 by voting for Home Rule. See Chapman, *Gordon*, p. 362—and for their earlier friendship, pp. 77, 359, 361.

23. Stanmore Papers, vols. XVIII–XXIII, XXVII, XXXVI–XXXVIII, BL Add. MSS. 49216–22, 49225, 49234–6.

24. Trying to arrange a visit, Wilberforce repeatedly wrote to Gordon, 25 July 1860 (fol. 63), 24 July (fol. 64), 23 July (fol. 65)—here they finally made the decision that they could get together—25 July (fol. 66), and 27 July (fol. 67). Gordon's next letters to Wilberforce are longer than usual, but they do not mention evolution; rather, they discuss the Maronite Church, the French, whether certain young acquaintances should get married, and long happy details of a country house party and the odd characters of Aberdeenshire—Gordon to Wilberforce, 31 July 1860, fos. 68–71, and 30 August 1860, fos. 77–84. Not long before, Gordon had written to Wilberforce about his visit to a Cistercian monastery in France, touching on a fellow traveller's description of life in Borneo—Gordon to Wilberforce, 3 April 1860, fos. 49–52. After the debate, Gordon penned a long account from the ruins of Damascus—Gordon to Wilberforce, 18 March 1861 (fos. 140–1) and 28 June 1861 (fos. 142–3). Nowhere is there any discussion of anthropological theories, race, or evolution. All letters in Stanmore Papers, vol. XVI, BL Add. MS 49214.

25. Gordon to Wilberforce, 25 January 1867, Stanmore Papers, vol. XVI, BL Add. MS 49214, fos. 170–4.

26. Wilberforce to Gordon, 24 November 1867, Stanmore Papers, vol. XVI, BL Add. MS 49214, fos. 174–81.

27. Gordon to Wilberforce, 24 April 1868, Stanmore Papers, vol. XVI, BL Add. MS 49214, fos. 182–7.

28. France, *Charter of the Land*, p. 105 n.

29. Gordon to his wife, [n.d.] 1868, Stanmore Papers, vol. XXVII, BL Add. MS 49225, fos. 4–5 at fol. 5.

30. Gordon's aristocratic paternalism and his feeling for native aristocracy have also struck Stuart Banner, in *Possessing the Pacific: Land, Settlers, and Indigenous People from Australia to Alaska* (Cambridge, Massachusetts: Harvard University Press, 2007), pp. 269–70.

31. As in his analysis of the problems of Jamaica: Gordon to Gladstone, 21 January 1882, Stanmore Papers, vol. XI, BL Add. MS 49209, fos. 21–3.

32. A very different view of Gordon, in which everything that he attempted to do to safeguard native populations and agricultural labourers is either omitted

or immediately undercut, is in Laurence Brown, 'Inter-Colonial Migration and the Fashioning of Indentured Labour: Arthur Gordon in Trinidad, Mauritius, and Fiji (1866–1880)', in David Lambert and Alan Lester (eds), *Colonial Lives across the British Empire: Imperial Careering in the Long Nineteenth Century* (Cambridge: Cambridge University Press, 2006), pp. 204–27. Gordon also did more for colonial hygiene and health than Brown gives him credit for (GP NYPL, Official Correspondence, I, Laws, no. 27 1867). For a more balanced picture of Gordon, see Heath, 'Toward a Reassessment of Gordon in Fiji'; this article corrects some of the factual errors in Peter France, *Charter of the Land*, Chapter 7. See also the favourable picture in Brereton, *Law, Justice, and Empire*, Chapters 3–5.

33. Arthur Gordon, *Paper on the System of Taxation in Force in Fiji* (London: Harrison and Sons, 1879), pp. 10–11. For Gordon on degeneration, see Gordon to Gladstone, 20 April 1883, given in Knaplund, 'Gladstone-Gordon Correspondence', pp. 88–9.

34. Ordinance to Authorize the Punishment of Whipping in Certain Cases, 8 February 1867, GP NYPL, Official Correspondence, I, Laws, no. 1 1867; Chapman, *Gordon*, p. 333.

35. Chapman, *Gordon*, pp. 164, 172–5. Two colonial governorships later, in 1884, Gordon was shocked when his colony of Ceylon was required to send money to London to support imperial military forces elsewhere—that meant siphoning money out of a colony—Chapman, *Gordon*, pp. 311–12. Gordon began planning his administrative program of economic development for Fiji as soon as he heard of his appointment to the colony. He took much of his programme from John Money's book setting out Dutch colonial practices in Java as a model for the British to follow in India. (Money discussed 'races' as a large variety of cultural or social groups, marked in India by colour difference; thus, Money bridged the old and new ways of using the word.) See Kelly, 'Gordon was no Amateur', pp. 84–7; J.W.B. Money, *Java, or How to Manage a Colony*, 2 vols (London: Hurst and Blackett, 1861), I, pp. 35, 39, 45, 71, 140–2, II, pp. 235–237, 240, 246–8.

36. James Stephen, Minute of 22 September 1841, quoted in Samuel Clyde McCulloch, 'Sir George Gipps and Eastern Australia's Policy toward the Aborigine, 1838–46', *Journal of Modern History* 33, 3 (September 1961), pp. 261–9 at p. 269.

37. See Paul Geraghty, 'The Ethnic Basis of Society in Fiji', in Brij V. Lal and Tomasi R. Vakatora (eds), *Fiji in Transition: Research Papers of the Fiji Constitutional Review Commission, Vol. 1* (Suva, Fiji: School of Economic and Social Development, University of the South Pacific, 1997), pp. 1–23.

38. Geoffrey Blomfield, *Baal Balbora: The End of the Dancing* (Chippendale, New South Wales: Apcol, 1981).

39. Gordon to Gladstone, 22 March–7 June 1876, given in Knaplund, 'Gladstone-Gordon Correspondence', p. 65.

40. Gordon to Gladstone, 12 October 1876, given in Knaplund, 'Gladstone-Gordon Correspondence', pp. 68–71. Gordon noted that the Queensland colonists—whose plan to enslave the peoples of New Guinea must be resisted—also used this offensive term; see Gordon to Gladstone, 20 April 1883, pp. 88–9.

41. Gladstone himself was beginning to pick up on that language, blaming the pro-Turkish agitation of 1877 on 'races' such as the Jews and Magyars, and on Disraeli's 'Jew feelings', which although 'he has been baptized', 'are the most radical & the most real, & so far respectable, portion of his profoundly falsified nature'. Gladstone to Gordon, 16 May 1877, given in Knaplund, 'Gladstone-Gordon Correspondence', pp. 74–5. As is well-known, Disraeli

himself stressed a racial Jewishness. See the essays in Todd M. Endelman and Tony Kushner, *Disraeli's Jewishness* (London: Vallentine Mitchell, 2002).

42. David Picker, 'Blood, Sweat, and Type O: Japan's Weird Science', *New York Times*, 14 December 2006.

43. Gordon to Gladstone, 17 May 1878, given in Knaplund, 'Gladstone-Gordon Correspondence', pp. 77–8. A similar passage appears in Gordon, *Taxation*, p. 9.

44. Edward Beasley, *Empire as the Triumph of Theory: Imperialism, Information, and the Colonial Society of 1868* (London: Routledge, 2005); idem., *Mid-Victorian Imperialists: British Gentlemen and the Empire of the Mind* (London: Routledge, 2005).

45. Tony Ballantyne has argued, correctly, that the overlapping and superimposed webs of webs of scientific, scholarly, and personal correspondence that developed under the British Empire could, some of them, be centred in Calcutta or New Zealand or anywhere else as well as they could be centred in England. And they could be centred on Maori and Bengali thinkers and scholars as much on the British. Ballantyne, *Orientalism and Race: Aryanism in the British Empire* (Basingstoke: Palgrave, 2002), pp. 14–16, 190–6.

46. Robert M. Young, 'Natural Theology, Victorian Periodicals, and the Fragmentation of a Common Context', in idem., *Darwin's Metaphor: Nature's Place in Victorian Culture* (Cambridge: Cambridge University Press, 1985), pp. 126–63, especially pp. 127–8, 152–61. For other thoughts on the passing of the old certainties and the coming of racial speculations, see John Burrow, 'Evolution and Anthropology in the 1860's: The Anthropological Society of London, 1863–1871', *Victorian Studies* 7, 2 (December 1963), pp. 137–54 at pp. 151–4; and Douglas Lorimer, 'Science and the Secularization of Victorian Ideas of Race', in Bernard Lightman (ed.), *Victorian Science in Context* (Chicago: University of Chicago Press, 1997), pp. 212–35. For the breaking up of the old intellectual consensus more generally—outside the question of any consensus on human unity—see T.W. Heyck, *The Transformation of Intellectual Life in Victorian England* (London: Croom Helm, 1982), pp. 42, 67–9, 75–6, 120–1, 184–6, 197–202.

47. Harriet Martineau, *How to Observe Manners and Morals* [1838] (New Brunswick, New Jersey: Transaction, 1989); Sarah Winter, 'Mental Culture: Liberal Pedagogy and the Emergence of Ethnographic Knowledge', *Victorian Studies* 41, 3 (Spring 1998), pp. 427–54. Catherine Hall shows that in her early writings, Martineau believed that people lived in changeable cultures, but that after the Indian Mutiny she adopted a more racialized thinking—Hall, 'Imperial Careering at Home: Harriet Martineau on Empire', in Lambert and Lester (eds), *Colonial Lives Across the British Empire*, pp. 334–59, especially pp. 348–9.

48. John Stuart Mill, *A System of Logic*, 2 vols (London: John W. Parker, 1843), II, pp. 516–24, 527–30 (Book VI, Chapter 5, sections 3–4 and 6)—the quotation is from section 6, p. 528. Mill's idea of the dialog between theory and evidence is clearest and most concrete at the end of section, 6, p. 529.

49. Mill, *A System of Logic*, 3rd edn, 2 vols (London: John W. Parker, 1851), II, p. 442 (Book VI, Chapter 5, section 4). The first edition says simply 'the formation of national character'; Mill had yet to add the world 'collective'—Mill, *A System of Logic*, 1st edn, II, 523. For Mill's rejection of the idea that 'negroes' cannot be civilized, see his discussion of fallacious generalization—II, p. 411 (Book V, Chapter 5, section 4); see also the 'negro' syllogism, I, p. 231 (Book II, Chapter 2, section 1). His main statement of the logic behind his skepticism about race is at I, pp. 168–71 (Book I, Chapter 7, section 5). Earlier in his career, he had flirted with French ideas of race: Peter Mandler,

The English National Character: The History of an Idea from Edmund Burke to Tony Blair (New Haven, Connecticut: Yale University Press, 2006), pp. 49–51.

50. Young, 'Natural Theology, Victorian Periodicals, and the Fragmentation of a Common Context', pp. 152–3. As Adrian Desmond has shown, atheistic radicals had accepted a more evolutionary or mechanistic view of the nature of life for some decades by the time Darwin published *The Origin of Species*. But more respectable Anglican opinion had shied away from these views as corrosive to respectable scientific theology—Desmond, *The Politics of Evolution: Morphology, Medicine, and Reform in Radical London* (Chicago: University of Chicago Press, 1989).

51. William Stanton long ago argued that there was no such consensus in the United States. Without the clerical influence, many thinkers could entertain notions of polygenism. He showed that the founders of the pre–Civil War 'American School' of racist, polygenist anthropology were strongly anticlerical. They *wanted* to reject the idea of a single Adamic heritage. Stanton, *The Leopard's Spots: Scientific Attitudes toward Race in America, 1815–59* (Chicago: University of Chicago Press, 1960), pp. 192–3.

52. Lorimer, 'Science and the Secularization of Victorian Images of Race'.

53. Gordon, *Taxation*, pp. 18–21, 30–3.

54. For examples from 1879 of Gordon employing the term 'race' without succumbing to it, see ibid., pp. 8–9, 11.

55. Laura Tabili, 'Race is a Relationship, and Not a Thing', *Journal of Social History* 37, 1 (2003), pp. 125–30 at p. 126.

56. Tabili, 'Race is a Relationship', p. 125.

57. Loïc J.D. Wacquant, 'For an Analytic of Racial Domination', in Diane E. Davis (ed.), *Political Power and Social Theory* 11 (Greenwich, Connecticut: JAI Press, 1997), pp. 217–234 at pp. 222–4.

58. Léon Poliakov, *The Aryan Myth: A History of Racist and Nationalist Ideas in Europe*, Edmund Howard (trans.) (London: Chatto Heinemann, 1974), p. 257.

59. In an essay that reached me too late to be mentioned elsewhere in this book, David Nirenberg develops some interesting thoughts on how the history of 'race' is discontinuous. That is, racial ideas are not handed down in an unbroken chain from earlier ages, but instead they reemerge in new ways in different historical periods. Scholars can compare and juxtapose the racial ideas of different ages without trying to fit them into a continuous genealogy down through time. I believe that Nirenberg's thinking dovetails nicely with the perspectives of this book—that racist ways of looking at the world can be reinvented. See Nirenberg, 'Was There Race before Modernity?: The Example of "Jewish Blood" in Late-Medieval Spain', in Miriam Eliav-Feldon, Benjamin Isaac, and Joseph Ziegler (eds), *The Origins of Racism in the West* (Cambridge: Cambridge University Press, 2009), pp. 232-64. Nirenberg's article is a good response to the claim of Benjamin Isaac that the 'proto-racism' of the early modern era did indeed come down from the Greco-Roman world. See also Isaac's treatise on 'proto-racism': Benjamin Isaac, *The Invention of Race in Classical Antiquity* (Princeton: Princeton University Press, 2004). I thank Elizabeth Pollard for pointing me in the direction of the Isaac controversy.

Bibliography

ARCHIVAL SOURCES

Avebury Papers, British Library
Gladstone Papers, British Library.
Gordon Papers, New York Public Library.
Murchison Papers, British Library.
Northbrook Papers, British Library: India Office Library and Records.
Stanmore Papers, British Library.

PRINTED PRIMARY SOURCES

Anonymous. 'Anthropology at the British Association, 1869', *Anthropological Review* 7, 27 (October 1869), pp. 414–42.
Anonymous. 'Discussion of "On the Negro's Place in Nature", by James Hunt', *Journal of the Anthropological Society of London* 2 (1864), pp. xv–lvi.
Arnold, Matthew. 'A Persian Passion Play', *Cornhill Magazine* 24 (December 1861), pp. 668–87.
Arnold, Thomas. *The Miscellaneous Works of Thomas Arnold, D.D.* (London: B. Fellowes, 1845; Farnborough, England: Gregg International Publishers, 1971).
Arnold, Thomas. *Introductory Lectures on Modern History* [1842], Henry Reed (ed.) (New York: D. Appleton, 1880).
Bagehot, Walter. *The Collected Works of Walter Bagehot*, Norman St. John-Stevas (ed.), 15 vols (London: The Economist, 1965–1986).
Barrett, Paul H., Peter J. Gautrey, Sandra Herbert, David Kohn, and Sydney Smith (eds). *Charles Darwin's Notebooks, 1836–1844: Geology, Transmutation of Species, Metaphysical Enquiries* (London: British Museum [Natural History], and Ithaca, New York: Cornell University Press, 1987).
Bock, Kenneth E. 'The Comparative Method in Anthropology', *Comparative Studies in Society and History* 8, 3 (April 1966), pp. 269–80.
Burkhardt, Frederick, et al. (eds). *The Correspondence of Charles Darwin*, 32 vols [projected] (Cambridge: Cambridge University Press, 1985–).
Burton, Richard. *The Lake Regions of Central Africa: A Picture of Exploration*, 2 vols (1860; New York: Horizon Press, 1961).
[Burton, Richard]. *Wanderings in West Africa from Liverpool to Fernando Po* (2 vols, London: Tinsley Brothers, 1863; facsimile edn in one volume, New York: Dover, 1991).
[Campbell, George Douglas, 8th Duke of Argyll]. 'The Administration of Justice in India', *National Review* 18 (1864), pp. 136–68.

Campbell, George Douglas, 8th Duke of Argyll. *India under Dalhousie and Canning* (London: Longman, Green, Longman, Roberts, & Green, 1865).

Campbell, George Douglas, 8th Duke of Argyll. *The Reign of Law* [1866], 5th edn (New York: A.L. Burt, n.d.).

Campbell, George Douglas, 8th Duke of Argyll. *Primeval Man: An Examination of Some Recent Speculations*, 3rd edn (London: Strahan & Co., 1870).

Campbell, George Douglas, 8th Duke of Argyll. *The Unity of Nature* (New York and London: G.P. Putnam's Sons, 1884).

Campbell, George Douglas, 8th Duke of Argyll. *Autobiography and Memoirs*, Dowager Duchess of Argyll [Ina Erskine Campbell] (ed.), 2 vols (London: John Murray, 1906).

Carlyle, Thomas. 'Occasional Discourse on the Negro Question', *Fraser's Magazine for Town and Country* 40 (December 1849), pp. 670–9.

[Chambers, Robert]. *Vestiges of the Natural History of Creation* (London: John Churchill, 1844; photographic reprint, Leicester: Leicester University Press, 1969).

Chambers, Robert. *Vestiges of the Natural History of Creation, with a Sequel* (New York: Harper and Brothers, [1857]).

Cole, G.D.H., and A.W. Filson. *British Working Class Movements: Select Documents, 1789–1875* (London: Macmillan; New York: St. Martin's, 1965).

Crawfurd, John. 'On the Aryan or Indo-Germanic Theory', *Transactions of the Ethnological Society of London* 1 (1861), pp. 268–86.

Darwin, Charles. *Journal of the Researches into the Geology and Natural History of the Countries Visited by H.M.S.* Beagle (1839; New York: Hafner, 1952).

Darwin, Charles. *On the Origin of Species by Means of Natural Selection, or the Preservation of Favoured Races in the Struggle for Life* (London: John Murray, 1859; reprinted in facsimile, with an introduction by Ernst Mayr, Cambridge, Massachusetts: Harvard University Press, 1964).

Darwin, Charles. *The Variation of Animals and Plants under Domestication*, 2 vols (London: John Murray, 1868).

Darwin, Charles. *The Descent of Man and Selection in Relation to Sex*, 2 vols (London: John Murray, 1871).

Darwin, Charles. *The Descent of Man, and Selection in Relation to Sex*, 2nd edn (1874; New York: Hurst, n.d.).

Darwin, Charles. *The Autobiography of Charles Darwin, 1809–1882*, Nora Barlow (ed.) (1958; New York: Norton, 1969).

Darwin, Francis. *More Letters of Charles Darwin*, 2 vols (New York: D. Appleton, 1903).

Denison, William. 'On Permanence of Type in the Human Race', *Journal of the Ethnological Society of London* (23 March 1869), pp. 194–8.

Dilke, Charles. *Greater Britain: A Record of Travel in English-Speaking Countries*, 2 vols (London: Macmillan, 1868).

Dilke, Charles. *Greater Britain: A Record of Travel in English-Speaking Countries*, 7th edn (London: Macmillan, 1880).

Drescher, Seymour (ed.). *Tocqueville and Beaumont on Social Reform* (New York: Harper & Row, 1968).

DuBois, W.E.B. 'The Conservation of Races', American Negro Academy Occasional Papers no. 2, 1897, in *W.E.B. DuBois: Writings*, Nathan Huggins (ed.) (New York: Library of America, 1986), pp. 815–26.

DuBois, W.E.B. *Dusk to Dawn* [1940], in *W.E.B. DuBois: Writings*, Nathan Huggins (ed.) (New York: Library of America, 1986), pp. 549–802.

Emerson, Ralph Waldo. *English Traits* [1856], in *Emerson: Essays and Lectures*, Joel Porte (ed.) (New York: Library of America, 1983), pp. 763–936.

Gobineau, Arthur de. *Essai sur la inégalité des races humaines*, 5 vols (Paris: Firmin-Didot, 1853–5).

Gobineau, Arthur de. *Essai sur la inégalité des races humaines* [1853–5], 2 vols (Paris: Firmin-Didot, 1940).

Gobineau, Arthur de. *The Inequality of Human Races*, Adrian Collins (trans.) (New York: G.P. Putnam's Sons, 1915).

Gobineau, Arthur de. *Selected Political Writings*, Michael D. Biddiss (ed.), Adrian Collins and Brian Nelson (trans.) (London: Jonathan Cape, 1970).

Gobineau, Arthur de. *Voyage à Terre-Neuve* [1861], *Literature des voyage, IV* (Paris: Aux Amateur des Livres, 1989).

Gordon, Arthur. *Wilderness Journeys in New Brunswick in 1862–3* (St. John, New Brunswick: J. & A. M'Millan, 1864).

Gordon, Arthur. *Paper on the System of Taxation in Force in Fiji* (London: Harrison and Sons, 1879).

Great Britain. Parliament. *Copies of the Recent Correspondence between Her Majesty's Secretary of State for the Colonies and the Acting Governor of New Zealand on the Subject of Responsible Government*, No. 160 (1854–1855).

Great Britain. Parliament. *Papers Relating to the Recent Disturbances in New Zealand, 1859–61*, No. 2798 (1861).

Grey, George. *Journals of Two Expeditions of Discovery in North-west and Western Australia, During the Years 1837, 38, and 39*, 2 vols (London: T. and W. Boone, 1841; facsimile reprint, Adelaide: Libraries Board of South Australia, 1964).

[Grove, William]. 'Natural History of Man', *Blackwood's Edinburgh Magazine 56* (September 1844), pp. 312–30.

Harris, John. 'Social Organization', in *Lectures Delivered before the Young Men's Christian Association, vol. 3, 1847–1848* (London: James Nisbet, 1878), pp. 37–63.

Hawkins, Angus, and John Powell (eds). *The Journal of John Wodehouse, First Earl of Kimberley, for 1862–1902*, Camden 5th ser., vol. 9 (London: Royal Historical Society, 1997).

Home, Henry, Lord Kames. *Sketches of the History of Man* [1788], James Harris (ed.), 3 vols (Indianapolis, Indiana: Liberty Fund, 2007).

Hunt, James. *Stammering and Stuttering, Their Nature and Treatment* (1861; New York and London: Hafner, 1967).

Huxley, Thomas Henry. *Evidence as to Man's Place in Nature* (New York: D. Appleton, 1863).

Huxley, Thomas Henry. *On Our Knowledge of the Causes of the Phenomena of Organic Nature* (London: Robert Hardwicke, 1863).

Huxley, Thomas Henry, and William Jay Youmans. *The Elements of Physiology and Hygiene* (New York: D. Appleton, 1868).

Huxley, Thomas Henry. *Lessons in Elementary Physiology*, 2nd edn (London: Macmillan, 1868).

Kingsley, Frances. *Charles Kingsley: His Letters and Memories of his Life*, one vol. edn (London: Macmillan, 1883).

Knaplund, Paul (ed.). 'Gladstone-Gordon Correspondence, 1851–1896: Selections from the Private Correspondence of British Prime Minister and a Colonial Governor', *Transactions of the American Philosophical Society*, new series 51, 4 (1961), pp. 1–116.

Knox, Robert. *The Races of Man: A Fragment* (Philadelphia: Lea and Blanchard, 1850; Miami, Florida: Mnemosyne Publishing Company, 1969).

Latham, Robert. *The Ethnology of the British Colonies and Dependencies* (London: John van Voost, 1851).

Latham, Robert. *The Germania of Tacitus, with Ethnological Dissertations and Notes* (London: Taylor, Walton, and Maberly, 1851).

Latham, Robert. *Man and His Migrations* (London: John van Voost, 1851).

Latham, Robert. *Descriptive Ethnology* [1859], reprinted as *Tribes and Races: A Descriptive Ethnology of Asia, Africa, & Europe*, 2 vols (Delhi: Cultural Publishing House, 1983).

Latham, Robert. *Opuscula: Essays Chiefly Philological and Ethnological* (London: Williams & Norgate, 1860).

Latham, Robert. *Elements of Comparative Philology* (London: Walton and Maberly, 1862).

Latham, Robert. *The Nationalities of Europe*, 2 vols (London: William H. Allen, 1863).

Livingstone, David. *Travels and Researches in South Africa* (Philadelphia: J.W. Bradley, 1858).

Long, Edward. *The History of Jamaica*, 3 vols (London: T. Lowndes, 1774; New York: Arno Press, 1972).

Lubbock, John. *Prehistoric Times* (London: Williams and Norgate, 1865).

Lubbock, John. *Primitive Man* (London: Williams and Norgate, 1865).

Lubbock, John. *The Origin of Civilisation and the Primitive Condition of Man* (London: Longmans, Green, 1870; Chicago: University of Chicago Press, 1978).

Lyell, Charles. *The Geological Evidences of the Antiquity of Man* (London: John Murray, 1863).

Maine, Henry Sumner. *Ancient Law*, 2nd edn (London: John Murray, 1863).

Martineau, Harriet. *How to Observe Manners and Morals* [1838] (New Brunswick, New Jersey: Transaction, 1989).

Maudsley, Henry. *The Physiology of Mind*, 2nd edn (London: Macmillan, 1868).

Maudsley, Henry. *Body and Mind* (London: Macmillan, 1870).

Mayhew, Henry. *London Labour and the London Poor*, 4 vols [1861–1862] (New York: Dover, 1968).

McIntyre, W. David, and W.J. Gardner (eds). *Speeches and Documents on New Zealand History* (Oxford: Clarendon Press, 1971).

M'Clennon, John F. *Primitive Marriage* (Edinburgh: Adam and Charles Black, 1865).

Mill, John Stuart. *A System of Logic*, 2 vols (London: John W. Parker, 1843).

Mill, John Stuart, *A System of Logic*, 3rd edn, 2 vols (London: John W. Parker, 1851).

Money, J.W.B. *Java, or How to Manage a Colony*, 2 vols (London: Hurst and Blackett, 1861).

Montesquieu, Charles-Louis de Secondat, Baron de. *The Spirit of the Laws*, Anne M. Cohler, Basia Carolyn Miller, and Harold Samuel Stone (trans and eds) (Cambridge: Cambridge University Press, 1989).

New Zealand. Parliament. *Appendices to the Journal of the House of Representatives of New Zealand*.

Nott, Josiah, and George Glidden. *Types of Mankind* (Philadelphia: Lippincott, Grambo, 1854; Miami, Florida: Mnemosyne, 1969).

Prichard, James Cowles. *Researches into the Physical History of Mankind*, 3rd edn, 5 vols (London: Sherwood, Gilbert, and Piper, 1836).

Robinson, George Frederick Samuel [Earl de Grey and Ripon]. 'Address to the Royal Geographical Society of London', *Proceedings of the Royal Geographical Society of London* 4, 4 (28 May 1860), pp. 117–209.

Spencer, Herbert. *Social Statics* (London: John Chapman, 1851).

Spencer, Herbert. *Principles of Psychology* (London: Longman, Brown, Green, and Longmans, 1855).

Spencer, Herbert. *Education: Intellectual, Moral, Physical* (1860; London: G. Manwaring, 1861).

Spencer, Herbert. *First Principles* (London: Williams and Norgate, 1862).

Spencer, Herbert. *Education: Intellectual, Moral, Physical* (1860; New York: D. Appleton, 1866).

Spencer, Herbert. *First Principles*, 2nd edn (London: Williams and Norgate, 1867).

Spencer, Herbert. *First Principles*, 3rd edn (London: Williams and Norgate, 1870).

Spencer, Herbert. *Principles of Psychology*, 2nd edn (London: Williams and Norgate, 1870).

Spencer, Herbert. *Principles of Sociology*, 2nd edn (London: Williams and Norgate, 1877).

Tocqueville, Alexis de. *De la démocratie en Amérique* [1835–40], 2 vols (Paris: Librarie de Médicis, 1951).

Tocqueville, Alexis de. *Democracy in America*, Arthur Goldhammer (trans.) (New York: Library Classics of the United States, 2004).

Tocqueville, Alexis de. *L'Ancien Régime et la Revolution Française* [1856], J.P Mayer (ed.) (Paris: Gallimard, 1967).

Tocqueville, Alexis de. *The Old Régime and the French Revolution* [1856], Stuart Gilbert (trans.) (New York: Anchor Books, 1955).

Tocqueville, Alexis de. *Oeuvres Complètes*, J. Mayer et al. (eds), 18 vols (Paris: Gallimard, 1952–2003).

Tocqueville, Alexis de. 'Travail sur l'Algérie (octobre 1841)', in Tocqueville, *Oeuvres*, vol. 1, André Jardin, Françoise Mélonio, and Lise Queffélec (eds) (Paris: Gallimard, 1992), pp. 691–759.

Tocqueville, Alexis de. *Alexis de Tocqueville: Writings on Empire and Slavery*, Jennifer Pitts (ed. and trans.) (Baltimore, Maryland: Johns Hopkins University Press, 2001).

Trollope, Anthony. *The West Indies and the Spanish Main*, 2nd edn (London: Chapman and Hall, 1860; facsimile edn, London: Frank Cass, 1968).

Tylor, Edward Burnett. *Anahuac: or, Mexico and the Mexicans, Ancient and Modern* (London: Longman, Green, Longman, and Roberts, 1861).

Tylor, Edward Burnett. *Researches into the Early History of Mankind* (London: John Murray, 1865).

Wakefield, Edward Gibbon. *A Letter from Sydney* [1829] (London: J.M. Dent, 1929).

Wallace, Alfred Russel. 'The Origin of Human Races and the Antiquity of Man Deduced from the Theory of "Natural Selection" ', *Journal of the Anthropological Society* 2 (1864), pp. clviii–clxx.

Weld, Frederick A. *Hints to Intending Sheep-Farmers in New Zealand* (London: Trelawny Saunders, 1851).

Weld, Frederick. 'On the Volcanic Eruption at Hawaii in 1855–56', *Quarterly Journal of the Geological Society of London* 13, 2 (No. 50, 1 May 1857), pp. 163–9.

Weld, Frederick A. *Notes on New Zealand Affairs* (London: Edward Stanford, 1869).

Weld, Frederick. 'The Straits Settlements and British Malaya', *Proceedings of the Royal Colonial Institute* 1884, reprinted in Paul H. Kratoska (ed.), *Honourable Intentions: Talks on the British Empire in South-East Asia Delivered at the Royal Colonial Institute 1874–1928* (Singapore: Oxford University Press, 1983), pp. 43–74.

Whately, Richard. 'Of the Origins of Civilisation', in *Lectures Delivered Before the Young Men's Christian Association in Exeter Hall*, vol. 10, *1854–1855* (London: James Nisbet, 1855), pp. 3–36.

SECONDARY SOURCES

Adams, James Eli. 'Woman Red in Tooth and Claw: Nature and the Feminine in Tennyson and Darwin', *Victorian Studies* 33, 1 (Autumn 1989), pp. 7–27.

Adas, Michael. *Machines as the Measure of Men* (Ithaca, New York: Cornell University Press, 1989).

Ali-Khodja, Mourad. 'Tocqueville Orientaliste?: Jalons pour une réinterpretation de ses écrits et de son engagement en faveur de la colonisation française en Algérie', *French Colonial History* 7 (2006), pp. 77–96.

Allen, Theodore W. *The Invention of the White Race*, vol. 1, *Racial Oppression and Social Control* (London: Verso, 2004).

Alter, Stephen G. *Darwinism and the Linguistic Image: Language, Race, and Natural Theology in the Nineteenth Century* (Baltimore: Johns Hopkins University Press, 1999).

Alter, Stephen G. 'Race, Language, and Mental Evolution in Darwin's *Descent of Man*', *Journal of the History of the Behavioral Sciences* 43, 3 (Summer 2007), pp. 239–55.

Alter, Stephen G. 'Separated at Birth: The Interlinked Origins of Darwin's Unconscious Selection Concept and the Application of Sexual Selection to Race', *Journal of the History of Biology* 40, 2 (Summer 2007), pp. 231–58.

Altick, Richard. *The English Common Reader: A Social History of the Mass Reading Public, 1800–1900* (Chicago: University of Chicago Press, 1957).

Altick, Richard. *The Shows of London: A Panoramic History of Exhibitions, 1600–1862* (Cambridge, Massachusetts: Belknap Press, 1978).

Anderson, Patricia. *The Printed Image and the Transformation of Popular Culture, 1790–1860* (Oxford: Clarendon Press, 1991).

Appiah, Anthony. 'The Uncompleted Argument: DuBois and the Illusion of Race', in Harry Louis Gates, Jr. (ed.), *"Race," Writing, and Difference* (Chicago: University of Chicago Press, 1986), pp. 21–37.

Appiah, Kwame Anthony. *In My Father's House: Africa in the Philosophy of Culture* (1992).

Arnold, David. 'Race, Place and Bodily Difference in Early Nineteenth-Century British India', *Historical Research* 77, 196 (May 2004), pp. 254–75.

Aubert, Guillaume. ' "The Blood of France": Race and Purity of Blood in the French Atlantic World', *William and Mary Quarterly* 61, 3 (July 2004), pp. 439–78.

Augstein, Hannah Franziska (ed.). *Race: The Origins of an Idea* (Bristol: Thommes Press, 1996).

Augstein, Hannah. *James Cowles Prichard's Anthropology: Remaking the Science of Man in Early Nineteenth-Century Britain* (Amsterdam: Editions Rodopi, 1999).

Balibar, Etienne. 'Is There a Neo-Racism?', in Etienne Balibar and Immanuel Wallerstein, *Race, Nation, Class: Ambiguous Identities* (Etienne Balibar trans. by Chris Turner) (1988; London: Verso, 1991).

Ballantyne, Tony. 'Empire, Knowledge, and Culture: From Proto-Globalization to Modern Globalization', in A.G. Hopkins (ed.), *Globalization in World History* (New York: W.W. Norton, 2002), pp. 116–40.

Ballantyne, Tony. *Orientalism and Race: Aryanism and the British Empire* (Basingstoke: Palgrave Macmillan, 2002).

Bank, Andrew. 'Losing Faith in the Civilizing Mission: The Premature Decline of Humanitarian Liberalism at the Cape, 1840–1860', in Martin Daunton and Rick Halpern (eds), *Empire and Others: British Encounters with Indigenous Peoples, 1600–1850* (Philadelphia: University of Pennsylvania Press, 1999), pp. 364–83.

Banner, Stuart. 'Two Properties, One Land: Law and Space in Nineteenth-Century New Zealand', *Law & Social Inquiry* 24, 4 (Autumn 1999), pp. 807–52.

Banner, Stuart. 'Conquest by Contract: Wealth Transfer and Land Market Structure in Colonial New Zealand', *Law & Society Review* 34, 1 (2000), pp. 47–96.

Banner, Stuart. *Possessing the Pacific: Land, Settlers, and Indigenous People from Australia to Alaska* (Cambridge, Massachusetts: Harvard University Press, 2007).

Banton, Michael. *The Idea of Race* (London: Tavistock, 1977).

Banton, Michael. *Racial Theories*, 2nd edn (Cambridge: Cambridge University Press, 1998).

Barbujani, Guido, and Elise M.S. Belle. 'Genomic Boundaries between Human Populations', *Human Heredity* 61 (2006), pp. 15–21.

Barkan, Elazar. *The Retreat of Scientific Racism: Changing Concepts of Race in Britain and the United States between the World Wars* (Cambridge: Cambridge University Press, 1992).

Barkan, Elazar. 'The Politics of the Science of Race: Ashley Montagu and UNESCO's Anti-racist Declarations', in Larry T. Reynolds and Leonard Lieberman (eds), *Race and Other Misadventures: Essays in Honor of Ashley Montagu in His Ninetieth Year* (Dix Hills, New York: General Hall, 1996), pp. 96–105.

Barker, Anthony J. *The African Link: British Attitudes to the Negro in the Era of the Atlantic Slave Trade, 1550–1807* (London: Frank Cass, 1978).

Barksdale, Richard K. 'Thomas Arnold's Attitude toward Race', *Phylon Quarterly* 18:2 (1957), pp. 174–80.

Barrington, Mrs. Russell. *The Works and Life of Walter Bagehot*, vol. 10, *The Life* (London: Longmans, Green, and Co., 1915).

Barzun, Jacques. *Race: A Study in Superstition* [1937], rev. edn (New York: Harper and Row, 1965).

Bate, Crispin. 'Race, Caste, and Tribe in Central India: The Early Origins of Indian Anthropometry', in Peter Robb (ed.), *The Concept of Race in South Asia* (Delhi: Oxford University Press, 1995), pp. 219–51.

Bayly, Susan. 'Caste and "Race" in the Colonial Ethnography of India', in Peter Robb (ed.), *The Concept of Race in South Asia* (Delhi: Oxford University Press, 1995), pp. 165–218.

Beasley, Edward. *Empire as the Triumph of Theory: Imperialism, Information, and the Colonial Society of 1868* (London: Routledge, 2005).

Beasley, Edward. *Mid-Victorian Imperialists: British Gentlemen and the Empire of the Mind* (London: Routledge, 2005).

Beatty, John. 'Speaking of Species: Darwin's Strategy', in David Kohn (ed.), *The Darwinian Heritage* (Princeton, New Jersey: Princeton University Press, 1985), pp. 265–81.

Beckingham, C.F. 'A History of the Royal Asiatic Society, 1823–1973', in Stuart Simmonds and Simon Digby (eds), *The Royal Asiatic Society: Its History and Treasures* (Leiden and London: E.J. Brill, 1979), pp. 1–77.

Beer, Gillian. *Darwin's Plots: Evolutionary Narrative in Darwin, George Eliot, and Nineteenth-Century Fiction* (London: Routledge and Kegan Paul, 1983).

Belgrave, Michael. 'Pre-emption, the Treaty of Waitangi, and the Politics of Crown Purchase', *New Zealand Journal of History* 31, 1 (April 1997), pp. 23–37.

Belich, James. *The Victorian Interpretation of Racial Conflict: The Maori, the British, and the New Zealand Wars* (Montreal and Kingston, Ontario: McGill-Queen's University Press, 1986).

Belich, James. 'The Victorian Interpretation of Racial Conflict and the New Zealand Wars: An Approach to the Problem of One-Sided Evidence', *Journal of Imperial and Commonwealth History* 15:2 (January 1987): pp. 123–47.

Belich, James. 'Myth, Race, and Identity in New Zealand', *New Zealand Journal of History* 31, 3 (April 1997), pp. 9–22.

Bell, Duncan. *The Idea of Greater Britain: Empire and the Future of World Order, 1860–1900* (Princeton, New Jersey: Princeton University Press, 2007).

Bernasconi, Robert. 'Who Invented the Concept of Race?: Kant's Role in the Enlightenment Construction of Race', in idem. (ed.), *Race* (Malden, Massachusetts: Blackwell, 2001), 11–36.

Bhabha, Homi K. *The Location of Culture* (London: Routledge, 1994).

Biddiss, Michael D. *Father of Racist Ideology: The Social and Political Thought of Count Gobineau* (New York: Weybright and Talley, 1970).

Biddiss, Michael D. 'Prophecy and Pragmatism: Gobineau's Confrontation with Tocqueville', *Historical Journal* 13, 4 (1970), pp. 611–33.

Biddiss, Michael D. 'History as Destiny: Gobineau, H.S. Chamberlain, and Spengler', *Transactions of the Royal Historical Society*, sixth series, 7 (1997), pp. 73–100.

Blackburn, Daniel G. 'Why Race Is Not a Biological Concept', in Berel Lang (ed.), *Race and Racism in Theory and Practice* (Lanham, Maryland: Rowman & Littlefield, 2000), pp. 3–26.

Blanckaert, Claude. 'On the Origins of French Ethnology: William Edwards and the Doctrine of Race', Susan Paulson and George W. Stocking, Jr. (trans.), in Stocking (ed.), *Bones, Bodies and Behavior: Essays in Biological Anthropology*, *History of Anthropology* 5 (Madison, Wisconsin: University of Wisconsin Press, 1988), pp. 18–55.

Blanckaert, Claude. 'Of Monstrous Métis?: Hybridity, Fear of Miscegenation, and Patriotism from Buffon to Paul Broca', in Sue Peabody and Tyler Stovall (eds), *The Color of Liberty: Histories of Race in France* (Durham, North Carolina: Duke University Press, 2003), pp. 42–70.

Blomfield, Geoffrey. *Baal Balbora: The End of the Dancing* (Chippendale, New South Wales: Apcol, 1981).

Blum, Edward J. *W.E.B. DuBois: American Prophet* (Philadelphia: University of Pennsylvania Press, 2007).

Bodian, Miriam. ' "Men of the Nation": The Shaping of Converso Identity in Early Modern Europe', *Past and Present* 143 (May 1994), pp. 48–76.

Boesche, Roger. 'The Dark Side of Tocqueville: On War and Empire', *Review of Politics* 67, 4 (Fall 2005), pp. 737–52.

Boissel, Jean. *Gobineau (1816–1882): Un Don Quichote Tragique* (Paris: Hachette, 1981).

Bolnick, Deborah A. 'Individual Ancestry Inference and the Reification of Race as a Biological Phenomenon', in Barbara A. Koenig, Sandra Soo-Jin Lee, and Sarah S. Richardson (eds), *Revisiting Race in a Genomic Age* (New Brunswick, New Jersey: Rutgers University Press, 2008), pp. 70–85.

Bolt, Christine. *Victorian Attitudes to Race* (London: Routledge & Kegan Paul; Toronto: University of Toronto Press, 1971).

Bolt, Christine. 'Race and the Victorians', in C.C. Eldridge (ed.), *The British Empire in the Nineteenth Century* (Houndsmills, Basingstoke, England: Macmillan, 1984), pp. 126–147.

Bonner, Robert E. 'Slavery, Confederate Diplomacy, and the Racialist Mission of Henry Hotze', *Civil War History* 51, 3 (2005), pp. 218–316.

Bonnett, Alastair. 'How the Working Class Became "White": The Symbolic (Re) formation of Racialized Capitalism', *Journal of Historical Sociology* 11, 3 (September 1998), pp. 316–40.

Borges, Jorge Luis. 'Funes the Memorious', Anthony Kerrigan (trans.), in *Ficciones* (New York: Grove Weidenfeld, 1962).

Boulton, Alexander O. 'The American Paradox: Jeffersonian Equality and Racial Science', *American Quarterly* 47, 3 (September 1995), pp. 467–92.

Bowker, Geoffrey, and Susan Leigh Star. *Sorting Things Out: Classification and Its Consequences* (Cambridge, Massachusetts: MIT Press, 1999).

Bowler, Peter J. 'Malthus, Darwin, and the Concept of Struggle', *Journal of the History of Ideas* 37, 4 (October–December 1976), pp. 631–50.

Bowler, Peter. *The Eclipse of Darwinism* (Baltimore: Johns Hopkins University Press, 1983).

Bowler, Peter J. *The Invention of Progress* (Oxford: Basil Blackwell, 1989).

Boyd, Richard. 'Tocqueville's Algeria', *Society* 38, 6 (September/October 2001), pp. 65–70.

Boyd, Richard. *Uncivil Society: The Perils of Pluralism and the Making of Modern Liberalism* (Lanham, Maryland: Lexington Books, 2004).

Brah, Avtar. 'Difference, Diversity, and Differentiation', in James Donald and Ali Rattansi (eds), *'Race', Culture, and Difference* (London: Sage, 1992), pp. 126–45.

Brantlinger, Patrick. 'Victorians and Africans: The Genealogy of the Myth of the Dark Continent', *Critical Inquiry* 12, 1 (Autumn 1985), pp. 166–203.

Brantlinger, Patrick. *Dark Vanishings: Discourse on the Extinction of Primitive Races, 1800–1930* (Ithaca, New York: Cornell University Press, 2003).

Brattain, Michelle. 'Race, Racism, and Anti-Racism: UNESCO and the Politics of Presenting Science to the Post-War Public', *American Historical Review* 112, 5 (December 2007), pp. 1386–1413.

Braun, Lundy, Anne Fausto-Sterling, Duana Fullwiley, Evelynn M. Hammonds, Alondra Nelson, William Quivers, Susan M. Reverby, and Alexandra E. Shields. 'Racial Categories in Medical Practice: How Useful Are They?', *PLoS Medicine* 4, 9 (September 2007), pp. 1423–28.

Brereton, Bridget. *Law, Justice, and Empire: The Colonial Career of John Gorrie, 1829–1892* (Mona, Jamaica: University of West Indies Press, 1997).

Brinton, Crane. *English Political Thought in the Nineteenth Century* [1933] (New York: Harper & Row, 1962).

Brogan, Hugh. *Alexis de Tocqueville: A Life* (New Haven, Connecticut: Yale University Press, 2006).

Brown, Alan Willard. *The Metaphysical Society: Victorian Minds in Crisis, 1869–1880* (New York: Columbia University Press, 1947; New York: Octagon Books, 1973).

Brown, Kathleen. 'Native Americans and Early Modern Concepts of Race', in Martin Daunton and Rick Halpern (eds), *Empire and Others: British Encounters with Indigenous Peoples, 1600–1850* (Philadelphia: University of Pennsylvania Press, 1999), pp. 79–100.

Brown, Laurence. 'Inter-colonial Migration and the Fashioning of Indentured Labour: Arthur Gordon in Trinidad, Mauritius, and Fiji (1866–1880)', in David Lambert and Alan Lester (eds), *Colonial Lives across the British Empire: Imperial Careering in the Long Nineteenth Century* (Cambridge: Cambridge University Press, 2006), pp. 204–27.

Buchan, Alastair. *The Spare Chancellor: The Life of Walter Bagehot* (East Lansing, Michigan: Michigan State University Press, 1960).

Buenzod, Janine. *La formation de le pensée de Gobineau et l'Essai sur l'inégalité des races humaines* (Paris: Librarie A.-G. Nizet, 1967).

Burrow, John. 'Evolution and Anthropology in the 1860's: The Anthropological Society of London, 1863–1871', *Victorian Studies* 7, 2 (December 1963), pp. 137–54.

Burrow, J.W. *Evolution and Society: A Study in Victorian Social Theory* (Cambridge: Cambridge University Press, 1966).

Butcher, Barry W. 'Darwinism, Social Darwinism, and the Australian Aborigines', in Roy MacLeod and Philip H. Rehbock (eds), *Darwin's Laboratory: Evolutionary Theory and Natural History in the Pacific* (Honolulu: University of Hawaii Press, 1994), pp. 371–94.

Castillo, Susan. ' "The Best of Nations?: Race and Imperial Destinies in Emerson's "English Traits" ', *Yearbook of English Studies* 34 (2004), pp. 100–111.

Castle, Kathryn. 'The Representation of Africa in Mid-Victorian Children's Magazines', in Gretchen Holbrooke Gerzina (ed.), *Black Victorians/Black Victoriana* (New Brunswick, New Jersey: Rutgers University Press, 2003), pp. 145–58.

Castleman, Bruce A. 'Social Climbers in a Mexican City: Individual Mobility within the *Sistema de Castas* in Orizaba, 1777–1791', *Colonial Latin American Review* 10, 2 (2001), pp. 229–49.

Cavalli-Sforza, Luigi Luca, and Francesco Cavalli-Sforza. *The Great Human Diasporas: The History of Diversity and Evolution*, Sarah Thorne (trans.) (Reading, Massachusetts: Helix Books, 1995).

Cavalli-Sforza, Luigi Luca. *Genes, Peoples, and Languages*, Mark Seielstad (trans.) (Berkeley and Los Angeles: University of California Press, 2000).

Ceaser, James W. *Reconstructing America; The Symbol of America in Modern Thought* (New Haven, Connecticut: Yale University Press, 1997).

Chaplin, Joyce E. 'Natural Philosophy and an Early Racial Idiom in North America: Comparing English and Indian Bodies', *William and Mary Quarterly* (January 1997), pp. 229–52.

Chaplin, Joyce E. "Race", in David Armitage and Michael J. Braddick (eds), *The British Atlantic World, 1500–1800* (Basingstoke: Palgrave Macmillan, 2002), pp. 154–72.

Chapman, J.K. *The Career of Arthur Hamilton Gordon, First Lord Stanmore: 1829–1912* (Toronto: University of Toronto Press, 1964).

Chew, Ernest. 'Sir Frank Swettenham and the Federation of Malay States', *Modern Asian Studies* 2, 1 (1968), pp. 51–69.

Claeys, Gregory. ' "The Survival of the Fittest" and the Origins of Social Darwinism', *Journal of the History of Ideas* 61, 2 (April 2000), pp. 223–40.

Clark, C.M.H. *A History of Australia*, IV, *The Earth Abideth Forever, 1851–1888* (Melbourne: Melbourne University Press, 1978).

Clinton, David. *Tocqueville, Lieber, Bagehot: Liberalism Confronts the World* (New York: Palgrave Macmillan, 2003).

Cohen, Mark Nathan. 'Race and IQ Again', *Evolutionary Psychology* 3 (2005), pp. 255–262.

Cohen, William B. *The French Encounter with Africans: White Response to Blacks, 1530–1880* (Bloomington, Indiana: Indiana University Press, 1980).

Collini, Stefan, Donald Winch, and John Burrow. *That Noble Science of Politics: A Study in Nineteenth-Century Intellectual History* (Cambridge: Cambridge University Press, 1983).

Colloms, Brenda. *Charles Kingsley: The Lion of Eversley* (London: Constable; New York: Barnes & Noble, 1975).

Cowles, Thomas. 'Malthus, Darwin, and Bagehot: A Study in the Transference of a Concept', *Isis* 26, 2 (March 1937), pp. 341–8.

Crais, Clifton. *White Supremacy and Black Resistance in Pre-Industrial South Africa, 1770–1865* (Cambridge: Cambridge University Press, 1992).

Craiutu, Aurelian. *Liberalism under Siege: The Political Thought of the French Doctrinaires* (Lanham, Maryland: Lexington Books, 2003).

Craiutu, Aurelian. 'Tocqueville's Paradoxical Moderation', *Review of Politics* 67, 4 (Fall 2005), pp. 599–629.

Crook, Paul. *Darwinism, War, and History: The Debate on the Biology of War from the 'Origin of Species' to the First World War* (Cambridge: Cambridge University Press, 1994).

Crook, Paul. 'Social Darwinism: The Concept', *History of European Ideas* 22, 4 (1996), pp. 261–74.

Curtin, Philip D. *The Image of Africa, British Ideas and Action, 1780–1850* (Madison: University of Wisconsin Press, 1964).

Curtis, L.P., Jr. *Anglo-Saxons and Celts: A Study of Anti-Irish Prejudice in Victorian England* (Bridgeport, Connecticut: Conference on British Studies at the University of Bridgeport, 1968).

Dain, Bruce. *A Hideous Monster of the Mind: American Race Theory in the Early Republic* (Cambridge, Massachusetts: Harvard University Press, 2002).

Dale, Leigh. 'George Grey in Australia, New Zealand, and South Africa', in Peter Hulme and Russell McDougall (eds), *Writing, Travel, and Empire in the Margins of Anthropology* (London: I.B. Tauris, 2007), pp. 19–41.

Dalton, B.J. *War and Politics in New Zealand, 1855–1870* (Sydney: Sydney University Press, 1970).

Day, Matthew. 'Godless Savages and Superstitious Dogs: Charles Darwin, Imperial Ethnography, and the Problem of Human Uniqueness', *Journal of the History of Ideas* 69, 1 (January 2008), pp. 49–70.

Desmond, Adrian. *Archetypes and Ancestors: Palaeontology in Victorian London, 1850–1875* (1982; Chicago: University of Chicago Press, 1984).

Desmond, Adrian. *The Politics of Evolution: Morphology, Medicine, and Reform in Radical London* (Chicago: University of Chicago Press, 1989).

Desmond, Adrian, and James Moore. *Darwin* (New York: Warner Books, 1991).

Desmond, Adrian, and James Moore. *Darwin's Sacred Cause: How a Hatred of Slavery Shaped Darwin's Views on Human Evolution* (Boston: Harcourt Mifflin, 2009).

Dewbury, Adam. 'The American School and Scientific Racism in Early American Anthropology', *Histories of Anthropology Annual* 3 (2007), pp. 121–47.

Dion, Stéphane. 'Durham et Tocqueville sur la colonisation libérale', *Revue d'études canadiennes/Journal of Canadian Studies* 25, 1 (Spring 1990), pp. 60–77.

Drescher, Seymour. *Tocqueville and England*, Harvard Historical Monographs 55 (Cambridge, Massachusetts: Harvard University Press, 1964).

Drescher, Seymour. *Dilemmas of Democracy: Tocqueville and Modernization* (Pittsburgh: University of Pittsburgh Press, 1968).

Drescher, Seymour. 'The Ending of the Slave Trade and the Evolution of European Scientific Racism', *Social Science History* 14, 3 (Autumn 1990), pp. 415–50.

Drescher, Seymour. 'British Way, French Way: Opinion Building and Revolution in the Second French Slave Emancipation', *American Historical Review* 96, 3 (June 1991), pp. 709–34.

Drews, Robert. *The Coming of the Greeks: Indo-European Conquests in the Aegean and Near East* (Princeton, New Jersey: Princeton University Press, 1988).

Driver, C.H. 'Walter Bagehot and the Social Psychologists', in F.J.C Hearnshaw (ed.), *The Social and Political Ideas of Some Representative Thinkers of the Victorian Age* (London: George E. Harrap, 1933), pp. 194–221.

Duffield, Ian. 'Skilled Workers or Marginalized Poor?: The African Population of the United Kingdom, 1812–52', *Immigrants and Minorities* 12, 3 (November 1993), pp. 49–87.

Edwards, John. 'Was the Spanish Inquisition Truthful?' *Jewish Quarterly Review*, new series 87, 3/4 (January 1997), pp. 351–66.

Ellingson, Ter. *The Myth of the Noble Savage* (Berkeley and Los Angeles: University of California Press, 2001).

Endelman, Todd M., and Tony Kushner. *Disraeli's Jewishness* (London: Vallentine Mitchell, 2002).

Eze, Emmanuel C. 'Hume, Race, and Human Nature', *Journal of the History of Ideas* 61, 3 (July 2000), pp. 691–8.

Farnsworth, Susan H. *The Evolution of British Imperial Policy During the Mid-Nineteenth Century: A Study of the Peelite Contribution, 1846–1874* (New York: Garland, 1992).

Faverty, Frederic. *Matthew Arnold the Ethnologist* (Evanston, Illinois: Northwestern University Press, 1951).

Fichman, Martin. *An Elusive Victorian: The Evolution of Alfred Russel Wallace* (Chicago: University of Chicago Press, 2004).

France, Peter. *The Charter of the Land: Custom and Colonization in Fiji* (Melbourne: Oxford University Press, 1969).

Francis, Mark. 'The "Civilizing" of Indigenous People in Nineteenth-Century Canada', *Journal of World History* 9, 1(1998), pp. 51–87.

Fraser, Alice M., Lady Lovat. *The Life of Sir Frederick Weld, GCMG, a Pioneer of Empire* (London: John Murray, 1914).

Frederickson, George M. *The Black Image in the White Mind: The Debate on Afro-American Character and Destiny, 1817–1914* (1971; Middletown, Connecticut: Wesleyan University Press, 1987).

Frederickson, George M. *The Comparative Imagination: On the History of Racism, Nationalism, and Social Movements* (Berkeley and Los Angeles: University of California Press, 1997).

Frederickson, Kathleen. 'Liberalism and the Time of Instinct', *Victorian Studies* 49, 2 (Winter 2007), pp. 302–12.

Fullerton, Stephanie Malia. 'On the Absence of Biology in Philosophical Considerations of Race', in Shannon Sullivan and Nancy Tuana (eds), *Race and Epistemologies of Ignorance* (Albany: State University of New York Press, 2007), pp. 241–58.

Fullwiley, Duana. 'The Molecularization of Race: U.S. Health Institutions, Pharmacogenetics Practice, and Public Science after the Genome', in Barbara A. Koenig, Sandra Soo-Jin Lee, and Sarah S. Richardson (eds), *Revisiting Race in a Genomic Age* (New Brunswick, New Jersey: Rutgers University Press, 2008), pp. 149–71.

Gale, Barry G. 'Darwin and the Concept of a Struggle for Existence: A Study in the Extrascientific Origins of Scientific Ideas', *Isis* 63, 3 (September 1962), pp. 321–44.

Gannett, Robert T. *Tocqueville Unveiled: The Historian and His Sources for the Old Regime and the Revolution* (Chicago: University of Chicago Press, 2003).

Gardner, W.J. 'A Colonial Economy', in Geoffrey W. Rice (ed.), *The Oxford History of New Zealand*, 2nd edn (Auckland: Oxford University Press, 1992), pp. 57–86.

Gargan, Edward T. 'Tocqueville and the Problem of Historical Prognosis', *American Historical Review* 68, 2 (January 1963), pp. 332–45.

Garnett, Richard. *Edward Gibbon Wakefield: The Colonoization of South Australia and New Zealand* (New York: Longmans, Green, 1898).

Garrigus, John D. 'Sons of the Same Father: Gender, Race, and Citizenship in French Saint-Domingue, 1760–1792', in Christine Adams, Jack R. Censer, and Lisa Jane Graham (eds), *Visions and Revisions of Eighteenth-Century France* (University Park, Pennsylvania: Pennsylvania State University Press, 1997), pp. 137–53.

Gates, Harry Louis, Jr. 'Talkin' that Talk', in idem. (ed.), *"Race," Writing, and Difference* (Chicago: University of Chicago Press, 1986), pp. 402–9.

Gay, Peter. *The Bourgeois Experience: Victoria to Freud*, III, *The Cultivation of Hatred* (New York: W.W. Norton, 1993).

Geraghty, Paul. 'The Ethnic Basis of Society in Fiji', in Brij V. Lal and Tomasi R. Vakatora (eds), *Fiji in Transition: Research Papers of the Fiji Constitutional Review Commission*, Vol. 1 (Suva, Fiji: School of Economic and Social Development, University of the South Pacific, 1997), pp. 1–23.

Ghiselin, Michael T. *The Triumph of the Darwinian Method* (Berkeley and Los Angeles: University of California Press, 1969; Chicago: University of Chicago Press, 1984).

Ghiselin, Michael T. 'Darwin, Progress, and Economic Principles', *Evolution* 49, 6 (December 1995), pp. 1029–37.

Gillespie, Neal C. 'The Duke of Argyll, Evolutionary Anthropology, and the Art of Scientific Controversy', *Isis* 68 (1977), pp. 40–54.

Gillespie, Neal C. *Charles Darwin and the Problem of Creation* (Chicago: University of Chicago Press, 1979).

Gissis, Snait B. 'When is "Race" a Race? 1946–2003', *Studies in History and Philosophy of Science Part C: Studies in History and Philosophy of Biological and Biomedical Sciences* 39, 4 (December 2008), pp. 437–50.

Glassman, Jonathon. 'Slower Than a Massacre: The Multiple Sources for Racial Thought in Colonial Africa', *American Historical Review* 109, 3 (June 2004), pp. 720–54.

Gould, Stephen Jay. *The Mismeasure of Man* (New York: W.W. Norton, 1981).

Gould, Stephen Jay. *Time's Arrow, Time's Cycle: Myth and Metaphor in the Discovery of Geological Time* (Cambridge, Massachusetts: Harvard University Press, 1987).

Graham, Jeanine. 'Pastoralist and Maoris: Frederick Weld at Wharekaka', *New Zealand Journal of History* 11, 1 (April 1977), pp. 28–53.

Graham, Jeanine. *Frederick Weld* (Auckland, New Zealand: Auckland University Press, 1983).

Graves, Joseph. L., Jr. *The Emperor's New Clothes: Biological Theories of Race at the Millennium* (New Brunswick, New Jersey: Rutgers University Press, 2001).

Greene, John C. *Science, Ideology, and World View: Essays in the History of Evolutionary Ideas* (Berkeley and Los Angeles: University of California Press, 1981).

Gruber, Howard E. *Darwin on Man: A Psychological Study of Scientific Creativity*, 2nd edn (Chicago: University of Chicago Press, 1981).

Guillaumin, Collette. 'Race and Nature: The System of Marks', in idem., *Racism, Sexism, Power, and Ideology*, Andrew Rothwell with Max Silverman (trans.) (London: Routledge, 1995), pp. 133–52.

Guillaumin, Collette. 'The Idea of Race and its Elevation to Autonomous Scientific and Legal Status', in idem., *Racism, Sexism, Power, and Ideology*, Andrew Rothwell with Max Silverman (trans.) (London: Routledge, 1995), pp. 61–98.

Gump, James. 'The Imperialism of Cultural Assimilation: Sir George Grey's Encounter with the Maori and the Xhosa, 1845–1868', *Journal of World History* 9, 1 (Spring 1998), pp. 89–106.

Hadari, Saguiv A. *Theory in Practice: Tocqueville's New Science of Politics* (Stanford, California: Stanford University Press, 1989).

Hall, Catherine. 'The Nation Within and Without', in Catherine Hall, Keith McClelland, and Jane Rendall, *Defining the Victorian Nation: Class, Race, Gender, and the Reform Act of 1867* (Cambridge: Cambridge University Press, 2000), pp. 179–233.

Hall, Catherine. *Civilising Subjects: Metropole and Colony in the English Imagination, 1830–1867* (Chicago: University of Chicago Press, 2002).

Hall, Catherine. 'Imperial Careering at Home: Harriet Martineau on Empire', in David Lambert and Alan Lester (eds), *Colonial Lives across the British Empire: Imperial Careering in the Long Nineteenth Century* (Cambridge: Cambridge University Press, 2006), pp. 334–59.

Hancher, Michael. 'An Imagined World: The Imperial Gazetteer', in Julie F. Codell (ed.), *Imperial Cohistories: National Identities and the British and Colonial Press* (Madison, New Jersey: Fairleigh Dickenson University Press, 2003), pp. 45–67.

Hannaford, Ivan. *Race: The History of an Idea in the West* (Washington, DC: Woodrow Wilson Center Press; and Baltimore: Johns Hopkins University Press, 1996).

Harris, José. 'Between Civic Virtue and Social Darwinism: The Concept of the Residuum', in David Englander and Rosemary O'Day (eds), *Retrieved Riches: Social Investigation in Britain, 1840–1914* (Aldershot, England: Scolar Press, 1995), pp. 66–87.

Harrison, Mark. *Climates and Constitutions: Health, Race, Environment and British Imperialism in India, 1600–1850* (Oxford: Oxford University Press, 1999).

Hasluck, Paul. *Black Australians: A Survey of Native Policy in Western Australia, 1829–1897*, 2nd edn (Melbourne: Melbourne University Press, 1970).

Hearnshaw, F.J.C. 'Herbert Spencer and the Individualists', in idem. (ed.), *The Social and Political Ideas of Some Representative Thinkers of the Victorian Age* (London: George E. Harrap, 1933).

Heath, Ian. 'Toward a Reassessment of Gordon in Fiji', *Journal of Pacific History* 9 (1974), pp. 81–92.

Heehs, Peter. 'Shades of Orientalism: Paradoxes and Problems in Indian Historiography', *History and Theory* 20, 3 (1986), pp. 169–75.

Heffernan, Michael J. 'The Parisian Poor and the Colonization of Algeria in the Second Republic', *French History* 3, 4 (December 1989), pp. 377–403.

Heffernan, Michael J., and Keith Sutton. 'The Landscape of Colonialism: The Impact of French Colonial Rule on the Algerian Rural Settlement Pattern, 1830–1987', in Chris Dixon and Michael Heffernan (eds), *Colonialism and Development in the Contemporary World* (London: Mansell, 1991), pp. 121–52.

Helly, Dorothy O. *Livingstone's Legacy: Horace Waller and Victorian Mythmaking* (Athens, Ohio: Ohio University Press, 1977).

Herbert, Christopher. *Culture and Anomie: Ethnographic Imagination in the Nineteenth Century* (Chicago: University of Chicago Press, 1991).

Herbert, Sandra. 'The Place of Man in the Development of Darwin's Theory of Transmutation, Part II', *Journal of the History of Biology* 10, 2 (Fall 1977), pp. 155–227.

Hereth, Michael. *Alexis de Tocqueville: Threats to Freedom in Democracy*, George Bogardus (trans.) (Durham, North Carolina: Duke University Press, 1986).

Heuman, Gad. *The Killing Time: The Morant Bay Rebellion in Jamaica* (Knoxville, Tennessee: University of Tennessee Press, 1994).

Heyck, T.W. *The Transformation of Intellectual Life in Victorian England* (London: Croom Helm, 1982).

Himmelfarb, Gertrude, *Darwin and the Darwinian Revolution* (New York: Doubleday, 1959).

Holt, Thomas C. *The Problem of Freedom: Race, Labor, and Politics in Jamaica and Britain, 1832–1938* (Baltimore, Maryland: Johns Hopkins University Press, 1992).

Horsman, Reginald. *Race and Manifest Destiny: The Origins of American Racial Anglo-Saxonism* (Cambridge, Massachusetts: Harvard University Press, 1981).

Hudson, Nicholas. 'From "Nation" to "Race": The Origin of Racial Classification in Eighteenth-Century Thought', *Eighteenth-Century Studies* 29, 3 (1996), pp. 247–64.

Hudson, Nicholas. '"Hottentots" and the Evolution of European Racism', *Journal of European Studies* 34, 4 (December 2004), pp. 308–32.

Hutchins, Francis. *The Illusion of Permanence: British Imperialism in India* (Princeton, New Jersey: Princeton University Press, 1970).

Hyman, Stanley Edgar. *The Tangled Bank: Darwin, Marx, Frazer, and Freud as Imaginative Writers* (1959; New York: Grosset & Dunlap, 1962).

Hyslop, Jonathan. 'The Imperial Working Class Makes Itself White: White Labourism in Britain, Australia and South Africa before the First World War', *Journal of Historical Sociology* 12, 4 (December 1999), pp. 398–421.

Inden, Ronald. *Imagining India* (Oxford: Blackwell, 1990).
Irvine, William. *Apes, Angels, and Victorians: The Story of Darwin, Huxley, and Evolution* (New York: McGraw-Hill, 1955).
Isaac, Benjamin. *The Invention of Race in Classical Antiquity* (Princeton: Princeton University Press, 2004).
Jablonski, Nina G., and George Chaplin. 'The Evolution of Human Skin Coloration', *Journal of Human Evolution* 39, 1 (2000), pp. 57–106.
Janara, Lauren. 'Brothers and Others: Tocqueville and Beaumont, U.S. Genealogy, and Racism', *Political Theory* 32, 6 (December 2004), pp. 773–800.
Jardin, André. 'Alexis de Tocqueville, Gustave de Beaumont, et le problème de l'inégalité des races', in Pierre Guiral and Émile Temime (eds), *L'idee de race dans la pensée politique française contemporaine* (Paris: Centre National de la Recherche Scientifique, 1977), pp. 199–219.
Jardin, André. *Tocqueville: A Biography*, Lydia Davis with Robert Hemenway (trans.) (London: Peter Halban, 1988).
Jones, H.S. *Victorian Political Thought* (Basingstoke: Macmillan, 2000).
Jordan, Winthrop. *White over Black: American Attitudes toward the Negro, 1550–1812* (Chapel Hill: University of North Carolina Press, 1968; New York: Pelican Books, 1969).
Joyce, Barry Alan. *The Shaping of American Ethnography: The Wilkes Exploring Expedition, 1838–1842* (Lincoln, Nebraska: University of Nebraska Press, 2001).
Juzeniene, Asta, Richard Setlow, Alina Porojnicu, Arnfinn Hykkerud Steindal, and Johan Moan. 'Development of Different Human Skin Colors: A Review Highlighting Photobiological and Photobiophysical Aspects', *Journal of Photochemistry and Photobiology B: Biology* 96 (2009), pp. 93–100.
Kahan, Alan S. *Aristocratic Liberalism: The Social and Political Thought of Jacob Burckhardt, John Stuart Mill, and Alexis de Tocqueville* (New York: Oxford University Press, 1992).
Kahan, Alan S. 'Tocqueville and the French Revolution', *History & Theory* 45, 3 (October 2006), pp. 424–35.
Kahn, Jonathan. 'Race in a Bottle', *Scientific American* 297, 2 (August 2007), pp. 40–5.
Kapila, Shruti. 'Race Matters: Orientalism and Religion, India and Beyond, c. 1770–1880', *Modern Asian Studies* 41, 3 (May 2007), pp. 471–513.
Katzew, Ilona. *Casta Painting* (New Haven, Connecticut: Yale University Press, 2004).
Kearns, Gerry. 'The Imperial Subject: Geography and Travel in the Work of Mary Kingsley and Halford Mackinder', *Transactions of the Institute of British Geographers*, new series 22 (1997), pp. 450–72.
Kelly, John D. 'Gordon Was No Amateur: Imperial Legal Strategies in the Colonization of Fiji', in Sally Engle Merry and Donald Brenneis (eds), *Law and Empire in the Pacific: Fiji and Hawai'i* (Santa Fe, New Mexico: School of American Research Press; Oxford: James Currey, 2003), pp. 61–100.
Kennedy, Dane. *The Highly Civilized Man: Richard Burton and the Victorian World* (Cambridge, Massachusetts: Harvard University Press, 2005).
Kenny, Robert. 'From the Curse of Ham to the Curse of Nature: The Influence of Natural Selection on the Debate on Human Unity before the Publication of *The Descent of Man*', *British Journal for the History of Science* 40, 3 (September 2007), pp. 367–88.
Kidd, Colin. *The Forging of Races: Race and Scripture in the Protestant Atlantic World, 1600–2000* (Cambridge: Cambridge University Press, 2006).
Kingsland, James. 'Colour-Coded Cures', *New Scientist* 186, 2503 (11 June 2005), pp. 42–7.

Kitson, Peter J. *Romantic Literature, Race, and the Colonial Encounter* (New York: Palgrave Macmillan, 2007).

Kittles, Rick. 'Nature, Origin, and Variation of Human Pigmentation', *Journal of Black Studies* 26, 1 (September 1995), pp. 36–61.

Koerner, Konrad. 'Schleicher and Trees', in Henry M. Hoenigswald and Linda F. Walker (eds), *Biological Metaphor and Cladistic Classification: An Interdisciplinary Perspective* (Philadelphia: University of Pennsylvania Press, 1987), pp. 109–13.

Kohn, David. 'Darwin's Ambiguity: The Secularization of Biological Meaning', *British Journal for the History of Science* 22, 2 (July 1989), pp. 215–39.

Kohn, Margaret. 'The Other America: Tocqueville and Beaumont on Race and Slavery', *Polity* 35, 2 (Winter 2002), pp. 169–93.

Kottler, Malcolm Jay. 'Alfred Russel Wallace, the Origin of Man, and Spiritualism', *Isis* 65, 2 (June 1974), pp. 145–92.

Kriz, Kay Dian. *Slavery, Sugar, and the Culture of Refinement: Picturing the British West Indies, 1700–1840* (New Haven, Connecticut: Yale University Press, 2008).

Kupperman, Karen Ordahl. 'Presentment of Civility: English Reading of American Self-Presentation in the Early Years of Colonization', *William and Mary Quarterly* (January 1997), pp. 193–228.

Lamberti, Jean-Claude. *Tocqueville and the Two Americas*, Arthur Goldhammer (trans.) (Cambridge, Massachusetts: Harvard University Press, 1989).

Landman, Otto E. 'Inheritance of Acquired Characteristics Revisited', *BioScience* 43, 10 (November 1993), pp. 696–705.

Larrimore, Mark. 'Race, Freedom, and the Fall in Steffens and Kant', in Sara Eigen and Mark Larrimore (eds), *The German Invention of Race* (Albany: State University of New York Press, 2006), pp. 91–120.

Legge, James. *Britain in Fiji, 1858–1880* (London: Macmillan, 1958).

Lehmann, William C. *Henry Hume, Lord Kames, and the Scottish Enlightenment: A Study in National Character and in the History of Ideas* (The Hague: Martinus Nijhoff, 1971).

Leopold, John. 'British Applications of the Aryan Theory of Race to India, 1850–1880', *English Historical Review* 89, 352 (July 1974), pp. 578–603.

Lester, Alan. 'British Settler Discourse and the Circuits of Empire', *History Workshop Journal* 54 (Autumn 2002), pp. 24–48.

Lewis, Bernard. *Race and Slavery in the Middle East: An Historical Enquiry* (New York: Oxford University Press, 1990).

Liebersohn, Harry. *Aristocratic Encounters: European Travelers and North American Indians* (Cambridge: Cambridge University Press, 1998).

Lively, Jack. *The Social and Political Thought of Alexis de Tocqueville* (Oxford: Oxford University Press, 1962).

Livingstone, David N. 'Human Acclimatization: Perspectives on a Contested Field of Enquiry in Science, Medicine, and Geography', *History of Science* 25 (1987), pp. 359–94.

Livingstone, David N. *Adam's Ancestors: Race, Religion, and the Politics of Human Origins* (Baltimore, Maryland: Johns Hopkins University Press, 2008).

Long, Jeffrey C., and Rick A. Kittles. 'Human Genetic Diversity and the Nonexistence of Biological Races', *Human Biology* 75, 4 (August 2003), pp. 449–71.

Lorimer, Douglas. *Colour, Class, and the Victorians: English Attitudes to the Negro in the Mid-Nineteenth Century* (Leicester: Leicester University Press, 1978).

Lorimer, Douglas. 'Theoretical Racism in Late-Victorian Anthropology, 1870–1900', *Victorian Studies* 31, 3 (Spring 1988), pp. 405–30.

Lorimer, Douglas. 'Science and the Secularization of Victorian Ideas of Race', in Bernard Lightman (ed.), *Victorian Science in Context* (Chicago: University of Chicago Press, 1997), pp. 212–35.

Lorimer, Douglas. 'Reconstructing Victorian Racial Discourse', in Gretchen Holbrooke Gerzina (ed.), *Black Victorians Black Victoriana* (New Brunswick, New Jersey: Rutgers University Press, 2003), pp. 187–207.

Lott, Tommy. 'DuBois's Anthropological Notion of Race', in Robert Bernasconi, *Race* (Malden, Massachusetts: Blackwell, 2001), pp. 59–83.

MacDougall, Hugh A. *Racial Myth in English History: Trojans, Teutons, and Anglo-Saxons* (Montreal: Harvest House, 1982).

McCulloch, Samuel Clyde. 'Sir George Gipps and Eastern Australia's Policy toward the Aborigine, 1838–46', *Journal of Modern History* 33, 3 (September 1961), pp. 261–69.

McGovern, William Montgomery. *From Luther to Hitler: The History of Fascist-Nazi Political Philosophy* (Boston: Houghton Mifflin, 1941).

McWhorter, Ladelle. 'Sex, Race, and Power: A Foucauldian Genealogy', *Hypatia* 19, 3 (Summer 2004), pp. 38–62.

Magali, M. Carrera. *Imagining Identity in New Spain: Race, Lineage, and the Colonial Body in Portraiture and Casta Paintings* (Austin: University of Texas Press, 2003).

Magubane, Zine. *Bringing the Empire Home: Race, Class, and Gender in Colonial South Africa* (Chicago: University of Chicago Press, 2004).

Malchow, H.L. 'Frankenstein's Monster and Images of Race in Nineteenth-Century Britain', *Past and Present* 139 (May 1993), pp. 90–130.

Mallory, J.P. 'A Short History of the Indo-European Problem', *Journal of Indo-European Studies* 1 (1973), pp. 21–65.

Maloney, Pat. 'Savagery and Civilization: Early Victorian Notions', *New Zealand Journal of History* 35, 2 (October 2001), pp. 153–76.

Mandler, Peter. ' "Race" and "Nation" in Mid-Victorian Thought', in Stefan Collini, Richard Whatmore, and Brian Young (eds), *History, Religion, and Culture: British Intellectual History, 1750–1950* (Cambridge: Cambridge University Press, 2000), pp. 222–44.

Mandler, Peter. *The English National Character: The History of an Idea from Edmund Burke to Tony Blair* (New Haven, Connecticut: Yale University Press, 2006).

Marriott, John. *The Other Empire: Metropolis, India, and Progress in the Colonial Imagination* (Manchester: Manchester University Press, 2003).

Martínez, María Elena. *Genealogical Fictions: Limpieza de Sangre, Religion, and Gender in Colonial Mexico* (Stanford, California: Stanford University Press, 2008).

Martínez, María Elena. 'The Language, Genealogy, and Classification of "Race" in Colonial Mexico', in Ilona Katzew and Susan Deans-Smith (eds), *Race and Classification: The Case of Mexican America* (Stanford, California: Stanford University Press, 2009), pp. 25–42.

Matysik, Tracie. 'International Activism and Global Civil Society at the High Point of Nationalism: The Paradox of the Universal Races Congress, 1911', in A.G. Hopkins (ed.), *Global History: Interactions between the Universal and the Local* (New York: Palgrave Macmillan, 2006), pp. 131–59.

May, Leila S. 'Monkeys, Microcephalous Idiots, and the Barbarous Races of Mankind: Darwin's Dangerous Victorianism', *Victorian Newsletter* 102 (Fall 2002), pp. 20–27.

Mayer, J.P. *Alexis de Tocqueville: A Biographical Essay in Political Science*, M.M. Bozman and C. Hahn (trans.) (New York: Viking Press, 1940).

Mayer, Ruth. 'The Things of Civilization, the Matters of Empire: Representing Jemmy Button', *New Literary History* 39 (2008), pp. 193–215.

Mays, Kelly J. 'Slaves in Heaven, Laborers in Hell: Chartist Poets' Ambivalent Identification with the (Black) Slave', *Victorian Poetry* 39, 2 (Summer 2001), pp. 137–63.

Mehta, Uday Singh. 'Essential Ambiguities of Race and Racism', in Diane E. Davis (ed.), *Political Power and Social Theory* 11 (Greenwich, Connecticut: JAI Press, 1997), pp. 234–46.

Mehta, Uday Singh. *Liberalism and Empire: A Study in Nineteenth-Century British Liberal Thought* (Chicago: University of Chicago Press, 1999).

Mélonio, Françoise. *Tocqueville and the French*, Beth G. Raps (trans.) (1993; Charlottesville, Virginia: University Press of Virginia, 1998).

Miller, John. *Early Victorian New Zealand: A Study of Racial Tension and Social Attitudes, 1839–1852* (London: Oxford University Press, 1958).

Misra, B.B. *The Bureaucracy in India: An Historical Analysis of Development up to 1947* (Delhi: Oxford University Press, 1977).

Morgan, Philip D. "British Encounters with Africans and African-Americans, circa 1600–1780", in Bernard Bailyn and Philip D. Morgan (eds), *Strangers within the Realm: Cultural Margins of the First British Empire* (Chapel Hill: University of North Carolina Press, 1991), pp. 157–219.

Morrell, W.P. *The Provincial System in New Zealand, 1852–1876*, 2nd edn (Christchurch, New Zealand: Whitcombe and Tombs, 1964).

Mudimbe, V.Y. *The Invention of Africa: Gnosis, Philosophy, and the Order of Knowledge* (Bloomington and Indianapolis: Indiana University Press; London: James Currey, 1988).

Murji, Karim, and John Solomos (eds). *Racialization: Studies in Theory and Practice* (Oxford: Oxford University Press, 2005).

Myers, Norma. *Reconstructing the Black Past: Blacks in Britain, c. 1780–1830* (London: Frank Cass, 1996).

Nasr, Mohammed Abdul-Muizz. *Walter Bagehot: A Study in Victorian Ideas*, Faculty of Arts Publication no. 9 (Alexandria, Egypt: Alexandria University Press, 1959).

Netanyahu, B. *The Origins of the Inquisition in Fifteenth Century Spain* (New York: Random House, 1995).

Newman, Judie. 'The Afterlife of *Dred* on the British Stage', in Denise Kohn, Sarah Meer, and Emily B. Todd (eds), *Transatlantic Stowe: Harriet Beecher Stowe and European Culture* (Iowa City: University of Iowa Press, 2006), pp. 208–24.

Nichols, Peter. *Evolution's Captain* (New York: Perennial, 2004).

Nightingale, Carl H. 'Before Race Mattered: Geographies of the Color Line in Early Colonial Madras and New York', *American Historical Review* 113, 1 (February 2008), pp. 48–71.

Nimtz, August. *Marx, Tocqueville, and Race in America: The 'Absolute Democracy' or 'Defiled Republic'* (Lanham, Maryland: Lexington Books, 2003).

Nirenberg, D. 'Mass Conversion and Genealogical Mentalities: Jews and Christians in Fifteenth Century Spain', *Past & Present* 174 (February 2002), pp. 3–41.

Nirenberg, David. 'Was There Race before Modernity?: The Example of "Jewish Blood" in Late-Medieval Spain', in Miriam Eliav-Feldon, Benjamin Isaac, and Joseph Ziegler (eds), *The Origins of Racism in the West* (Cambridge: Cambridge University Press, 2009), pp. 232–64.

Nussbaum, Felicity A. 'The Theatre of Empire: Racial Counterfeit, Racial Realism', in Kathleen Wilson (ed.), *A New Imperial History: Culture, Identity, and Modernity in Britain and the Empire, 1660–1840* (Cambridge: Cambridge University Press, 2004).

O'Brien, Michael. *Conjectures of Order: Intellectual Life in the American South, 1810–1860*, 2 vols (Chapel Hill: University of North Carolina Press, 2004).

Olby, R.C. 'Charles Darwin's Manuscript of Pangenesis', *British Journal for the History of Science* 1, 3 (June 1963), pp. 251–63.

Olby, R.C. *Origins of Mendelism* (New York: Schocken Books, 1966).

Onuf, Peter S. '"To Declare Them a Free and Independent People": Race, Slavery, and National Identity in Jefferson's Thought', *Journal of the Early Republic* 18, 1 (Spring 1998), pp. 1–46.

Ospovat, Dov. *The Development of Darwin's Theory: Natural History, Natural Theology, and Natural Selection, 1838–1859* (Cambridge: Cambridge University Press, 1981).

Parker, C.J.W. 'The Failure of Liberal Racialism: The Racial Ideas of E.A. Freeman', *Historical Journal* 24, 4 (December 1981), pp. 825–46.

Parsonson, Ann R. 'The Expansion of a Competitive Society: A Study in Nineteenth-Century Maori Social History', in D.A. Hamer (ed.), *New Zealand Social History: Papers from the Turnbull Conference on New Zealand Social History, 1978* (Auckland, New Zealand: Auckland University Press, 1978), pp. 83–98.

Patton, Mark. *Science, Politics, and Business in the Work of Sir John Lubbock: A Man of Universal Mind* (Aldershot: Ashgate, 2007).

Paz, D.G. 'Anti-Catholicism, Anti-Irish Stereotyping, and Anti-Celtic Racism in Mid-Victorian Working-Class Periodicals', *Albion* 18, 4 (Winter 1986), pp. 601–16.

Peabody, Sue. *'There Are No Slaves in France': The Political Culture of Race and Slavery in the Ancien Régime* (New York: Oxford University Press, 1996).

Pecora, Vincent P. 'Arnoldian Ethnology', *Victorian Studies* 41:3 (Spring 1998), pp. 355–79.

Peires, J.B. *The Dead Will Rise Again: Nongqawuse and the Great Xhosa Cattle-Killing Movement of 1856–7* (Johannesburg: Ravan Press, 1989).

Perkin, Joan. *Women and Marriage in Nineteenth-Century England* (London: Routledge, 1989).

Petrusic, Christopher. 'Violence as Masculinity: David Livingstone's Radical Racial Politics in the Cape Colony and the Transvaal, 1845–1852', *International History Review* 26, 1 (March 2004), pp. 20–55.

Peyre, Henri. 'Three Nineteenth-Century Myths: Race, Nation, Revolution', in idem., *Historical and Critical Essays* (Lincoln, Nebraska: University of Nebraska Press, 1968), pp. 24–61.

Pick, Daniel. *Faces of Degeneration: A European Disorder, c. 1848–c. 1918* (Cambridge: Cambridge University Press, 1989).

Picker, David. 'Blood, Sweat, and Type O: Japan's Weird Science', *New York Times*, 14 December 2006.

Pierson, George Wilson. *Tocqueville in America* ([*Tocqueville and Beaumont in America*, 1938]; Baltimore: Johns Hopkins University Press, 1996).

Pitts, Jennifer. 'Empire and Democracy: Tocqueville and the Algeria Question', *Journal of Political Philosophy* 8, 3 (September 2000), pp. 295–318.

Pitts, Jennifer. *A Turn to Empire: The Rise of Imperial Liberalism in Britain and France* (Princeton, New Jersey: Princeton University Press, 2005).

Poliakov, Léon. *The Aryan Myth: A History of Racist and Nationalist Ideas in Europe*, Edmund Howard (trans.) (London: Chatto Heinemann, 1974).

Poole, Stafford. 'The Politics of Limpieza de Sangre: Juan de Ovando and His Circle in the Reign of Philip II', *Americas* 55, 3 (1999), pp. 359–89.

Poovey, Mary. *Making a Social Body: British Cultural Formation, 1830–1864* (Chicago: University of Chicago Press, 1995).

Popkin, Richard H. 'The Philosophical Bases of Modern Racism', in Craig Walton and John P. Anton (eds), *Philosophy and the Civilizing Arts: Essays Presented to Herbert W. Schneider* (Athens, Ohio: Ohio University Press, 1974), pp. 126–65.

Popkin, Richard H. *Isaac La Peyrère (1596–1676): His Life, Work, and Influence* (Leiden: E.J. Brill, 1987).

Porter, Andrew. *Religion Versus Empire?: British Protestant Missionaries and Overseas Expansion, 1700–1914* (Manchester: Manchester University Press, 2004).

Posel, Deborah. 'What's in a Name?: Racial Categorisations under Apartheid and Their Afterlife', *Transformation* 47 (2001), pp. 45–74.

Pratt, Mary Louise. *Imperial Eyes: Travel Writing and Transculturalization* (London: Routledge, 1992).

Price, Richard. *Making Empire: Colonial Encounters and the Creation of Imperial Rule in Nineteenth-Century South Africa* (Cambridge: Cambridge University Press, 2008).

Rainger, Ronald. 'Race, Politics, and Science: The Anthropological Society of London in the 1860s', *Victorian Studies* 22, 1 (Autumn 1978), pp. 51–70.

Ransford, Oliver. *David Livingstone: The Dark Interior* (New York: St. Martin's Press, 1978).

Reardon, Jenny. 'Decoding Race and Human Difference in a Genomic Age', *Differences: A Journal of Feminist Cultural Studies* 15, 3 (2004), pp. 38–65.

Reece, R.H.W. *Aborigines and Colonists: Aborigines and Colonial Society in New South Wales in the 1830s and 1840s* (Sydney: Sydney University Press, 1974).

Regard, Frédéric. 'The Catholic Mule: E.B. Tylor's Chimeric Perception of Otherness', *Journal of Victorian Culture* 12, 2 (2007), pp. 225–37.

Rehbock, Philip F. *The Philosophical Naturalists: Themes in Early Nineteenth-Century British Biology* (Madison: University of Wisconsin Press, 1983).

Rehin, George F. 'Blackface Street Minstrels in Victorian London and Its Resorts: Popular Culture and Its Racial Implications as Revealed in Polite Opinion', *Journal of Popular Culture* 15, 1 (Summer 1981), pp. 19–38.

Reinhardt, Mark. *The Art of Being Free: Taking Liberties with Tocqueville, Marx, and Arendt* (Ithaca, New York: Cornell University Press, 1997).

Reisman, David. 'Psychological Types and National Character: An Informal Commentary', *American Quarterly* 5, 4 (Winter 1953), pp. 325–43.

Rekdal, Ole Bjørn. 'When Hypothesis Becomes Myth: The Iraqi Origin of the Iraqw', *Ethnology* 37, 1 (Winter 1998), pp. 17–38.

Resh, Richard. 'Alexis de Tocqueville and the Negro: *Democracy in America* Reconsidered', *Journal of Negro History* 48, 4 (October 1963), pp. 251–59.

Reynolds, Henry. 'Racial Thought in Early Colonial Australia', *Australian Journal of Politics and History* 20, 1 (1974), pp. 25–53.

Richards, Evelleen. 'The "Moral Anatomy" of Robert Knox: The Interplay between Biological and Social Thought in Victorian Scientific Naturalism', *Journal of the History of Biology* 22, 3 (Fall 1989), pp. 373–436.

Richards, Robert J. 'The Emergence of Evolutionary Biology of Behaviour in the Early Nineteenth Century', *British Journal for the History of Science* 15, 3 (November 1982), pp. 241–80.

Richards, Robert J. *Darwin and the Emergence of Evolutionary Theories of Mind and Behavior* (Chicago: University of Chicago Press, 1987).

Richter, Melvin. 'The Study of Man—a Debate on Race: The Tocqueville-Gobineau Correspondence', *Commentary* 25, 2 (February 1958), pp. 151–60.

Richter, Melvin. 'Tocqueville on Algeria', *The Review of Politics* 25, 3 (July 1963), pp. 362–98.

Richter, Melvin. 'The Uses of Theory: Tocqueville's Adaptation of Montesquieu' in idem. (ed.), *Essays in Theory and History: An Approach to the Social Sciences* (Cambridge, Massachusetts: Harvard University Press, 1970), pp. 74–102.

Ritvo, Harriet. *The Platypus and the Mermaid, and Other Figments of the Classifying Imagination* (Cambridge, Massachusetts: Harvard University Press, 1987).

Ritvo, Harriet. 'Classification and Continuity in *The Origin of Species*', in David Amigoni and Jeff Wallace (eds), *Charles Darwin's The Origin of Species: New Interdisciplinary Essays* (Manchester: Manchester University Press, 1995), pp. 47–67.

Robinson, Gloria. *A Prelude to Genetics: Theories of a Material Substance of Heredity, Darwin to Weismann* (Lawrence, Kansas: Coronado Press, 1979).

Rogers, James Allen. 'Darwinism and Social Darwinism', *Journal of the History of Ideas* 33, 2 (April–June 1972), pp. 265–80.

Romani, Roberto. *National Character and Public Spirit in Britain and France, 1750–1914* (Cambridge: Cambridge University Press, 2002).

Rosaldo, Renato. 'Imperialist Nostalgia', *Representations* 26 (Spring 1989), pp. 107–22.

Rowbotham, Arnold. *The Literary Works of Count de Gobineau.* (Paris: Librarie Ancienne Honoré Champion, 1929).

Rupke, Nicolaas A. *Richard Owen: Victorian Naturalist* (Yale and London: Yale University Press, 1994).

Ruse, Michael. 'Social Darwinism: The Two Sources', *Albion* 12, 1 (Spring 1980), pp. 23–36.

St. John-Stevas, Norman. *Walter Bagehot* (London: Longmans, Green, and Co., 1963).

Sanders, Edith R. 'The Hamitic Hypothesis: Its Origin and Functions in Time Perspective', *Journal of African History* 10, 4 (1969), pp. 521–32.

Scarr, Deryck. *Fragments of Empire: A History of the Western Pacific High Commission, 1877–1914* (Canberra: Australian National University Press, 1967).

Schleifer, James T. *The Making of Tocqueville's Democracy in America* (Chapel Hill: University of North Carolina Press, 1980).

Schwartz, James. *In Pursuit of the Gene: From Darwin to DNA* (Cambridge, Massachusetts: Harvard University Press, 2008).

Schweber, Sylvan. 'The Origins of the *Origin* Revisited', *Journal of the History of Biology* 10, 2 (Fall 1977), pp. 229–316.

Schweber, Silvan S. 'The Wider British Context in Darwin's Theorizing', in David Kohn (ed.), *The Darwinian Heritage* (Princeton, New Jersey: Princeton University Press, 1985), pp. 35–69.

Secord, James A. *Victorian Sensation: The Extraordinary Publication, Reception, and Secret Authorship of 'Vestiges of the Natural History of Creation'* (Chicago: University of Chicago Press, 2000).

Semmel, Bernard. *The Governor Eyre Controversy* (London: MacGibbon and Kee, 1962).

Semmel, Bernard. 'The Issue of "Race" in the British Reaction to the Morant Bay Uprising of 1865', *Caribbean Studies* 2, 3 (October 1962), pp. 3–15.

Sepinwall, Alyssa Goldstein. *The Abbé Grégoire and the French Revolution: The Making of Modern Universalism* (Berkeley and Los Angeles: University of California Press, 2005).

Seton, Malcolm C.C. *The India Office* (London and New York: G.P. Putman's Sons, 1926).

Shapin, Steven, and Barry Barnes. 'Darwin and Social Darwinism: Purity in History', in Barry Barnes and Steven Shapin (eds), *Natural Order: Historical Studies of Scientific Culture* (Beverly Hills, California: Sage, 1979), pp. 125–42.

Smith, Mark M. *How Race Is Made: Slavery, Segregation, and the Senses* (Chapel Hill: University of North Carolina Press, 2006).

Smith, Woodruff D. *Politics and the Sciences of Culture in Germany, 1840–1920* (New York: Oxford University Press, 1991).

Sorrenson, M.P.K. *Maori Origins and Migrations* (Auckland, New Zealand: Auckland University Press, 1979).

Sorrenson, M.P.K. 'Maori and Pakeha', in Geoffrey W. Rice (ed.), *The Oxford History of New Zealand*, 2nd edn (Auckland: Oxford University Press, 1992), pp. 141–66.

Stamos, David N. *Darwin and the Nature of Species* (Albany: State University of New York Press, 2007).

Stanton, William. *The Leopard's Spots: Scientific Attitudes toward Race in America, 1815–59* (Chicago: University of Chicago Press, 1960).

Staum, Martin S. *Labeling People: French Scholars on Society, Race, and Empire, 1815–1848* (Montreal and Kingston: McGill-Queen's University Press, 2003).

Stenhouse, John. 'The Darwinian Enlightenment and New Zealand Politics', in Roy MacLeod and Philip H. Rehbock (eds), *Darwin's Laboratory: Evolutionary Theory and Natural History in the Pacific* (Honolulu: University of Hawaii Press, 1994), pp. 395–425.

Stenhouse, John. 'Imperialism, Atheism, and Race: Charles Southwell, Old Corruption, and the Maori', *Journal of British Studies* 44 (October 2005), pp. 754–74.

Stepan, Nancy. *The Idea of Race in Science: Great Britain, 1800–1960* (New York: Archon Books, 1982).

Stepan, Nancy Lys. *Picturing Tropical Nature* (London: Reaktion Books, 2001).

Stewart, James Brewer. 'The Emergence of Racial Modernity and the Rise of the White North, 1790–1840', *Journal of the Early Republic* 18, 2 (Summer 1998), pp. 181–217.

Stix, Gary. 'Human Origins: Traces of Distant Past', *Scientific American* 299, 1 (July 2008), pp. 56–63.

Stocking, George. *Race, Culture, and Evolution: Essays in the History of Anthropology* (New York: The Free Press, 1968).

Stocking, George. 'What's in a Name?: The Origins of the Royal Anthropological Institute, 1837–71', *Man*, new series, 6, 3 (September 1971), pp. 369–90.

Stocking, George. Introduction to James Cowles Prichard, *Researches into the Physical History of Man* [1813], George Stocking (ed.) (Chicago: University of Chicago Press, 1973).

Stocking, George. *Victorian Anthropology* (New York: The Free Press, 1987).

Stokes, Curtis. 'Tocqueville and the Problem of Racial Inequality', *Journal of Negro History* 75, 1/2 (Winter/Spring, 1990), pp. 1–15.

Stoler, Ann Laura. *Race and the Education of Desire* (Durham, North Carolina: Duke University Press, 1995).

Stoler, Ann Laura. 'Racial Histories and Their Regimes of Truth', in Diane E. Davis (ed.), *Political Power and Social Theory* 11 (Greenwich, Connecticut: JAI Press, 1997), pp. 183–206.

Streets, Heather. *Martial Races: The Military, Race, and Masculinity in British Imperial Culture, 1857–1914* (Manchester: Manchester University Press, 2004).

Sweet, James H. 'The Iberian Roots of American Racist Thought', *William and Mary Quarterly* 54, 1 (January 1997), pp. 143–66.

Tabili, Laura. 'Race Is a Relationship, and Not a Thing', *Journal of Social History* 37, 1 (2003), pp. 125–30.

Tallant, Harold B. *Evil Necessity: Slavery and Political Culture in Antebellum Kentucky* (Lexington, Kentucky: University Press of Kentucky, 2003).

Tessitore, Aristide. 'Tocqueville and Gobineau on the Nature of Modern Politics', *Review of Politics* 67, 4 (Fall 2005), pp. 631–57.

Thapar, Romila. 'The Theory of Aryan Race and India: History and Politics', *Social Scientist* 24, 1–3 (January–March 1996), pp. 3–29.

Thomson, Keith. *Before Darwin: Reconciling God and Nature* (New Haven, Connecticut: Yale University Press, 2005).

Thompson, Dorothy. *Outsiders: Class, Gender, and Nation* (London: Verso, 1993).

Todorov, Tzvetan. ' "Race," Writing, and Culture', in Harry Louis Gates, Jr. (ed.), *"Race," Writing, and Difference* (Chicago: University of Chicago Press, 1986), pp. 370–80.

Todorov, Tzvetan. 'Introduction: Tocqueville et la doctrine coloniale', in Alexis de Tocqueville, *De la Colonie en Algérie* (Paris: Éditions Complexe, 1988), pp. 9–34.

Todorov, Tzvetan. *Nous et les autres: La réflexion française sur la diversité humaine* (Paris: Éditions du Seuil, 1989).

Trautmann, Thomas R. *Aryans and British India* (Berkeley and Los Angeles: University of California Press, 1997).

Trilling, Lionel. *Matthew Arnold* [1939], The Works of Lionel Trilling: Uniform Edition (New York: Harcourt Brace Jovanavich, 1977).

Turnbull, Paul. 'British Anatomists, Phrenologists, and the Construction of the Aboriginal Race, c. 1790–1830', *History Compass* 5, 1 (2007), pp. 26–50.

Twells, Alison. *The Civilising Mission and the English Middle Class, 1792–1850* (Basingstoke: Palgrave Macmillan, 2009).

van Arkel, D. 'Racism in Europe', in Robert Ross (ed.), *Racism and Colonialism: Essays in Ideology and Social Structure* (The Hague: Martinus Nijhoff, 1981), pp. 11–31.

van den Boogaart, Ernst. 'Colour Prejudice and the Yardstick of Civility: The Initial Dutch Confrontation with Black Africans, 1590–1635', in Robert Ross (ed.), *Racism and Colonialism: Essays in Ideology and Social Structure* (The Hague: Martinus Nijhoff, 1981), pp. 33–54.

Varouxakis, Georgios. *Victorian Political Thought on France and the French* (Basingstoke: Palgrave Macmillan, 2002).

Wacquant, Loïc J.D. 'For an Analytic of Racial Domination', in Diane E. Davis (ed.), *Political Power and Social Theory* 11 (Greenwich, Connecticut: JAI Press, 1997), pp. 217–34.

Ward, Alan. *A Show of Justice: Racial 'Amalgamation' in Nineteenth Century New Zealand* (Toronto: University of Toronto Press, 1974).

Waters, Hazel. *Racism on the Victorian Stage: Representation of Slavery and the Black Character* (Cambridge: Cambridge University Press, 1977).

Watson, George. *The English Ideology: Studies in the Language of Victorian Politics* (London: Allen Lane, 1973).

Welch, Cheryl B. 'Colonial Violence and the Rhetoric of Evasion: Tocqueville on Algeria', *Political Theory* 31, 2 (April 2003), pp. 235–64.

Welch, Cheryl B. 'Tocqueville's Resistance to the Social', *History of European Ideas* 20 (2004), pp. 83–107.

Wheeler, Roxann. *The Complexion of Race: Categories of Difference in Eighteenth-Century British Culture* (Philadelphia: University of Pennsylvania Press, 2000).

Wiener, Martin J. *An Empire on Trial: Race, Murder, and Justice under British Rule, 1870–1935* (Cambridge: Cambridge University Press, 2009).

Williams, Daniel G. *Ethnicity and Cultural Authority from Arnold to DuBois* (Edinburgh: Edinburgh University Press, 2006).

Williams, Elizabeth A. *The Physical and the Moral: Anthropology, Physiology, and Philosophical Medicine in France, 1750–1850* (Cambridge: Cambridge University Press, 1994).

Wilson, Kathleen. *The Island Race: Englishness, Empire, and Gender in the Eighteenth Century* (London: Routledge, 2003).

Winter, Sarah. 'Mental Culture: Liberal Pedagogy and the Emergence of Ethnographic Knowledge', *Victorian Studies* 41, 3 (Spring 1998), pp. 427–54.

Wolf, Eva Sheppard. *Race and Liberty in the New Nation: Emancipation in Virginia from the Revolution to Nat Turner's Rebellion* (Baton Rouge: Louisiana State University Press, 2006).

Wood, Donald. *Trinidad in Transition* (London: Oxford University Press, 1968).

Wood, Marcus. *Blind Memory: Visual Representation of Slavery in England and America, 1780–1865* (London: Routledge, 2000).

Young, Robert J.C. *Colonial Desire: Hybridity in Race, Theory, and Culture* (London: Routledge, 1995).

Young, Robert J.C. *The Idea of English Ethnicity* (Malden, Massachusetts: Blackwell, 2008).

Young, Robert M. 'Darwinism *Is* Social', in David Kohn (ed.), *The Darwinian Heritage* (Princeton, New Jersey: Princeton University Press, 1985), pp. 609–38.

Young, Robert M. 'Natural Theology, Victorian Periodicals, and the Fragmentation of a Common Context', in idem., *Darwin's Metaphor: Nature's Place in Victorian Culture* (Cambridge: Cambridge University Press, 1985), pp. 126–63.

Zachernuk, Philip S. 'Of Origins and Colonial Order: Southern Nigerian Historians and the "Hamitic Hypothesis" c. 1870–1970', *Journal of African History* 35, 3 (1994), pp. 427–55.

Zeitlin, Irving M. *Liberty, Equality, and Revolution in Alexis de Tocqueville* (Boston: Little, Brown, and Co., 1971).

Zemka, Sue. 'Spiritual Authority and the Life of Thomas Arnold', *Victorian Studies* 38, 3 (Spring 1995), pp. 429–62.

Zetterbaum, Marvin. *Tocqueville and the Problem of Democracy* (Stanford, California: Stanford University Press, 1967).

Zimmerman, Andrew. *Anthropology and Antihumanism in Imperial Germany* (Chicago: University of Chicago Press, 2001).

Index

civilization (stages of), 32–3, 42, 78,
113, 115, 197
civil service recruitment (India), 125
Clapham Sect, 155
Clarke, Andrew, 144
class, 30–1, 73, 83–4, 92, 108–9, 157
classifications of humanity. *See* categorizations of humanity
Clifford, Charles, 130
climate: causing human differentiation, 17, 20, 26, 31–2, 72, 75–7;
effects on humanity denied, 49,
52, 75, 85–6, 90
Collini, Stefan, 74
colonial ideas of race, 10, 12, 17,
35–41, 104, 130, 136–8, 149–50
Colonial Reform Movement, 133–4
colour differences. *See* skin colour
colour-races: for Bagehot, 75–6, 85–6;
in British thought, 18–20, 63;
in colonies, 17, 149–50; for
Darwin, 97–8, 102–5; in 18th
century, 12; for Gobineau, 46,
48, 53–7, 60; in modern U.S.,
30–1, 110; for Weld, 144–5
colour-races (rejection of), 65–6, 101,
114, 122
common sense, 74, 76–7, 110
communications (growth in), 155–6
Condorcet, Nicolas de Caritat, Marquis
de, 32
Confederate States of America, 18, 69
conflict (racial). *See* racial conflict
conquest, 33, 47, 57–8, 86–9, 107, 122,
139–40
continental groups, 110
coolie labourers, 149, 155
Cornish (people), 79
Corsicans, 150
Courtet de l'Isle, Victor, 27, 49
Crawfurd, John, 18, 60, 101
Crévecoeur, J. Hector St. John de, 26
Crimean War, 62, 135
Crook, Paul, 87–8
Crowther, Samuel Ajayi, 19
cultural decline, 38, 50, 87. *See also*
degeneration
cultural evolution, 81–2, 107–8
cultural groups, 3, 64–5, 86–7, 149–51.
See also the names of individual
places or peoples
Curtin, Philip, 173n111
custom, 86–7, 89
Cuvier, Georges, 26, 49–50, 67, 92

D
Dahomeys, 58
Dalhousie, James Broun Ramsay (1st
Marquess of), 126
Darwin, Charles: abolitionism of, 97,
99; *Beagle*, 19, 97–8; and Brazil,
97; criticism from Argyll, 111,
121; and Bagehot, 107–8, 122;
on classes, 108; on eugenics, 108; and extermination,
102, 107; on Eyre, 99; and the
Fuegians, 98, 105, 114; funeral
of, 122–3; on inheritance of
acquired characteristics, 82–3,
105–6; human races (ambivalence on), 103–5, 109, 160;
human races (argues against),
100–1; human races (argues for),
97–8; human races (assumptions
of), 97–8, 102, 106–9; inconsistent language of, 102–3, 160;
methodology, 82, 103; on racial
conflict, 106–7; social Darwinism of, 191n7, 191n8; social
evolutionism of, 81–2, 107–8,
122; species (definition of),
97–9; tree of life, 98–9
Darwin, Erasmus, 106
Darwin, Robert (father of Charles Darwin), 19–20
decline of civilizations, 48, 50. *See also*
degeneration
degeneration (opinions on): Argyll,
112–14, 123–7; Bagehot, 87, 90;
Darwin, 114; in French thought,
92; Gobineau, 56, 60, 62; Gordon, 154; Whately, 112
determinism (racial), 17, 60–2
Denison, William, 146
Desjobert, Amédée, 36
determinism, 19, 45, 60–1
Dilke, Charles Wentworth (second
Baronet), 20, 203n81
discussion (importance of), 89–91, 95
Drescher, Seymour 25, 28
DuBois, W.E.B., 22
Dyaks, 75

E
East Africa, 18, 124
economic development: in Fiji, 154; in
India, 124–6
Economist, 77
Edinburgh, 67

An environmentally friendly book printed and bound in England by www.printondemand-worldwide.com

This book is made entirely of sustainable materials; FSC paper for the cover and PEFC paper for the text pages.

#0167 - 300915 - C0 - 229/152/14 - PB - 9780415652780